Elder Horror

Also edited by Cynthia J. Miller
and A. Bowdoin Van Riper
and from McFarland

Terrifying Texts: Essays on Books of Good and Evil in Horror Cinema (2018)

Divine Horror: Essays on the Cinematic Battle Between the Sacred and the Diabolical (2017)

Edited by A. Bowdoin Van Riper

Learning from Mickey, Donald and Walt: Essays on Disney's Edutainment Films (2011)

Elder Horror

Essays on Film's Frightening Images of Aging

Edited by Cynthia J. Miller *and* A. Bowdoin Van Riper

McFarland & Company, Inc., Publishers
Jefferson, North Carolina

LIBRARY OF CONGRESS CATALOGUING-IN-PUBLICATION DATA

Names: Miller, Cynthia J., 1958– editor. | Van Riper, A. Bowdoin, editor.
Title: Elder horror : essays on film's frightening images of aging / edited by Cynthia J. Miller and A. Bowdoin Van Riper.
Description: Jefferson, North Carolina : McFarland & Company, Inc., Publishers, 2019 | Includes bibliographical references and index.
Identifiers: LCCN 2018060574 | ISBN 9781476675374 (paperback : acid free paper) ∞
Subjects: LCSH: Aging in motion pictures. | Older people in motion pictures.
Classification: LCC PN1995.9.A433 E43 2019 | DDC 791.43/654—dc23
LC record available at https://lccn.loc.gov/2018060574

BRITISH LIBRARY CATALOGUING DATA ARE AVAILABLE

ISBN (print) 978-1-4766-7537-4
ISBN (ebook) 978-1-4766-3507-1

© 2019 Cynthia J. Miller and A. Bowdoin Van Riper. All rights reserved

No part of this book may be reproduced or transmitted in any form or by any means, electronic or mechanical, including photocopying or recording, or by any information storage and retrieval system, without permission in writing from the publisher.

Front cover: Lorna Raver as Mrs. Sylvia Ganush in *Drag Me to Hell* (2009, Universal Pictures/Photofest)

Printed in the United States of America

*McFarland & Company, Inc., Publishers
Box 611, Jefferson, North Carolina 28640
www.mcfarlandpub.com*

For everyone who believes that getting old
still beats the alternative.

Acknowledgments

As with any scholarly work, this collection owes its existence to all those colleagues, in and out of the horror genre, who have been thinking and writing about cinematic depictions of the elderly. From memory and cognition, to health and disability, to social issues, to death itself, the body of literature on aging and the aged has much to offer as we think about its many portrayals on screen. To all of those scholars, we extend our thanks. Additionally, thanks to our fine contributors, for their energy, hard work, and creativity. And of course, our deep thanks to Charlie Perdue and the team at McFarland for their unfailing support of this project, from start to finish.

Contents

Acknowledgments   vi

Introduction
   Cynthia J. Miller *and* A. Bowdoin Van Riper   1

I. Victims No More

"Ask not what your rest home can do for you": Self-Agency and Public Service in *Bubba Ho-Tep*
   Philip L. Simpson   12

Panic in Detroit: *Don't Breathe* and the Fear of Old Cities, Homes and Men
   Isaac Rooks   22

"It's the work of a crazy old woman": Revenge of the Elderly in *The Devil-Doll*
   Martin F. Norden   32

From Beneficent Elderly to Vile M'others: Familial Relations and Cannibalism in Troma's *Rabid Grannies* (1988)
   Steve J. Webley   46

II. Aesthetics of Decay

The Shock of Aging (Women) in Horror Film
   Dawn Keetley   58

"To Grandmother's house we go": Documenting the Horror of the Aging Woman in Found Footage Films
   Maddi McGillvray   70

"More like music": Aging, Abjection and Dementia at the Overlook Hotel
   Sue Matheson   81

The Skeleton Key, the Southern Gothic and the Uncanny Decay of Teleological History
   Jessica Balanzategui   92

III. Elders as Others/Outsiders

Making the Hard Choices: The Economics of Damnation in *Drag Me to Hell*
    CYNTHIA J. MILLER   108

"Mirror, mirror on the wall, who is the ugliest of them all?" The Elderly as "Other" in *Countess Dracula*
    JENNIFER RICHARDS   119

Old and In the Way: Torments of the Aging Male in *Psycho II*
    HANS STAATS   129

The Limits of "Sundowning": M. Night Shyamalan's *The Visit* and the Horror of the Aging Body
    STEPHANIE M. FLINT   140

IV. Fighting Back Time

"The powers of time can be altered": The Ambiguities of Aging in *Bram Stoker's Dracula* (1992)
    THOMAS PRASCH   152

"You can be young forever": The Dread of Aging in Tony Scott's Art-Horror Film *The Hunger*
    JAMES J. WARD   165

The Brittle Body: The Elderly and Cars in *The Brotherhood of Satan*
    BRIAN BREMS   179

The Evil Aging Women of *American Horror Story*
    KAREN J. RENNER   189

V. What the Old Folks Know

Disturbing the Past: Horror and Historical Memory in *Ghost Story* (1981)
    A. BOWDOIN VAN RIPER   202

Becoming Dr. Caligari
    ROBERT B. LUEHRS   212

"Some kind of special": Queering Death Through Elder/Child Relationships in *The Haunting in Connecticut 2: Ghosts of Georgia*
    OLIVIA OLIVER-HOPKINS   222

Flowers in the Attic: The Elderly as Monster
    LIAM T. WEBB   233

About the Contributors   243

Index   245

Introduction

CYNTHIA J. MILLER *and* A. BOWDOIN VAN RIPER

> I have seen the moment of my greatness flicker
> And I have seen the eternal Footman hold my coat, and snicker
> And in short, I was afraid[1]

Fear.... Of death? Yes. But if we're honest, there's something that, as a culture, we fear more: aging. Or, specifically, aging badly. The aging process would not seem anywhere near as daunting if we all knew we could do so with grace, dignity, and our bodies and minds relatively intact; if opportunities didn't dwindle, abilities and memories didn't fail; and if the face staring back in the mirror looked a bit more like the "us" we remembered. Unfortunately, no matter how many times Baby Boomers reassure themselves that "60 is the new 40," for many of us, that's just not true. We age with the same diversity with which we all live, and whether we attribute the outcome to genetics, lifestyle, or luck, the body quite often does what it will, and we live (and live with) the results. Still, many of us would agree, it beats the alternative.

As the Baby Boom generation grays, representations of elderly characters on screen are increasing, and are receiving significant attention in the scholarly literature that considers them. Cinematic depictions of aging as a degenerative process, along with othering, marginalization, and victimization of the elderly, and fears tied to the finality of death have all been increasingly highlighted and analyzed as we attempt to sort out the complex social, psychological, economic, and emotional consequences of—and responses to—growing old.

Absent from these considerations, however, is a genre in which our fears of growing and being old, and of the elderly, take on fantastic proportions: horror. Here, the threats of aging are made manifest and bloody—by the eccentric harbinger of doom, the crone who seeks to restore her vitality, the pensioners who bargain with the supernatural to cheat death, and ancestors who return from the grave to curse the living—as well as threats *to* the aged, whether cast as frail victims or as stalwart gatekeepers and repositories of Old-World knowledge.

This volume features essays that focus on films in which these horrors of aging are prominently featured. The authors here explore the ways in which cinematic horror texts reflect—and shape—our ambivalent attitudes toward growing old, exploring presentations of aging as the ultimate, inescapable horror destined to overtake us all, as a terrifying time of reckoning with past sins, and as a portal to unexpected (even unimaginable) powers. They also pose new questions about our complex relationship with the aged, whose role as keepers of wisdom and experience simultaneously intrigues and unsettles us.

The Elderly on Screen

As scholars of film, gerontology, and disability studies have increasingly begun to note, the "cinema of old age" has been problematic. "Getting old," as Amir Cohen-Shalev notes, "is something for which Western culture has a long history of avoidance and denial … we prefer to disengage, or worse, quarantine the aging."[2] Our culture has been one that valorizes youth, shunning the aging body and mind; one in which old age, limitation, disability, and illness all readily collapsed into each other, or, as Martine Beugnet argues, "old age *is* a disease."[3] As a result, elderly characters in film have historically been defined in easy (or more accurately, "uneasy") contrast against their younger counterparts, with central narratives emphasizing the difference between the old and the young.[4] Stereotypical portrayals frame these aging characters as hindrances, helpers, or recipients of help, providing sources of narrative tension and drama.[5] These images, reflections of failed men and "hackneyed characterizations of old women," populated the screen well into the 1960s, and have continued to do so to the present day.[6]

Over time, however, challenges to these images have been increasingly mounted. Demographics have shifted, lifespans have extended, workforce years have increased, and our notions of what constitutes "elderly" or "the aged" have altered, forcing us, as a society, to reevaluate our understandings and representations of the aging process and old age. This was especially true as we approached the close of the 20th century and the older members of the Baby Boom generation—those born between the mid–1940s and mid–1960s—approached senior citizen status. As a culture, we became increasingly aware that perceptions of agedness rely much more on "contextual or situational age,"[7] as Shary and McVittie argue, than on chronological age; that "old age" is more about our understandings of age appropriateness and established age contrasts than about capacity, suitability, or ability. Yet still, we resist. Actor Harrison Ford, best known for his portrayals of Indiana Jones, has lamented in interviews that "what astonishes me is that people can't imagine Indiana Jones aging at all. Why expect any character to be frozen in time? The appeal of Indiana Jones isn't his youth, but his imagination, his resourcefulness."[8]

This awareness of both the power of portrayal and the complexities of reception makes cinematic depictions of the aging process and advanced age particularly important to carefully consider, particularly in terms of perpetuating stereotypes and discourses of limitation. Moving image media has a singular ability to carefully control both context and situation, and so, is uniquely able to reinforce or challenge stereotypes about elderly individuals. While scholars such as Cohen-Shalev, Pamela Gravagne, and Sally Chivers argue for broad changes in the cultural "narrative[s] of decline" used to frame aging and the elderly in order to "denaturalize" age and "uproot the pervasive assumptions" about age, aging, and the life course,[9] portrayals in film tend to shift slowly, and diversely. Those that challenge assumptions of decline and offer positive possibilities for their elderly characters still generally do so in clear reference to cultural "givens," marking their elderly characters as exceptions, rather than the norm.[10]

Thus, while cinematic portrayals of aging and the elderly have become increasingly complex, they have done so within a fairly narrow range of images which, as is the case with most cinematic texts, say as much or more about the society in which they have been produced than about the identities and lived realities of individuals. Amir Cohen-Shalev observes:

> Trapped between life and death, personal experience and social time, old people occupy a unique cultural symbolic space. This space is characterized by many ambiguities: the demarcation between the aged and the rest of society, the phenomenon of social roles devoid of content, the gap between social and biological death, the tension between meaning and control, the incongruence between social image and self-image…[11]

Such a level of ambiguity can be challenging to portray, and also to view, lacking the comforting simplicity of easy stereotypes. We find it occasionally in films such as *Providence* (1977), *Nelly and Mr. Arnaud* (1995), and *Away from Her* (2006), where the distinct, ongoing *un*ease of elderly characters' lives—difficult choices, unresolved relationships, and troubled inner worlds—are not only focal points, but drive the films' narratives.

As narratives of "old and in the way" are increasingly questioned, the tension between ability and disability in the elderly has also begun to receive more nuanced and focused consideration on screen and in the scholarly analyses of those cinematic texts. Films such as *Pauline and Paulette* (2001), *The Savages* (2007), and the aforementioned *Away from Her* all amply illustrate the fear that an aging body will be accompanied by a failing mind. Sally Chivers provocatively questions both notions and portrayals of "cultural fitness," asking why claims of physical and mental ability are necessary for older actors, and by extension, older people more generally.[12] Potential answers abound, ranging from our inner struggles with identity and reflexivity to economics. As Martine Beugnet explains: "In the context of a late capitalist culture old age is … equivalent to the categories of low consumer value and low productivity; a social stigma that is acutely reflected in its status in terms of representation."[13] Each of these possibilities—vulnerabilities in memory, physical and cognitive abilities, economic viability—has potential for evoking terror even when deployed in mainstream cinematic narratives. Horror cinema goes further, seizing hold of them and pushing them to extremes.

The Elderly in Horror Film

Horror cinema is, by its nature, an exercise in thrusting the grotesque into the midst of the banal, and rendering familiar settings and situations uncanny. Fantasy and science fiction—the other two elements of the "fantastic cinema" triad—*may* keep one foot in the audience's reality, but horror, with rare exceptions, *must* do so.[14] Horror, as Robin Wood famously argued, can be seen as "the struggle for recognition of all that our civilization represses or oppresses, its reemergence dramatized, as in our nightmares, as an object of horror, a matter of terror, and the happy ending (when it exists) signifying the return of repression."[15] It achieves its emotional effect on the viewing audience by putting them, along with the characters, in a comfortably familiar situation and then demonstrating that the "rules" that render it familiar and comfortable have, without warning or reason, been suspended.

Filmmakers working in the idiom of horror are thus free to push fears about the consequences of "aging badly" to grotesque extremes, and to transmute everyday anxieties into elaborate nightmares. Elderly characters in horror films do not simply suffer from failing bodies, but decay and (rendering Genesis 3:19 chillingly literal[16]) even crumble to dust before audiences' eyes. They carry with them not just the telltale signs of routine bodily functions slipping beyond their control, but the rot and stench of death. The beautiful, naked young woman who Jack Torrance eagerly embraces in *The Shining* (1980) transforms not just into an elderly hag, but an animated corpse. The "dead hand" of the old that, metaphorically, controls the behavior of the young is rendered horrifyingly literal in *Psycho* (1960) when Norman Bates' tyrannical mother—the guiding force that pushes him to commit acts of shocking brutality—is revealed as a withered, wizened body in the dusty basement of his home. Even when indisputably alive, the debilitated and decaying bodies of the elderly function as a symbol of abjection in films as coolly stylish as *Nosferatu* (1922) and *The Hunger* (1983) and as extravagantly grotesque as *The Texas Chainsaw Massacre* (1974), in which the Sawyer family's cannibalistic travesty of the idealized American family includes Grandpa—so old and infirm that he seems to be a lifeless corpse until he hungrily sucks the blood oozing from a captive victim's body.

The eccentricities of thought, speech, and behavior that accompany old age are exaggerated, in horror films, until they transcend the labels—endearing, eccentric, or irritating—applied to them in real life and become disturbing, even terrifying. The quirks of the once-glamorous, now deranged older women in "hag horror" films like *Whatever Happened to Baby Jane?* became audible signals of their insanity and markers of their capacity for psychological and physical abuse of those around them.[17] The Tall Man, the gray-haired, dark-suited figure from the *Phantasm* films whose mortuary conceals a gate to Hell, achieves the same disturbing effect with his near-silence and uncanny stillness of manner. Like an elderly person who spends hours at a time disengaged from those around them, lost in an inner world invisible to and impenetrable by outsiders, his blank mien reveals nothing of his motives, intentions, or desires. They are accessible only through his actions: bloody acts of vengeance perpetrated against intruders in his domain, rendered all the more terrifying because his blankness leaves them unsignaled and unexplained.

When they *do* explain themselves, the graying villains of horror cinema often mimic, in extreme fashion, the cultural stereotypes of elders as emotionally mercurial (alternately stern and giddily childlike), unconstrained by everyday logic, and disdainful of the filters of politeness, propriety, and discretion. Henry Frankenstein, the transgressive researcher whose desire to "play in God's domain" drives the action of James Whale's *Frankenstein* (1931), is displaced from that role in *Bride of Frankenstein* (1935) by Dr. Septimus Pretorius (Ernst Thiesinger): a visibly older, and considerably madder, scientist.[18] Rail thin, white-haired, and wild-eyed, Pretorius rushes into forbidden territory with the glee of a child newly released from school on the first day of summer. Before goading Frankenstein to create a reanimated mate for the Creature from the first film, he casually shows off his own creation: five homunculi—tiny, perfectly formed living humans—imprisoned under glass bell jars in his laboratory. Unconnected to the larger story, they blur the line between Pretorius' cutting-edge science and black magic, turning "old and in the way" into "old and out of control." Their existence establishes Pretorius as sufficiently unhinged make Frankenstein himself seem like the film's sober, cautious rationalist.

Pretorius, like the brownstone-dwelling Satanists in *Rosemary's Baby* (1968), embodies a dark version of a familiar trope about the elderly: that their knowledge and experience extends into areas of which the young know nothing. The knowledge that horror-film elders possess, however, need not be forbidden or destructive. Quite the opposite. Rosemary becomes the sacrificial victim of her elderly neighbors—drugged, raped, and impregnated by the Prince of Darkness at their direction—but the protagonists of both *The Exorcist* (1973) and *The Omen* (1976), confronted by the forces of darkness, turn to elderly priests (played by Max von Sydow and Leo McKern, respectively) who are keepers of the ancient knowledge the modern Church has cast aside. The family menaced by the malevolent title figure in *Krampus* (2015) turn to, and are ultimately defended by, grandmother Omi, who once confronted it as a young girl in Germany. Her hard-won wisdom and experience matters more, in the face of supernatural evil, than her aging and weakened body.

Elder Horrors and Horrific Elders

The 20 essays in this volume survey the range of roles—from victims to villains to wise saviors and fierce warriors—that elderly characters play in horror cinema. It begins with a part focused on feisty senior citizens, "Victims No More," led off by Philip L. Simpson's essay "'Ask not what your rest home can do for you': Self-Agency and Public Service in *Bubba Ho-Tep*." Don Coscarelli's cult horror film pits two aging residents of an East Texas nursing home against an ancient Egyptian soul-sucking mummy in a tale of masculinity and agency lost and found. Simpson's essay explores the characters' discovery of newfound dignity and purpose, as they struggle to save the souls of their fellow residents. The central figure of the part's next essay adds a new, and notably dark, dimension to an aging character's refusal to be victimized. Isaac Rooks' essay, "Panic in Detroit: *Don't Breathe* and the Fear of Old Cities, Homes and Men," examines the controversies surrounding the film's nameless Blind Man, as he terrorizes three young intruders who break into his home with the intention of robbing it. What begins as a tale of a heroic aging victim protecting his property turns unexpectedly horrific as the Blind Man's terrible secret is revealed. Contextualizing the narrative's setting not only in a decaying home, but a decaying city, Rooks explores the anxieties that the old man evokes in not only the three young characters, but in viewers, as well.

Moving deeper into revenge—and madness—Martin F. Norden's essay, "'It's the work of a crazy old woman': Revenge of the Elderly in *The Devil-Doll*," analyzes Tod Browning's classic 1930s horror melodrama, which stars Lionel Barrymore as a banker who steals a mad scientist's formula to exact revenge on former colleagues who framed him for embezzlement. Barrymore's cross-dressing performance is of particular interest here, enabling him to construct the alternate persona: the elderly female proprietor of the toy store that serves as a front for his nefarious scheme. Madness continues to take its toll as the part closes with Steve J. Webley's examination of a Troma Studios classic in "From Beneficent Elderly to Vile M'others: Familial Relations and Cannibalism in Troma's *Rabid Grannies* (1988)." Known for over-the-top gore, Troma uses its gleefully transgressive film as a vehicle for extended cultural commentary about families' relationships with their elder members. Webley draws on psychoanalytic theories in order to shed light on the ways in which family roles, rituals, and relationships can become not only toxic, but monstrous, as he looks at the story of two elderly aunts and a birthday celebration that won't soon be forgotten.

The next part, "Aesthetics of Decay," draws together four essays that focus on the relationship between the elderly and abjection. Dawn Keetley's essay, "The Shock of Aging (Women) in Horror Film," opens by taking a broad approach to the horror genre, asking incisive questions regarding the use of aging and elderly women to create jump scares and other genre effects to elicit shock in viewers. Keetley observes that, through such uses, aging is presented as a kind of trauma—not as a gradual process, but as an assault to the senses. Keetley's essay ranges widely through contemporary horror films, drawing on a diversity of titles that rely on the shock value of old women, in order to illustrate her analysis. Horror films that present the elderly as abject focus particularly on old women, as Maddi McGillvray discusses in "'To Grandmother's house we go': Documenting the Horror of the Aging Woman in Found Footage Films." McGillvray's work examines the ways in which *The Visit* and *The Taking of Deborah Logan* not only embrace the found-footage subgenre of horror, but also use its tropes to depict the transformation of their older female characters into abject and monstrous old crones.

The next entry in the part, Sue Matheson's "'More like music': Aging, Abjection and Dementia at the Overlook Hotel," shows that abjection can take many forms—in this case, that of the Overlook Hotel, home to Jack Torrance and his family in Stanley Kubrick's classic film *The Shining*. Using a framework drawn from the musical concept of the fugue, where a motif is introduced and then repeated or revisited throughout the piece in different forms or pitches, Matheson examines the themes of abjection and dementia as they, also, recur and repeat in different forms throughout the narrative. The part's discussion of abjection, decay, and decrepitude closes with Jessica Balanzategui's essay "*The Skeleton Key*, the Southern Gothic and the Uncanny Decay of Teleological History." The film's narrative centers on the ghosts of two enslaved African Americans, violently murdered, who assume multi-generational ownership over the plantation where they were enslaved by continuously possessing young members of the family. Here, Balanzategui analyzes the ways in which the film uses spectrality to unsettle traditional paradigms of growth and aging, and in so doing challenge modernist visions of historical progress.

The third part, "Elders as Others/Outsiders," takes a close look at the ways in which the aged in horror films are made strange, uncanny, and thus terrifying. It opens with Cynthia J. Miller's "Making the Hard Choices: The Economics of Damnation in *Drag Me to Hell*," in which an ambitious young woman working in the mortgage department of a bank confronts an older woman with a physical appearance she finds grotesque and Old-World ways she finds incomprehensible. Rejecting the old woman's desperate pleas for financial relief, she finds herself cursed, and forced to confront demons in a battle where the stakes are not the material success she pursued so avidly, but control of her immortal soul. Jennifer Richards' essay, "'Mirror, mirror on the wall, who is the ugliest of them all?' The Elderly as 'Other' in *Countess Dracula*," turns its attention to a deranged elderly woman willing to sacrifice her own children to keep a dark secret. In this classic Hammer Studios release, the countess accidentally discovers the restorative powers of virgins' blood, and embarks on an endless series of murders to retain her newfound youth, not even sparing her own daughter. Richards' essay examines the film's narrative commentary on both the stigma of aging and our desperate struggle to avoid its visible consequences.

The part continues with "Old and In the Way: Torments of the Aging Male in *Psycho II*." Richard Franklin's 1983 film, a distant sequel to Alfred Hitchcock's 1960 classic, picks up the story of Norman Bates, cinema's most famous maniac as, in late middle age, he is declared cured and returned to society. Hans Staats' close reading focuses on Norman's predicament as an aging man thrown—like many older adults—into a world that has no place for him, in which he is surrounded by people indifferent to (or actively contemptuous of) his attempts to maintain his mental stability. The part closes with Stephanie M. Flint's "The Limits of 'Sundowning': M. Night Shyamalan's *The Visit* and the Horror of the Aging Body," which turns a critical eye on the popular director's tale of two children's first visit with the maternal grandparents they have never met. The film's meticulous development of the grandparents' increasingly bizarre behavior, and the children's divergent reactions to it—teenage Becca accepting it as a natural result of the mental changes that come with aging, while her younger brother Tyler is disturbed and repulsed by it— is, Flint argues, undone by Shyamalan's trademark last-act twist, which validates Tyler's repulsion and Others the grandparents on the basis of both their age and their (unrelated) mental illness.

Elders clinging desperately to youth, or even attempting to reverse the ravages of time, is an evergreen theme in horror cinema, and the essays that make up the next part, "Fighting Back Time," consider four divergent takes on it. In "'The powers of time can be altered': The Ambiguities of Aging in *Bram Stoker's Dracula* (1992)," Thomas Prasch unpacks the multi-layered treatment of time and aging in Francis Ford Coppola's version of the evergreen horror tale. Coppola's version of the Count, Prasch notes, appears able to control or even reverse the flow of time, altering his age to suit his circumstances. Other characters—notably Mina—are reborn, both in body and spirit, after lapses of centuries, giving them a different kind of quasi-immortality. Layered over both, Prasch notes, is Coppola's own revitalization and use of visual tropes from early silent cinema, born at precisely the same historical moment as Bram Stoker's novel. Tony Scott's *The Hunger* (1983) revels in its presentism every bit as much as Coppola's *Dracula* revels in its historicity. James J. Ward's "'You can be young forever': The Dread of Aging in Tony Scott's Art-Horror Film *The Hunger*" shows how Scott's choice to root his tale of two vampires—seemingly ageless but pointedly *not* immortal—in the image-obsessed Manhattan club scene of the early 1980s enables him to take a fresh approach to the idea that eternal youth is, for vampires, both a blessing and a nightmarish burden.

The latter two essays in the part move away from classical vampire tropes, to consider the battle against aging in a variety of other supernatural-horror settings. The monsters in Brian Brems' "The Brittle Body: The Elderly and Cars in *The Brotherhood of Satan*," for example, are elderly citizens of a forgotten desert town who kidnap children for use in the satanic rituals that prolong their lives. Brems explores how the film uses the bodies of automobiles—complex, expensive, and perpetually decaying—as proxies for the aging bodies of cult members who, through their pact with the Devil, seek to regain the lost vitality of body and freedom of action mockingly symbolized by the seemingly endless road that runs past their forgotten desert town. Rounding out the part, Karen J. Renner addresses "The Evil Aging Women of *American Horror Story*." Acknowledging the widely held position that the series' older female characters exhibit degrees of power and agency unusual in television, Renner tacks strongly against it. Far from transcending the limits Hollywood imposes on "women of a certain age," Renner argues, the characters remain subject to, and in some cases even reinforce, those limits.

The final part, "What the Old Folks Know," considers films about aging characters empowered—or trapped—by the lifetime of knowledge they possess. The four old men at the heart of A. Bowdoin Van Riper's essay "Disturbing the Past: Horror and Historical Memory in *Ghost Story* (1981)," for example, are haunted—literally and figuratively—by a terrible act committed in their youth and forgotten by everyone in their small New

8   Introduction

England town, save them and the vengeful ghost of their victim. Van Riper considers how the quartet's attempts to erase the woman from their town's history, and the ghost's horrific attempts to force her way back into it, shed light on the ways in which, individually and collectively, we remember the past. Stepping further back in time, Robert B. Luehrs' essay "Becoming Dr. Caligari" focuses on one of early cinema's iconic horror films. Luehrs examines how the title character of *The Cabinet of Dr. Caligari*—a deranged psychiatrist who dispatches his sleepwalking patient/henchman Cesare to murder his enemies—functions in the film not only as a prototypical mad genius, but as an embodiment of the qualities that, in the eyes of onlookers, render the elderly horrifying. Cesare may menace the onscreen heroes of *Caligari*, but the elderly doctor—whose bizarre appearance, shuffling gait, and unpredictable moods evoke the mental ravages of age—is disturbing in his uncanny familiarity.

The final two essays in the volume take up the intersection of old age with secret histories and forbidden knowledge. Mama Kay, the elderly African American woman featured in Olivia Oliver-Hopkins' "'Some kind of special': Queering Death Through Elder/Child Relationships in *The Haunting in Connecticut 2: Ghosts of Georgia*," is blind but—like the young white girl at the center of the story—possesses "the sight," and so the ability to see what lies below the surfaces where others' vision stops. Together, the two characters form a unique bond while confronting an evil, tied to America's "original sin" of slavery, that transcends death and time. Olivia Foxworth, the wealthy matriarch who terrorizes the four young protagonists of *Flowers in the Attic* (1987), is consumed by a different kind of "original sin": the incestuous marriage between her daughter and brother-in-law that, in her view, renders the children irredeemably corrupt. In the concluding essay in the volume—"*Flowers in the Attic:* The Elderly as Monster"—Liam T. Webb argues that the grandmother's twisted religiosity and determination to keep the family's dark secret hidden leads her to horrific acts of neglect, abuse, and ultimately murder.

Notes

1. Eliot, "The Love Song of J. Alfred Prufrock."
2. Cohen-Shalev, *Visions of Aging*, 9.
3. Beugnet, "Screening the Old," 4.
4. Shary and McVittie, *Fade to Gray*, 19.
5. Ibid.
6. Beugnet, "Screening the Old," 3.
7. Shary and McVittie, *Fade to Gray*, 16.
8. Harrison Ford, quoted in TheRaider.net, "Frequently Asked Questions."
9. See Chivers, *Silvering Screen*; Cohen-Shalev, *Visions of Aging*; Gravagne, *The Becoming of Age*.
10. For example, in films such as *The Straight Story* (1999), *The Best Exotic Marigold Hotel* (2011), *The Intern* (2015), or *Finding Your Feet* (2018).
11. Cohen-Shalev, *Visions of Aging*, 37.
12. Chivers, *Silvering Screen*, xii.
13. Beugnet, "Screening the Old," 4.
14. The most prominent semi-exceptions—*Alien* (1979) and John Carpenter's remake of *The Thing* (1982)—are horror/science fiction hybrids set in environments disconnected from the everyday world, for which audiences have no frame of reference for "normal."
15. Wood, "American Nightmare," 75.
16. "Dust thou art," God reminds Adam after his expulsion from Eden, "and unto dust shalt thou return."
17. For an overview of the subgenre, see Shelley, *Grand Dame Guignol*.
18. Manguel, "Bride of Frankenstein," 303, 307–314.

Bibliography

Beugnet, Martine. "Screening the Old: Femininity as Old Age in Contemporary French Cinema." *Studies in the Literary Imagination* 39, no. 2 (Fall 2006): 1–20.

Chivers, Sally. *The Silvering Screen: Old Age and Disability in Cinema.* Toronto: University of Toronto Press, 2011.
Cohen-Shalev, Amir. *Visions of Aging: Images of the Elderly in Film.* Brighton: Sussex Academic Press, 2009.
Eliot, T. S. "The Love Song of J. Alfred Prufrock." In *Collected Poems 1909–1962*, 6. New York: Harcourt, Brace, Jovanovich, 1991.
Gravagne, Pamela H. *The Becoming of Age: Cinematic Visions of Mind, Body and Identity in Later Life.* Jefferson, NC: McFarland, 2013.
Manguel, Alberto. "Bride of Frankenstein." In *British Film Institute Classics: The Best of International Cinema, 1916–1981* [2 volumes], edited by Rob White, I:297–316. London: Taylor and Francis, 2002.
Shary, Timothy, and Nancy McVittie. *Fade to Gray: Aging in American Cinema.* Austin: University of Texas Press, 2016.
Shelley, Peter. *Grand Dame Guignol: A History of Hag Horror from Baby Jane to Mother.* Jefferson, NC: McFarland, 2009.
Wood, Robin. "The American Nightmare: Horror in the 70s." In *Hollywood from Vietnam to Reagan.* New York: Columbia University Press, 1986, 70–94.

I.
Victims No More

"Ask not what your rest home can do for you"
Self-Agency and Public Service *in* Bubba Ho-Tep

PHILIP L. SIMPSON

Don Coscarelli's cult horror film *Bubba Ho-Tep* (2003) examines as poignantly as any mainstream tearjerker drama what it means to grow old, sick, frail, and abandoned in an American nursing home. The film is told from the point of view of an aged man who may or may not be Elvis Presley. In accordance with a persistent urban legend, he insists that he has traded places with one of his many impersonators to escape the unmanageable burden of his fame. The former King now lives in Mud Creek Shady Rest Convalescence Home in East Texas with no way to prove his real identity. As the plot unfolds, he must join forces with an elderly black man named Jack, who claims, implausibly, to be President John F. Kennedy, to combat an ancient Egyptian Soul Sucker (the titular Bubba Ho-Tep) who preys upon the aged.

The film's premise, while absurd on one level, is the foundation upon which Coscarelli constructs an elaborate allegory of the universal fear of not aging well. Through the voiceover reflections of Elvis, the film evokes the quiet despair of suffering helplessly as our formerly reliable bodies progressively fail in a myriad of painful (and often humiliating) ways. Our friends and family members die. Our interest in and engagement with the outside world vanishes. Our agency and autonomy irrevocably decline, leaving us dependent upon indifferent or condescending caregiver strangers. Our sexuality diminishes. Perhaps most frightening of all, our grown children, let alone the rest of the world, consign us to the living death of a backwater nursing home where they never come to visit. Even fame is no insulation against being forgotten by the world, as foregrounding the highly public characters of the King of Rock 'n' Roll and the President of Camelot suggests. Elvis' narration captures a horror more chilling, and relatable, than the cartoon evil of a reanimated mummy in cowboy duds who sucks souls through any bodily orifice—*any*—and then defecates the soul residue into the nursing home toilets while scrawling Egyptian hieroglyphic graffiti on the stall wall.

As the nature of its antagonist illustrates, *Bubba Ho-Tep* grafts one persistent strain in the horror genre—what might be called "elder horror," or the fear of aging, the decrepitude that accompanies it, and the aged—upon the dusty, linen-wrapped bones of the mummy subgenre of horror. The juxtaposition is not as incongruous as it first may appear. In that the old people in the nursing home are near natural death and the mummy has a supernaturally extended life, they are natural foils to one another. While one nearer to death may long for immortality, the monstrous Bubba Ho-Tep shows the undesirable outcome of actually achieving it. While Bubba Ho-Tep's parasitic relationship to the elderly as "easy targets" sets him in inimical opposition to Elvis and Jack, the men and the mummy share outsider status in a world that belongs to the young. From the perspective of those who are younger, both the elderly and the mummy share a certain uncanny quality: generally human in appearance, but otherwise sick unto death, dry, dusty, and moldering. The mummy is on the further end of the same continuum of slow decay upon which the elderly exist. As a metaphor of the marginalization and obscurity of advanced old age, the mummy is ideal. Elvis and Jack as sick old men cast away into a nursing home removed from and forgotten by the rest of the world recognize something of themselves and their eventual corporeal destiny in Bubba Ho-Tep's shambolic physical state as a mummy.

Old Versus the New, East Versus West

As Chris Vander Kaay and Kathleen Fernandez-Vander Kaay argue, mummy films are "almost always stories about people from later generations who have to deal with the mummy and its dark practices" originating in magical rituals from thousands of years ago.[1] Typically, mummy narratives are built upon the defilement of the Egyptian mummy's place of origin and/or burial place by Westerners, which activates an ancient magical curse that victimizes the defilers. *Bubba Ho-Tep* acknowledges this trope by opening with vintage faux-newsreel footage from Germany showing "adventurers" (a code word for Western intruders) lording over a crew of native laborers excavating the tomb of King Amen Ho-Tep near Luxor and Thebes. As a rule in mummy films, the Westerners unwisely bring back relics from the mummy's homeland/tomb to the Western world, thus bringing the curse with them. Accordingly, *Bubba Ho-Tep*'s opening newsreel concludes by showing King Amen Ho-Tep's remains being prepared for export and a caption (or a warning) that the mummy "will be coming soon to a museum near you."

These magical rituals and curses related to mummification are also associated in the Western cultural imagination with the exotic East. According to Charles Martin, for example, "the mummy represented an exotic Orient once magnificent in its power but now conquered and dissolute, a silent East that refused to reveal its mysteries."[2] By transposing an ancient Eastern world villain into a modern Western world setting, as Western mummy films tend to do, a number of dichotomies are created that produce dramatic tension, such as old versus the new and East versus West. Even in its very title, *Bubba Ho-Tep* foregrounds this oppositional tension between East and West. The opening title cards help unpack the meaning of the title by defining Ho-Tep for the audience as a "relative or descendant of the 17 Egyptian Dynasties, 3100–1550 B.C." and the "Family surname of an Egyptian pharaoh (king)," and Bubba as a "Male from the Southern U.S.," a "Good ole boy," and a "Cracker, red neck, trailer park resident." As a title, *Bubba Ho-Tep* both establishes the mortal combatants of its cultural collision as the Egyptian royal class on one side and the working-class, uneducated rural Americana in which Elvis Presley was the commoner King on the other side. It's a stark contrast, both echoing and playfully satirizing the tropes of earlier mummy films in which educated, relatively sophisticated white Westerners of privilege square off against the undead Egyptian royal and his exotic priests, acolytes, and minions.

Hannah Thompson, surveying the extensive range of Western mummy stories of the 19th century and movies of the 20th century, links the conventions established by the literary and cinematic predecessors to Bubba Ho-Tep when she identifies the following elements in the film: Bubba Ho-Tep's live mummification apparently as punishment for a forbidden love affair; flashback scenes revealing the desecration of Bubba Ho-Tep's tomb and the transportation of his body from Egypt to the United States, where he is put on display from museum to museum until a bus wreck releases him from his sarcophagus near the nursing home; the initial rational skepticism of and then gradual acceptance of the reality of the supernatural mummy's curse by Elvis; the learned guide to the lore of the mummy and how to fight it as represented by Jack; and the final destruction of Bubba Ho-Tep by fire at the hands of Elvis and Jack.[3] As a nightmare manifestation of a foreign Other, then, the film's mummy is set in opposition against two of the Western world's most iconic figures: the King of Rock and Roll and JFK. Their struggle represents not just a personal one, but a clash of civilizations: the kind of populist American cultural imperialism represented by Elvis Presley (popular music) and John F. Kennedy (presidential politics) against the undead vengeance of a conquered Eastern people represented by the monstrous Bubba Ho-Tep, transplanted into the Western world. From this perspective, then, pitting the living eldest of the later generations—the broken, infirm residents of a rural nursing home trapped in a kind of living death themselves—against an ancient, undead soul-sucking mummy makes metaphoric sense. The film's resolution of this conflict in favor of the partnership between Elvis and Jack over the mummy shows the West in ascendance over the ancient evil of the East. More specifically, the kind of

An ancient mummy (Bob Ivy) threatens elderly nursing home residents in *Bubba Ho-Tep* (2002).

rural populism embodied in Elvis vanquishes the foreign threat. Further, Elvis' reclamation of the King's crown is endorsed by Jack, a man who is both black and white in terms of his own claimed identity, implying a sweeping, biracial mandate for Elvis' victory.

Elvis and Jack: The Near Dead Versus the Undead

The dual protagonists of the film—Elvis and Jack, or the former King and JFK—literalize the cultural anxiety of aging even before the soul-sucker invades their nursing home. What they face, with the comedic and supernatural elements stripped away from the narrative, is what many elderly people endure in a society that often has no better solution to the problem of what to do with an aged population than to warehouse them in decrepit facilities (usually given pastoral names that belie their grim, institutional nature). Jack states the essence of the solution in stark terms: "That's what they brought us here for, to get us out of the way until we die." The elderly are barely maintained in their needs by underpaid, overwhelmed, and sometimes callous staff until such time as the patients die, to the unspoken relief of both staff and whatever family members may still be around.

This abandonment theme is introduced early in the film when Elvis' roommate Bull dies. Bull's daughter Callie shows up to collect his meager belongings, prompting Elvis to chide her for not having visited him once in the three years since Bull had been checked into the nursing home. She reacts defensively: "Don't lay some guilt trip on me, mister. I did what I could. I mean, if it hadn't been for Medicaid or Medicare, whatever that stuff was, he'd have been in some ditch somewhere. And I sure didn't have the money to take care of him." While Elvis views Callie as an unsympathetic character (clearly seeing in her a reflection of his own daughter's absence in his life), her words nevertheless summarize the dilemma of many grown children who must find a way, with insufficient individual financial means and only a couple of overburdened governmental health care programs as a safety net, to support aging parents. Often, the solution is to institutionalize these parents—and that is only if the families are lucky enough to qualify for Medicaid to pay for long-term residency in institutions such as Shady Rest.

The callousness of the system toward the aged persists even after they die. Bodies of the elderly are often unceremoniously disposed of with little respect for their dignity or the lives they lived. Two hearse drivers, who function in the narrative as comic versions of psychopomps for the characters who die in the nursing home, embody the system's callousness. Clad in the institutional white that signifies the cold indifference of the system in which they labor, the drivers are first seen wheeling Bull's body out on a gurney to the hearse. One of the drivers briefly ruminates about Bull's mortality: "Makes you wonder, doesn't it, what kind of life this old guy had?... His kids, his grandkids, his legacy. Look at him now." The other driver, clearly harried and on a schedule, barks, "Oh, who gives a shit," and slams the hearse doors shut. As an agent of the over-extended institutions charged with warehousing the elderly at the barest subsistence level and then clearing their bodies out of the system to make room for more, the second driver through his words and actions symbolically cuts off both Bull's legacy and the first driver's brief moment of humanism. By the time the drivers return to the nursing home for the body of the old woman killed by the mummy, the first driver demonstrates that he too has been de-sensitized by the system, a necessary condition of remaining employed in it. When his co-worker asks if he's "gonna get all weepy on me again," the driver replies, "No. I was merely gonna suggest that you some of this here deodorizer and spray it on that corpse because she's smellin' pretty ripe." The third time the drivers return—to cart away the body of Kemosabe, a resident who believed he was the Lone Ranger and died in the hallway firing toy pistols at Bubba Ho-Tep—they accidentally dump the body in the bushes carrying it from the facility and are only concerned if someone saw their careless act, not about the dignity of Kemosabe himself. What happens to Kemosabe, Bull, Elvis, Jack, and all the other patients in Shady Rest—victimized by a faceless uncaring health-care system and an ancient Egyptian mummy—is a metaphoric indictment of what happens to millions of aging Americans in a country unable or unwilling to provide for them as their health declines and their medical costs escalate.

Elvis and Jack's failing bodies are only part of the horrific conditions they must endure in Shady Rest, of course. Their mental state is also called into question, both by characters within the narrative and by the narrative itself. Are these men senile or otherwise brain damaged? Or are they really who they claim to be? Each man has an elaborate explanation for the unlikely circumstances that led them to Shady Rest: explanations that no one, including each other, gives any credence to. Their general lack of credibility further marginalizes them to the point where any self-agency is functionally impossible. Jack, for instance, believes himself to have been driven from power by a global conspiracy intent on murdering him. Pointing to his temple where he supposedly received the would-be assassin's bullet, he explains his unlikely survival in terms of a conspiracy theory even more outlandish than the ones already swirling around the shooting of the President: "They took a piece of my brain. They got it back in D.C. in that goddamn jar. I got a little bag of sand up there now." Elvis, though skeptical, raises an even bigger objection to Jack's story: "Jack, no offense, but President Kennedy was a white man." Jack indignantly retorts: "That's how clever they are! They dyed me this color. All over! Can you think of a better way to hide the truth than that?" Jack is perpetually afraid the conspiratorial "they" who tried to kill him in Dallas will return even now to finish the job. He does not trust the hospital staff or administration as agents of the same state that tried to kill him; "suits and white starches," he calls them. "I trusted them when I was back in Dallas," he laments, "and look where that got my brain and me. I'm thinkin' with sand here." Nor does he trust his fellow nursing home residents, including Elvis, whom Jack believes hates him. Jack's latent paranoia is fully engaged when he is assaulted in his sleep by a shadowy figure who snatches him from his bed to the floor. Jack exclaims to Elvis "they" have come for him. When Elvis asks who "they" are, Jack proposes a few likely suspects—Castro, or Lyndon Johnson, ultimately settling on Johnson because the assailant was "real goddamn ugly." When Elvis reasonably counters that Johnson is dead, Jack scoffs: "Shit. That ain't gonna stop him."

Of course, an elderly black man who insists he is JFK and believes an undead Lyndon Johnson is coming to finish off killing him is only slightly more ludicrous than an elderly white man, no matter how impressively pompadoured, who says he is Elvis. Advancing a theory in its own way no less conspiratorial than Jack's, Elvis explains that when he tired of the parasitic friends and promoters and women who were "suckin' me dry," he drove to Nacogdoches to sign over his life and fortune (most of it) to the Elvis impersonator Sebastian Haff, who contractually agreed to inhabit Elvis' identity until such time as Elvis wanted to take his life back. When a copy of the contract was lost in "a barbeque accident" that blows up Elvis' trailer and everything in it, however, Elvis didn't mind. He was content to be "Elvis playing Sebastian Haff playing Elvis," reaping the rewards of the impersonator's lifestyle—women, road trips, stage performances in front of adoring audiences, modest financial returns—without the pressure of the actual Elvis' life.

Just as the narrative suggests that Jack is not really JFK, the narrative also insinuates that Elvis may actually be Haff, who in his dotage has come to believe he was and is Elvis. For instance, if one is to believe his nurse, who insists on calling him Mr. Haff over Elvis' insistence to call him "Mr. Presley," Elvis is still suffering the physical and psychological after-effects of a fall from a stage, 20 years before (when he was performing as Haff performing as Elvis), that broke his hip and landed him in a coma. She claims that he "came out [of the coma] with a few—problems." Elvis calls her out on her euphemisms: "You're tryin' to say my brain's messed up, aren't you?" But when Haff, who enjoyed drugs and hard living even more than Elvis did, died from a heart attack, Elvis had no credible ground on which to take back his true identity. None of the staff or administration at Shady Rest believe Elvis' story, of course, which leaves him in an even more powerless state than his bodily infirmities have reduced him to. As a man with no solid identity and no way to prove to his skeptics that he is who he says he is, he has no real self-agency left. While the narrative ultimately leans toward verifying the authenticity of Elvis' identity as Elvis Presley, the ambiguity established in the opening scenes lingers. It is even possible that Elvis may be "no one" at all—an obscure everyman who seeks solace in his last years by believing that once upon a time he was not a nobody, but rather the most famous, influential American rock star of them all.

The film begins with this maybe–Elvis' voice-over narration as he transitions from a dream state to a decidedly unpleasant reality. His condition as an elderly, now asexual man in a nursing home bitterly contrasts with his memories of what it was like to be a virile younger man (and not just any man, but the hip-gyrating, sexualized figure of the King of Rock 'n' Roll himself) in his sexual prime. He dreams of his erect penis being "out and ... checking to see if that infected bump on the head of it had filled with pus again. If it had, I was gonna name that bump after my ex-wife Priscilla and bust it by jackin' off.... Or I'd like to think that's what I'd do. Dreams let you think like that. Truth was, I hadn't had a hard-on in years." He ruefully wonders if he is even capable of sex anymore: "If Priscilla discovered I was alive, would she come and see me? Would we still wanna fuck? Or would we merely have to talk about it?" His memory of sexual activity with his famous and beautiful wife, albeit bittersweet because the marriage ended in divorce, is spoiled by two factors. One, he is so remote from the prospect of any kind of sexual life that he no longer gets erections. Two, even if he could, if only to masturbate, his penis is corrupted, or literally being consumed to eventual nothingness, by some kind of foul infection or cancer (no one seems to know or care what it is) that makes sex even more of an impossibility. Elvis' penile affliction is a metaphor for his overall loss of potency and masculine energy. Accordingly, like the wounded Fisher King, he lives in a bed-ridden twilight state where he is neither dead nor alive, sinking daily into further entropy and ultimate dissolution.

His lack of a sex life, however, does not imply he has no interest in sex. The film directly questions the common stereotype of the elderly as having somehow outlived the sex drive. Though he still feels occasional stirrings of desire, Elvis is always acutely aware that women no longer view him as a potential sexual partner. When Elvis' deceased roommate's attractive young daughter Callie comes to collect her father's meager belongings, for example, Elvis catches a glimpse of her panties as she bends over and reflects: "The revealin' of her panties wasn't intentional or unintentional. She just didn't give a damn. She saw me as … physically and sexually non-threatenin.'" He thinks much the same when his unnamed nurse applies doctor-prescribed steroid cream to his penis to heal the inflammation: "A doll like this handlin' me without warmth or emotion. Twenty years ago. Just twenty, man. I could've made with the curly-lip smile and had her eatin' out of my asshole…. Where'd my youth go?" Elvis equates the loss of his virility and youth with a corresponding loss of agency. He feels powerless as a man. Largely confined to a sick bed and lost in bitter nostalgic longing for what once was, he is the most unlikely of heroes to take on the supernatural potency embodied by Bubba Ho-Tep. Uncertain of what he is seeing, for example, he literally and metaphorically turns his back on Bubba Ho-Tep's first victim, the elderly woman who is killed in the hallway outside Elvis' room and vainly pleads for Elvis to help her, to go back to sleep.

However, the conflict with the mummy ultimately reinvigorates both the minds and bodies of the protagonists, Elvis and Jack. The life-and-death struggle rouses them from their semi-somnolent state near death to give them a renewed sense of purpose, which in turn fills their aged limbs with energy. Given that this story focuses on male protagonists, their revitalization is coded as life-affirming, masculine re-empowerment. Their male revitalization through conflict with a supernatural force both parallels that of and contrasts with the undead mummy, which sustains its own prolonged, unnatural existence through consuming the energy of the living. Elvis' first stirring from his somnolent, living-death state occurs shortly after he battles the large scarab beetle in his room and is signified by his first erection in many years as his nurse rubs cream on his infected penis. Elvis reflects: "There'd been two presidential elections since I had a boner like that one. What gave here? Then I realized what gave. I was thinkin' about something that interested me. Not my next meal or going' to the crapper. I'd been given a dose of life again." He then invites his nurse to take a shower with him and to keep "pulling." While she declines, she does not take offense and playfully calls him an "old rascal" who should be ashamed of himself. Of this scene, Hannah Thompson writes that "it is only when [Elvis] begins to fight supernatural forces that he regains his masculinity, defiantly asserting his true identity as Elvis and assuming the additional role of hero."[4]

Jack, by contrast, is a more cerebral protagonist than Elvis. If Elvis is the action hero of the movie, Jack is the scholarly sidekick who imparts knowledge needed by the primary hero to act. Though Jack initially suspects his nocturnal attacker is Lyndon Johnson or another member of the cabal he believes tried to kill him, a few scenes later it is Jack who puts the evidence together to realize that his would-be assassin is not Johnson, but "an Egyptian soul-sucker of some sort," in Jack's words. As Jack begins to research what attacked him and the other residents, he rediscovers his sense of agency and purposeful action in the service of others—in this case, the supernaturally beleaguered residents of a nursing home. Identifying Elvis as his ally in the fight, Jack calls Elvis' attention to hieroglyphics scrawled on a bathroom wall. Jack explains that he looked them up in books he keeps in his room and is now able to (roughly) translate the writing, which includes such lines as "Pharaoh gobbles donkey goobers" and "Cleopatra does the nasty." Through further delving into the books that in essence serve as his grimoires for decoding the supernatural mystery, Jack discovers the connection between mummification and soul-sucking: "To stay alive, [the mummy] has to suck on the souls of the livin', and that if the souls are small, his life force doesn't last long." As Elvis' teacher, Jack coaches Elvis to see the counterintuitive reason why Bubba Ho-Tep has chosen Shady Rest and its slowly dying population: "Small souls are those that don't have much fire for life. You know a place like that?... It's perfect, you see? We're small souls, so we can't provide him much. But if that thing comes back two or three times in a row and wraps his lips around some elder's asshole, that elder is going to die pretty soon. And who would be the wiser?" Jack details his explanation of the mummy's reasons for consuming elderly life forces: "A mummy can't be getting too much energy from all this ... but the prey is easy. With new people comin' all the time, he can keep this up forever." Later, Jack solves the mystery of how the mummy ended up in East Texas: stolen while on a cross-country tour from a train by two thieves looking to ransom the body, only for their silver bus to be washed into a creek near the nursing home during a terrible storm. Jack speculates that when the coffin broke open during the crash, the mummy was "free of coffin and curse" but still needs souls. When Elvis asks what to do about this, Jack proposes flight: "Changing rest homes might be a good idea." However, Elvis has regained enough semblance of pride by this point in the narrative to reject flight. Albeit slowly and reluctantly, he chooses fight.

Elvis' reawakening to a sense of purpose, like his emergence from the coma after his fall, does not happen immediately but in stages. Following the example of Kemosabe, who fought the good fight against Bubba Ho-Tep and died with dignity restored and soul intact, Elvis takes his first tentative steps toward the personal re-empowerment he will need to fight the mummy by rejecting the infantalization the institutional system imposes upon him and those in his plight. When his nurse notes he's looking stronger but in the same breath chides him to come inside for his nap, he lashes out at her: "You fuck off, you patronizing bitch! I'm sick of your shit! I'll lube my own crankshaft from now on. You treat me like a baby again, I'll wrap this goddamn walker right around your head!" While Elvis' newfound sense of dignity is expressed in aggressively hypermasculine language and directed at a woman the film consistently portrays in a humiliatingly sexualized manner, the scene nevertheless demonstrates, however problematically in its gender dynamics, the return of Elvis' agency as a man and a human being.

Later that night, when he chances across a television commercial advertising a marathon of Elvis Presley movies in which the "two-fisted Hound Dog" is promised to "out-strum, outrace, out-fight, and outwit the bad guys," Elvis realizes that his films were not only badly made, but phony depictions of celluloid, traditionally masculine heroism that covered for his own lack of courage to fire the exploitative Colonel Parker, to treat his wife right, and to tell his daughter he loved her. Part of his reawakening to his sense of self is a belated reckoning with how badly he treated the two most important women in his life; he wishes he could somehow talk to his daughter again and tell her he loves her to "try and make things right somehow." That being impossible because of a lifetime of bad decisions and selfishness, he comes to a resolution that all he has left in life is the Shady Rest nursing home and its residents: "It ain't much of a home, but it's all I got. Well, goddamn it, I'll be damned if I let some foreign, graffiti-writin', soul-suckin', son of a bitch in an oversized cowboy hat and boots take my friends' souls and shit 'em down the visitor's toilet." He determines he will live up to his heroic on-screen persona: "In the movies, I always played heroic types. But when the stage lights went out, it was time for drugs and stupidity and the coveting of women. Now it's time ... to be a little of what I had always fantasized bein': a hero." He enlists Jack to defend the nursing home against

20   I. Victims No More

Elvis (Bruce Campbell) and JFK (Ossie Davis) prepare for the final showdown in *Bubba Ho-Tep*.

the mummy by addressing him as "Mr. Kennedy," reminding him of his former identity as a public servant, and then paraphrasing to him JFK's most famous call to civic service in his 1961 inaugural address: "Ask not what your rest home can do for you. Ask what you can do for your rest home."

Elvis concludes with an affirmation of his own identity as the King: "Let me paraphrase one of my own [best lines.] Let's take care of business." The climactic showdown with the mummy ensues, resulting in the dispatch of Bubba Ho-Tep and the deaths of both Elvis and Jack—but as Elvis lays dying looking up at the starry East Texas night sky, he finds comfort in the salvation of not only his soul but the souls of the dying residents of the nursing home, now forever safe from the soul-sucker's threat of total oblivion. Elvis' last words are both a celebration of communal redemption and his final affirmation of reclaimed identity through recitation of one of his most famous lines as a celebrity: "But I still have my soul. It's still mine. All mine. And the folks up there at Shady Rest, they have theirs too. And they're gonna keep 'em. Every single one. Thank you. Thank you very much."

So, while the film begins with a grim portrait of elderly men and women waiting to die (which makes their weakened souls easy pickings for the predatory Bubba Ho-Tep), it concludes on a more positive note, in spite of the deaths of both Elvis and JFK. Part of the elder angst with which both men must contend is that their apparent deaths in the glare of the public spotlight decades ago were meaningless, further casting their historical reputations into ignominy. Sacrificing themselves now, even if the rest of the world will never know it, to save the nursing home residents from an ancient evil which would even deny their souls an afterlife is a redemptive and fitting end for both. Thus, the misery of the first half of the film, in which the elderly are exiled and warehoused and forgotten by all of society, is ameliorated by the restoration of their dignity in the second. Through this arc, the film argues that the prescription for not aging well is to recommit in one's last years to an active life of purpose and self-agency in the service of others.

NOTES

1. Vander Kaay and Fernandez-Vander Kaay, *Horror Films by Subgenre*, 117.
2. Martin, "Can the Mummy Speak?"
3. Thompson, "'You Nasty Thing from Beyond the Dead,'" 242–244.
4. *Ibid.*, 246.

BIBLIOGRAPHY

Martin, Charles. "Can the Mummy Speak? Manifest Destiny, Ventriloquism, and the Silence of the Ancient Egyptian Body." *Nineteenth Century Contexts* 31, no. 2 (2009): 113–28.
Thompson, Hannah. "'You Nasty Thing from Beyond the Dead': Elvis and JFK Versus The Mummy in *Bubba Ho-Tep*." In *Undead in the West: Vampires, Zombies, Mummies, and Ghosts on the Cinematic Frontier*, edited by Cynthia J. Miller and A. Bowdoin Van Riper, 237–52. Lanham, MD: Scarecrow Press, 2012.
Vander Kaay, Chris, and Kathleen Fernandez-Vander Kaay. *Horror Films by Subgenre: A Viewer's Guide*. Jefferson, NC: McFarland, 2016.

Panic in Detroit
Don't Breathe *and the Fear of Old Cities, Homes and Men*

Isaac Rooks

Don't Breathe opens on a high-angle view of a quiet suburban street. The golden light hitting the trees and rooftops gives the scene a dreamy early-morning quality. Then the camera descends, and the audience realizes something is wrong. Overgrown sidewalks border an ill-maintained road patched with veins of tar. On closer inspection, the houses appear shabby, their windows boarded up. Most disturbingly, an old man walks along this empty street, dragging an unconscious young woman by her hair.

Fede Alvarez's 2016 thriller centers on a trio of teenage home invaders terrorized by the blind man they attempt to rob, an inversion of the classic *Wait Until Dark*. Our protagonists are Detroit residents who burglarize affluent homes. Rocky (Jane Levy) comes from a poor dysfunctional family and steals to support her younger sister. The middle-class Alex (Dylan Minnette) is motivated by unrequited love for Rocky, while Money (Daniel Zavatto) wants to cultivate his thuggish persona. Hoping to escape their dead-end city, they target a blind veteran (Stephen Lang) for their final heist. They know the Blind Man's house hides the settlement he received from the wealthy family of a young woman who killed his daughter in a car accident. They fail to anticipate, however, the Blind Man's capacity for violence or his secret: he has imprisoned and impregnated his daughter's killer, Cindy. This minimal plot motivates a series of high-concept set pieces as the young anti-heroes try to escape the Blind Man's home.

Reviews of *Don't Breathe* frequently praised it as a well-crafted and stripped-down thriller, but the appeal and efficacy of its thrills rely as much on its resonance with contemporary anxieties as on slick production.[1] The film addresses a range of issues related to disability, gender, class, and race, but—while touching on those topics—this essay engages intergenerational tensions. My reading does not negate the controversies and criticisms surrounding the film; in many ways, *Don't Breathe* remains a complicated and problematic text, but it is, I will argue, a deceptively rich one.

Don't Breathe exploits different ways that fears of the elderly are manifested in horror cinema. It addresses generic fears young people have about aging, monstrously personified by the Blind Man—bodily anxieties related to mortality and the inevitability of physical breakdown—as well as political and social fears of the elderly grounded in the cultural zeitgeist. The elderly in the United States are sometimes associated with reactionary and outdated worldviews, and their presence also serves as a reminder of how rapidly the world is changing. Old social infrastructure crumbles while the economy shifts in ways that eradicate once-thriving markets, leaving many disenfranchised and angry. These latter elements of elder horror became especially relevant in the polarized run-up to the 2016 election, when *Don't Breathe* was released. In the summer of 2016, the prospect of a Trump presidency existed for many as a frightening (but unlikely) possibility. Lang's character, an old white man waving a gun and literally blind to the world around him, feels like a grotesque parody of a Trump voter.

Other contemporary films, like *Purge: Election Year* and *Get Out*, signal their political engagement explicitly, but *Don't Breathe* is just as much a product of its time and just as capable of providing insight into its cultural moment. Given the political climate during and since the film's release, a movie about a young woman fighting to escape a Rust Belt hell and the violence of a terrible patriarch intent on controlling her reproduction takes on a powerful resonance.

This essay's structure mimics *Don't Breathe*'s opening shot: it starts wide and then moves in close, each section dealing with a different type of elder horror on display in the film. The first discusses the film's depiction of Detroit as an old, broken-down city suffering from the devastating consequences of economic restructuring and infrastructural collapse. The film's protagonists hope to leave it for California, a generic paradise for the young. The second addresses the old house: a labyrinthine structure that makes the Blind Man's madness manifest. The protagonists face the threat of becoming trapped in this structure, which houses a grotesque parody of patriarchal domesticity and gender roles. The final section focuses on the Blind Man, a crippled veteran and the film's villain. Though he initially appears to be an unlikely threat, he embodies young people's anxieties about the failure of the physical body, and the rage of disenfranchised aging people who cannot keep pace with a mutable and apathetic world.

The City

Don't Breathe is hardly the first film to use Detroit and the fallout of its economic hardships to enhance its eerie atmosphere. Several genre films, in fact, used the troubled city as a backdrop shortly before *Don't Breathe*'s release (*Only Lovers Left Alive*, *Lost River*, and *It Follows*). Detroit's residents and defenders are understandably sensitive about how outsiders depict and use the city. When Pedro Luque's cinematography lovingly showcases derelict buildings, it suggests another iteration of the derided practice of "ruin porn" photography.[2] Dora Apel notes that the ruin porn label tends to be applied to artistic works seen "as voyeuristic and exploitative, feeding off the city's misery while understanding little about its problems, histories, or dreams."[3] Ruin porn lacks context and betrays a disinterest in the city's people. This largely applies to *Don't Breathe*, which does little to engage the specifics of Detroit and its situation. No one expects a pacey thriller to offer extended lectures about the downfall of American manufacturing. However, *Don't Breathe* was barely even shot in Detroit. The cast and crew shot exteriors in Detroit for a week, but the "bulk of filming was done in Budapest, Hungary, in 2015 over the course of seven weeks."[4]

If the film is not grounded in the specifics of Detroit, what does it get out of using the city as a narrative setting? One possibility is that the city's steadily diminishing population enables the filmmakers to use it as an uncanny urban environment—a large city with few people. Consider the disturbing first shot of a street of empty houses. This "ghost city" setting lends the film's events an extra eerie quality. However, I argue that the location choice matters for reasons beyond the aesthetic. What the film wants from Detroit, or at least what it unavoidably gets from Detroit, is a broad idea.

While exploiting Detroit's name and reputation, *Don't Breathe* ultimately uses it as a generic depressed city. There are no distinct or iconic landmarks; nothing clearly marks the location as Detroit. Notably, the film also features no black actors, despite Detroit's mostly African American population.[5] Yet setting the film in Detroit carries weight. While it is hardly the only U.S. city affected by the atrophy of manufacturing, Detroit exemplifies the economic and infrastructural problems in the contemporary United States, conjuring up dramatic images of urban decay more vividly than similarly blighted Rust Belt towns. The film does not linger on derelict buildings for purely aesthetic purposes. A city's emptiness speaks of the economic forces that killed the way of living upon which that city depended, and *Don't Breathe*'s Detroit feels very empty.

Upon hearing that another peer has left Detroit, Rocky observes: "Everybody's leaving." This does not feel like an exaggeration. Rocky, Alex, and Money seem to be some of the few residents left. Rocky's comment follows another high-angle shot showcasing wide streets with few cars, bordered by vacant lots and shabby buildings. Later, the crew loudly plan their robbery at a diner where they are the only customers, sitting in a sea of empty tables. The film never features background extras until the final scene in a bus station (Detroit's only active spot being where people go to leave). Of course, part of what makes Detroit a compelling site is the fact that it has not always been in its current depressed state.

Don't Breathe provides some details that hint at what the city was once. The most striking example of this is an uncommented-upon background detail early in the film. Money meets a dealer to sell some stolen goods in an abandoned factory. Visible in the background is a mural on the derelict factory's walls, depicting smokestacks, gears, and workers. It is a stylized, romanticized depiction of the labor that might once have occurred in this gutted space. It exists now merely as a ghostly echo, emphasizing the building's current decrepitude and the ignoble business done there. Our protagonists are left to make a living in the ruins of a way of life and labor confined to the nostalgic past. They work not to make a living here, but to escape.

If Detroit stereotypically suggests hopelessness, a different generic buzz surrounds another key location for the film, one referenced but never seen: California. California is where our protagonists hope to find a better life. Saying that one plans to move to "California" does little to narrow things down. California is a large and diverse state, one with its own economic hardships and inequity. At this point, the California dream seems like a played-out cliché. U.S. pop culture has thoroughly explored the darker side of the Golden State; think of the many film noirs set in major cities like Los Angeles and San Francisco. Yet, in broad strokes, California makes sense as Detroit's opposite.

California represents the young and the vigorous, while Detroit signifies a dying way of life. By no means is Detroit a terribly old city. However, in a bit of poetic coincidence, Detroit resembles an aging human body. It enjoyed its greatest vitality in the post–World War II boom years. Over the course of about 70 years, this thriving metropolis became a crumbling husk. Detroit's collapse essentially played out in the "threescore

While Money (Daniel Zavatto) makes a shady deal in an abandoned factory, a mural speaks to a more glorious past for the building and Detroit in *Don't Breathe* (2016).

years and ten" that the Bible suggests humans should expect to live. Meanwhile, California is literally a younger part of the United States. Throughout the country's history, California was associated with different manifestations of vitality and youth, from westward expansion, to beach and hotrod culture, to tech-savvy progressivism. This notion of California's promise is as much a construct as the film's futureless Detroit. *Don't Breathe* is not concerned with the subtleties and complexities of reality. Based on popular stereotypes, Detroit is dying and California is for the young.

Don't Breathe centers its conflict on class and age. Without prospects of gainful employment or any discernable social support system, our hopeless protagonists finance their ambitions through criminal activities. In order to reach the Promise Land, they must rob an even more marginalized member of their community: the Blind Man. They know he is aging, believe him to be infirm, and suspect he possesses huge amounts of cash, a settlement from an elite family (who offer monetary compensation to excuse the trauma caused by their carelessness). While others leave Detroit, the Blind Man remains a lone holdout clinging to the past. And, as the youths discover, that isolation allows him to engage in horrific activities in the privacy of his home.

The Home

The Blind Man's well-maintained and unspectacular two-story home seems like an unlikely house of horrors. The surrounding area is what makes it unsettling. Before introducing the home, *Don't Breathe* offers an extended montage of the abandoned structures and rundown neighborhood around it. That context turns the house into the suburban equivalent of a Gothic castle in an ominous wilderness. Without belaboring the point, this street tells a story, illustrating the fallout of the grand-scale processes affecting cities

The Blind Man's well-maintained suburban home sits surrounded by decay and holds dark secrets in *Don't Breathe*.

like Detroit. Looking at the Blind Man's home, one can imagine that this was once a nice residential street. However, the economy and infrastructure that once supported this neighborhood and its community has withered away, and now these abandoned homes decay from neglect. The initial scene invites the audience to question who this lone holdout is, refusing to leave and keeping his home in good condition. Aging and isolated, the Blind Man clings to a bygone age that will not return. This offers early clues about his deeper pathology.

The interior of the home, the film's main arena, provides further insights into its reticent resident's psyche. The audience gets little concrete information about him, but becomes well acquainted with his home. When our protagonists first enter, the film provides an extensive tour in a sequence made to look like a single Steadicam shot. This sequence not only orients the audience to the structure, it also encourages them to read the house and its set dressings in order to understand the Blind Man.

As one expects in narrative cinema, the protagonists' actions largely dictate the camera's movements during this sequence. It follows them as they explore the house, and the audience sees what they see. However, the knowing camera will move beyond them or lag behind to highlight relevant details. When it drifts over Alex's head to focus on a set of sharp tools on the wall before rejoining him, the audience (knowing the genre) anticipates that these props will play a grim role in the future. As Money goes upstairs, the camera floats up through the crawlspace to the next floor. Rocky will eventually enter this space during an escape attempt, so this camera move provides information that will be relevant later. However, it also hints that dark secrets lie hidden behind the visible in this house. When Money peeks into the Blind Man's room, the camera shows him in bed. It then glides under his bed to reveal a hidden pistol. While the Blind Man sleeps, apparently helpless, an easily accessible instrument of death lies concealed within his reach.

The intimate bond between the Blind Man and his home, a structure reflecting and externalizing his mental state, speaks to a long history between the two. The home itself is a relic of the past, preserved long past the expiration date of its surroundings. The Blind Man's intimate knowledge of it—a product of his blindness and everyday need to navigate the space—becomes most obvious during a chase scene in the basement. Shelves packed with junk turn the space into a maze. When the Blind Man shuts off the lights, it further compromises the teens' ability to navigate the unfamiliar environment. The extent of the clutter, indeed the clutter itself, suggests how long the Blind Man has lived in the house, and the ease with which he maneuvers through it suggests that he knows it as thoroughly as he does his own body. Bits of junk possess great meaning for him. As he pursues his prey, he runs his hand along the wall. When it brushes against a piece of bric-a-brac, it gives a clear indicator of place, allowing him to abruptly change direction. The disorderly basement also suggests a chaotic and disturbed mind. As in horror films like *Psycho* and *Silence of the Lambs*, this subterranean space contains the ultimate manifestation of his madness and inability to let go of the past.

Aboveground, the Blind Man's collection of photos and home movies speak to a harmless nostalgia. When the teens enter, the Blind Man has fallen asleep to the antiquated technology of a VHS tape featuring his dead daughter. Yet there is an ominous edge to the mementos surrounding him. On the mantelpiece, Rocky finds a framed picture of his daughter placed upside down, signaling the warped nature of the Blind Man's grief. It also acknowledges that he cannot appreciate or draw comfort from such items in the same way a sighted person would.

While the VHS offers a simulated recreation of the past, the Blind Man hopes to literally restore his lost child. His plan also satisfies a primitive notion of retribution-based justice. In the basement, Rocky and Alex find Cindy, the daughter's killer, muzzled and chained to the wall. The pair tries to help her escape, but during their attempt, the Blind Man accidentally shoots and kills her. When the Blind Man captures Rocky, he reveals that he had impregnated Cindy and was going to force her to deliver the baby before freeing her. As he sees it, since she "took my child away from me, I thought it only fair that she give me a new one." Viewing Rocky as responsible for Cindy and the fetus's death, it now falls on Rocky to become an unwilling mother.

Prior to this point, the film illustrates how the *unhomely* home connects Rocky and the Blind Man, making them complementary and opposed figures.[6] The Blind Man lost his wife and daughter. Rocky lost her father. Each deals with their broken homes differently. During an early robbery, Rocky enters a teenage girl's room. While the boys loot and steal, she puts on the girl's clothes and collapses into her bed. This momentary masquerade takes on greater significance when the audience learns that Rocky's father left her and her sister with an abusive mother. As a result, Rocky adopted a maternal role in relation to her sister, a responsibility ostensibly beyond her years that left her fantasizing about escape. This coping method allows her to imagine moving on to a different way of life. On the other hand, the aging Blind Man cannot imagine any other way of life and only seeks to recreate the past. Significantly, it seems to be both a personal and social past that he wants to resurrect.

The setup devised by the Blind Man resembles a grim parody of familial roles and patriarchal power. He silenced Cindy and made her a domestic prisoner. For him, she existed only to make a baby. After she dies, the Blind Man dumps her into a tomb full of oil-like liquid under the basement floor. When he covers that with tiles, Cindy disappears into the house. The threat posed by the Blind Man is particularly acute for Rocky, already weighed down by the responsibilities of de-facto motherhood and determined to escape her dead-end town. The Blind Man threatens to trap her there in (literally constraining) domesticity, forcing her to serve a pregnancy-based prison sentence. There is also no guarantee that the Blind Man will keep his word and not condemn her, as he did Cindy, to be in and of his home forever.

The film avoids giving the rape scene any sense of latent eroticism. It removes the fleshiness from the potential encounter, rendering it disturbingly clinical. On a hot plate, the Blind Man thaws his frozen semen, pictured in a close-up that reveals pubic hairs floating in the milky slime, and draws this substance into a turkey baster, an artificial phallus.[7] Further demonstrating his perverse attitudes toward women, the Blind Man argues that his intended rape is not a rape, claiming there is nothing sexual about his plan to forcibly inseminate Rocky. Like many rapes, this is about power, not sex.

The threat of the Blind Man's misogynistic violence pays off with a cathartic act of retribution. With Alex's help, Rocky escapes and handcuffs the Blind Man to the rig he used to bind the women. Having escaped his trap, she appropriates his phallic instrument, and rams the baster into the Blind Man's mouth, causing him to choke on his own semen. Though controversial, Rocky's plight and retaliation fit conventional patterns in horror cinema. In many ways, *Don't Breathe* neatly illustrates Carol Clover's conception of the sadomasochistic thrills of watching the "Final Girl" fight back against a sexually dysfunctional monster. Of course, also in keeping with classic horror, the monster's defeat proves less conclusive than the hero hopes.

The Blind Man escapes and shoots Alex, but Rocky manages to get the money and leaves the Blind Man for dead in his basement. While Rocky waits in the bus terminal with her sister, a story on the local news reveals that the Blind Man survived. The news story celebrates the Blind Man for killing the teenage intruders who assaulted him. The media thus creates a different version of our protagonists' mistake. The teen trio saw the Blind Man's age and disability and assumed he would be a frail victim. He was not. The media see an innocent elderly man acting in justified self-defense against youthful assailants to protect the sanctity of his home. Rocky and the audience know better. Outsiders fail to understand how unsanctified that home is. They also fundamentally misunderstand the home's resident.

The Man

The audience can, perhaps, sympathize with the reporter's confusion, since the film offers few details about the Blind Man and his life. It never even names him properly. As a result, the few bits of information provided take on disproportionate significance in terms of how the audience thinks about the character. The audience learns three significant things about the Blind Man. The first is that he lost his daughter. His wife's fate remains a mystery, but his daughter's death provides his primary motivation and explains his madness. The second, which the film repeatedly emphasizes, is that he is a veteran. The last is that he is blind.

The film's treatment of disability is problematic, but critical to its function as a work of elder horror, as the Blind Man's disability codes him as monstrous and reflects his personal failings. Tellingly, the thing marking him as physically different affects his eyes, a body part typically associated with an individual's character, humanity, and soul. His blindness also crudely indicates the character's inability to move on. He literally cannot see and appreciate the world around him. Ableist anxieties run through the film, and manifest in different ways. The Blind Man's sightless eyes are presented as disturbing and disgusting. The film frequently emphasizes them through close-ups and dramatic lighting. Indeed, his eyes are not just a significant bit of iconography within the film. They were featured prominently in advertisements selling *Don't Breathe* as a horror film.[8] The Blind Man's disability makes him both a more and less effective antagonist. His blindness has not elevated his other senses (although the title *Don't Breathe* suggests he possesses unusually sensitive hearing), but it allows him to comfortably navigate the familiar dark while our protagonists stumble about in terror. The film also mines his blindness for black comedy. There is grim humor in Alex pressing up against a wall to avoid the Blind Man as he stalks past obliviously, or the reveal that the Blind Man accidentally stabbed the already dead Money when he thought he was stabbing Alex. While *Don't Breathe*'s treatment of disabilities is troubling, it is inflected by the film's elder horror, and the commentary introduced by the Blind Man's wounded warrior status.

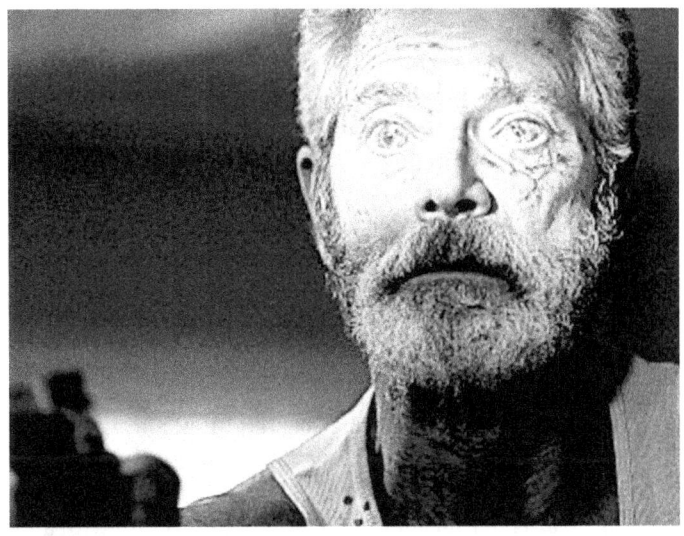

The Blind Man's (Stephen Lang) mutilated eyes mark him as monstrous, but also speak to a traumatic past in service of his country in *Don't Breathe*.

As a horror film, *Don't Breathe* displays a general fascination with the spectacle of wrecked bodies. The film features few deaths, but renders each in gruesome detail. The most jarring example is the early death of Money. The Blind Man shoots him pointblank in the head. In a close-up, the audience watches in slow motion as the flesh of Money's face ripples at the bullet's impact. His mouth glows from the muzzle flash and blood flies from his mouth and head. The deaths of Cindy and Alex are not as brutally rendered, but the film uses slow motion for both in order to extend the moment's horror, as blood flies and bodies fall. Death hovers over most horror films, as the audience anticipates the next act of violence, and this becomes especially notable in horror films featuring elderly villains. Their very presence reminds the audience that death comes to all, sooner or later.

Numerous qualities make elderly people such as the Blind Man prime horror antagonists; their apparent vulnerability rendering their threat unexpected and shocking. The Blind Man's disability, in fact, makes him seem vulnerable. Indeed, Alex expresses reservations about victimizing a blind person. The crew thinks of the Blind Man as a helpless victim, right up until he takes away Money's gun and turns it on him. Even as it shocks the audience to have an elderly person turn out to be dangerous, however, it feels appropriate when embodiments of mortality become dealers of death. The elderly signal the inevitability of aging, and the way people's bodies and minds change and become strange. Amelia DeFalco describes aging as an inherently uncanny experience: "For many aging becomes a process of alienation, producing a doubling of self."[9] Young people can disavow, but never escape, this inevitable process, resulting in an increasingly untenable "simultaneous belief/nonbelief" in aging.[10] Given youth culture's impotent denial of aging and death, elderly antagonists fit well with Robin Wood's classic conception of the monster representing the return of the repressed.

The question of what constitutes "elderly" is subjective and relative, but at the time of filming in 2015, Lang was in his early 60s, his hair and beard visibly graying. More importantly, Lang is considered "old" to the protagonists, who presumably also represent the film's target audience. The film codes his advanced age in various ways, including the various mementos that testify to the pain and loss he has experienced in his life, and the familiar clutter that suggests the accumulation of years. However, the most important qualifier is his blindness, which signals his body's failing and vulnerability.

His eyes are framed by scarred flesh, and in some shots the eyes themselves appear cut and mutilated. The film explains that he lost his sight in the Gulf War. In the final news report, it elaborates that a grenade fragment blinded him. Linking his injury to the Gulf War is significant in two ways: It aligns him with a military intervention that returned to haunt a new generation, but also lets the audience know that his blindness came late in life, presumably after a long period of physical ability and fitness.

The Blind Man's military past makes him intimidating and formidable, and explains why this sightless older man easily bests younger men in physical combat and handles weapons adroitly. It also hints at another layer of trauma contributing to his disturbed mental state. The character's disability seems to reflect his madness, and the film emphasizes the connection between his military service and blindness repeatedly. Even if this terrible injury is unrelated to his mental condition, it adds layers to the character that make him more than a simple devil.

While the Blind Man is monstrous, he is also a victim. His actions are not wholly unjustified—the teens are invading his home to steal money meant to compensate him for a horrible tragedy—but the justification depends on perverse logic. Given the teens' age and economic status, the mere fact that he owns a home makes him seem privileged, but he makes it clear that he sees the money as a reflection of how the justice system failed him. "She should have gone to prison," he says of Cindy, "but rich girls don't go to jail." Society has failed him in other ways too. He was crippled while, as the final news story puts it, he "fought for our country." Despite his sacrifice, the whole world has moved on and left him behind. As a result, he lashes out, violently struggling to keep what belongs to him. Ominously, at the end of the film, nothing much has changed. Rocky may escape, but the Blind Man will remain. Ultimately, the film's horror stems from the struggle of this pathetic and terrible relic to not just continue, but to monstrously reproduce. The prospect of his perpetuation terrifies those hoping to escape what he, his home, and his city represent.

NOTES

1. Kim Newman, "Don't Breathe Review," *Empire Online*, September 5, 2016, http://www.empireonline.com/movies/breathe-2/review/. Brian Rafferty, "We Need to Talk About That Awful Don't Breathe Twist," *Wired*, September 2, 2016, https://www.wired.com/2016/09/dont-breathe-twist-talk/.

2. Two editorials about the recent spate of genre films set in Detroit applied the "ruin porn" label to

Don't Breathe. One was written by Justine Smith for Rogerebert.com, and the other by Julie Hinds for *Detroit Free Press*. Critic Kirk Michael felt the film looked as if "one of those 'ruin porn' coffee table books has come to life."

3. Apel, *Beautiful Terrible Ruins*, 23.

4. Hinds, "'Don't Breathe' Is the Latest Movie." Hinds cites producer Rob Tapert's explanation that the elimination of Michigan's tax incentives affected where the relatively low budget film could afford to shoot. Still, the decision leaves the film open to criticism. Kirk Michael jokingly speculates that the decision was made "because the filmmakers wanted to assure that Detroit was denigrated, but in no way enriched by the film's production."

5. Census data from 2016 registers over 80 percent of Detroit's population as African American, one of the highest percentages for a U.S. city (https://www.census.gov/quickfacts/fact/table/detroitcitymichigan/PST045216).

6. "Uncanny" translates from Freud's original term "*unheimlich*," denoting the opposite of "homely" and therefore the opposite of what is known, familiar, and comforting. The strange, sinister house therefore makes an excellent uncanny subject (Freud, "The Uncanny," 220).

7. Timothy Shary and Nancy McVittie note, in *Fade to Gray*, that the "inappropriate" sexuality of older women tends to find its place in horror, while the "dirty old man" is seen as a more comic figure. They note that older men in horror tend to be "notably desexualized and, as a result, presented as far less sinister and disturbing" than their female counterparts (86). The Blind Man's dysfunctional sexuality and grotesque impotence can be seen as an interesting inflection of common cinematic trends related to seeing older people's sexuality as somehow wrong.

8. The official trailer ends with a close-up on the Blind's Mans wide, mutilated eyes. One version of the film's poster features his disembodied all-white eyes hovering over the house.

9. DeFalco, *Uncanny Subjects*, 5.

10. *Ibid.*, 4.

Bibliography

Apel, Dora. *Beautiful Terrible Ruins: Detroit and the Anxiety of Decline*. New Brunswick: Rutgers University Press, 2015.

DeFalco, Amelia. *Uncanny Subjects: Aging in Contemporary Narrative*. Columbus: Ohio State University Press, 2010.

Don't Breathe. Directed by Fede Alvarez. 2016. Culver City, CA: Sony Pictures, 2016. DVD.

Freud, Sigmund. "The Uncanny." In *The Standard Edition of the Complete Psychological Works of Sigmund Freud. Vol. XVII (1917–1919)*, 219–253. Translated by James Strachey. London: The Hogarth Press and the Institute of Psychoanalysis, 1955.

Hinds, Julie. "'Don't Breathe' Is the Latest Movie to Use Detroit as Its Scary Setting." *Detroit Free Press*. 25 August 2016. https://www.freep.com/story/entertainment/movies/julie-hinds/2016/08/25/dont-breathe-horror-film-detroit/89304296/.

Michael, Kirk. "Film Review: 'Don't Breathe.'" *Sonoma Index-Tribune*. 1 September 2016. http://www.sonomanews.com/entertainment/6035826-181/film-review-dont-breathe.

Newman, Kim. "Don't Breathe Review." *Empire Online*. 5 September 2016. http://www.empireonline.com/movies/breathe-2/review/.

Rafferty, Brian. "We Need to Talk About That Awful Don't Breathe Twist." *Wired*. 2 September 2016. https://www.wired.com/2016/09/dont-breathe-twist-talk/.

Shary, Timothy, and Nancy McVittie. *Fade to Gray: Aging in American Cinema*. Austin: University of Texas Press, 2016.

Smith, Justine. "Detroit: The New City of American Horror." Rogerebert.com. 24 August 2016. https://www.rogerebert.com/balder-and-dash/detroit-the-new-city-of-american-horror.

"It's the work of a crazy old woman"
Revenge of the Elderly in The Devil-Doll

MARTIN F. NORDEN

Leo Townsend, fan magazine scribe and aspiring screenwriter, couldn't help but chuckle as he trotted away from a Metro-Goldwyn-Mayer backlot on a late spring day in 1936. A dapper young man with a pencil mustache and a penchant for double-breasted suits, Townsend had been collecting material at MGM's Culver City complex for stories to publish in *Modern Screen* and was now scribbling a few notes to himself on the fly. "Came across an old woman smoking a cigar on the MGM lot recently," he wrote. "Stopped for a second look and it turned out to be Lionel Barrymore, all made up for the title role in *The Witch of Timbuctoo*. The cigar wasn't part of the make-up; it was merely part of Lionel's between-scenes relaxation." Townsend concluded his commentary with a familial kicker: "Just before a crowd gathered someone told him he looked the picture of his sister, Ethel. For some reason or other the statement didn't seem to please him one bit."[1]

In a sense, the incongruous situation that Townsend had encountered—the spectacle of an elderly Ethel Barrymoresque woman puffing away on a tobacco product associated almost exclusively with men—was a thematic preview of the horror-fantasy film on which Ethel's elder brother was then working: *The Witch of Timbuctoo,* later retitled *The Devil-Doll*. Directed by Tod Browning and featuring a large number of performers in their 50s or older, the film gleefully tweaks a number of assumptions about gender and old age. Though the film includes such well-worn character types as polished but corrupt middle-aged businessmen, it also features a trio of decidedly different elders: an embittered and vengeful man disguised as a gentle old woman, and a husband-and-wife team of mad scientists who defy gender expectations. This essay examines the relationship of old age to horror in *The Devil-Doll* with attention paid to the film's intersecting concerns of advanced age and gender. It also investigates *The Devil-Doll*'s relationship to its literary source material and its troubled production history as they relate to the elderly characters.

Literary Origins

The Devil-Doll can trace its age- and gender-bending roots to a novel titled *Burn, Witch, Burn!* Penned by journalist-*cum*-fiction writer Abraham Merritt, it was initially published in four parts in the pulp magazine *Argosy Weekly* in late 1932 and as a freestanding book the following year. Similar to Bram Stoker's *Dracula* in its occasional use of diary entries to propel the narrative, *Burn, Witch, Burn!* is mostly a first-person account of highly unsettling supernatural occurrences in contemporary Manhattan. The narrator of the piece, a physician who goes by the pseudonym "Dr. Lowell," is an expert in neurology and brain pathology. Julian Ricori, a Prohibition-era crime boss, has asked him to minister to his right-hand man, Thomas Peters, who has become inexplicably paralyzed. Peters dies of unknown causes, and the doctor eventually learns from fellow physicians that other people have been similarly stricken. The common denominator among the victims is strange, to say the least; they were all patrons of a Manhattan toyshop operated by a mysterious figure named Madame Mandilip. Readers later learn that Mandilip has used dark magic to inject the souls of her victims into dolls that become subject to her murderous will. Laschna, the proprietor's adoptive niece and assistant, reveals late in the book that Mandilip lived in many European cities—Berlin, Paris, London, Prague, Warsaw—before moving to New York and had created dolls that had killed in each of them. Twenty new dolls have fatally struck in Manhattan, but Mandilip's motivation for creating the lethal figures is never made clear. To Dr. Lowell's question "Why do the dolls kill?" Laschna haltingly replies under hypnosis, "To ... please ... her." With no point to the murders, Mandilip and her miniaturized minions are not unlike an ever-spreading plague that kills indiscriminately.

Browning, who had been casting about for a horror-film follow-up to his 1935 film *Mark of the Vampire* and turned to the pulp press before for inspiration,[2] was fascinated by a number of the book's qualities: among them, its deployment of witchcraft in a modern urban setting, its convoluted moral struggles, and the androgyny of the elderly Madame Mandilip. The physician narrator characterizes her as "a giantess whose heavy face with its broad, high cheek bones, mustached upper lip and thick mouth produced a suggestion of masculinity grotesquely in contrast with the immense bosom." Mandilip's physically imposing qualities are in direct contrast to her advanced age, a situation of which the character is keenly aware. When Dr. Lowell, Ricori, and the gangster's henchmen arrive at her toyshop near the end of the novel, for instance, the powerful six-footer mockingly says to them, "I would have met you at my outer door—but I am an old, old woman and timid!" Browning could not help but be intrigued.

Though *Burn, Witch, Burn!* alludes to the supposed pervasiveness and long history of the "dark flame of evil wisdom," it does not explain the immediate source of Mandilip's supernatural powers. Instead, much of the book dwells on Dr. Lowell's refusal to believe that witchcraft is involved. "No, Madame Mandilip was no 'witch,' as Ricori thought her," he opined. "She was mistress of some unknown science—that was all." Though Merritt was perhaps interested in showing the folly of such thinking—there are some things in this world that science cannot explain, a concept that Lowell eventually accepts—Browning saw the indeterminacy as an opportunity to create a full-blown horror film.

From Novel to Screenplay

With his studio's assent, Browning purchased the movie rights to the Merritt novel in June 1935, less than two months after the premiere of *Mark of the Vampire*. When word got around Hollywood about the sale, pundits quickly picked up on the connections between *Burn, Witch, Burn!* and the industry's then-recent spate of horror films. "The Frankenstein influence is spreading," wrote the *Los Angeles Times'* Edwin Schallert. "Evidences of this are found in the purchase by MGM of a story called *Burn, Witch, Burn* ... which concerns the animation of the human manner of dolls. It is a real horror story, part of it being laid in a hospital as well as a doll shop. So you can imagine the goings on there will be."[3]

Using the Merritt novel as his basis, Browning began developing a voodoo-themed story with the help of screenwriter Guy Endore, who had written *Mark of the Vampire* and contributed to the scripts for the 1935 horror films *Mad Love* and *The Raven*. Eager to exploit the novel's darkly supernatural qualities, Browning even consulted with a Haitian "voodoo medicine man" known simply as Owoli to add greater authenticity to the narrative.[4] After an MGM reader had deemed the resulting 37-page story "superlative horror stuff ... completely realized in the rough,"[5] the director added another writer to his creative team: principal *Frankenstein* screenwriter Garrett Fort, who had collaborated with Browning on the script for *Outside the Law* in 1930 and written the adapted screenplay for Browning's *Dracula* the following year. Working in close collaboration, Browning, Endore, and Fort developed a shooting script during July and August of 1935. They tentatively titled their film *The Witch of Timbuctoo*.[6]

Browning and his screenwriters moved the action to locations far beyond the limited settings of Merritt's novel. Taking their cue from the prevailing Hollywood interest in faraway lands,[7] they jettisoned the book's sole location—lower Manhattan—in favor of settings in South America, Africa, and Europe. Even before Browning, Endore, and Fort had completed their script, MGM began publishing advertisements in the trade press that trumpeted the anticipated film's globe-spanning narrative. One such ad read: "Fantastic Voodoo rites in Africa, the horrors of Devil's Island and the mysteries of the Paris underworld. To be directed by Tod Browning as one of the most important mystery-horror thrillers of the year."[8]

The narrative cultivated by the Browning-Endore-Fort team veered far from the novel and hinged to a large extent on Browning's conception of the pivotal character of Madame Mandilip. After briefly considering the tall and stately British actress Constance Collier for the role, Browning went in a distinctly different direction. Looking for an excuse to revive a character concept that he had developed with the late Lon Chaney in *The Unholy Three* (1925)—a man disguises himself as an elderly woman to avoid arrest—Browning made a decision that displeased the novel's author; he converted the Mandilip figure into a vengeful male who assumes the guise of a kindly old woman to elude the police.[9]

Browning's choice for the role was the renowned stage and screen actor Lionel Barrymore. He had worked with Barrymore on *The Show* (1927), *West of Zanzibar* (1928), and *Mark of the Vampire* and had admired the actor's work as the revenge-minded Duke Cathos de Alvia in *Drums of Love*, a 1928 film directed by Browning's mentor and fellow Kentuckian, D.W. Griffith. Though Barrymore did not possess Chaney's chameleon-like performative talents, he was a redoubtable actor who had won an Oscar for his performance in 1931's *A Free Soul* and had high name-recognition value. With Barrymore in mind for the role that would unquestionably have gone to Chaney in an earlier day, Browning introduced a powerful revenge streak to the film-in-progress that was completely lacking in the novel.

Having worked with many aging actors such as Chaney, Barrymore, Bela Lugosi,

Edward Van Sloan, Lionel Atwill, Jean Hersholt, and Owen Moore late in his career, Browning had absolutely no misgivings about centering his new film on a character played by an actor who was then in his late 50s. In a 1933 interview, Browning scoffed at the idea that younger was better than older. For him, filmmaking was all about character and story regardless of the age of the actors:

> Age means nothing if character is there and if the story given the actor is interesting. It stands to reason that the popular seasoned actors were as good artists a few years ago as now. But now it happens that they are put in the right vehicles. As a matter of fact the player of middle age has the best chance of permanent success. I directed the late Lon Chaney for years. He would have been popular forever. The love the public bears for Marie Dressler will never die; it will increase as the years go on. In other words, the character actor is the foundation of the drama whether on stage or screen. And the ripe experience of this type of artist insures success when once it is allowed to flower.[10]

The premise that Browning and his screenwriters developed can be summarized as follows: Paul Duval, a well-to-do Parisian bank president, is wrongfully convicted of murder and embezzlement. Incarcerated on Devil's Island and consumed with hatred for the three former banking colleagues who had set him up, Duval befriends a young man named Ba-oola, a fellow prisoner from colonial Africa.[11] Duval and Ba-oola escape from the *Île du Diable* and journey to the latter's home country, where Ba-oola is reunited with his mother, Nyleta, a high priestess of voodoo. Duval witnesses a number of her dark-arts rituals, which inspire him to develop a diabolical plan against the bankers who framed him. Nyleta is so grateful to him for helping her son escape that she agrees to accompany him to Paris to help him carry out a bizarre revenge scheme that includes, among other things, the abduction of Parisian "Apache" street thugs, miniaturizing them into doll-sized assassins with no will of their own, and dispatching them to murder Duval's former banking colleagues. Through all of his time in Paris, Duval maintains an elaborate disguise as "Madame Mandilip," a sweet old lady who runs a toyshop in the city's Montmartre district. The masquerade not only allows him to evade the gendarmes but also enables him to get close to his estranged daughter Lorraine, who believes he was guilty of the criminal charges and blames him for the misery the Duval family endured in the years that followed. His plan is to clear the family name, make amends with his daughter, and then commit suicide to atone for the supernatural havoc he had unleashed.

Censorship Problems

Despite their efforts to deliver on what promised to be a top-flight horror film, Browning and his writers were stymied by censorship concerns that ultimately led to changes in the elderly characters. As film historian Bret Wood has observed, Joseph Breen, head of Hollywood's self-regulatory Production Code Administration, expressed concerns about the proposed film. Some of the issues dealt with the explicitness of Nyleta's ceremonies, while others were related to Duval's suicide. On this latter point, Breen wrote the following in a letter to MGM head Louis B. Mayer: "In the present treatment Duval, after effecting his revenge through the murder of several characters, commits suicide and thereby escapes due legal apprehension, trial and punishment. Such a solution to this present story is, of course, not acceptable. It would be most advisable to indicate that Duval is captured and does, or is to suffer, the penalties of the proper legal trial. We also suggest that in attempting to fight off the police and escape, he is killed."[12]

MGM was accustomed to receiving such dicta from the PCA but was unprepared for the bombshell response from another regulatory agency: the British Board of Film Censors. The board raised serious objections to the film, particularly its witchcraft angle. The BBFC believed that the film's references to voodoo and witchcraft would agitate blacks living under colonial rule and thus were unacceptable. According to *Los Angeles Times* writer Philip K. Scheuer, the BBFC opposed the film for another geopolitical reason; Britain's rival, Italy, had declared its intent to eradicate voodoo and witchcraft in Ethiopia, and the BBFC feared that, if it allowed the film to be shown, its decision might be viewed as a validation of Italy's claim that voodoo and witchcraft actually exist and thus misconstrued as an endorsement of Italy's October 1935 invasion of the East African nation.[13]

Since the British empire represented a huge market for MGM's films, the studio felt it had little choice but to comply with the BBFC's demands. The trade journal *Variety* reported in late March 1936 that significant changes were underway: "Recently Metro was called to task by Great Britain over *The Witch of Timbuctoo*. Subject matter of the story was voodooism. To offend the British possessions would mean a serious crimp in the picture's revenue were it banned, so the changes were made to eliminate the objectionable angles."[14]

The changes, however, did not come from Browning, Endore, and Fort. Instead, MGM stepped in and essentially took the script out of their hands. While the director and his handpicked writers looked on with dismay, the studio assigned an ever-growing number of staff writers to "fix" the screenplay. These new writers—including Robert Chapin, Richard Schayer, and Erich von Stroheim, who worked independently of each other—toned down the film's reference to suicide by having Duval utter a few veiled comments to Lorraine's boyfriend near the end of the film, such as "Where I'm going, Toto, I won't need any money." More significantly, they dutifully followed a suggestion by MGM story editor Sam Marx and replaced the witchcraft dimension with a mad science angle that had been popularized in such films as the Universal studio's *Frankenstein* (1931) and *Bride of Frankenstein* (1935). Breen's PCA office and the British Board of Film Censors found these changes acceptable.

The decision to eliminate the dark magic material in favor of mad science had a profound effect on the film's representation of elderly characters. The cadre of writers dumped Nyleta, presumably a middle-aged woman, and her offspring Ba-oola and replaced them with two French mad scientists: Malita and Marcel. They are not just any mad scientists, however; they are an elderly husband-and-wife team of mad scientists. The creation of Marcel and Malita added a completely new level of elder activity to the film, and these characters warrant a closer look.

Mad Marcel and Malita

The now-retitled film *The Devil-Doll*, released on July 10, 1936, after much tinkering, introduces us to Marcel almost immediately; he and fellow fugitive Paul Lavond (formerly "Duval" in the various treatments and scripts) have just escaped from prison and are being pursued by guards across swampy terrain.[15] According to an earlier screenplay draft prepared by the MGM rewriters, Marcel has a history of violence; he had been convicted on charges of cruelty to wild animals and seriously injuring the police who had come to arrest him.[16] These references were expunged from the release version of the

Marcel (Henry B. Walthall, right) explains his mad scheme to a skeptical Paul Lavond (Lionel Barrymore) in *The Devil-Doll* (1936).

film, however, and Marcel, as played by the 58-year-old actor Henry B. Walthall, comes across as a somewhat doddering and enfeebled old man.

Marcel is one of the most selfless mad scientists in movie history. Far from wanting to control the world for his own nefarious purposes, he wants to help it by shrinking humans and animals to one-sixth their normal size so that, in his skewed view of things, the world's food supply will go farther. Holding no hidden agenda whatsoever, the wild-haired scientist draws a sharp distinction between Lavond and himself: "You have only hatred in your heart. My work will help the world to live." Though he is as obsessed with his work as any other of moviedom's mad scientists, Marcel, unfettered by anything resembling a moral conflict, is far removed from such archetypal figures as the aggressive Dr. Pretorius and the agonized Dr. Frankenstein of Universal's *Frankenstein* franchise.

Having eluded the Devil's Island guards, Lavond and Marcel arrive at a nearby hidden laboratory maintained by Marcel's wife Malita (former Grand-Guignol actress Rafaela Ottiano), who conspicuously uses a crutch throughout the movie. Lavond learns that Marcel has, with Malita's help, actually developed an experimental procedure for shrinking humans and animals, though it includes an unintentional side effect; the subjects lose their individual wills once they have been reduced to doll-size and become quite susceptible to control by others. He watches with concern, and then with high interest, as Marcel and Malita take their developmentally disabled servant Lachna (Grace Ford) and shrink her, turning her into the film's first devil doll. She is in fact the film's title character.[17]

Before Lavond can think about using this scientific breakthrough for his own purposes, fate steps in; Marcel, represented as a well-meaning but rather fragile elder, expires of a heart attack in the midst of the excitement.[18] With this narrative development occurring less than 15 minutes into the film, the burden of Marcel's plan to shrink the world's population quickly falls on Malita. Recognizing the enormity of the task, she agrees to accompany Lavond to Paris and assist him with his vengeful scheme in the misguided belief that he will return the favor after taking his revenge and help her carry out Marcel's mad dream.

The saucer-eyed Malita is one of an extremely unusual movie breed: the female mad scientist. Indeed, film historian David Skal lists only two women in his 1998 pantheon of nearly 80 mad scientists, many of whom, like Dr. Frankenstein, went through multiple incarnations over the decades.[19] In a sense, Malita and Marcel have swapped traditional gender roles. Stripped of the violent behavior attributed to him in an earlier script draft, Marcel is a somewhat feminized male; he is other-oriented, kind, gentle, compassionate, benevolent. Malita maintains some stereotypical female qualities, too; for instance, she watches with wide-eyed girlish delight as two miniaturized people, dressed in French Apache garb, dance to the strains of a music-box rendition of Jacques Offenbach's "Valse des rayons." When she believes that Lavond has crossed her, however, she turns vengeful and malevolent. Alarmed that Lavond no longer wants to continue their miniaturization experiments and has in fact informed the police of their activities, Malita plans to order one of Lavond's former banking colleagues who has been shrunken to doll-size—Victor Radin (Arthur Hohl)—to stab Lavond in the ankle with a poisoned stiletto that she has prepared. "We've served his purpose, Radin, now he'll serve ours. Reduced to your size, I'll control him as easily as I control you," she cackles. Lavond thwarts her plan and castigates his erstwhile accomplice: "Why, you poor insane wretch! I should destroy you with all the rest of this horror." He begins wrecking the toyshop's lab, whereupon Malita tries to stop him by threatening to hurl a bottle of explosive fluid. In a line of dialogue cut from the final film, she says succinctly to Lavond, "You must die now." Malita thus lives up to her "Bad Girl" name by taking on violent characteristics that Hollywood filmmakers have far more typically associated with male figures than female ones.

Browning added a related dimension to Malita's characterization by often showing her walking stiffly while leaning on a crutch, a trope that carries considerable cultural baggage. Browning had long been known for conflating visible disability and moral impairment in his many movies with Lon Chaney, and he continued that tradition with the criminally insane Malita. Not only is she an atypical mad scientist due to her gender, but she is also an exceptionally rare female amid the multitude of Hollywood's disabled movie characters whose physical differences symbolize deformed morality if not outright evil.[20]

Though the filmmakers pushed Marcel and Malita in different directions by finessing gender-related assumptions about the geriatric couple, it is reasonably clear that the *Devil-Doll* rewriters, working under intense deadline pressure, drew heavily on *Bride of Frankenstein* for inspiration. Released in early May 1935, *Bride* bears a number of similarities with *The Devil-Doll*: scientific experiments with miniaturized humans, a highly "Otherized" woman with a pronounced white streak in her dark hair, obsessed and borderline-psychotic scientists working in phantasmagorical laboratories, montages of

"It's the work of a crazy old woman" (Norden) 39

Armed with a flask of explosive fluid, Malita (Rafaela Ottiano) threatens Paul Lavond (Lionel Barrymore) near the conclusion of *The Devil-Doll* **(1936).**

bubbling beakers and related paraphernalia, and an apocalyptic explosion in the laboratory near the end of each film. On this latter point, even the dialogue is similar. In *Bride,* an enraged Frankenstein monster (Boris Karloff) grabs a lever in the doctors' lab and threatens to pull it, which prompts one of the film's mad scientists, the elderly Dr. Pretorius (Ernest Thesiger), to shout, "Get away from that lever. You'll blow us all to atoms." When Malita threatens to throw a bottle of explosive liquid in an attempt to stop Lavond from wrecking the lab, he barks back at her with "Put that down. You'll blow yourself to atoms." Wittingly or not, MGM solidified the two movies' connection through another decision; it recruited composer Franz Waxman to write the musical score for *The Devil-Doll* in the hope that he could duplicate the success of his quirky and evocative score for *Bride* the previous year.[21]

Lavond and Laughter

Despite *The Devil-Doll*'s ill-advised gravitation toward daffy science and the significant changes arising therefrom, its central character, Paul Lavond (né Duval), was remarkably consistent throughout the film's tortuous production process; he is an embittered middle-aged man, unjustly convicted and incarcerated, who escapes from Devil's Island

and, while masquerading as an elderly toyshop proprietress, plots revenge by shrinking people to doll-size and ordering them to carry out his dirty work. Satisfied with the outcome, he sees suicide as the only honorable exit after restoring the family name. He, too, deserves closer scrutiny.

Lavond is quite aware of the effectiveness of his elderly female disguise. "A hundred thousand francs reward for my capture," he says to Malita while referring to a wanted poster bearing his image. "Who do you think is offering all this money for me? The same three swine that sent me to prison before. They're frightened to death, Malita. They know that my freedom means they're finished." He then gleefully adds, "But what they don't know is the Paul Lavond they're looking for is Madame Mandilip, a poor, tottering old woman." Lavond later slips back into character as Mandilip when a gendarme shows up at the toyshop, but he is able to relax upon learning that the cop merely wants to relay neighbors' complaints about the glue pots that Mandilip had left outside. While exiting the gendarme says, "Well, good day and good luck, Madame," to which Lavond replies, "I'm amazed at my good luck, M'sieur," and sweetly laughs. His tone abruptly shifts, though, after the cop has departed. "Amazed is the word—eh, Malita? Stupid policeman—to let an old white wig cost him a hundred thousand francs."

Paul Lavond (Lionel Barrymore) issues telepathic commands while disguised as the kindly Madame Mandilip in *The Devil-Doll* (1936).

Lavond/Mandilip's pointed dialogue, laden with innuendo and dramatic irony and delivered by Barrymore in a bravura falsetto, provided much of the film's appeal to 1936 audiences. Consider, for instance, the following assessment offered by Norbert Lusk, a New York City–based correspondent for the *Los Angeles Times*. After describing the film, then playing at the Capitol Theater on Broadway, Lusk reported on the audience's intriguing reaction to it:

> For some reason it is amusing instead of sinister, but it is entertaining always. The audience enjoys it to the accompaniment of frequent laughter, especially when Mr. Barrymore makes a remark with a double meaning to one of his victims. It is laughter of enjoyment at the fate in store for the unsuspecting dupe and is never ridicule. But it is laughter none the less. This makes the picture a melodramatic comedy rather than the macabre yarn it starts out to be. Perhaps the change was intentional though suspense might have been enhanced had the story been developed to the accompaniment of terror and gathering doom. It is rattling good entertainment, though, with trick photography fascinating the beholder.[22]

Examples of Lavond's double-meaning remarks abound. A key set of them occurs after he in his Mandilip guise has talked Victor Radin, one of the three villainous bankers, into visiting the toy store under the pretense of proposing a business deal. The audience knows that Lavond is planning to set Radin up for some unpleasantness but does not know precisely what it will be. The oblivious Radin says, "But remember—I'm making no promises," to which Lavond replies with the frisson-producing lines, "You don't have to. Once you're in my shop, I'll wager you'll do anything I ask." When Radin shows up at the appointed hour, he and Lavond engage in the following conversation:

> LAVOND [in character as Madame Mandilip]: Well, I can hardly believe it. I feel like pinching myself to see if I'm awake or dreaming. To think that I really have you here.
> RADIN: Huh?
> LAVOND: I mean—that you're going to be my partner and help me.
> RADIN: Oh yes, but remember if I do, it will only be financially. My name must not appear.
> LAVOND: Oh, I wouldn't dream of using your name. You'll just be my silent partner.

After leading Radin down a flight of steps to the toy workshop ("This is the room where we keep all our little secrets," Lavond says cheerily), he permanently silences his former colleague by jabbing a miniature poisoned knife into his leg, paralyzing him. Radin thus falls under Lavond's complete control and is later reduced to doll size to carry out another phase of his plans.

Later, after Lavond in disguise as Madame Mandilip has finagled his way into the palatial home of another villainous banker, Emile Coulvet (Robert Greig), and persuaded him to purchase a doll, he says, "Thank you a thousand times, Monsieur. You'll never know how happy it makes me to leave one of my dolls in your beautiful home." Lavond later wills the doll—Lachna, the young woman whom Marcel and Malita had miniaturized near the beginning of the film—into stabbing Coulvet with a tiny poisoned stiletto, thereby paralyzing him as well.

When a middle-aged police detective shows up at the toyshop later in the film to ask questions about a robbery that might be related to Coulvet's paralysis, Lavond says, "Oh, dear, an old woman like me—mixed up in such a thing. What will the neighbors say? They gossip! I'll lose all my customers. Why, you might as well accuse one of my little dolls as accuse me." The detective states that he has no plans to arrest Mandilip, however, and Lavond's chatter takes on a friendlier tone. He remarks on the things that may happen when women are separated from the men in their lives and adds, "You see, you men never know what's going on behind your backs." As the detective gets ready to depart, Lavond says, "As long as my shop is here, you'll always know where to find me." About a dozen minutes later, however, an explosion obliterates the shop and the Mandilip character disappears. "Well, that's the end of Madame Mandilip," says a fireman while surveying the smoking wreckage of the toyshop. His companion, the police detective who had visited the shop minutes before in the film, adds ruefully, "We're pretty smart, eh? Got everything pinned on Lavond, only to find out it's the work of a crazy old woman."

Lavond and Post-Traumatic Embitterment Disorder

As *Philadelphia Inquirer* movie critic Mildred Martin observed in her review of *The Devil-Doll*, Tod Browning was known for his expertise as a purveyor of revenge-driven melodrama. Browning, she wrote, "the man who made *Freaks* and *The Unholy Three*, knows his way around in these tales of warped minds and strange physical aspects, of bitter grudges and horrible revenge."[23] Lavond, whose behavior is by turns vengeful and suicidal, was the latest in a long line of obsessed, embittered characters that Browning had cultivated. Though it might be tempting to write off Lavond merely as an exaggerated figment of Browning's feverish imagination, the character's behavior almost perfectly—indeed, uncannily—matches the characteristics of Post-Traumatic Embitterment Disorder (PTED), a psychiatric syndrome identified in 2003. Michael Linden, the psychiatrist who proposed the disorder, observed that a major negative life event can cause some people to become so embittered that their normal day-to-day functioning is seriously impaired. Linden defined the major elements of PTED as follows:

- a single exceptional negative life event precipitates the onset of the illness;
- the person's present negative state has developed in the direct context of this event;
- the person's emotional response is embitterment and feelings of injustice;
- the person experiences repeated intrusive memories of the event;
- the person's emotional modulation is unaffected; a patient can even smile when engaged in thoughts of revenge;
- no obvious other mental disorder can explain the reaction.[24]

Other PTED symptoms identified by Linden include aggressiveness, dysphoria, and the formation of suicidal thoughts—items highly consistent with Lavond's behavior. In a follow-up study to Linden's groundbreaking work, researchers Carsten Wrosch and Jesse Renaud suggested that elders who have difficulty adapting to new challenges and pursuing alternative life-goals are particularly susceptible to the disorder. "Although undesirable life circumstances may elicit bitterness at any age in an adult life, theories of lifespan development suggest that there are age-graded opportunities for overcoming difficulty and attaining personal goals," they wrote. "From this perspective, it is important to consider that developmental losses and goal-related challenges typically increase with advancing age and opportunities for overcoming problems show sharp age-related declines." The researchers added that "not all older adults are capable of managing their emotional well-being through the engagement in self-protective and goal adjustment processes.... There is a substantial proportion of older adults who do not succeed in the adaptive management of age-related challenges and who experience high levels of negative affect" such as embitterment.[25]

Put another way, the happiest older adults are typically those who have adapted to their changing situations and adjusted their goals; they have revised their outlook on life and are better off for it. Elders who dwell on traumatic events and embark on vengeful quests to undo them, however, may experience intense regret and plummeting levels of emotional well-being that, if left unchecked, may lead to suicidal ideation. This is the Post-Traumatic Embitterment Disorder in a nutshell, and no filmmaker, before or since, intuitively understood it better than Tod Browning.

Concluding Thoughts

The Devil-Doll was released on July 10, 1936, a mere two days before Browning's 56th birthday. It was hardly the birthday present to himself that he wanted. Desperate to re-establish his reputation as a top master of Hollywood horror, the director could only watch from the sidelines as critics began offering their opinions of the watered-down film.

The vast majority of reviews were mixed. They tended to praise *The Devil-Doll* for its generally entertaining qualities but came down on it for its lack of true horror. For example, a reviewer for the *Brooklyn Daily Eagle* wrote,

> Mr. Browning has always displayed a fancy taste for the bizarre, and this current confection, it must be said, has a literary lineup that should have made it a masterpiece of goose-flesh. For in addition to Garrett Fort there is Guy Endore, who rose to best-sellerdom and Hollywood on the strength of his horrific *The Werewolf of Paris*, and there is also Erich von Stroheim, who has demonstrated on occasion that his own tastes run somewhat in this direction. Yet *The Devil-Doll* is not nearly as provocative of chills as one might have expected it to be.

The writer concluded the review thusly: "After you have been introduced to the devil dolls, you may regard their subsequent activities with complete indifference."[26]

Other critics offered similar perspectives. "Tod Browning is up to his old tricks, turning out a fantastic horror drama," wrote Eileen Creelman for the *New York Sun*. "He has pulled his punches, however, in *The Devil-Doll*, dwelling less on the macabre than the romantic elements of his story. The miniature humans of the film, instead of appearing sinister, are only cute. Even the crimes they are forced to commit are quaint rather than horrible." A reviewer for the *Naples* (NY) *News* opined that "the picture is mechanically excellent, but fails photographically in getting across an atmosphere of brooding and evil and leaves the spectator amused rather than horrified.... While the picture is not Tod Browning at his best, it is good fun."[27]

A reviewer for the London *Times*, while not mentioning the film's British censorship struggles, echoed these views:

> It is a reasonably good idea, and gives an opportunity for much excellent trick photography, but the film makes a very timid use of the supernatural. The dolls might have been really alarming, or the consequences of the idea might have been worked out with that amusing logic which Mr. [H. G.] Wells understands so well. But as it is, and apart from some few occasions when Mr. Lionel Barrymore's acting somehow convinces one that his dolls are strange, the idea is merely used as a means of bringing a conventional situation to a sentimental conclusion.[28]

Hard-core fans of movie horror condemned the film. An example of their displeasure is a harsh review that appeared in the December 1936 issue of *Thrilling Wonder Stories*, a fantasy-oriented pulp magazine. The reviewer, Henry Kuttner, called *The Devil-Doll* a "dull picture," a "disappointment" and "a run-of-the-mill thriller which does not attempt to recapture the unique fantasy of Merritt's novel." Kuttner appreciated several shots of the dolls, though he underscored their derivative nature. "These are merely further developments of the homunculus scenes in *The Bride of Frankenstein*," he wrote.[29]

No doubt discouraged by such reviews and aware that his stock with MGM was sinking, Browning directed only one more film—the otherwise forgettable *Miracles for Sale*—in 1939 before retiring from the film business. He was 59. He probably took some consolation in the knowledge that his penultimate film featured his favorite type of characters: elders with resonant life experiences. Nevertheless, he and the generations of horror-film aficionados to follow—the present author very much included—could only mourn the truly macabre film that might have been.

Notes

The author wishes to thank William Gorman of the New York State Archives and Veronica Golden of Hampshire College's Harold F. Johnson Library for their assistance.

1. Townsend, "Good News," 112.
2. Most famously, Browning employed Tod Robbins' short story "Spurs," published in a 1923 issue of *Munsey's Magazine*, as the literary basis for his 1932 film, *Freaks*.

3. Schallert, "'Burn, Witch, Burn' Purchased for Filming," 19.
4. Schallert, "Browning Preparing Voodoo Thriller," 9.
5. Quoted in Wood, "The Witch, the Devil, and the Code," 52.
6. Greville Bain, a London-based film reviewer for the *Times of India*, found this title particularly unappealing. "The title seems to be a dangerous one for a picture which is intended to be taken very seriously," he wrote, "and it would not be surprising if it were changed to something less suggestive of the old-fashioned penny-dreadful." See Bain, "H. G. Wells Joins Chaplin," 11.
7. For a fascinating examination of the "Hollywoodization" of exotic locales during this time, see Cooper and Meeuf, eds., *Projecting the World*, particularly the first section, "Islands and Identity."
8. Advertisement, *Motion Picture Herald*, 45.
9. According to Ben Indick, Merritt was unhappy with the idea of a man playing Mandilip: "Madame Mandilip suffered an extreme sex change when her part was played by Lionel Barrymore, all of it much to Merritt's distaste." See Indick, "A. Merritt: A Re-Appraisal," 153.
10. Browning quoted in Jessie Henderson, "Door Not Closed in Hollywood to Faces That Show Wrinkles," 10.
11. Confusion exists as to Ba-oola's and Nyleta's country of origin. The film's proposed title, *The Witch of Timbuctoo*, would suggest Mali, then a French colony, but historian Bret Wood, who conducted a thorough history of the making of *The Devil-Doll*, claimed the characters were from the Belgian Congo (now the Democratic Republic of the Congo). See Wood, "The Witch, the Devil, and the Code," 52.
12. Wood, "The Witch, the Devil, and the Code," 53–54; Joseph Breen, letter to Louis B. Mayer.
13. Scheuer, "A Town Called Hollywood," C1.
14. "H'wood's Foreign Jams," 3. For some context on British concerns during the 1930s, see "Britain Disturbed by Outbreaks of 'Black Magic,'" 6.
15. In light of the film's new title, MGM may have changed the lead character's name to "Lavond" to avoid the similarly sounding "Devil" and "Duval."
16. This earlier screenplay draft served as the basis for a movie tie-in published in Britain: a photo-laden, heavily detailed short story that includes a considerable amount of material cut from the final film. See "The Devil Doll," 13.
17. Though Lachna and the book's Laschna are young female underlings with similar names, they serve very different functions. Laschna, who Madame Mandilip had rescued from a European slum as a child, serves mainly as an informational conduit; Lachna, on the other hand, is a mute servant to Marcel and Malita, the latter of whom characterizes her as an "inbred peasant half-wit." Marcel and Malita shrink her to doll-size as a kind of test, a fate that does not befall her near-namesake in the Merritt novel.
18. In a sad parallel, Henry B. Walthall, the actor who played Marcel, died of intestinal influenza on June 7, 1936, about a month before the film opened.
19. See Skal, *Screams of Reason*, 319–333. The two women that Skal lists are Elaine Frederick (Veronica Lake) in *Flesh Feast*, and Jane Tiptree (Diane Ladd) in *Carnosaur*. He erroneously lists the German actress Hilde Wolter as having played a mad scientist in the 1918 film *Alraune*.
20. For more on the movie connection between disability and evil, see Norden, *Cinema of Isolation*; and Norden and Cahill, "Violence, Women, and Disability."
21. For further discussion of this famous installment in Universal's *Frankenstein* film series, see Norden, "'We're Not All Dead Yet.'"
22. Lusk, "Studio and Theater Comings and Goings," C3. Audiences of the time may have responded with laughter for another reason; they may have associated Robert Greig, the actor who played chief villain Emile Coulvet, with his many comedic roles in such films as *Animal Crackers* (1930), *Horse Feathers* (1932), *The Cohens and the Kellys in Hollywood* (1932), and *Cockeyed Cavaliers* (1934).
23. Martin, "Lionel Barrymore Film Opens," 15.
24. Linden, "Posttraumatic Embitterment Disorder," 195.
25. Wrosch and Renaud, "Self-Regulation of Bitterness Across the Lifespan," 135–136.
26. "The Screen," 7.
27. Creelman, "The New Talkie," 8; "Movie Hits in N.Y.," 4.
28. "New Films in London," 8.
29. Kuttner, "Scientifilm Review," 119.

Bibliography

Advertisement. *Motion Picture Herald*, May 29, 1935, 45.
Bain, Greville. "H. G. Wells Joins Chaplin." *Times of India*, November 16, 1935, 11.
Breen, Joseph. Letter to Louis B. Mayer, September 13, 1935, *Devil Doll* file, PCA collection, Margaret Herrick Library, Academy of Motion Picture Arts and Sciences.
"Britain Disturbed by Outbreaks of 'Black Magic.'" *Albany Times-Union*, June 4, 1938, magazine sec., 6.
Cooper, Anna, and Russell Meeuf, eds. *Projecting the World: Representing the "Foreign" in Classical Hollywood*. Detroit: Wayne State University Press, 2017.

Creelman, Eileen. "The New Talkie." *New York Sun*, August 8, 1936, 8
"The Devil Doll." *Boy's Cinema*, October 24, 1936, 13–20, 26.
Henderson, Jessie. "Door Not Closed in Hollywood to Faces that Show Wrinkles." *Springfield Sunday Union and Republican* (Springfield, MA), February 12, 1933, 10.
"H'wood's Foreign Jams." *Variety*, March 25, 1936, 3.
Indick, Ben P. "A. Merritt: A Re-Appraisal." In *Classic Fantasy Fiction: Essays on the Antecedents of Fantastic Literature*, edited by Darrell Schweitzer, 76–87. Gillette, NJ: Wildside Press, 1996.
Kuttner, Henry. "Scientifilm Review." *Thrilling Wonder Stories*, December 1936, 119.
Linden, Michael. "Posttraumatic Embitterment Disorder." *Psychotherapy and Psychosomatics* 72, no. 4 (July–August 2003): 195–202.
Lusk, Norbert. "Studio and Theater Comings and Goings." *Los Angeles Times*, August 16, 1936, C3.
Martin, Mildred. "Lionel Barrymore Film Opens." *Philadelphia Inquirer*, August 2, 1936, 15.
Merritt, Abraham. *Burn, Witch, Burn!* New York: Liveright, 1933.
"Movie Hits in N.Y." *Naples News* (Naples, NY), August 26, 1936, 4.
"New Films in London." *Times* (London), August 24, 1936, 8.
Norden, Martin F. *The Cinema of Isolation: A History of Physical Disability in the Movies*. New Brunswick: Rutgers University Press, 1994.
_____. "'We're Not All Dead Yet': Humor Amid the Horror in James Whale's *Bride of Frankenstein*." In *The Laughing Dead: The Horror-Comedy Film from Bride of Frankenstein to Zombieland*, edited by Cynthia Miller and Bowdoin Van Riper, 102–120. Lanham, MD: Rowman & Littlefield, 2016.
_____, and Madeleine Cahill. "Violence, Women, and Disability in Tod Browning's *Freaks* and *The Devil-Doll*." *Journal of Popular Film & Television* 26, no. 2 (Summer 1998): 86–94.
Schallert, Edwin. "Browning Preparing Voodoo Thriller." *Los Angeles Times*, July 16, 1935, 9.
_____. "'Burn, Witch, Burn' Purchased for Filming; Constance Collier May Do Lead." *Los Angeles Times*, June 23, 1935, 19.
Scheuer, Philip K. "A Town Called Hollywood." *Los Angeles Times*, March 29, 1936, C1.
"The Screen." *Brooklyn Daily Eagle*, August 10, 1936, 7.
Skal, David J. *Screams of Reason: Mad Science and Modern Culture*. New York: W. W. Norton, 1998.
Townsend, Leo. "Good News." *Modern Screen*, July 1936, 112.
Wood, Bret. "The Witch, the Devil, and the Code: A Horror Story of Hollywood in the Golden Age." *Film Comment* 28, no. 6 (November–December 1992): 52–56.
Wrosch, Carsten, and Jesse Renaud. "Self-Regulation of Bitterness Across the Lifespan." In *Embitterment: Societal, Psychological, and Clinical Perspectives*, edited by Michael Linden and Andreas Maercker, 129–141. Vienna: Springer-Verlag Wien, 2011.

From Beneficent Elderly to Vile M'others

Familial Relations and Cannibalism in Troma's Rabid Grannies *(1988)*

Steve J. Webley

> A glimpse into the world proves that horror is nothing other than reality.
> —Alfred Hitchcock

In 1988 Troma Entertainment released an obscure Belgian horror film titled *Rabid Grannies*. A natural choice for a company already well known for releasing independent films that blended the ridiculous with underlying social commentary, it was an instant success. Troma aficionados enthusiastically celebrated the film's adolescent combination of wit, gore, and familial subject matter, while it topped the list of "video-nasties" in the UK and Canada. Initially banned in those nations and pilloried by the mainstream media globally, it remains notorious to this day.

The film follows the 92nd birthday party of two beneficent elderly aunts, Victoria and Elizabeth Remington (Anne-Marie Fox and Danielle Daven) attended by grasping family members who hope to inherit the family estate. Their ostracized, devil-worshipping nephew sends a mysterious gift that transforms the aunts into twin cannibalistic demons, and what follows is a night of hell, in which the relatives are hunted down and consumed in a surreal display of grotesquery and slapstick cannibalism.

Rabid Grannies is a surreal inversion of Freud's primal act of murder and cannibalism. The Freudian primal "obscene Father" is an archetypal character used to explain the origins of societal laws and religion through prohibitions, transgressions, and guilt. Freud draws parallels between the origins of civilization and the Oedipal scene, with the alpha father figure dominating access to the society's females and thus controlling and curtailing the desire of his sons and other males. In Freud's story, this domination over desire is the ultimate anxiety-inducing prohibition. It is a prohibition with such palpable ambivalence between respect for power and hatred of control that it drove the sons to transgress any notion of law or order—they murder and consume the father. This act allowed for the symbolic absorption of his strength, but also gave rise to the need for prohibitions grounded in guilt. It is from this dialectic that new structures of meaning emerge.

Heavily influenced by both structural anthropology and linguistics, the French psychiatrist Jacques Lacan diverged from Freud's work by linking the emotion of anxiety to the function of desire in the unconscious mind. Lacan used this coupling to create the phase of human subjectivity he called the *Symbolic* register of language and social authority. Rather than follow Freud's insistence on sex and libidinal impulses, Lacan's *Symbolic* is somewhat comparable to Freud's notion of the super ego, and is formed by the colonizing power of language. It is the register of human subjectivity. We first enter what Lacan called the *Imaginary* register of image identification—a register comparable to the Freudian Ego, where early subjectivity is formed through identification with the imaginary otherness of our fathers and mothers. It is also in this nascent phase of identity that we lay the foundations of our own conflicting relationships with authority, and are dominated by the otherness of social authority—a perspective from which our unconscious minds are being gazed upon by a relentless and invisible prescience.

Freud was consumed by fear of the breakdown of the authority of patriarchal society. However, Troma's *Rabid Grannies* confronts viewers with a subversive inversion and surreal doubling of his ideas. The story of *Rabid Grannies* is dominated by a dualistic and cannibalistic twin maternal image. The dominating "Otherness" of the father is replaced by a surreal dualism of maternal authority—one that oscillates uncannily between beneficial "nannas" who we know and love as the "spoilers" of children and the "rabid" elderly persecutors of familial desires and guilt.

Faced with these conflicting images, viewers are continually unsure of the perspectives from which to interpret the film. Whether beneficent or obscene, the desire of this maternal authority dominates the despicable family and film narrative; it is a portrayal of an aged M'othering desire, and its guilty enjoyment functions to hold together meaning.

> All sorts of things in this world behave like mirrors.—Jacques Lacan,
> *Seminar II*

Troma had, by 1988, a vast stable of distributed films—including *The Toxic Avenger* (1984), which featured a nerdy social misfit transformed by chemical waste into a type of rhetorical superhero who evolved over numerous sequels to espouse "viewpoints that are anti-religion, anti-police, anti-capitalist, anti–Washington, anti-hippie, anti–Hollywood, anti-woman, anti-good taste, and anti-pretty much everything!"[1] In short, Troma offered the type of releases that college students of the 1980s, in search of meaningful countercultural icons, skipped class to see simply because they were considered so bad they *had* to be good.

Cult films are strange creatures. To many non–Troma aficionados *Rabid Grannies* appeared to be the ultimate Troma release, in that it went out of its way to defy audience expectations. The film contains neither grandmothers nor a case of rabies. Moreover, it did not contain the visceral horror that was promised during promotion, with gore cutscenes released separately from the main feature. The film was so heavily censored and edited by third parties to remove scenes of cannibalism that the original Troma release seemingly contained little in the way of a working narrative. The film's first-time director Emmanuel Kervyn even complained about the film's lack of meaning, arguing that the excision of the special effects—intended to hold the text of the film together as parodic mimicry of old B movies—left him feeling as if he was watching John Travolta in *Saturday Night Fever* with all the dance sequences removed.[2] However, for Troma's audiences the film was still an exquisite spectacle despite, or even because of, its meaninglessness. Even severely cut, the film reflected Troma's flair for the transgressive and comically absurd, the obscure, the burlesque, the gratuitous, the grotesque, the titillating, and the downright disgusting (all frequently combined within a single title).[3]

Falling out of vogue in the 1970s, Lacanian film theory missed the advent of the splatter films of the 1980s. This essay however, furthers a renewed interest in Lacanian criticism by reintegrating the role of the spectator through the irrepressible effects of the *Real* inherent in film's text.[4] The *Real* is the third of Lacan's registers of subjectivity and is similar to the Freudian id. It is the register of human subjectivity that resists articulation; a range of bodily affects that can neither be signified nor controlled which, together with the *Imaginary* and *Symbolic*, fully constitutes the human condition. Encounters with the *Real* are destabilizing—simultaneously enthralling and intolerable—like the repeated picking of a scab or the realization one has been unconsciously picking one's nose in public.[5] The unearthing of the *Real* is similar to the destabilizing bodily affects we encounter when confronted with Freud's *uncanny*—the surfacing of dark entities from the unconscious mind. This essay frames *Rabid Grannies* as an encounter with the *Real*, and a means through which the uncanny prompts viewers to negotiate understandings of their own identities. If, as McGowan and Kunkle contend, the Self is the "stumbling block of sense,"[6] then the cinematic fantasy of *Rabid Grannies* exists in the space between the interior identity created by the Self and the social identity promoted by American culture in the 1980s.

> If youth knew; if age could.—Sigmund Freud

The ambivalent emotions we harbor toward the elderly contort our lives and our fantasies. Freud, intent on tracing the origins of the stories we embrace about ourselves, repeatedly found himself excavating the complicated networks of family histories that reached back over generations.[7] The individual in a family is already situated before birth within a constellation of networks of kinship. How we love within the family unit is not a simple exercise; we are all at the mercy of the ambivalence of emotions and the language of expression. Simultaneously, we love and hate those who provide for us and for whom we provide. We wish them success, yet envy their good fortune and wish them ill. We revere them, yet unconsciously wish them dead as part of the natural progression of kinship, so that we may consume (and thus absorb) the power and authority that they wield(ed) in life.

These ambivalences of death and desire, particularly the unconscious wish for the death of our parents, cause us terrible anxiety. For Freud, this did much to cement the foundations of civilization and simultaneously cause society-wide neuroses. He theorized that desire for the death of our elderly, and the consummation of their desires as our own, formed the spiritual belief systems of early civilizations, and that it rooted fear of the dead, and of their demonic return, in the repressed origins of societal laws, customs, and rituals. Belief in the need for religion to contain and control the violent retribution of the dead, fear of demonic forces, and anxiety over transformational powers such as lycanthropy originated, for Freud, in the unconscious psychic mechanisms of the familial unit.[8]

It is within this strange world of kinship and unconscious perspectives that we are situated, as viewers, within Kervyn's *Rabid Grannies*. We enter via a shaky and improperly lit long-shot of a gothic cathedral, as Father Percival requests leave to attend his aunt's birthday party. What follows sets the scene for the entire cutting and editing style of the film. It is a segue into a world continually viewed from divergent and doubling angles. Scenes are quick-cut from off-angled third person perspectives to first person perspectives and back again, often shifting in height and scope with disconcerting irregularity. Jumps to first-person perspectives vary in height, while including shots of autonomous disembodied hands, leaving viewers in a peculiar relation to the images on the screen. They are forced unconsciously to ask on whose authority, and from whose perspective, they are being forced to view the events unfolding on screen.

> When someone abuses me I can defend myself, but against praise I am defenseless.—Sigmund Freud

This spectral discord seems to give the film's characters, locations, and props divergent proportions that are uncannily redoubled by badly dubbed and lip-synced audio. The surrealist imagery then ups its own game. We are introduced to a cast of characters straight from the gothic naturalist oeuvre in the rapid-fire exposition of 1980s contextual filmmaking. The elderly twin spinsters, raised in an era when public demonstrations of faith were routine and expected, faithfully attend prayers at a gothic cathedral. They live in an aging chateau staffed by a pompous Indian Raj butler, an earthy cook who likens the family to a maggot infested stillborn calf, and a demure but pathetic maid (Patricia Davia) whose peculiarly captivating lazy eye gives her the air of a broken doll.

We are then introduced to the party guests as they begin their journey to the aunts' home. Kervyn's dizzy visual style and exposition giving the narrative a sense of stilted forward motion. We meet a corpulent industrialist and his trophy wife, who make a living manufacturing condoms, polluting the environment, and profiting from the AIDS epidemic. There is a slick armaments manufacturer who wishes to sell weapons in the Middle East in order to propagate World War Three. We are also introduced to a bullying middle-aged fashion mogul, accompanied by an attractive personal assistant who is also her jealousy controlled lesbian lover. There is the middle-class liberal family with young son and daughter, who in an argument over sharing cookies unmask their parents' contemptuous greed. We also meet a tragic middle-aged spinster—the "family virgin"—who cycles to the party while carrying on an out-of-place internal monologue with her own domineering mother. She is run off the road by an arrogant young playboy in a sports car, who proves to be the final invitee. Picking sides for the upcoming contest is simply not possible. None of the characters are likeable; a generation earlier, before the late 1980s cultural moment from which the film is inseparable, they would have been inconceivable.

Comprehension is shattered and fragmented in *Rabid Grannies*, mirroring the social fragmentation and cultural upheavals that came to a climax in America as the Reagan era drew to a close. Grasping greed had become "good," and consumption had been enshrined as virtuous, as the monied elites abandoned the broad-based manufacturing economy of that sustained the "American century" for the creation of wealth through elaborate financial manipulations encouraged by "Reaganomics." New ideas of authority emphasized deregulation and the unfettered production of capital, not for reinvestment in society, but for hoarding and public display as vast *personal* wealth. The Cold War

50   I. Victims No More

(and the ever-present threat of actual war) was profitable, and the military-industrial complex completed its decades-long takeover of the economy. Its pursuit of high-tech weapons drove the burgeoning digitization of Western civilization, and laid the foundations for a post-industrial, knowledge-based society defined, for it rank-and-file workers, by debt and perpetual job insecurity. Freud's patriarchal society—defined by restraint and prohibition—had begun to unravel in the late 1960s, and was, two decades later, gone entirely. In its place stood a society that, though equally beholden to patriarchal authority, was defined by its embrace of unfettered consumption. By the late 1980s, prohibition was out; fun and self-gratification, regardless of their social cost, were in.

The plot of *Rabid Grannies* hinges on wealth and its unbridled pursuit, but the film is not, ultimately, a commentary on wealth—or even economics. The Aunts' estate is a McGuffin, and thus narratively meaningless, except as a catalyst for the action. The filmmakers' real interest, and the film's real meaning, is hidden in the fractured family dynamics onscreen.

As the party begins, guests drink heavily and make underhand comments to each other that seem to go unnoticed by their elderly hosts, until a mystery guest arrives at the gate. An elderly lady with strange unblinking eyes delivers a gift from the long-disinherited, devil-worshiping Christopher: a plain and unspectacular jewelry box. There is an outbreak of contrived morality among the guests as presents—including Christopher's seemingly innocuous box—are opened and the cake arrives at the table.

What follows is as bizarre as it is enthralling: As the family begins a ritual hand-clapping chant for "a knife for a cake," the aunts transform into rubber-faced demons. One grows an arm that shoots the length of the table, grabs the elder of the lesbians in

Another mysterious guest at the Chateau. A mysterious old woman (Cindy Rimoe) delivers the magical mystery box that transforms the beneficent elders into *Rabid Grannies* (1988)!

a clawed hand, eats her head, belches and giggles. The young boy laughs and says, "That's smashing," Percival shouts, "Holy shit," and quite literally all hell breaks loose. Viewers are again left with nowhere to turn.

From the opening scenes, when we meet the elderly ladies, the film explicitly places them as being simultaneously at home and not at home. In a brief exposition, they inform the audience that after 92 years of residence, they know their own home, and they clearly have significance as elders in the wider community. Yet the reality that viewers can plainly see is that their despicable relatives are attending the birthday party simply to scheme their way into the lion's share of the inheritance. From the outset, Kervyn's story and techniques trouble the deeply rooted social norms that govern family gatherings: being homely, familial and politely blind to the reality of how unhomely home can be. The film—a cascade of discombobulating perspectives, obsessed with eyes, seeing, and scopic doubling—forces the audience into the realm of the psychoanalytic uncanny. Freud, who coined the concept in 1919, argued that we can grasp the reality of the uncanny in fiction, yet appeared to deny that fiction can play a role in our search to uncover something of who we really are.[9] Immersion in the uncanny world of *Rabid Grannies* suggests, however, that Freud's embrace of fiction as a path to understanding is more plausible than his denial.

Enjoying the party, Victoria and Elizabeth Remington (Anne-Marie Fox, left, and Danielle Daven) about to "get rabid" in *Rabid Grannies*. The movie was filmed in the middle of winter without heating, and with a cast wearing summer clothes, some of the actors struggled to perform without shivering!

> In his essay.... Das Unheimliche, Freud said that the uncanny is the only feeling which is more powerfully experienced in art than in life. If the horror genre required any justification, I should think this alone would serve as its credentials...—Stanley Kubrick

Kervyn's style was, by his own admission, shaped by the film's ultra-low-budget and other constraints imposed from outside the set. The directorial techniques they necessitated all but guaranteed a sense of disruption.[10] *Rabid Grannies* was made on a budget of $150,000 with a 79-cent advance from Troma for exclusive distribution rights. No one was paid for the any work on the production, cast and crew were interchangeable, often fulfilling multiple production roles as well as acting. There was only a smattering of professional actors on set, with most roles being played by amateurs and friends of the director. The chateau itself had minimal improvised lighting, and camera setups were chosen and executed "on-the-fly" to maximize atmosphere and minimize expense and the whole production was shot over six weeks of 16-hour work days.[11]

Having set out with his crew to film "the most horrific horror film ever," Kervyn quickly realized that time, budget, and special effects would not allow for it. He responded by making the film a parodic horror-comedy with grotesque special effects and minimal alterations to the script and dialogue. The special effects and horror scenes could only be shot in one take, so careful consideration was given to selecting the most efficient camera angles to optimize the effects, hide props and tricks from the camera, and save costs and time.[12] What resulted is a film filled with uncanny visual perspectives that mimicked gothic B-movie horror conventions while combining them with surreal folkloric grotesquery.

The film's visual ambiguity is compounded by auditory dissonance. Only two of the actors could speak English, so Kervyn made the cast pronounce the words of their lines phonetically, and then had the lines dubbed by Belgian actors who *did* speak English, albeit as a second language.[13] The result is a disconcerting meaninglessness in word and image, intensified by third-party editing and Troma's own censoring of the gore effects. When the main investor in the film demanded that it include a sex scene and a nude, Kervyn quickly added one involving the young lesbian (now bisexual) personal assistant and the arrogant playboy, which was reduced by editors to two people disliking each other and then quickly jumping into bed together. The changes erased any trace of motivation from an already arbitrary scene, turning the film's supposed heroine into someone willing to casually sleep with a distasteful misogynist.[14]

As the aunts change into slavering, vomiting, cannibalistic party animals, the guests fight back, cutting off hands that quickly grow back and gouging out eyes that *don't* grow back. The rabid aunts also exhibit animalistic behavior swinging from light fixtures in their old nursery, where they capture, dismember, and eat the legs of the young niece.[15] They devolve into childlike entities who partake in games of riddles, rhymes, and spite. They survive multiple gunshots and function with their internal organs removed—at one point throwing them onto the floor for guests to slip on like slapstick banana skins, while the spinster delivers a soliloquy about being unable to escape one's destiny.

One by one the guests and house staff are killed and consumed, in as many unique ways as Kervyn's intuitive style, budget, and knowledge of horror repertoire would allow. The industrialist is eaten alive from the waist down; the arms dealer is dismembered and castrated with a medieval weapon. The father of the children, who has fled from his family to save himself, is the last to die. Admitting his cowardice, he sacrifices himself to the aunts—literally bent over backwards and snapped in half—in order that the spinster can flee to the chapel and destroy the mystery box. Eventually, only the spinster, the (now nymphomaniac) bisexual assistant, the son, and his now-insane mother remain, and the curse is broken. The aunts revert to banal normality, with organs and appendages intact and no memory of their rampage.

The film's ending is equally surreal. The day dawns and the grannies are back to

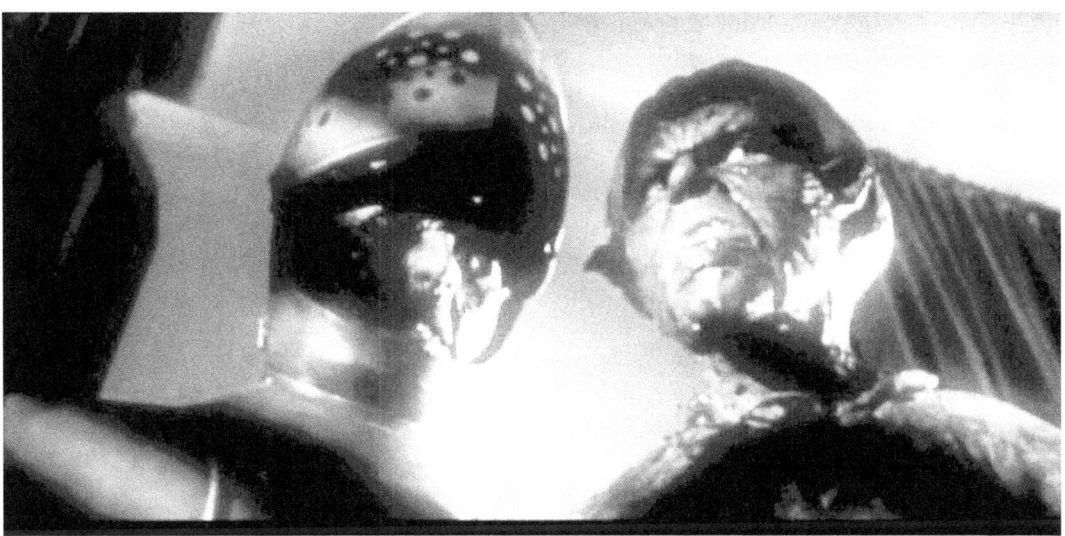

Rabid Grannies go to war, one (Anne-Marie Fox) wearing medieval armor! Director Kervyn utilized his genre mastery to create as many gruesome scenes as quickly as possible. Shots and cuts are used to hide prosthetics and effects from the camera and creates a style of dizzying irregularity.

normal, the chateau is full of dead and partially-eaten relatives, the police are called, and the personal assistant—our nominal heroine—and the young boy sit together pondering the night's events. The boy remarks on his now-certain knowledge that God does not exist, to which our heroine replies that he had to go through this ordeal to prove how brave he is: "Nobody could ever prove anything if the solutions were handed down from above.....see what I mean?" Meanwhile, the spinster, whose destruction of the box with a crucifix broke the curse, catches a taxi out of town. The driver asks if they should stop to eat, at which point she suddenly transforms into a bile-vomiting demon and eats the driver.

> Mimicry reveals something in so far as it is distinct from what might be called an itself that is behind. The effect of mimicry is camouflage....
> It is not a question of harmonizing with the background … [it's] like the technique of camouflage practiced in human warfare.—Jacques Lacan, *Of the Gaze*

In contemporary psychoanalytic film theory, mimicry, surrealism, and cannibalism have a direct relationship to clinical concepts of the uncanny. Lacan was influenced by Roger Caillois fascination with mimicry and his discovery that mimicry in nature had no evolutionary benefit. For Lacan mimicry was not a case of evolutionary biology but a violent cannibalizing of an image to structure identity.

There is no conceptual word for "uncanny" in French, so Lacan developed the concept of *extimité*: the point of meaninglessness between interiority and exteriority—the barrier between mind/body subject/object conscious/unconscious.[16] It leads back to what is old and familiar in the self, to the formation of self-identity. It is at this point we begin to develop the gamut of repulse and fascination at our own interiority: the gag at the site of vomit, the recoil at the sight of excrement, the vertigo at the sight of blood and internal organs. Lacan framed this concept to account for Freud's theory that the death drive compels individuals to compulsively repeat troubling and traumatic occurrences in their lives. This urge to return to a "non"-existence is what Lacan called "*between the two deaths*," an existence between symbolic and real death linked to the world of the undead.

It is why we unconsciously fear our elderly, especially those beneficent elderly who accept that, in the eyes of a youth-obsessed society, they are no longer truly alive, and await the finality of death without fear. Having embraced this status, they become not-of-reality, able to tap into the intuitive psychic insights of childhood and access childlike knowledge that makes conformity appear foolish. We visit this realm in horror fiction every chance we get, because—as Freud knew—we cannot imagine our own death, but merely conceive of it as spectators. Repulsed and drawn to it, we watch the death of the Other repetitively, compulsively; there is no death in the unconscious, no negation of life. Even our notions of afterlife connote this psychic realm between two deaths—we die to exist as undead-selves in an afterlife, awaiting the further non-death of final judgment.

Kervyn's style is relentless in its uncanniness. Not only is the visual content overtly parodic in its relation to folkloric tales and the thematic content of tragic myth, the imagery and spectral experience is also uncanny in the form of its own medium, as if the very celluloid is itself uncanny. It is as if the viewer has no locus or fixed perspective. In this, Kervyn moves beyond Troma's trademark mimicry of previous B-movie titles, lifting genre concepts wholesale from past generations of Gothic horror narratives with a zesty, youthful, self-referential twist. His style prefigures Troma's later penchant for recycling scenes, props, artifacts, effects, and locations from the company's own stable of films. Cultural theorists have noted that this mimicry plays a critical role in canonizing and formalizing genre conceits,[17] just as Troma films have been credited with establishing the genre specifics of "splatter-cinema." *Rabid Grannies*, however, goes beyond such play with genre-boundaries, transgressing—and thus calling attention to—social boundaries as well.

The quick-fire mimicry and uncanniness of Kervyn's film taps into the need for identifying a text as a frame for social action—that is in developing typified responses and rhetorical [re]actions to a singular crisis or anxiety that perturbs the real world.[18] In *Rabid Grannies,* this forces audiences to recognize that the ongoing social desires of the community in which they operate are meaningful signifiers of social behavior. *Rabid Grannies* is, therefore, a key film in the Troma stable. It identifies who benefits from the text of its commentary, who cannot participate in its meanings, and who has the power to recreate, alter, censor, and ultimately mimic its defining tropes.[19]

The "so bad it's good" appeal of *Rabid Grannies* lies in its ludicrous grotesquery, which situates the viewer in the midst of exactly what was repressed in the late 1980s drive for commodification and unfettered consumption: guilt over the destruction of relationships and diminishing of humanity brought about by those drives. The film is an example of the high-water mark of postmodernity and its cinema. It is an example of how a film that received cult status due to its "badness" was in fact "good" because it demonstrates the independent filmmaker's intuitive ability to surreally mimic, *uncannily* through notions of repressed affects and their relation to subjectivity, films visual power to challenge and critique the dominant ideology of its epoch.

Postmodernity in the late 1980s was identified by its repression of guilt and unqualified access to greed and desires of all kinds. It has been equated with the rise of the maternal super ego, a social authority that denies greed, and offers full access to the fulfillment of desire, in stark contrast to the prohibitive laws and ideologies of a patriarchal modernity. Psychoanalysis offers two subjective positions in relation to transgression, guilt, and desire, and unfettered access to the all-consuming desire of the M'otherer offers a forced choice between them. Knowing no desire of their own, the subject of the M'others desire is consumed as an all-encompassing truth and is manifest as psychosis. Alternately, the subject's enjoyment becomes the object cause of the M'others desire; and manifests as clinical perversion. In his intuitive approach, Kervyn really had no choice but to mimic the very constellation of primal fears and repressions at the heart of this choice and present them in the very context that they appeared in 1988.

Viewed through the lens of psychoanalysis, *Rabid Grannies* illustrates that we can still see the primordial narratives that dominate our social lives and witness how these narratives have been further developed and elaborated by postmodern cinema and its conceits. *Rabid Grannies* is a narrative about greed and desire and the repressed emotions at the heart of the postmodern family, but it is also indicative of something more—this is a film that is a direct descendent of the independent "midnight movies" of the late 1960s and early 1970s—it is a film that brings together a constellation of tropes from postcolonial and modernist narratives, with new concerns about the changing nature of family and social institutions. Subversive in terms of filmmaking through its own reflexivity, *Rabid Grannies* is also a commentary on the workings of guilt, shame, sex, and rapacious enjoyment that have come to be a well-cited embodiment of our postmodern condition.

Notes

1. Bramesco, "Toxic Avenger Franchise."
2. Kervyn, "Director's Commentary."
3. "Film Catalog," *Troma Entertainment: 40 Years of Disrupting Media*, https://www.troma.com/films/.
4. See McGowan and Kunkle, *Lacan and Contemporary Film*.
5. Žižek, *For They Know Not What They Do*.
6. McGowan and Kunkle, *Lacan and Contemporary Film*, xvii–xviii.
7. Kennedy, *The Psychic Home*, 24–27.
8. Freud, *Totem and Taboo*.
9. For discussions of Freud's essay on the uncanny and its providence in modernist literature see: Vine, "Uncanny Literature"; Cixous, "Fiction and its Phantoms"; Koffman, "The Double is/and the Devil"; Masschelein, "Unconcept"; Moller, "The Sandman."
10. Kervyn, "Director's Commentary," *Rabid Grannies*.
11. *Ibid.*
12. *Ibid.*
13. *Ibid.*
14. *Ibid.*
15. In keeping with an "uncanny" tradition a scene reminiscent of the dismemberment of Olimpia in the Powell and Pressburger epic *Tales of Hoffman* (1951).
16. Dollar, "I Shall Be with You," 6.
17. Žižek, "The Act and Its Vicissitudes."
18. Miller, "Genre as Social Action," 155–158.
19. Paré, "Rhetorical Genre Theory and Academic Literacy," A84.

Bibliography

Bramesco, Charles. "The Toxic Avenger Franchise is a Monument to Putridness." *The AV Club*. May 19, 2016. https://film.avclub.com/the-toxic-avenger-franchise-is-a-monument-to-putridness-1798247621.
Cixous, Hélén. "Fiction and its Phantoms: A Reading of Freud's "Das Unheimlich."" In *Literature in Psychoanalysis: A Reader*, edited by Steve Vine, 84–96. London: Palgrave Macmillan, 2005.
Dollar, Mladen. "'I Shall Be with You on Your Wedding-Night': Lacan and the Uncanny." *Rendering the Real* 58 (Autumn 1991): 5–23.

Freud, Sigmund. *Totem and Taboo: Resemblances between the Psychic Lives of Savages and Neurotics.* London: Routledge, 1919.
Kennedy, Roger. *The Psychic Home: Psychoanalysis, Consciousness and the Human Soul.* London: Routledge, 2014.
Koffman, Sarah. "The Double is/and the Devil: The Uncanniness of 'The Sandman.'" In *Literature in Psychoanalysis: A Reader*, edited by Steve Vine, 68–83. London: Palgrave Macmillan, 2005.
Masschelein, Anneleen. *Unconcept: The Freudian in Late-Twentieth-Century Theory.* New York: State University of New York Press, 2011.
McGowan, Todd, and Sheila Kunkle. *Lacan and Contemporary Film.* New York: Other Press, 2004.
Miller, Carolyn R. "Genre as Social Action." *Quarterly Journal of Speech* 70 (1984): 151–167.
Moller, Lis. "'The Sandman': The Uncanny as Problem of Reading." In *Literature in Psychoanalysis: A Reader*, edited by Steve Vine, 97–110. London: Palgrave Macmillan, 2005.
Paré, Anthony. "Rhetorical Genre Theory and Academic Literacy." *Journal of Academic Language & Learning* (AALL) 8, no. 1 (2014): a83-a94. journal.aall.org.au/index.php /jall/article/download/313/189.
Rabid Grannies. Directed by Emmanuel Kervyn. 1988. Schwadorf, Germany: XT Video, 2012. DVD.
Roye, Nicholas. *The Uncanny.* Manchester: Manchester University Press, 2003.
Vine, Steve. "Uncanny Literature—Freud and the "Uncanny." In *Literature in Psychoanalysis: A Reader*, edited by Steve Vine, 60–67. London: Palgrave Macmillan, 2005.
Žižek, Slavoj. "The Act and Its Vicissitudes." *The Symptom.* 2005. http://www.lacan.com/symptom6_articles/zizek.html.
_____. *For They Know Not What They Do: Enjoyment as a Political Factor*, 2nd ed. London: Verso, 1991.
_____. *The Pervert's Guide to Cinema: Parts 1, 2 & 3.* Directed by Sophie Fiennes. Performed by Slavoj Žižek. 2006.
_____. *The Pervert's Guide to Ideology.* Directed by Sophie Fiennes. Performed by Slavoj Žižek. 2012.

II.
Aesthetics of Decay

The Shock of Aging (Women) in Horror Film

DAWN KEETLEY

There is a recurring figure, filmed with the express intent of shocking the audience, that has appeared in horror film after horror film since 2010—not a supernatural monster, but a thoroughly human-looking old woman. James Wan's *Insidious* (2010) is a powerful case in point, parsing out its jump scares between dark maleficent shapes, an orange-faced demon, and an old woman dressed in black. What makes these figures—the visibly unnatural and the visibly human—at all equivalent? Why is an old woman as shocking as a demon? This question is only made more urgent by the proliferation of high-profile 21st-century films—among them *Paranormal Activity 3* (2011), *The Woman in Black* (2012), *The Conjuring* (2013), *It Follows* (2014), and *The Witch* (2015)—that use the sudden appearance of old women to create jump scares.[1] Using old women to elicit cinematic shock has a much longer history, however—one that extends at least as far back as Edward Dein's *The Leech Woman* (1960) and includes *Psycho* (1960), *The Exorcist* (1973), and *The Shining* (1980).

On one level, a jump cut to an old woman is sheer sensationalism. More substantively, though, as this essay will argue, employing visual representations of women's aging as shock effects within horror film serves to illuminate philosopher Catherine Malabou's exploration of aging as a kind of trauma. In her *Ontology of the Accident* (2012), Malabou claims that aging can divest the self almost as fully and suddenly as a catastrophic brain injury. Against the prevailing notion that aging is experienced as a gradual process, she argues that aging happens all of sudden, like a trauma, transforming us into someone unrecognizable. It's not surprising, then, that this idea—aging as shock—would make its way into the horror film.

Shock has been an important cinematic concept since Walter Benjamin's work in the early 20th century. For Benjamin and many of the film theorists who have been influenced by his theories, shocks explode from the modern, crowded urban environment. Ben Singer, for instance, in *Melodrama and Modernity* (2001), ties melodrama and early sensational cinema to the shock of living in the city with its repeated sensory assaults and life-and-limb-threatening accidents: this new "violence, suddenness, randomness (and, in a sense, the humiliating public character) of accidental death in the metropolis" had "intensified and focalized" the fear of unnatural death, he writes.[2] But it is not only the stimuli of the external world, and not only unnatural death, that can shock—so can

June Talbot (Coleen Gray) realizes with horror that her new youth has gone (*The Leech Woman*, 1960).

our own bodily interiors and our own "natural" aging. Indeed, the shock of age is equally capable (with the shocks of the city) of assailing the human subject and defying the ability of consciousness to process it.

This essay begins by exploring how 1960's *The Leech Woman* embodies Malabou's theory of aging as sudden and shocking "accident." The film features a middle-aged woman, June Talbot (Coleen Gray), who discovers a way to make herself young again. Since the process of rejuvenation is only temporary, however, the film features three shocking scenes in which June suddenly becomes old again (aging more in each transformation). What June experiences throughout the second half of the film is far from a gradual process of aging but its repeated sudden and horrific onset. *The Leech Woman* thus gets not only at what aging feels like for everyone but, specifically, at what it feels like for women in a society that continues to value youth and beauty. Above all, though, the film demonstrates that we are all vulnerable not only to assaults emanating from the external environment but also to those that come from our own interior.

As horror films have continued to frame the old woman as shock, they do more than represent what it means to age (especially as a woman). I will go on to read more recent horror films, notably James Wan's *Dead Silence* (2007), through the lens of Tom Gunning's well-known theory of the "cinema of attractions," a term he coined to describe a technique of very early (pre–1908) and avant-garde cinema. The shocking appearance of the old woman in horror, I argue, represents not only an ontology of aging but also a narrative strategy, serving as a fleeting rupture in the diegesis of the film. The figure of the old woman serves, specifically, to rupture the classical narrative arc that centers and privileges the heterosexual couple and the reproductive family. The old woman, thrust upon the audience as jump scare, often in self-aware and fleetingly avant-garde moments, threatens the dependence of the seamless classical Hollywood narrative on the reproductive couple framed in an illusory eternal youth. The old woman refuses to go quietly, rejecting the mantle of invisibility she is supposed to take up once she reaches her 50s. She comes back not only to terrify viewers (especially the young) but also to disrupt the privileged romance plot that is predicated on youth.

The Leech Woman *and Monstrous Aging*

The Leech Woman begins by focusing on Dr. Paul Talbot (Phillip Terry), who is searching for a way to slow the aging process and thus make himself a wealthy man. He also loathes aging women: "Old women always give me the creeps," he tells his young, attractive assistant early in the film, making it clear that his scientific drive is also personal. One day, an elderly African American woman, Malla (Estelle Hemsley), who claims she is a 152-year-old former slave, arrives at his office. Her story of a substance that can stave off aging and death, held secret by her tribe in Africa, lures Talbot into the jungle. He brings along his wife, June, who is a decade older than he is and whom he had coerced into filing for a divorce just before realizing he needed her as a human guinea pig. Once they find the Nandos tribe and discover that Malla's story is true, however, June ends up turning the tables on Paul, sacrificing him to ensure her own return to youth. While Malla's powder by itself only delays aging, when it is mixed with fluid from a man's pineal gland in a ritual that involves that man's violent death, it precipitates a transformation from age to youthfulness in a moment. June unhesitatingly sacrifices the dubious pleasures of her marriage for an instant return to youth and beauty. The transformation is temporary, however, and June is forced to kill again and again to stave off increasing age and to maintain her renewed youth and beauty.

On one level, June's shocking transformation into an old woman continues the horror film's longstanding project of disrupting the classical cinematic narrative predicated on and driven by the attractive young woman who is the linchpin of the heterosexual romance and the reproductive family. Horror films of the 1930s through the 1950s are particularly structured by the threat the monster poses to the heterosexual couple: Henry and Elizabeth (*Frankenstein*, 1931), Mina and Jonathan (*Dracula*, 1931), Jack and Ann (*King Kong*, 1933), Oliver and Alice (*Cat People*, 1942), David and Kay (*The Creature from the Black Lagoon*, 1954), and Becky and Miles (*Invasion of the Body Snatchers*, 1956). *The Leech Woman*, in a twist on this classic plot, features a monster that is not external to the couple but is June herself, in her twinned function as both young and beautiful heterosexual woman and monstrous hag: she *herself* thus drives the narrative forward *and* violently disrupts it.[3]

All three of June's transformations back to an increasingly aged woman occur immediately after moments of intimacy, emphasizing how aging upsets heterosexuality. The first time, June is still in the jungle with guide Bertram Garvey (John Van Dreelen), who helped her escape from the Nandos tribe. They have already developed an intimate relationship, but when he sees that she has become devastatingly old, he is repelled: "Take your hands off me. Don't touch me. Don't touch me. Get away from me," he yells at her in horror. In the second instance, June pre-emptively wrenches herself away from Neil Foster (Grant Williams), the young lawyer whom she is seducing, and slams the door on him. Her third violent metamorphosis occurs immediately after Neil has proposed marriage, and she runs upstairs and throws herself out of her bedroom window rather than reveal herself as old. All three of these moments of precipitous aging on June's part represent the repeated and violent disruption of the heterosexual romance by a "monster" that parallels, say, Frankenstein's creature or King Kong but that is, in the end, nothing but aging itself. Aging does not just halt but destroys the narrative trajectory upon which the classical Hollywood romance plot depends: it is what makes *The Leech Woman* a horror film.

As well as dramatizing how old women stop the romance narrative dead in its tracks, *The Leech Woman* also presents, midway through its running time, a striking indictment of the gendered double standard that makes aging catastrophic to women while offering men other options. Malla overtly voices this feminist message: "For a man, old age has rewards. If he is wise, his gray hairs bring dignity and he is treated with honor and respect. But for the aged woman, there is nothing. At best she's pitied. More often, her lot is of contempt and neglect." Malla follows this message, however, with a less empowering claim: "What woman lives who has passed the prime of her life who would not give her remaining years to reclaim even a few moments of joy and happiness and know the worship of men. For the end of life should be its moment of triumph. So it is with the aged women of Nandos, a last flowering of love, beauty—before death." Despite the film's radical recognition of how aging men and women are treated very differently, its imagined solution is women's grasping, by whatever means possible, a few moments of renewed youth and beauty and thus men's "worship." The ambivalence of the film's politics is maintained, however, in the deadly anger that shadows women's otherwise regressive desire for the "worship" of men. It is not insignificant, for instance, that a *man* must die to provide the pineal gland fluid that effects Malla's and June's sudden return to youth. And it is even more significant that June chooses to sacrifice her own contemptible husband. As the (now young) Malla (Kim Hamilton) says, approvingly, when June chooses to exchange her husband for youth: "You will have beauty and revenge at the same time." Women might clutch at beauty and the worship of men, then, but they are prepared to kill men in the process—another way in which *The Leech Woman* functions as a horror film.

Vivian Sobchack has astutely written about the way that *The Leech Woman* reflects the gendered double standard of aging. She argues that the film "can be seen as a feminist indictment of the premium men put on female youth and beauty" and, in a second and more sustained analysis, that the film shows how women become the repository of everyone's fears about aging—that the film is about "the explicit engendering of the cultural fear, loathing, and anger directed at the mortal fact and process of physical aging" and embodied in the "scary" woman.[4] When aging women are depicted as objects of terror in low-budget horror films, Sobchack argues, they illustrate how women (alone) come to bear the burden of anxieties surrounding "abjection and death."[5] Objects of desire when they are young, women slide easily into becoming objects of horror when they age: in both instances, they are spectacles caught in the male gaze. Indeed, as Linda Williams has pointed out, there is not "that much difference between an object of desire and an object of horror as far as the male look is concerned." When women are "considered too old to continue as spectacle-objects," she writes, they "persevere as horror objects."[6]

Aging as Shock

The Leech Woman does more, though, than present aging women as disruptors of the romance/reproduction plot or exemplars of mortality and the "horror objects" of the male gaze. The film also speaks to women's own experience of aging, especially in a society that prefers to turn away from the elderly woman. Specifically, *The Leech Woman* captures what Malabou describes as the "suddenness," even the "trauma," of aging. In her two essays on the film, Sobchak repeats that June "soon starts to age," as the effect of the serum wears off.[7] This language is imperfect, however, because what June experiences throughout the second half of the film—three times, in fact—is not a gradual process of aging ("soon starts") but its sudden and horrific onset. June experiences the *shock* of becoming old. This dynamic taps into the way women experience aging as well as refracting the visceral horror with which old women, who should remain invisible, are viewed—when they are viewed—in a western society that, as Malla perfectly articulates, values (only) youth and beauty in women. The horror film, which trades in shock as part of the affect it routinely elicits, is indeed the perfect venue through which to explore *aging* as *shock*.

It is significant that each of the three times June reverts back to old age—getting older and older each time—it is she who sees herself first and who bears the first shock. In the first instance, June wakes up in the jungle with Garvey, who remains sleeping while she looks at her hands and experiences on her own the full horror of her sudden aging. The second time, June is seducing Neil in her bedroom and, as they are clasped in an embrace, she sees her own suddenly wrinkled hand on his shoulder and pushes the oblivious man out of the room in terror. The third and last time, which comes shortly after another seduction scene with Neil, June again sees her hand and rushes upstairs to her room, only to then have the shocking experience described by so many older women: she looks in the mirror and sees, with horror and without recognition, an old woman. As Lori Day puts it, "You'll catch your reflection and your breath at the same time and be abruptly reminded that your exterior no longer matches how you feel inside."[8] In all of these moments, June has to *see* herself to grasp her sudden change, making it clear that nothing inside, nothing about the way she feels, has changed. The figure she sees in the mirror is a stranger.

In its visual representation of women's aging as shock, *The Leech Woman* represents Malabou's argument that aging can alienate the self almost as fully and suddenly as a catastrophic brain injury. Malabou's *Ontology of the Accident* explores what it means to the notion of the self that an "accident" always threatens to make it permanently other: there is "a sort of death that is not death but that appears instead as a radical personality change."[9] Malabou claims, moreover, that calling a brain injury and its consequences "contingent" is actually not quite the right way to think of it, since the "possibility of an identity change by destruction" is inherent—"a constant virtuality of being, inscribed in it as an eventuality, understood within its biological and ontological fate." The accident is "unpredictable," and yet "it must be acknowledged as a law."[10] It is a law of being, in other words, that we suffer the kind of "accident" that turns us into someone else. Although it is not her focus, Malabou offers some suggestive comments about how the "accident" of identity loss is in fact a constitutive part of the developmental cycle. Who, for instance, recognizes themselves in the infant they once were?[11] Most importantly, Malabou suggests that "ageing [sic] itself may be thought of as a lesion. In the end it may be that for each one of us, ageing arises all of a sudden, in an instant, like a trauma, and that it suddenly transforms us, without warning, into an unknown subject."[12] She elaborates that "old age remains fundamentally a rupture; it breaks being at an unlocatable point, forcing it to change direction, leading it to become other."[13] For Malabou, then, the inexorability of the "accident" not only illuminates the experience of aging, which "arises all of a sudden," but it also fundamentally destabilizes the notion that identity is continuous from birth to death. The "history of being itself," she concludes, "consists perhaps of nothing but a series of accidents which, in every era and without hope of return, dangerously disfigure the meaning of essence."[14]

As June transitions among three different selves—middle-aged woman (before she starts taking the rejuvenating concoction), a woman so young she has to masquerade as June's niece, and the shockingly old hag that the young June reverts to when the serum wears off—*The Leech Woman* both depicts aging as a trauma that hits "all of a sudden" and—to the extent that June is dramatically different, "other" than herself, in virtually every scene—illuminates the profound instability of identity. Malabou's theory of the stark change instantiated by an "accident" that is innate to being itself offers a view of selfhood as harboring a perennial other, something so alien it seems inhuman—what theorists of the "nonhuman turn" have articulated as a blind nonhumanity buried within the "human." Rosi Braidotti, for instance, argues that the paradigm shifts effected by Darwin and Freud "opened up a profound *nonhumanness* at the heart of the subject." And Roberto Esposito has described how the "person" is "traversed by a power that is foreign to it" what he calls a "*non-human*" organic life.[15] Aging is one aspect of this interior unrecognizable "nonhuman" lurking within the "human" that we recognize ourselves to be. Our aging is a blind force of nature that not only makes us alien to ourselves but challenges the very notion of ourselves as "human" (knowable and singular) at all.

This "nonhuman otherness" inherent in the self finds in aging perhaps its perfect example, and *The Leech Woman* (despite its undeniably low-budget origins) visually represents this nonhuman within the human in a paired set of scenes. Shortly after June and her husband arrive in Africa, June realizes her husband only wanted her along so he could test the age-defying powder on her. She runs out of the tent and into the jungle and is chased by a leopard, which is finally shot by Garvey. Later, after the effects of June's first transformation into a young beauty wear off and she begs Garvey for help, he runs away from her, utterly repelled by her aged appearance, and she chases him through the jungle in a repetition of the earlier scene. As June becomes something other than who she had been, then, as she becomes the alienating "hag" that had been lurking within all along, she takes on the position of the predatory animal. The aged self that waits for us, paralleled in the film by the leopard, is something inhuman within the human, and the human is shown to be, as Esposito puts it, "traversed by a power that is foreign to it."

Aging as Shock in 2010s Horror

The Leech Woman represents through one character (played by one actress) the way in which aging falls upon us—"all of a sudden, in an instant, like a trauma," as Malabou puts it—suddenly transforming us, "without warning, into an unknown subject."[16] Although in a slightly different way, the horror film since around 2007 has likewise taken up the shocking image of the old woman. She is divided from the young woman, however,

Jay Height (Maika Monroe) is followed inexorably by an old woman (*It Follows*, 2014).

not embodied in the same character; the shock of aging is externalized as the young protagonist is shadowed by her uncanny elderly double. One of the most iconic scenes in David Robert Mitchell's *It Follows*, for instance, shows Jay (Maika Monroe) inexorably pursued by an old woman, and the camera captures them together in a hallway in a way that highlights how the woman is, if Jay survives, her possible future self. As Jay turns anxiously back to look at what follows her, her face is obscured, replaced by the old woman who is the face of a future she does not want to recognize.

Interwoven with the shots of the old woman pursuing Jay is a classroom scene in which the teacher reads part of T. S. Eliot's "The Love Song of J. Alfred Prufrock," which meditates on an encroaching mortality that is like a death in life ("Would it have been worth while … / To say: 'I am Lazarus, come from the dead'"). The sight of the old woman, eliciting a dread deepened by the lines of poetry, are so disturbing to Jay that she runs from both—avoiding confronting an aging she's already intimated is unsettling to her. "Now that we're older," she laments to Hugh, "where do we go?" Besides this line, though, the fear of becoming old is not explicitly part of the plot of *It Follows* (as it is in *The Leech Woman*); instead, the story ostensibly concerns a fatal "it" that is passed on through sex. Fears about aging are thus displaced from the young protagonists themselves onto the old woman and the many other elderly followers of the film, all of whom are used to create dread through Mitchell's distinctive panning and tracking shots.

Shock (rather than dread) is more explicitly exploited in *Paranormal Activity 3*, in which one of the principal jump scares occurs near the end as Dennis (Chris Smith) is searching for his girlfriend, Julie (Lauren Bittner), and opens a door to find a group of middle-aged and elderly women; they're witches, but the shock of this moment is generated by the women's age, notable in a film that has focused on the young Julie and Dennis and Julie's still-younger daughters, all of whom are drawn into plots involving reproduction from which the older women are excluded. In both of these films, the fear induced by old people is about not only the shock of aging, then, but the shock of aging in a world in which the fact of aging is increasingly refused.

Indeed, this splitting of youth and age into different characters in 2010s horror film (unlike their incorporation in one character in *The Leech Woman*) marks the increasing repression of aging in the United States as life expectancy continues to lengthen and as products designed to extend youth (along with the worship of youth) proliferate exponentially: while the elderly woman inexorably follows the young protagonist of *It Follows*, there's the hope that she won't catch her—that maybe aging and death are not inevitable. The relentless search by scientists for the technologies that might reverse aging and extend life drives this plot—and we see other manifestations of it in, for instance, Jordan Peele's *Get Out* (2017), which maps race onto the desperate desire of wealthy white baby boomers to defeat aging and death.[17] The reiterated scene of the old woman in 2010s horror films—encroaching inexorably or appearing suddenly, but always threatening young people—can be read, moreover, as expressing a collective anxiety about the sheer numbers of elderly Americans. As the baby boomers age, they are being viewed as a potential economic burden, threatening to overwhelm social services and put the well-being of the young at risk. Between 2000 and 2050, for instance, a 135 percent increase in the number of Americans over 65 is projected to occur, along with a 350 percent increase in those over 85 (compared to only a 33 percent increase in those aged 16 to 64).[18] The mainstream media are already running stories about the dire consequences that will ensue as the numbers of those who are dependent on social services dramatically start to outpace the wage-earners who support them.[19] A heightened denial of aging in the 21st century, then, along with increased anxiety about the growing number of the elderly, are the twinned forces driving the proliferating trope of the old woman, framed as shock, as jump-scare, in post–2010 horror films.

Aging as Grand Guignol

What is striking about post–2010 films is not only the repeated appearance, "all of a sudden," of the old woman but also the way in which the jolting shot of her sagging body, her white, wrinkled face, her gray hair is explicitly framed to shock the audience. This use of the old woman as jump scare serves, in fact, to mark one particular contemporary manifestation of what Tom Gunning famously called a "cinema of attractions." Gunning argues that, although the era of cinematic attractions lasted only through 1907, it did not disappear but went "underground," reappearing in "certain avant-garde practices and as a component of narrative films, more evident in some genres (e.g., the musical) than in others."[20] While Gunning himself does not mention the horror film, Adam Lowenstein has argued that the horror genre, "with its multiple and varied investments in shocking, terrifying, disturbing, and haunting its viewers, has more to teach us than perhaps any other about the fearful attractions of film."[21] The old woman, I argue, has become one of the "fearful attractions" of 2010s horror.

According to Gunning, the cinema of attractions is defined by spectacle, the disruption of narrative, and the direct address of the spectator. As he puts it: "Theatrical display dominates over narrative absorption, emphasizing the direct stimulation of shock or surprise at the expense of unfolding a story or creating a diegetic universe." Gunning adds that an "attraction aggressively subjected the spectator to 'sensual or psychological impact'" and that its relation to the spectator is one of "exhibitionist confrontation rather than diegetic absorption."[22] Horror films have always dealt in attractions. Indeed, Sergei Eisenstein, one of attractions' earliest theorists, argued that their "emotional shocks" relied on "the tradition of the French Grand Guignol Theater that was notorious for its horror and special effects."[23] In recent horror films, the spectacle of bodies being dismembered has been supplemented by the old woman, filmed in such a way that she provides those visceral and emotional shocks.[24]

This figure, this visual effect, contains a multitude of meanings: the existential experience of aging as shock (as Malabou has described it), the fear of old *women* in particular as repositories of dread about mortality, and the collective cultural anxiety about the increasing numbers of the elderly in the United States. The visual practice of old-woman-as-shock is substituted for the bodily mutilations of eyes being gouged out and legs amputated (part of the attractions of Grand Guignol): indeed, both forms trade in the horrific deformation of the healthy, youthful body. And such scenes not only break narrative absorption, a crucial component of the cinema of attractions, but they specifically (as in *The Leech Woman*) disrupt the heterosexual romance plot that is the heart of classical narrative. Indeed, part of breaking narrative absorption is breaking the driving force of heterosexuality and reproductivity.

James Wan's 2007 film *Dead Silence* perfectly exemplifies these uses of the old woman. The film begins with young newlywed couple, Jamie and Lisa Ashen (Ryan Kwanten and Laura Regan), who are starting their lives away from their hometown. Lisa, as it turns out, is pregnant. Her baby is never born, though, because the opening scene shows her being grotesquely murdered after a ventriloquist's dummy arrives at their door in a mysterious box. The doll is an uncanny substitute, offered to the couple who will never reproduce. In grief, Jamie returns to their hometown of Raven's Fair and uncovers the history behind the stories of Mary Shaw (Judith Roberts). Mary, the monstrous old woman, is the center of the film, and a flashback halfway through discloses the origin of her reign of terror. As local mortician Henry Walker (Michael Fairman) recounts the story to Jamie, in the 1940s, Raven's Fair had a "grand old" lakeside theater, not insignificantly called the Guignol Theater, which staged live attractions. Mary Shaw was one of those attractions—a ventriloquist with a dummy named Billy. At one fateful show, a local boy named Michael broke the spell of her performance, calling out from the audience, "I can see your lips moving." As consternation rippled through the spectators, Mary tried to restore the illusion, making Billy repeat over and over, "I'm as real as you!" and delivering a bravura performance that led to spontaneous applause. Mary then turned to look at Michael and the rest of the theater audience (along with the viewers of the film) and asked, "Now, who's the dummy?"

Michael subsequently vanished and, not long after, Mary was herself murdered, the victim of a group of vigilantes convinced she was responsible for Michael's disappearance. Her dying wish was to be buried with her 101 dolls, her "children," and to be turned into a doll herself. Her aging, non-reproductive body—highlighted by her association with inanimate dolls who are self-evidently not "children"—then becomes the source of the

Mary Shaw (Judith Roberts) and Billy at the Guignol Theater (*Dead Silence*, 2007).

jump scares interspersed throughout the rest of the film. Shortly after he tells the story about the Guignol performance, for instance, Henry, who had been a boy at the time, tells Jamie how he went to see her coffin, which fell off the table spilling the dead Mary Shaw—at this point, part dead human, part inhuman doll—onto the floor besides him, a flashback that is shot for maximum terror.

Dead Silence thus does several things simultaneously. It violently disrupts a plot of heterosexual romance and procreation with the perverse story of the unmarried Mary Shaw and her inanimate dolls-as-children; it deploys Mary Shaw's old, white, wrinkled body as jump scare; and it thematizes both of the above, enacting a "cinema of attractions" through its central scene at the Guignol Theater. In that scene, Mary Shaw's performance with her "child" Billy, no matter how "real" she claims it is, is revealed to be artificial, not least through Michael's shouted accusation, which breaks narrative absorption and the story she tried to tell about her reproductive "family." Her knowing (and threatening) stare out at both the theater audience (and the film audience) perfectly embodies the ways in which the old woman has been used in horror as sensational jump scare and as a figure that breaks narrative realism along with the heterosexual romance/reproductive plot. Her repeated shocking appearances throughout the rest of the film also manifest an ontology of aging in which humans neither age gradually nor maintain a singular coherent identity over the course of a lifetime, but instead age suddenly, becoming someone else—transformed by a "nonhuman" core, the alien and incontrollable fact of aging, that is allegorized aptly by Mary Shaw's dolls (and by her own transformation into a doll).

Philip Nickel has argued that the project of horror film in general is to offer a "skeptical alternative to belief in everyday reality." Or, as he puts it in a more violent metaphor, horror's "bite" lies in "a *malicious* ripping-away of this intellectual trust [that stands behind our actions], exposing our vulnerabilities in relying on the world and on other people."[25] Indeed, Nickel argues that horror films perfectly dramatize "philosophical skepticism"—that is, the idea that "no human being can have any knowledge or justification in a given area, for example, on questions of religion, the future, morality, or the external world."[26] According to Nickel, the horror film forces us to confront the fact that the everyday world as we know it can suddenly be utterly transformed. *The Leech Woman* and the old women in horror films of the last decade go further, however, reminding us that we cannot even rely on the integrity of our own bodies or the persistence of identity. As Malabou explains, as we age, we are forced to give up a commonsense faith in our bodies and in the ways they serve as the foundations of identity. We inevitably experience the rupture, the malicious ripping-away, that Nickel claims horror exploits so expertly.

NOTES

1. The figure of the old woman in these films is a diverse and rich one and could be analyzed extensively for the way in which it functions in each of these individual films. For purposes of this essay, I am just making the point that the old woman appears frequently in recent horror and is always filmed in such a way as to produce a shock in the spectator.
2. Singer, *Melodrama and Modernity*, 70–71.
3. The way in which June as female protagonist/love object also doubles as the monster is similar to the way in which Irena functions in *Cat People* and Becky in *Invasion* (after she is taken over by the pods). The dominant trend in horror films before the 1960s, though, was clearly to demarcate the female protagonist (an exemplar of "normality") from the monster.
4. Sobchack, "*The Leech Woman*'s Revenge," 255; Sobchack, "Revenge of *The Leech Woman*," 338.
5. Sobchack, "Revenge of *The Leech Woman*," 337. The other films Sobchack discusses are *Attack of the 50 Ft. Woman* (1958) and *The Wasp Woman* (1960).
6. Williams, "When the Woman Looks," 21.
7. Sobchack, "*The Leech Woman*'s Revenge," 253; Sobchack, "Revenge of *The Leech Woman*," 341.
8. Day, "Aging While Female."
9. Malabou, *Ontology*, 33.
10. Ibid., 30.
11. Ibid., 32.
12. Ibid., 49. In a third chapter that touches more briefly on *The Leech Woman*, Sobchack calls old age an "injury." See Sobchack, *Carnal Thoughts*, 36.
13. Malabou, *Ontology*, 52.
14. Ibid., 91.
15. Braidotti, "Animals, Anomalies," 528, and Esposito, *Third Person*, 24; emphasis mine.
16. Malabou, *Ontology*, 49.
17. For a recent survey of efforts to reverse the aging process, see Friend, "Silicon Valley's Quest."
18. Wiener and Tilly, "Population Ageing," 776.
19. See, for example, Casselman, "What Baby Boomers' Retirement Means," and Tankersley, "Baby Boomers."
20. Gunning, "Cinema," 382.
21. Lowenstein, "Living Dead," 107.
22. Gunning, "Cinema," 384.
23. Strauven, "Introduction," 18.
24. In his book *Grande Dame Guignol Cinema*, Peter Shelley identifies a sub-genre of film, "Grande Dame Guignol," defined by three criteria, "that it be a horror movie which uses grande guignol effects and stars an actress in a leading role playing a character with the airs and graces of a grande dame." He identifies 45 such films released between 1962 and 2007, ending just before the (different) trend involving old women that I identify in this essay.
25. Nickel, "Horror and the Idea of Everyday Life," 25, 28.
26. Ibid., 18.

BIBLIOGRAPHY

Braidotti, Rosi. "Animals, Anomalies, and Inorganic Others." *PMLA* 124, no. 2 (2009): 526–32.
Casselman, Ben. "What Baby Boomers' Retirement Means for the U.S. Economy." *FiveThirtyEight*, May 7, 2014. https://fivethirtyeight.com/features/what-baby-boomers-retirement-means-for-the-u-s-economy/.
Day, Lori. "Aging While Female Is Not Your Worst Nightmare." *Feminist Current*, March 10, 2015. http://www.feministcurrent.com/2015/03/10/aging-while-female-is-not-your-worst-nightmare-2/.
Esposito, Roberto. *Third Person: Politics of Life and Philosophy of the Impersonal.* Trans. Zakiya Hanafi. Malden, MA: Polity Press, 2012.
Friend, Tad. "Silicon Valley's Quest to Live Forever." *The New Yorker*, April 3, 2017. https://www.newyorker.com/magazine/2017/04/03/silicon-valleys-quest-to-live-forever.
Gunning, Tom. "The Cinema of Attraction[s]: Early Film, Its Spectator and the Avant-Garde." In Strauven, *Cinema of Attractions*, 381–88.
Lowenstein, Adam. "Living Dead: Fearful Attractions of Film." *Representations* 110, no. 1 (2010): 105–28.
Malabou, Catherine. *Ontology of the Accident: An Essay on Destructive Plasticity.* Trans. Carolyn Shread. Malden, MA: Polity Press, 2012.
Nickel, Philip J. "Horror and the Idea of Everyday Life: On Skeptical Threats in *Psycho* and *The Birds*." In *The Philosophy of Horror*, edited by Thomas Fahy, 14–32. Lexington: University Press of Kentucky, 2010.
Shelley, Peter. *Grande Dame Guignol Cinema: A History of Hag Horror from Baby Jane to Mother.* Jefferson, NC: McFarland, 2009.
Singer, Ben. *Melodrama and Modernity: Early Sensational Cinema and Its Contexts.* New York: Columbia University Press, 2001.
Sobchack, Vivian C. *Carnal Thoughts: Embodiment and Moving Image Culture.* Berkeley: University of California Press, 2004.
_____. "*The Leech Woman*'s Revenge, or a Case for Misrepresentation." *Journal of Popular Film* 4.3 (1975): 236–57.
_____. "Revenge of *The Leech Woman*: On the Dread of Aging in a Low-Budget Horror Film." In *The Horror Reader*, edited by Ken Gelder, 336–45. New York: Routledge, 2000.
Strauven, Wanda. "Introduction to an Attractive Concept." In Strauven, *Cinema of Attractions*, 11–27.
_____, ed. *The Cinema of Attractions Reloaded.* Amsterdam: Amsterdam University Press, 2006.
Tankersley, Jim. "Baby Boomers Are What's Wrong with America's Economy." *The Chicago Tribune*, November 7, 2015. http://www.chicagotribune.com/news/opinion/commentary/ct-baby-boomers-american-economy-20151107-story.html.
Wiener, Joshua M., and Jane Tilly. "Population Ageing in the United States of America: Implications for Public Programmes." *International Journal of Epidemiology* 31, no. 4 (2002): 776–781.
Williams, Linda. "When the Woman Looks." In *The Dread of Difference: Gender and the Horror Film*, edited by Barry Keith Grant, 15–34. Austin: University of Texas Press, 1996.

"To Grandmother's house we go"

Documenting the Horror of the Aging Woman in Found Footage Films

Maddi McGillvray

> If you want to strike fear into the hearts of both men and women, bring out the crone.
> —Kristen Sollée in *Witches, Sluts, Feminists: Conjuring the Sex Positive*

For as long as people have been telling stories, the face of evil has often been that of an older woman.[1] From witches and hags to spell-casting gypsies and evil stepmothers, elderly women have been frequently depicted as sites of monstrosity, cruelty, and even doom. The crone is a prominent figure from fairy tales and folklore often portrayed as a sinister old woman with magical or supernatural abilities.[2] Although the mythological crone was traditionally thought of as a wise Goddess, she has evolved over the years into a spiteful witch or hag. In most stories, the crone is depicted as old, thin, and ugly, with a penchant for feasting on children. This is epitomized in folk tales such as "Hansel and Gretel" (1812) by the Grimm brothers, where an old woman lures children into her home with candy in the hopes of cooking and eating them.[3] Over the last hundred years, cinema has joined folklore, myth, and gothic fiction as one of the primary vehicles for the telling of stories about monstrous beings.[4] These images are seared into our imaginations from an early age, as is exemplified in classic Disney adaptations of fairy tales that feature older female characters: The evil queen in *Snow White and the Seven Dwarfs* (1937) turns into an old hag and poisons Snow White, Ursula in *The Little Mermaid* (1989) gives Ariel legs in exchange for her voice, and Maleficent in *Sleeping Beauty* (1959) merges both woman and monster in a literal sense by turning into a gigantic fire-breathing dragon. In each of these stories, older women play the role of foul villains intended to scare or harm children.

Although these examples stem from children's literature and film, representations of malevolent older women are also common in the horror genre. Horror films twist the familiar and benign into the unsettling, alienating, or taboo, creating an experience that Sigmund Freud described as "the uncanny."[5] Freud frames the uncanny as "that class of the frightening which leads back to what is known of old and long familiar."[6] The uncanny is thus something that is both familiar and foreign at the same time, resulting in feelings of unease and confusion. The "grannies gone bad" horror narrative evokes the uncanny by presenting a seemingly sweet older woman who is also revealed as something more heinous. The older women of *Friday the 13th* (1980), *Troll 2* (1990), and *Krampus* (2015), for example, are harbingers of doom or warning signs of horrible things to come. In *Rosemary's Baby* (1968), *The House of the Devil* (2009), and *Paranormal Activity 3* (2011), they share unholy or demonic alliances. Finally, in other cases like *Suspiria* (1977), *Drag Me to Hell* (2009), and *Hocus Pocus* (1993), they are hideous witches or gypsies out to seek revenge and (sometimes simultaneously) to restore their youth.

There have been many such "grannies gone bad" throughout horror cinema, but the 2010s have seen a proliferation of evil older women, particularly within the found-footage subgenre. This essay investigates the representation of elderly women in two prominent examples of the trend: M. Night Shyamalan's *The Visit* (2015) and Adam Robitel's *The Taking of Deborah Logan* (2014). Both filmmakers begin by presenting their aged female characters as sympathetic victims who cannot control their decaying minds and bodies. By the end of each film, however, it is revealed that something more sinister may be responsible for their strange behaviors and changing bodies. These elderly women are gradually revealed to be modern versions of the vile old crone or witch—archetypal depictions of Barbara Creed's "monstrous-feminine" and its reflection of patriarchal anxieties about the female body.[7] This process of "othering" not only reflects ambivalent attitudes toward growing old, but also emphasizes a connection between monstrosity and aging women. Unlike most horror subgenres, which are rooted in fiction and fantasy, conventions of the found-footage subgenre give the monstrous figures embodied by the elderly women in these two films an extra level of concreteness and reality. This essay considers how and why the anxieties spurred by aging are being projected specifically onto women, and why found-footage horror is such fertile cinematic ground for doing so.

Found Footage Horror

The Blair Witch Project (1999) popularized the contemporary found-footage horror technique, in which a film is presented as discovered video recordings of actual events. The recordings are often framed as the only surviving record of the events portrayed, with the characters in them now either missing or presumed dead. They take the form of a pseudo-documentary, consisting of interviews or some sort of investigative recording of the events, drawing on the aesthetic of amateurism to reinforce the illusion that the footage is real. As such, the camera's presence within the diegesis is crucial to this construction of verisimilitude.[8] The events are typically represented through the shaky handheld camera footage of one or more characters, a surveillance feed, or news footage, and are often accompanied by off-camera commentary. The films are generally produced on very low budgets, feature unknown casts, and reject the use of non-diegetic sounds or music. The subgenre covers almost every horror trope imaginable: possession, exorcisms, ghosts, aliens, cults, zombies, cannibalism, monsters, serial killers, and infectious diseases.[9] Although they mimic an amateur filmmaking style, found-footage horror films have been some of the most successful in the genre, with box office receipts far exceeding their modest production costs.[10]

The Visit and *The Taking of Deborah Logan* not only follow the found-footage formula, but also use its tropes to depict the transformation of their older female characters into abject and monstrous old crones. In *Powers of Horror,* Julia Kristeva frames the abject as that which is rejected by and disturbs social reason, and outlines how it functions as a source of horror within patriarchal societies.[11] Representing the horror induced when the boundaries of what is self and what is "other" are threatened, whether by a corpse—a body without a soul—or by substances such as feces, blood, pus, or vomit, Creed states that "abject things are those which highlight the fragility of the law, and humans exist on the other side of the border, which separates out the living subject from that which threatens its extinction."[12] The abject threatens life and must be "radically excluded" from the place of the living subject, deposited on the other side of an imaginary border which separates the self from that which threatens it.[13] Consequently, ancient figures of abjection such as the wicked witch or evil crone continue to provide some of the most compelling images of horror in modern cinema.[14]

Creed argues that all societies have a conception of the monstrous-feminine: an image of a woman that is "shocking, terrifying, horrific, and abject."[15] She sees the monstrous-feminine reflected in horror films in the amoral vampire, witch, monstrous womb, possessed body, castrating mother, and other stock characters. Accordingly, "the presence of the monstrous-feminine in the popular horror film speaks to us more about male fears than about female desires or feminine subjectivity."[16] One of Creed's central arguments is that feminine monstrosity in horror is directly linked to the reproductive and mothering female body. But what about those women who are past their prime and no longer fertile? Medical science in early modern Britain and America rested on the idea that good health resulted from a balance (and disease from an imbalance) between blood and three other bodily fluids, collectively known as "the four humors." Older women, whose bodies were no longer purged of excess blood through menstruation, were therefore thought to possess unquenchable, even demonic sexual drives.[17] The women of *The Visit* and *The Taking of Deborah Logan* embody similar anxieties, and their monstrosity is directly rooted in the abject process of aging.

The Visit

After releasing a series of poorly received films including *The Village* (2004), *Lady in the Water* (2006), and *The Happening* (2008), Shyamalan took a new approach with *The Visit*—an entirely self-funded independent film that blends conventions from both horror and comedy. It follows 15-year-old Becca (Olivia DeJonge) and her eccentric younger brother Tyler (Ed Oxenbould), as they spend the week with their estranged grandparents, while their mother Loretta (Kathryn Hahn)—who has not spoken to her parents in 15 years—goes on a cruise with her new boyfriend. Becca, an aspiring filmmaker, enlists her brother to help record a documentary about their visit with their grandparents (whom they have not previously met) in the hopes that it will bring their family back together.

At the train station, Becca and Tyler meet the elderly couple, who they refer to as "Nana" (Deanna Dunagan) and "Pop Pop" (Peter McRobbie). When they arrive at their isolated farmhouse in the snow-covered countryside, Becca and Tyler are instructed that bedtime is strictly 9:30 p.m. They are also ordered to never go into the basement due to toxic mold. Nana and Pop Pop are kindhearted at first. However, Becca and Tyler notice strange things happening to their grandparents at night. Pop Pop reveals that both he and Nana suffer from sundowning, a form of dementia that results in late-night confusion and agitation. As Pop Pop explains: "We're old, and old people have trouble with their bodies sometimes." Over the course of their visit, Becca and Tyler notice their grandparents exhibiting increasingly disturbing behavior. The day before the children are supposed to leave, they video chat with their mother to convince her that she needs to pick them up right away. They hold their laptop up to the window so that Loretta can see Nana and Pop Pop, only to discover that the situation is far worse than they realized when she responds: "Those aren't your grandparents." With this knowledge, the children decide to finally venture into the basement. They discover the dead bodies of their real grandparents, a bloody hammer, and uniforms from the nearby mental hospital where their grandparents volunteered.

Pop Pop appears in the basement and reveals that Nana once had children of her own, but that she drowned them years before. Their charade was intended to allow her to experience a week of being a grandmother. He threatens that Becca and Tyler are going to join their children in the water, and then attacks Becca and drags her up the stairs, locking her inside a bedroom with Nana. A chilling cackle is heard off-screen and Nana suddenly crawls across the floor toward Becca. Just as Nana opens her suddenly-monstrous jaws to bite her, Becca breaks a piece of glass from a nearby mirror and stabs her to death. Meanwhile, Pop Pop torments Tyler downstairs in the kitchen by rubbing his soiled diaper in his face. In a fit of rage, Tyler forces Pop Pop onto the floor and proceeds to slam the refrigerator door on his head until he is dead. Becca and Tyler escape the home unharmed before being rescued by their mother and police officers the next morning.

The Visit addresses the characters' reason for filming (a motivational plot point that plagues many found footage films) at the very outset of the narrative: Becca wants to record footage of what she calls an "elixir," which is to get her grandparents to talk about and forgive her mother on camera. The footage shot from Becca's hand-held camera adopts a shaky-cam aesthetic, but Shyamalan still employs elaborate lighting and composition throughout. Unlike most found-footage horror films—the result is often quite beautiful.[18] The film accounts for this visual style by presenting Becca as an aspiring filmmaker, eager to showcase her craftsmanship and expertise.

Despite its lush aesthetic, *The Visit* tells a macabre story. From the moment the children arrive and Becca's camera starts rolling, it is abundantly clear that Nana and Pop Pop are both struggling with growing older. Signs of Pop Pop's deteriorating condition are woven through the narrative, ranging from the physically repulsive (feces-soaked diapers piled in a shed) and socially disturbing (accosting a group of strangers on the street) to the merely sad (putting on a three-piece suit to attend an event that happened years before). The old man frequently appears confused and defensive when the children question his actions in these moments, explaining them away as things that happen as one gets older. In keeping with representational conventions, however, *The Visit* dwells more extensively on Nana's age, and its role in making her a heinous old crone.

At first glance, Nana seems to be a sweet grandmotherly figure. She is kind, nurturing, and is constantly offering to cook and bake for the children. Her age is emphasized in early conversations with the children that serve to illustrate that she is not in tune with the times—as Tyler proclaims, "she doesn't even know who One Direction is!" The film also plays upon the age-old stereotype of elderly people not understanding how to use technology. Tyler needs to explain what YouTube is when he tries to teach Nana how to use their laptop, and constantly complains that she does not have wi-fi set up in their home. Shyamalan's misdirect initially makes it appear as though old age had made Nana charmingly out of touch with these modern elements, when in reality, it is most likely due to her isolation in the mental health facility. Despite such differences, Pop Pop expresses how thrilled Nana is to have the children around, claiming, "I haven't seen your grandmother this happy in years."

Nana, however, is also a vile crone. On the first night of the children's visit, Becca goes in search of a cookie and, when she opens the bedroom door, finds Nana projectile vomiting on the floor. The process of aging has left her without the ability to monitor and police her body, and such actions have become routine and involuntary for her—simply a part of growing old. Pop Pop explains: "She's an old lady. She gets sick sometimes." On Becca and Tyler's last night, as the four begin to play a game of Yahtzee, Nana and Pop Pop's strange behavior intensifies. Pop Pop defecates in his pants, and Nana begins shoving several cookies into her mouth in rapid succession, then launches herself towards Becca's camera and screams "Yahtzee!" (signaling a winning play) as half-eaten cookies spill out of her lips. The process of aging, and the deterioration of mind and body associated with it, has turned Nana's once-pure body to an abject space of horror and disgust. She is sickly, polluting, and unclean—that is, abject—the opposite of what is traditionally considered as acceptable feminine behavior.

Elderly female nudity is also a key source of horror in *The Visit*. Creed argues that bodily disfigurement, scars, or blemishes are visible markers of impurity, and Nana's aged and frail naked body is presented as something that the viewers, as well as the characters in the film, are meant to wince at in disgust. Early in their stay, Becca and Tyler hear strange noises in the hall after their 9:30 curfew and discover Nana scratching at her bedroom door completely naked. Elder nudity has long been an anxiety—particularly for women, whose sagging skin, faces, breasts, and abdomens represent a loss of fertility.[19] Films such as *The Visit* demonstrate that these anxieties are still very much alive and well.

The Visit also documents the decline of Nana's mind, as well as her body. In a particularly unsettling scene, Becca and Tyler start playing a game of hide-and-seek under their grandparents' deck. As they are maneuvering through the claustrophobic crawl space, they start to hear growling noises. Becca crawls as fast as she can, causing her camera to shake rapidly back and forth, obstructing the audience's view of what is approaching behind her. Alarmed that it might be an animal, Becca looks behind her through the camera lens, which reveals that the sounds are actually coming from Nana, who is chasing her. As Nana draws closer to Becca, she eerily whispers, "I'm going to get you," in a tone more chilling than playful. Just as Nana approaches Becca, she exits the deck, laughs and says, "I'm making chicken pot pie for dinner." Nana turns around to walk back into the house, but her skirt is caught,

Nana (Deanna Dunagan) terrifies with increasingly grotesque behaviors in *The Visit* (2015).

revealing her bare buttocks. Nana's final interview with Becca is, in contrast, disturbing in what it implies rather than what it shows. Little white lights in the pond, she explains, take people and store them until they can, one day, take them back to their home planet. Nana shrugs it off by claiming it is just a story, but the audience is left to conclude that this belief led her to drown her own children.

Nana's alarming behavior intensifies until, in the film's final act, it becomes abundantly clear that something is wrong with her. Nana explains to Becca that she needs help cleaning the oven and asks her to get inside. Becca agrees, and Nana closes the oven door behind her. In this moment, the viewer automatically fears the worst: that Nana is about to cook Becca alive, like the witch in "Hansel and Gretel." While it might have been hinted at or implied earlier in the film, this scene directly solidifies Nana's affiliation with the monstrous-feminine: simultaneously the vile old crone and the sweet grandmother. She is monstrous in the way aging has transformed her mind and body into an abject space, but also because she is literally a child-murdering (and -eating?) psychopath. We typically expect the elderly to become monstrous in the abject sense, but not in the latter. Shyamalan plays upon our expectations of (and perhaps experiences with) the elderly, then pushes the resulting feeling of unease to its extreme by revealing—in the film's final twist—that Nana is much more "not right" than we had suspected.

The Taking

Released a year before *The Visit,* Adam Robitel's *The Taking of Deborah Logan* is framed as a medical documentary gone horribly wrong. The film follows a tenacious PhD candidate named Mia (Michelle Ang) who, for her dissertation, is producing a documentary about Alzheimer's sufferer Deborah Logan (Jill Larson) and her daughter Sarah (Ann Ramsay). Deborah is reluctant to be filmed at first, but then agrees after Sarah reminds her that the house is on the verge of being repossessed and Mia's compensation for their participation could help ease their financial problems. Deborah soon embraces the filming process, exclaiming, "they want to make a movie about me!" Robitel adopts the customary found-footage visual techniques, including shaky footage from handheld cameras, security footage, and archival exposition. The film begins by mimicking a medical documentary through a montage of supporting documents, medical charts, and seemingly "real" hospital footage outlining the side effects and facts about Alzheimer's disease. This footage is accompanied by a voice over from Mia, who introduces her work, which is a study on how the disease affects both the patient and their surrounding loved ones.

At first, audiences are led to believe that Deborah's failing health is the result of aging and the diseases associated with it. Over the course of Mia and her film crew's time in Deborah's home, however, it becomes clear that things are not quite as they seem. Mia's subject is initially presented as a dignified older woman who carries herself with grace and refinement. She wears elegant clothing and pearl jewelry, and her hair is neatly curled. In her preliminary interview with Mia, Deborah describes the earlier years of her life where she operated a telephone answering service business from her home, the attic of which still houses the old equipment. When the conversation turns to the present, Deborah turns her attention to her medical condition, detailing the actions she takes to help combat the disease and expresses her frustration at her mind's inevitable decline.

76　II. Aesthetics of Decay

She states, "I do all my little puzzles. I do crosswords. I'm lifting weights. I am doing everything that I have read will help to stave off the progression of this disease. Stave it off. There is no cure." Robitel establishes a strong sense of verisimilitude around Deborah's mental decline. She forgets things or does not remember moments that Sarah can vividly recall. As the plot unfolds, however, it becomes increasingly clear that something (or someone) else is trying to take over her mind and body.

As the audience watches through the film crew's lens, Deborah's behavior becomes increasingly bizarre in ways that defy normal, medical explanations. The team members express their concerns to Mia, who also fears that an evil presence might be at work. They record audio of Deborah speaking, in foreign languages, about sacrifices and snakes. Line 337, which once belonged to local physician Henry Desjardins, continually rings on the switchboard in the attic, despite the fact that the doctor disappeared years before, following the ritualized murders of four young girls. After several alarming incidents, Sarah decides to hospitalize Deborah. A physician runs a series of tests and informs Sarah that her mother's symptoms are not typically associated with Alzheimer's disease. After doing some research, Mia and Sarah discover that Desjardins was trying to recreate an ancient demonic ritual that would make him immortal—a process that required the deaths of five girls who recently had their first menstrual period. Their investigation also reveals a secret Deborah has kept from her daughter: that she, along with her neighbor Harris (Ryan Cutrona), murdered Desjardins after finding out that he wanted to use Sarah as his fifth victim.

Deborah, now possessed by Desjardins, abducts a teenage cancer patient named Cara (Julianne Taylor) from the hospital and takes her to the abandoned mine where he had murdered his previous victims. Mia and Sarah believe that if they burn Desjardin's remains they can free Deborah from his control. They exhume the body and find Deborah in the mines just as she is about to eat Cara. They manage to stop Deborah and burn Desjardins' corpse, freeing Deborah from her trance. The film then cuts to news footage describing how Deborah was deemed unfit to stand trial for her abduction of Cara. An additional news story shows that Cara is in remission and is celebrating her birthday. As the reporter begins to conclude the segment, Cara gives a sinister grin, suggesting that Desjardins' spirit may have fled Deborah's body for hers.

Similar to *The Visit*, *The Taking of Deborah Logan* documents Deborah's daily life as she declines physically and mentally in front of the camera. Initially beautiful and poised, Deborah almost immediately begins to deteriorate: her hairline recedes, her face becomes sunken and wrinkled, and her nails grow long and discolored. She also exhibits extreme weight loss between shootings and develops a mysterious condition that leaves the skin on her

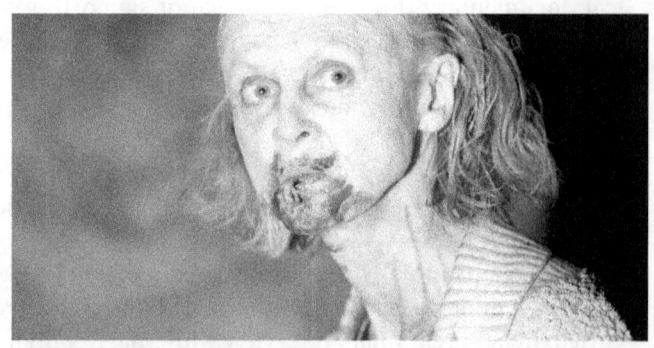

Deborah (Jill Larson), now barely recognizable from the once poised and gracious woman she was at the beginning of Mia's documentary, has completely transformed into an old crone in *The Taking of Deborah Logan* (2014).

back red and scaly. Despite Mia's initial intentions to examine how the disease impacts Deborah's relationship with her daughter, her documentary quickly shifts to focus on Deborah's behavior and changing body as it worsens at an alarming (and unnatural) rate. The longer the film crew stay at her home, the more hideous and grotesque Deborah becomes. In *Six Women of Salem,* Marilynne K. Roach cites nine traits that marked someone as sharing a potential relationship with the devil, one of which was simply being beyond middle age.[20] Deborah's age is thus a marker of her transgressive nature. She is rendered monstrous both by her physical appearance—a grotesque caricature of the changes aging bodies go through—and by her possession by Desjardin's demonic spirit.

Beyond the toll aging takes on Deborah, there are also several scenes in the film where she inflicts harm towards her own body. This begins subtly, as when she scratches at the soil in her garden to the point that her hands are raw and bloody, but rapidly escalates until, in a fit of rage and confusion, she tears a large piece of skin off of her neck with her bare hands. Creed argues that women are often sites of abjection in horror films because they "may appear pure and beautiful on the outside, but evil may, nevertheless, reside within,"[21] a sentiment echoed by the film's tag line: "evil lives within." The idea of "evil within" evokes both the grip of Alzheimer's on her mind and the eventual possession of her body by Desjardins' spirit. Both maladies break Deborah from her proper feminine role and link her to the figure of the crone. Instead of her typically poised and gracious behavior, she makes a spectacle of herself and puts her unruly body on display—behavior that, in early modern Europe, often led to accusations of witchcraft.[22]

The Taking of Deborah Logan also connects aging with a loss of control over one's body. In one scene, after hearing what sounds like vomiting noises in the bathroom offscreen, Sarah opens the door to check on her mother. After hearing Sarah's loud scream, the camera crew rushes over to find that Deborah has both defecated a reddish-brown fluid and vomited up soil and worms all over the floor. Kristeva argues that the mother's first role of authority is when the child learns about the body.[23] In this stage, the mother educates her child about the task of toilet training, which Kristeva argues is a "primal mapping of the body."[24] This scene is shocking in its display of abjection, but also in its reversal of the roles of mother and child. It is Sarah who witnesses, and has to take care of, the filth of her mother's body.

The film begins by connecting such moments of abjection to aging, but as it progresses and transitions into a possession narrative, the film focuses less on her age, other than to suggest that Deborah might be too week to fend off Desjardins' spirit. Heartbreaking, yet realistic, moments in which Deborah attacks the camera crew because she has forgotten them and thinks that they are robbing her evolve into scenes involving snakes appearing out of nowhere. While the film-within-a-film documentary shifts according to the bizarre circumstances surrounding Deborah, it still achieves Mia's original objective. The sacrifices that Deborah and Sarah make for one another remain the central theme: Deborah's rescue of her daughter is the reason for her possession, and Sarah's saving of her mother constitutes the dramatic the arc of the entire film.[25] Sarah supports Deborah every step of the way, from seeking financial aid and bringing her to medical appointments to performing an exorcism.[26] In the film's climax, Sarah encourages her mother to throw off Desjardins' possession by shouting, "Fight him, Mom! Fight him!" Horror films often present maternal figures as abject and separation from them as a natural part of independent adulthood, but Sarah—far from rejecting the increasingly abject Deborah—steps in to act as her caregiver, leaving behind the life that she has established for herself.[27] The film thus illustrates how traditional familial structures and hierarchies change when dealing with an elderly loved one, along with the extreme lengths we are willing to go to protect and support the aged in their battles against diseases and complications of the aging process.

While horror films about possession commonly feature vulnerable young girls as their victims, Robitel instead focuses on an older woman. In the moments when Deborah leaves the hospital with Cara in hand, she appears more terrifying than ever; looking more monstrous than feminine, or human for that matter. In the film's bone-chilling climax, Mia's camera catches a brief glimpse of Deborah trying to eat Cara's head like a snake swallowing its prey whole. It is at this point in the film where Deborah has crossed the line from sweet older woman suffering from an illness to a hideous evil crone. She is both unnatural and grotesque, as well as filled with an abject evil. Much like Nana in *The Visit*, Deborah is, on one hand, represented as a monster simply because she is old and riddled with disease. By the end of the film, however, she transforms into a witchlike figure—a literal monster—as a result of her possession. Robitel is playing upon the common assumption that "something is just not right" with a lot of elderly people. We often even excuse it by politely hiding our frustration or repulsion because we know, as Pop Pop tells Becca in *The Visit*, "That is just how old people are sometimes."

Why Found Footage?

The crone has been prominent in found-footage horror films, as is exemplified by the subgenre's precursor, *The Blair Witch Project*. However, the makers of the films within *The Visit* and *The Taking of Deborah Logan* do not begin with the intention that they will be recording a crone. Becca sees a sweet, kindly grandmother, and Mia a poised and elegant woman battling a debilitating mental condition. However, in the process of recording their documentaries, both young women stumble upon tales of monstrosity and danger that they never could have anticipated. Films like *The Visit* and *The Taking of Deborah Logan* exemplify the fears we all have about growing old. Both films strip away the layers of protection we collectively use to hide from those fears, and instead force us to take a hard look at them by using the found footage technique.[28] Anyone who has had to care for a family member suffering from dementia, or watched someone cease to be the vigorous person they once were, will no doubt recognize Nana and Deborah at times, making their strange actions seem to be based in reality.[29]

The presence of wicked older women in contemporary films such as *The Visit* and *The Taking of Deborah Logan* suggests that there is a heightened interest in this longstanding archetype. Perhaps this is because it embodies what Dafina Lemish and Varda Muhlbauer deem "the double marginalization of age and gender," where female monstrosity functions as a reflection of larger social fears and acts of violent provocation towards women as a whole.[30] Kathleen Woodward notes that "at the same time as the material conditions of aging undergoing change, so too our culture is producing new representations of aging."[31] While the witch or crone is traditionally thought of as a symbol of female persecution, she has also been appropriated by some feminists as a positive symbol of female subversiveness. *The Visit* and *The Taking of Deborah Logan* may not have been produced with a particular feminist orientation, but they can be viewed within a feminist framework, revealing an alternative discourse regarding elderly women and their transgressive abilities to disrupt patriarchal structures and visual culture. What is more terrifying than finding out that the kindly old lady is anything but?[32]

NOTES

1. Blaire, "Why Are Old Women Often the Face of Evil in Fairy Tales and Folklore?"
2. The word "crone," known from about 1390 onward, is derived from the Anglo-French word *carogne*, meaning an insult. This originates from the Old North French term *caroigne*, which translates to a disagreeable old woman.
3. The crone appears in a variety of different cultural contexts from across the globe. Perhaps the most terrifying rendition of the crone comes from Russia in the form of the Baba Yaga, who is a deformed and ferocious-looking supernatural woman. Likewise, in Persia the crone called Bakhtak (which means nightmare) is rumoured to sit on upon a sleeper's chest making them waken unable to move or breathe in the night. In Scotland the crone appears in the form of the Cailleachan, which are a group of "storm hags" who are believed to personify the destructive elements and forces of nature. Despite the many variations on the archetype, they all share one common feature: they are old women.
4. Creed, *Phallic Panic*, vii.
5. Freud, "The 'Uncanny' (1919)."
6. Ibid.
7. Creed, *Monstrous-Feminine*, 1.
8. Heller-Nicholas, *Found Footage Horror Films*, 3.
9. "What Are Found Footage Films."
10. J.T. Velikovky, "Two Successful Transmedia Case Studies."
11. Kristeva, *Powers of Horror*, 4.
12. Creed, *The Monstrous-Feminine*, 5.
13. Ibid., 5.
14. Ibid., 4.
15. Ibid., 1.
16. Ibid., 7.
17. Norton, *In the Devil's Snare*; Karlsen, *The Devil in the Shape of a Woman*.
18. Such an approach follows Alexandra Heller-Nicholas' observation that just because these films might look like amateur productions, does not exactly mean that they are amateur. In this case, *The Visit* a prime example of how found footage horror can be replicated by professional Hollywood directors and production teams.
19. Norton, *In the Devil's Snare*.
20. Roach, *Six Women of Salem*.
21. Creed, *Monstrous-Feminine*, 42.
22. Roper, *Witch Craze*, 160.
23. Kristeva, *Powers of Horror*, 72.
24. Ibid.
25. Blinde, "The Taking of Deborah Logan."
26. Ibid.
27. One particularly compelling storyline in the film is Sarah's sexual orientation. Sarah is a lesbian and in a private conversation with Mia she informs her that she has a partner back home, who she has left to take care of her mother. Deborah's disease has not only affected her mind and body, but it prevents Sarah from living her own life. Unbeknownst to Sarah, Deborah expresses her disproval of this to Mia, in a tone that appears unnervingly threatening. While the film does not return to this concept, it does reflect the traditional values that are commonly associated with older people, as well as the assumption that they are unwilling or unaccepting of alternative lifestyles.
28. Riendeau, "M. Night Shyamalan's The Visit Is This Year's Babadook."
29. Ibid.
30. Lemish and Muhlbauer, "'Can't Have It All,'" 165.
31. Woodward, *Aging and Its Discontents*, 194.
32. Mackie, "The Visit."

BIBLIOGRAPHY

Blaire, Elizabeth. "Why Are Old Women Often the Face of Evil in Fairy Tales and Folklore?" *NPR Special Series: The Changing Lives of Women*. 2015. http://www.npr.org/2015/10/28/450657717/why-are-old-women-often-the-face-of-evil-in-fairy-tales-and-folklore.
Blinde, Mychael. "'The Taking of Deborah Logan': Possession, Alzheimer's and Mother/Daughter Love." *Bitch Flicks*, December 15, 2014. www.btchflicks.com.
Creed, Barbara. *The Monstrous-Feminine: Film, Feminism, and Psychoanalysis*. New York: Routledge, 1993.
_____. *Phallic Panic: Film, Horror and the Primal Uncanny*. Melbourne: Melbourne University Press, 2005.

Freud, Sigmund. "The 'Uncanny.'" *The Standard Edition of the Complete Psychological Works of Sigmund Freud* 17 (1917–1919). London: Hogarth Press, 1955.
Heller-Nicholas, Alexandra. *Found Footage Horror Films: Fear and the Appearance of Reality*. Jefferson, NC: McFarland, 2014.
Karlsen, Carol F. *The Devil in the Shape of a Woman: Witchcraft in Colonial New England*. New York: W.W. Norton, 1987.
Kristeva, Julia. *Powers of Horror: An Essay on Abjection*. New York: Columbia University Press, 1980.
Lemish, Dafna, and Vurda Muhlbauer. "'Can't Have It All': Representations of Older Women in Popular Culture." *Women & Therapy* 35, no. 3–4 (2012).
Mackie, Drew. "The Visit and 13 Other Movies Starring Scary Old Ladies." *People Movies*. www.people.com/movies.
Mallan, Kerry. "Witches, Bitches and Femmes Fatales: Viewing the Female Grotesque in Children's Film." *Explorations into Children's Literature* 10, no. 1 (2000): 26–35.
Norton, Mary Beth. *In the Devil's Snare: The Salem Witchcraft Crisis of 1962*. New York: Vintage Books, 2002.
Riendeau, Danielle. "M. Night Shyamalan's *The Visit* Is This Year's *Babadook*." *Polygon*, 2015. https://www.polygon.com/2015/9/16/9322075/the-visit-shyamalan-babadook.
Roach, Marilynne K. *Six Women of Salem: The Untold Story of the Accused and Their Accusers in the Salem Witch Trials*. Boston: Da Capo Press, 2013.
Roper, Lyndal. *Witch Craze: Terror and Fantasy in Baroque Germany*. New Haven: Yale University Press, 2004.
Velikovky, J. T. "Two Successful Transmedia Case Studies: *The Blair Witch Project* (1999) and *The Devil Inside* (2012)." School of Humanities and Communication Arts, University of Western Sydney, NSW Australia, 2013.
"What Are Found Footage Films." *Found Footage Critic*, 2017. http://foundfootagecritic.com/found-footage-film-genre/.
Woodward, Kathleen M. *Aging and Its Discontents: Freud and Other Fictions*. Bloomington: Indiana University Press, 1991.

"More like music"
Aging, Abjection and Dementia at the Overlook Hotel

Sue Matheson

The story of a man's descent into homicidal madness during a winter at a snowbound resort hotel, Stanley Kubrick's *The Shining* (1980) is, at its base, about psychological horror. As Diane Johnson points out in *View from The Overlook: Crafting The Shining* (2007), Kubrick wanted the film "to make sense in real psychological terms just as the great horror tales do. They all have some underlying paradigm which can explain why they touch us or scare us."[1] This essay investigates the underpinnings of the paradigm that Kubrick used, arguing that the fundamental horror formula that Kubrick adopted for *The Shining*—that of an innocent family isolated and trapped in an evil dwelling with a bloody history—is informed, intensified, complicated, and sustained by the film's terrifying layers of elder horror. Subtle, sophisticated, a-logical, and synchronistic, elder horror in *The Shining* is an intensive, contrapuntal investigation of aging, abjection, and dementia, "lightly illustrated," as Kubrick would say, in a series of simple visual statements. As Kubrick notes to Michel Ciment in *A Voix Nue: Stanley Kubrick*, "Reason doesn't help you [in *The Shining*]. You're in an area where it's more like music than rational thought."[2] Peter Klimpton's experience of watching *The Shining* as a teenager is a prime example of the effectiveness of the psychic strains that are produced by conceptualizing our own ends and conveyed in what should considered a cinematic fugue. "The film ended," he says, "and as Jack sat frozen in the maze, I sat frozen in a cold sweat to the sofa. I didn't sleep at all that night. My parents came home and I locked my bedroom door, but that wouldn't have stopped Jack. And when I eventually did sleep the next night, it was far from restful then, or for several weeks."[3]

The Shining begins as Jack Torrance (Jack Nicholson), a recovering middle-aged alcoholic and aspiring novelist, drives through the Colorado Rockies to the Overlook Hotel. At the Overlook, he interviews for the position of the winter caretaker. Jack is warned that he and his family will be snowbound during the winter, that the secluded hotel's solitude and isolation could become a problem for his family, and that in 1970 winter caretaker Charles Grady (Philip Stone) suffered a complete mental breakdown and killed his family with an axe before committing suicide. Experiencing a mid-life crisis, Jack, who has recently broken his young son's arm, should have paid close attention to these warnings, but he disregards them and unwisely accepts the position. When he and his family arrive on the last day of the season to take up residence in the old building, they tour their new home. While Jack and his wife Wendy (Shelley Duvall) inspect the basement of the Overlook, hotel chef Dick Hallorann (Scatman Crothers) takes their son Danny (Danny Lloyd) to the kitchen for chocolate ice cream. There they talk about the telepathic abilities they share, but skirt around the reasons for Danny's reluctance to live in the Overlook over the winter. Hallorann also warns the boy to stay out of Room 237, which houses the ghost of a murder victim. During his first months of living in the Overlook, Danny, who keeps encountering the ghosts of two girls, seems to take Hallorann's advice to heart, pedaling his plastic tricycle through the hotel's long empty corridors and cavernous lobbies, while his father attempts to write a novel and interacts with other ghosts that also haunt the hotel. When the Overlook becomes snowbound, however, Danny enters Room 237, encountering the ghost and setting off a terrifying chain of events. As Jack slips deeper into madness and Wendy becomes aware of—and alarmed by—his fragile mental state, Hallorann's psychic abilities alert him that the Grady tragedy may be about to repeat itself. He returns to the Overlook to intervene, but Jack murders him with a fire axe and attempts to kill Wendy and Danny after chopping through the door of the bathroom where they have barricaded themselves. They temporarily elude him and flee through the hotel's corridors and out onto the snow-covered lawn where Jack chases Danny into an ornamental hedge maze. Danny escapes, fleeing with Wendy in Hallorann's SnowCat; Jack, who quickly becomes disoriented and lost in the maze, remains behind, frozen to death in the snow. Kubrick's final shot reveals an old photograph in the hotel hallway dated July 4, 1921. In it, a young, smiling Jack Torrance dressed in a tuxedo is foregrounded, standing in the middle of a crowd of party-goers in the Overlook's elegant ballroom.

Generally, the elderly symbolize the terrors of aging (and death) in horror movies, but, in *The Shining*, the source of the Torrances' terror and misadventures is the elderly hotel. Despite (or arguably because of) "its illustrious past," the hotel contains what Hallorann calls "traces" of its aging, the many "bad things" that happened there. As in a fugue, which is canonically constructed (the first voice introduces the subject that a second voice repeats at a different pitch, and other voices repeat in the same way), horrific events at the Overlook echo those of the past.[4] The hotel's general manager, Mr. Ullman (Barry Nelson) introduces Jack (and the audience) to the Grady family's tragedy, and as the Torrances travel to the Overlook, the surrounding mountain wilderness reminds Wendy of the Donner Party disaster. When the Torrances, like the Donner Party, are imprisoned by a blizzard and struggling to survive in a place from which they cannot escape, they find themselves living like the elderly, whose advanced years first isolate and then oppose them. Danny is haunted by an image of a wave of blood pouring from the open doors of a hotel elevator, and of Grady's twins (Lisa and Louise Burns) lying dead in a bloody hallway. Jack discovers the rotting corpse of a woman in Room 237 and, in a blood-red men's room, encounters the ghost of Grady himself, who counsels Jack to follow his example and "correct" his wife and son.

Creating and sustaining the audience's horror of death, the film's enlarged narrative scope conflates past and present. At first, Wendy regards the Overlook as a place in which she and her family can reinvent themselves, but she discovers that she cannot escape the complicated history of her marriage and her own personal past. Her memory of Jack breaking Danny's arm cannot be erased. Jack, too, cannot forget the incident, which continually reminds him of his failings as a father and as a man. When the family begins suffering from cabin fever, the memories of Jack's unhappy experience with child abuse escalate. Haunted by their own history, the Torrances are doomed to repeat the past. Jack begins having nightmares about killing his family, and Wendy—sensing that her husband is again becoming a monster—screams, "You did this to him, didn't you?!" when Danny is mysteriously injured in Room 237.

The Torrance family is also haunted by the old hotel's past. Early in their stay, the unsettling ghosts of the Overlook appear to be passive and their haunting benign. Even though the uncanny twins appear and re-appear in the elderly hotel's corridors and lobby, they do not attempt to speak with or injure Danny. As the winter wears on, Jack, who regularly visits the Gold Room (the hotel's beautiful ballroom) increasingly falls under the influence of the hotel's history. A dry alcoholic, he haunts the bar, finding himself to be on friendly terms with Lloyd (Joe Turkel), a demonic bartender, who assures him that the management has determined the new caretaker's drinks are on the house. The ghosts of hotel guests who inhabit the Gold Room and litter the hotel's hallways with streamers and balloons do not visit the family's apartment or interfere with Jack's attempts to write his novel, but they do not remain benign for long. The hotel's monstrous embodiments of the past, like Homeric and Roman ghosts, must have blood.

When physical violence occurs (and escalates), Kubrick's elder horror is foregrounded. The ghosts of the young twins do not physically harm Danny; it is the ancient, animated corpse in Room 237 that attempts to strangle him. When Jack, carrying an axe, chases Danny through the Overlook, Wendy finds the Colorado Lounge, the hotel lobby's sprawling salon, filled with decrepit cadavers and encounters the apparition of an elderly hotel guest (Norman Gay) with a head injury who chirps, "Great party, isn't it?"

An elderly ghost (Horace Derwent) toasts Wendy Torrance (Shelley Duvall) in *The Shining* (1980), exclaiming, "Great party, isn't it?"

84   II. Aesthetics of Decay

Cognitively, every ghost at the Overlook blurs the distinction between the past and the present, violating common knowledge and challenging the foundations of our thinking about time. Jack's horrifying encounter with the ghost that inhabits Room 237 is particularly instructive in this regard. Building on Jeffrey Cohen's earlier work, Peter Hutchings points out that the horror monster, a thing that simply should not be, is a kind of pollutant because it embodies a crossing of borders and a transgressive mixing of categories.[5] Room 237's rotting, walking corpse, a thing that clearly should not be, breaches so many borders (to name only two, those between the living and the dead, the past and the present) that Danny cannot tell his mother what happened to him. He attempts to re-establish normative categories, saying "[a] crazy woman" tried to strangle him. When Jack cautiously investigates Room 237, he is delighted (rather than horrified) to discover an attractive naked woman in the bathroom who attempts to seduce him.

A prime example of the abject not simply designating that which is disgusting and threatens identity, this woman fascinates Jack. Although her desirability makes her status ambiguous, her attempt to seduce him marks her as a predator. At first, his awkward attempt at adultery flouts only social norms and forms. Almost immediately, however, Kubrick's zip pan to the bathroom mirror violates much broader (and arguably more important) categories when Jack's reflection reveals that he is actually embracing the final product of old age—a decomposing corpse. McAvoy argues that Kubrick uses mirrors throughout *The Shining* to explore the duality of the main characters, Jack and Danny,[6] but in Room 237, the bathroom's mirror also reveals the abominable nature of the Other that is old age. As Jack's horrified gaze continues in the mirror, the corpse becomes animated, morphing into a hag that cackles like a witch and then chases him out of the bathroom and into the hallway, its repulsive arms gruesomely extended.[7]

Jack Torrance (Jack Nicholson) reacts in disgust when he realizes he has been consorting with an elderly abject (Billie Gibson) in *The Shining*.

Generally malevolent, the hags of folklore are vicious (and often malicious) embodiments of death that represent the dissolution of the body, the destructive, devouring nature of time, and the mindless persistence of the past.[8] As the rotting appearance of Kubrick's hag suggests, the abjection or subjective horror that the viewer experiences when confronted by the unpleasant corporeal reality of aging expresses what we fear most about decay—the breakdown of distinctions between self and other, even self and the world. As Hutchings remarks, "the ultimate abjected object becomes the human corpse, an object from which identity itself has been expelled."[9] Presented as Other, the prurient hag in Room 237 emblematizes the disintegration of the individual's sense of being an entity distinct from nature via the decay most commonly associated with death. Covered in green and brown patches of congealed blood and revealing gobs of rotting flesh, her moldering skin cannot act as a boundary between self and the world. Both Jack and the viewer are confronted with abjection—what Hutchings would call "various bodily fluids and substances passing from the inside to the outside [that] become abject inasmuch as they breach the body's borders"—and reminded of the "biological world against which—according to Kristeva at least—our identities have been constructed."[10]

As Robert Kilker points out, Jack fears the abject, which Julia Kristeva equates with death.[11] Not surprisingly, Jack backs away from the rotting body he has been caressing and flees. Because abjection (as described by Kristeva) is integral to the formation of the self, via the exclusion of elements that might threaten or undermine the individual's sense of him- or herself as a distinct entity,[12] when Jack reaches the safety of the hallway, he re-establishes boundaries between himself and the world by slamming the door shut and locking the abject inside her room.

In the abject, we have a concept that has the potential to help us understand the biological nature of many horror monsters, not only in the way in which they confound distinctions between human and animal but also in their association with gross biological practices.[13] Jack can flee from the horror he discovers in Room 237, but not from the horror in himself. As he transforms into a murdering monster, physical and psychological boundaries between himself and the world are discarded. At the beginning of *The Shining*, Jack looks every inch the sophisticated urbanite; nattily and formally dressed in a tweed jacket, he wears an impeccable shirt, tie, and perfectly pressed trousers for his job interview—his polished shoes gleam as he enters the Overlook, and his hair is carefully brushed. Over the course of the film, however, his appearance deteriorates along with his mental state, and by the time he chops down the bathroom door of his apartment with the intention of murdering his wife and child, he is visibly coming apart at the seams. Close up, he looks like a wolfish predator: his sweating, unshaven, disheveled visage sports an inordinate amount of hair: long, greasy strands that fall into his rolling blood-shot eyes, and prominent grey whisker stubble that frames his horribly white teeth and big, red tongue. Tellingly, it is the dearth of boundaries between Jack and the biological world that causes his death. Lacking a winter jacket while chasing Danny through snowdrifts at the end of the movie, he simply freezes to death.

As Jack deteriorates physically, he also fails socially and psychologically. Aware of his social abjection, Jack confides to Lloyd that breaking Danny's arm was "a mistake" which continues to haunt him. "That bitch," he tells the bartender. "She'll never let me forget what happened. I did hurt [Danny] once okay? It was an accident. Completely unintentional." He becomes, in effect, a Barthean scriptor—a socially and historically constituted being, capable only of imitating that which is anterior, which, in the case of the Overlook, is the elderly hotel's bloody history. Jack's repeated visits to the Gold Room, where he finds release among ghostly revelers, clearly signals his insanity. As his visits multiply, the hallways of the Overlook, which should be empty, become littered with confetti, party streamers, and balloons as celebrations taking place in the ballroom spill out into the hotel. Introduced to well-dressed party-goers from the Roaring Twenties, Jack ceases to distinguish between the dead and the living.

In many ways, Jack's psychological deterioration resembles the elderly's loss-of-self, with the impaired memory and trouble communicating that lead to depression, apathy, confusion, and a sense of disorientation. He has trouble getting out of bed in the morning, he does not spend time with his wife and his child, and at times he appears to be suffering from senile dementia or even Alzheimer's, unable to remember where he is and speaking to hotel guests who do not exist. When Wendy discovers the manuscript, it becomes apparent that the decline in his thinking has been a steady one. She is horrified to discover that every page of his novel-in-progress repeats what has come before. Over *and* over *and* over again, page upon page only reiterates their novel's opening statement—"All work and no play makes Jack a dull boy." Like the elderly, who once demented circle back, again and again, to the same stories and questions, without realizing they are doing so, Jack has been typing the same phrase over and over.

In a fugue, once each voice has entered the composition, the *exposition* is complete. The exposition is often followed by an *episode*, developed from previously heard material. Then further entries of the subject are heard in related keys. In a similar manner, the Overlook's ghosts heighten *The Shining*'s psychological horror by intensifying dysfunction throughout the movie. Inviting Danny to "come and play with us ... for *ever and ever and ever*" (italics mine), Charles Grady's identical twins appear and reappear in the hallways. During an excruciatingly long and luridly lit conversation with Jack in the crimson-colored men's washroom just off the Gold Room, Grady himself informs Jack that he (Jack) has always been a part of the Overlook. Jack does not question the truth of this statement, although he and the audience know that he has only recently been employed—and that his term of employment ends on May 1. Convinced that he is, in fact, a part of the elderly hotel, Jack becomes completely psychotic. He takes Grady's advice. Re-enacting the former caretaker's actions, he picks up an axe and stumbles upstairs to repeat the tragedy that occurred in 1970.

Grounded in his need to relive earlier times, Jack's madness is marked by obsessive-compulsive behavior (he refuses to leave the hotel), psychotic episodes (he communicates with people who do not exist), and depression, states often associated with the elderly. Terrifying and inexplicable outbreaks of these behaviors are further complicated by Kubrick's leitmotif of mazes and labyrinths at the Overlook. This system of micro-macrocosmic correspondences found within the hotel's corridors, inscribed in its carpeting, its hallways, and outside in its topiary garden not only reveals the mechanisms of the hotel, it also informs the workings of Jack's demented mind. "There are two principal mazes in *The Shining*," P. L. Titterington notes, "the garden maze outside the hotel ... and the maze of the hotel itself, its endless winding corridors explored by Kubrick's camera and its Steadicam system."[14] Presented as a warren of corridors and rooms, the Overlook offers its visitors a number of pathways that appear to advance numerous choices of transit. Each door, however, opens into a room that is revealed to be a cul-de-sac, offering no passage by which the hotel may be exited. The only means of transit forces one to return to the maze itself. One is required to make choices, but every room that is entered leads to error, confusion, entanglement, and finally, entrapment. Notably, the physical layout of the hotel itself is designed to confound the present with the past—for the only way to exit the Overlook in *The Shining* is to retrace (or repeat) one's steps and leave via its entrance.

Jack acts in error many times. His first mistake is his decision to accept the job and move into the old hotel; he errs when he sabotages the SnowCat so his wife and son cannot leave the Overlook. His final (and fatal) mistake occurs when he chooses to follow his son into the topiary garden's labyrinth. Here it is important to note that the maze at the Overlook is designed so that the guests who walk its halls have to make wrong choices. As Danny pedals his tricycle around the hotel's passageways, he passes through what appears to be every possible track in the hotel. When he enters Room 237, it becomes evident that the guest rooms are dead ends (so to speak), emphasizing that passage is horrifying because it must end in death—Wendy encounters this truth when she finds the Colorado Lounge covered in cobwebs and filled with skeletal cadavers seated on its chairs and couches. Hallorann's error in returning to rescue Danny is particularly instructive. Knowing that the Grady tragedy is in the process of being re-enacted, he goes back, and takes the place of the caretaker's victims.

The temporal stasis within which the Overlook exists enables the past to intrude on the present: The angry ghost of Grady's victim still lurks in Room 237 and Grady's own homicidal madness possesses Jack as he chops his way through the bathroom door toward Wendy and Danny. Movement, throughout *The Shining*, is equated with characters' abilities to advance into the future. Danny, for example, is an extremely mobile character, and so, his youthfulness keeps him out of harm's way. It is only when Danny stops moving that he sees the twins and encounters the corpse in Room 237. Older, Jack, on the other hand, is often immobile, seen sitting at his typewriter, sitting at the bar talking to Lloyd, or lounging in bed when depressed. A forward-looking individual, Wendy is more mobile than her husband, but she, too, spends a good deal of her time sitting, watching television; standing, cooking in the kitchen; and lying in bed asleep. Because Danny continually moves about, mapping the Overlook, the old hotel's hallways become legible—a pattern, arranged in a series of internal, intercommunicating, and most importantly, repeating planes. First, the transit from the lobby to the caretaker's quarters becomes apparent; then the passage on the second floor, through the Colorado Lounge, and down the corridor past Room 237 to the Lounge is made evident; finally, the overall scheme of the hotel floors is fully revealed. As the links from room to room and floor to floor are uncovered by the camera that follows Danny (and also his parents), the psychological horror of *The Shining* is sustained; the correspondences at work create a horrifying homology of the hotel's past and its present. Well before he descends into madness, Jack says to Wendy, "When I came up here for my interview it was as though I had been here before. I mean we all have moments of déjà vu but this was ridiculous. It was almost as if I knew what was going to be around every corner."

Jack's identification with these mazes increases the movie's elder horror. On a sunny afternoon, while Wendy and Danny explore the Overlook Maze, Jack remains in the Colorado Lounge. As Wendy and Danny walk through the Maze, the Steadicam, tracking them through the garden's pathways, recreates Danny's movement through the hotel's corridors. Holding his mother's hand, Danny unerringly leads his mother to the center of the labyrinth. Kubrick carefully positions mother and child walking away from the camera in the center of these shots, framed on either side by tall green topiary hedges,

88   II. Aesthetics of Decay

Jack Torrance (Jack Nicholson) overlooks the model of the maze located outside the old hotel in *The Shining*.

before slowly dissolving to a corresponding shot of Jack in the Colorado Lounge. In this dissolve, Jack eerily also appears to be walking through the garden maze. Centered in the frame as well, he, like Wendy and Danny, walks away from the camera, the room's columns on his right appearing in the place of the topiary's hedges and the centered figures of his wife and child dissolving into his figure.

After the dissolve ends, Jack stops playing with a tennis ball and wanders over to the model of the Maze. Kubrick shows him leaning over the model, intently studying its intricacies, then cuts to a shot in which the model appears to become the Maze itself. From a great height, Wendy and Danny (in miniature) are seen arriving at the center of the puzzle. "We made it," Wendy says, fixed in Jack's imagination, "isn't it beautiful?"

Here it is important to note that in this shot, the Maze is larger and far more intricate than the model on the table or the actual Maze that is located outside the hotel's window. In Jack's imagination, the Maze contains many more passages and dead ends, which repeat the larger pattern of the Maze over and over again. Bordered by the camera's frame, Jack's Maze lacks an entrance/exit and retaining walls that separate it from the outside world. As the shot slowly zooms in, Wendy and Danny's tiny figures can be seen walking the length of the center of the Maze. It is impossible to determine how they will be able to leave the labyrinth. Overlooking the actions of his wife and child, Jack appears to be omniscient—looking down from above, situated like the hotel, which offers its visitors a bird's-eye view of the land beneath. Intensifying the film's psychological horror, this homology of garden-brain-hotel declares there is no exit available in the situation at the Overlook and prepares the viewer for Wendy's horrifying discovery of her husband's cognitive impairment.

It seems there is certainly no exiting the situation in which Jack finds himself. Ironically, when he pursues Danny across the hotel grounds, he finds himself unable to navigate the Maze he previously surveyed and becomes lost in a dead end—unable even to backtrack and follow his own footsteps to its entrance. As John Baxter comments, Jack's inability to distinguish the past from the present, reality from illusion, the world from himself, proves to be his Achilles' heel: Jack "kills himself," Baxter says. "The madness consumes him."[15] Having walked the Maze with his mother, Danny knows better and ensures his own survival by not repeating the actions of others and thereby becoming a part of the Overlook's past. Mastering his trauma, he carefully walks backward in his own footprints and in doing so lays a false trail for his father; he then breaks the pattern dictated by the Overlook by stepping off the path, exiting through the hedgewall, and retracing his own footsteps. When Wendy and Danny drive away from the Overlook in Hallorann's SnowCat, Jack, who suffers from repetition compulsion, irrationally continues to walk the Overlook Maze. Trapped therein, he freezes into an uncanny image of the abject, his corpse sitting in a snowdrift, ice and snow frozen to its face, its eyes rolled upwards, its teeth showing. In this shot, Kubrick ensures that everything antisocial about Jack Torrance as a father and husband that has been *unheimlich* and that ought to have remained secret and hidden is now evident for all to see. Speaking with Michel Ciment, Kubrick points out that Jack "doesn't have very much further to go for his anger and frustration to become completely uncontrollable. He is bitter about his failure as a writer. He is married to a woman for whom he has only contempt. He hates his son."[16] The Torrances' history of family violence and the Grady murders are matters are rarely spoken of by the snowbound family at the Overlook, because Jack, having abused his son, is a social pariah. In *The Shining*, as Hugh Hudson would say, elder horror is found "across the dinner table, across the breakfast table."[17] Frank Manchel similarly argues that mitigating circumstances (his "precarious economic situation," "troubled home life" and "'honorable" responsibilities) encourage viewers to empathize with Jack's crisis at the Overlook, but any sympathy for Jack ends when he becomes a shambling, axe-wielding, apelike monster.[18] He is patriarchal authority run amok. Lying beneath the fundamental horror formula of an innocent family isolated and trapped in an evil dwelling with a bloody history, one finds the chilling, elderly figure of Cronus. Like Cronus, Jack deliberately attempts to kill his son. As he chops through the door of the bathroom in which Danny is hidden, it is apparent that Jack Weinberg could not have been more correct in cautioning America's youth not to trust anyone over the age of 30.

Arguably, the most unsettling moment of *The Shining* is its final shot. In a fugue, the coda or closing material, which follows the final entry of the subject, repeating the chords or bars attached to the canon and rendering it finite, should offer a harmonious conclusion. Instead, emphasizing that the Overlook has claimed Jack, Kubrick's camera cuts to the Gold Room before the Steadicam tracks over to a close up of a framed photograph of the hotel's 1921 July 4th ball that is hanging on the wall in the corridor outside the ballroom's door. Sophisticated and refined, a young Jack Torrance stands front and center in the picture, popular and surrounded by a happy crowd, smiling and waving at the viewer. This picture, which Kubrick says to Ciment, "suggests the reincarnation of

II. Aesthetics of Decay

Jack,"[19] ensures the open-endedness of the film that Roger Ebert finds "so strangely disturbing."[20] At the last, *The Shining* proposes the well-dressed monster is particularly American ... with the power to return. Completely contemporary, the film makes a simple, eloquent statement regarding what has become the ultimate taboo subject in the United States. As Lawrence R. Samuel says, death and dying "are viewed as profoundly 'un–American' experiences ... not to be brought up in polite conversation."[21] In the final analysis, *The Shining*'s psychological horror must be considered anything but polite, offering America and its youth culture a frighteningly frank examination of the horrors of aging and death. *The Shining* shows Kubrick's comment in 1968 during a *Playboy* interview to be true: we are still generally incapable of coming to grips with the "awareness of our own mortality and all its implications" and that "our ability, unlike other animals, to conceptualize our own end creates terrible psychic strains within us."[22]

Notes

1. See Johnson *View from the Overlook*.
2. Kubrick speaking with Michel Ciment in *A Voix Nue: Stanley Kubrick (Rare Radio Interview)* at https://www.youtube.com/watch?v=wvoxjkTNOXE.
3. See Klimpton, "*The Shining*."
4. Kubrick says to Michel Ciment, "I have a feeling that you could have a story that had much greater narrative scope. Certain things would merely be illustrated and other things would be dramatized. I mean, in most films, everything is dramatized and nothing is just lightly illustrated." According to Kubrick, *The Shining* is structured in a conventional way. He tells Ciment that he "would still like to make a movie which is structured more the way silent movies were structured, than the way sound movies were. We started to talk earlier about sound and the price that has been paid for sound is that you owe movies think of scenes in terms of theatrical sciences you know even if they're short they're thought of as a scene whereas in the silent movies you could make a little simple statement like saying Bill's uncle and you illustrate there's Bill's uncle on the back porch into something else ... you had a much greater scope... I certainly would like to make a movie that told a story differently than a series of scenes which in most movies could be told on the stage." In *A Voix Nue: Stanley Kubrick (Rare Radio Interview)*, https://www.youtube.com/watch?v=wvoxjkTNOXE.
5. Hutchings, *Horror Film*, 35. See also Cohen, "Monster Culture: Seven Theses."
6. McAvoy, "The Uncanny, the Gothic and the Loner."
7. Smith, "'Real Horrorshow,'" 302.
8. Etymologically, hag is a shortened version of the Old English term for witch, *hægtesse*, and closely associated with crone, a term from the Latin, *caro*, means meat or the decaying, dead flesh of an animal.
9. *Ibid.*
10. *Ibid.*
11. Kilker, "All Roads Lead to the Abject," 57; Kristeva, *Powers of Horror*, 26. Designating that which is disgusting and threatens identity, the abject is not only physically repulsive; it is also frightening.
12. Hutchings, *Horror Film*, 36.
13. *Ibid.*
14. Titterington, "Kubrick and 'The Shining.'"
15. Hutchings, *Horror Film*, 36.
16. *Kubrick on the Shining: An Interview with Michel Ciment*, http://www.visual-memory.co.uk/amk/doc/interview.ts.html.
17. In *View from the Overlook*, Hugh Hudson says about *The Shining* that "horror is across the dinner table, across the breakfast table. Actually, horror is in the family it can be and often is. And it's always hidden, it's always repressed."
18. Manchel, "What About Jack?"
19. *Ibid.*
20. Ebert, "Reviews."
21. Samuel, "Death, American Style."
22. Stanley Kubrick speaking with *Playboy* during his 1968 Interview on page 192 and 195. See https://archive.org/stream/USPlayboy196809/U.S._Playboy_1968_09.

Bibliography

Cohen, Jeffrey Jerome. "Monster Culture: Seven Theses." In *Monster Theory: Reading Culture*, ed. Jeffrey Jerome Cohen, 3–25. Minneapolis: University of Minnesota Press, 1996.

Ebert, Roger. "The Shining." rogerebert.com, June 18, 2006. https://www.rogerebert.com/reviews/great-movie-the-shining-1980.
Hutchings, Peter. *The Horror Film*. Harlow, Essex: Pearson, 2004.
Manchel, Frank. "What About Jack? Another Perspective on Family Relationships in Stanley Kubrick's *The Shining*." *Literature/Film Quarterly* 25, no. 4 (1995): 68–78.
McAvoy, Catriona. "The Uncanny, the Gothic and the Loner: Intertextuality in the Adaptation Process of *The Shining* (1980)." *The Journal of Literature on Screen Studies* 8, no. 3 (2015): 345–60. http://citeseerx.ist.psu.edu/viewdoc/download?doi=10.1.1.963.1610 &rep=rep1&type=pdf.
Samuel, Lawrence R. "Death, American Style." *Psychology Today*, June 23, 2013. https://www.psychologytoday.com/blog/psychology-yesterday/201306/death-american-style.
The Shining. 1980. Dir. Stanley Kubrick. Burbank, California: Warner Home Video, 2015. DVD.
Smith, Greg. "'Real Horrorshow': The Juxtaposition of Subtext, Satire and Audience Implication in Stanley Kubrick's *The Shining*." *Literature Film Quarterly* 25, no. 4 (1997): 300–306.
"Stanley Kubrick: Playboy Interview (1968)." *Playboy: Entertainment for Men*, September 1968. https://archive.org/stream/USPlayboy196809/US_Playboy_1968_09#page /n5/mode/1up.
Titterington, P.L. "Kubrick and 'The Shining.'" *Sight and Sound* 50, no. 2 (Spring 1981): 117–21.
View from the Overlook: Crafting "The Shining" (2007). Dir. Gary Leva. Leva Filmworks, 2007. DVD.

The Skeleton Key, the Southern Gothic and the Uncanny Decay of Teleological History

JESSICA BALANZATEGUI

The turn of the millennium saw the emergence of a transnational cycle of supernatural horror films preoccupied with ideologies of historical time. This group of films—which includes *The Sixth Sense* (1999), *The Devil's Backbone* (2001), *The Ring* (2002), and *The Others* (2001)—interrogates the aesthetic and thematic properties of spectrality to work through anxieties about historical continuity. Fixated on Gothic topes and multi-layered, self-reflexive ghost narratives, these films are characterized by what James Kendrick describes as "a backbone of terror, dread, suspense, and spiritual contemplation."[1] Their complex use of ghost narratives tends to challenge modernist assumptions about the progression of historical time. As Jeffrey Weinstock writes, this "millennial explosion of supernatural cultural production ... seems to suggest that what is as frightening as the unknown field of the future is the tenacious tendrils of a past we cannot shake."[2] In *The Skeleton Key* (2005), one of the later films of this cycle, the ghosts take on an overtly subversive function: in a concealed narrative fabula that only becomes clear towards the end of the film, *The Skeleton Key* centers on two spirits who possess the bodies of children and young adults, inhabiting these bodies until they are elderly. The ghosts thus incite an unsettling disjuncture between corporeal growth and decline, and spectral intransience.

Indicative of the film's use of Gothic ghost themes to trouble assumptions about historical continuity, the ghosts of *The Skeleton Key* are African American house servants Mama Cecile and Papa Justify, who were lynched in the 1920s by the white owners of the plantation house in which they worked for teaching Hoodoo spells to the children of their employers. As is revealed in the film's final twist, Cecile and Justify took possession of the two young children just prior to their violent murder. Their spirits inhabited the bodies of the children until they reached old age, then discarded them for the bodies of a younger couple. Cecile and Justify thus challenge the very definition of ghost, assuming and sustaining multi-generational ownership of the plantation house originally owned by their white murderers. Ultimately, *The Skeleton Key* fuses Southern Gothic themes and aesthetics with those of the millennial supernatural horror cycle to form dissident specters who deconstruct teleological narratives of history.

This essay explores how *The Skeleton Key* deploys spectrality to unsettle traditional paradigms of growth and aging, and in so doing to challenge modernist visions of historical progress. As Peter Buse and Andrew Stott assert: "anachronism might well be the defining feature of ghosts ... because haunting, by its very structure, implies a deformation of temporal linearity.... Ghosts are a problem for historicism precisely because they disrupt our sense of a linear teleology in which the consecutive movement of history passes untroubled through the generations."[3] In *The Skeleton Key*, aging and decay assume a significant aesthetic and ideological function that aligns with the film's narrative twist, gradually revealing to the viewer an altered perception of time passing outside of hegemonic narratives of historical advance. In so doing, the film impels us to experience the eerie (re)emergence of previously concealed counter-memories, a form of memory which, in the words of Foucault, enacts "a transformation of history into a totally different form of time."[4] *The Skeleton Key*'s subversive specters impel such a transformation by troubling the naturalized connections between growth, inter-generational continuity, and historical progression.

The Gothic Cycle, Historical Temporality, and the Turn of the Millennium

That such supernatural horror films emerged around the turn of the millennium suggests much about their thematic preoccupations. As Weinstock articulates, the moment seemed to be a "haunted one"[5]: a juncture at which ghost narratives became a popular means of expressing ontological uncertainty about the shifting relationships between the past, present, and future. As Weinstock expands: "the ghost is that which interrupts the presentness of the present, and its haunting indicates that, beneath the surface of received history, there lurks another narrative, an untold story that calls into question the veracity of the authorized version of events. As such, the contemporary fascination with ghosts is reflective of an awareness of the narrativity of history."[6] These supernatural horror films of the turn of the millennium circulate around a new recognition of the 20th century as "history." Thus, the ghost—which "calls into question the linearity of history"[7]—becomes a cinematic means of inquiry into the uncertain temporal conditions of millennial shift.

The Skeleton Key centers on two elderly characters—Violet and Ben Deveraux—whose shifting relationships to the past, present, and future drive the film's temporal complexity. The historical implications of *The Skeleton Key*'s construction of spectrality are more overt and pointed than many other millennial horror films due to the film's self-conscious engagement with Southern Gothic conventions. Gothic fiction generally is associated with a troubling of teleological historical consciousness: as Carol Margaret Davison suggests, the Gothic tends to "stage various dreams and nightmarish dreads about history."[8] However while the Gothic has come to represent a rather amorphous and regionally non-specific mode (despite the fact that Gothic fiction does indeed have historically and geographically rooted origins), the Southern Gothic is a genre inherently bound to the historical conditions of its regional context. As Karen Horsley suggests, the genre engages "with a regional specificity," interrogating how the American South is "heavy with the burden of a history that has resulted in the positioning of the South as a benighted and troubled space."[9]

Thus while the Gothic mode generally is preoccupied with the unsettled slip-zones between histories, presents, and futures, the Southern Gothic revolves around the specific horrors of slavery and African American oppression that are an inescapable specter of the American past. As Matthew Wynn Sivils suggests:

> As the history and culture of the South indicate, this racism mingles with a host of other horrors so that, ultimately, the landscapes of the South are haunted by the threat of a shallowly buried cultural contagion, one that threatens to expose humanity's monstrous legacy and to spread that legacy from the past to the present. That is the great fear of the Southern landscape: that its pestilence will not merely frighten us with horrors exhumed from days gone by, but that even buried those horrors continue to poison the land, as well as those who reside within its influence.[10]

It is this intermingling of cultural anxieties about the disturbing undercurrents of national history with the geographical conditions of the American South that shape the Southern Gothic. By participating in this tradition, *The Skeleton Key* harnesses the preoccupations of millennial horror to unsettle the relationship between the history of the American south and the new, 21st-century American present.

The film evokes all of the major themes of the Southern Gothic, as identified by Kellie Donovan-Condron: "slavery, history, and the relationship between past and present, individual, familial, and social relationships, ties between bodies and property."[11] As will be seen, it approaches these themes in a way that is almost baroque in its layers of self-recognition, as the relationships between property ownership, bodies, and racial identities—and the way that these relationships both shape and deconstruct historical narratives—are foregrounded as a key source of dread. The film's combination of three settings pervasive in the Southern Gothic—New Orleans, the rural bayous of Louisiana, and the decaying plantation house—succinctly conjure the distinct thematic and aesthetic archaeology of Southern Gothic fiction, a genre defined by the inscription of dichotomous historical preoccupations with oppression, rebellion, violence, and freedom onto the unique landscapes of the American south.

The Skeleton Key engages in such conflicted ways with Southern Gothic themes that some scholars have questioned the motivations behind the film's negotiation of the genre's anxieties. Maisha Wester suggests that the film "recalls and reproduces white America's conflicting racist stance, illustrating both a desire to fall into and be consumed by dark otherness as well as a fear of destruction and contamination by that same dark other."[12] Likewise, David Greven suggests that *The Skeleton Key* takes part in a cycle of ideologically problematic Southern Gothic works in which "the abused and violated become the truly monstrous oppressors and horrifying entities," and that thus "bizarrely revise" historical trauma.[13] While I concur that the film is "ideologically troubling"[14] in the ambivalent way that it confronts historical trauma, I suggest that this ideological distress is self-consciously central to the film's horrors. When read in relation to the transnational cycle of ghost films in which the film takes part, *The Skeleton Key*'s ambiguous confrontation of historical anxieties is not only clarified, but exposed as subversive of the very epistemic structures that tend to sustain the ongoing suppression of America's more disturbing histories.

While the film starts in New Orleans, the South's "gothic capital,"[15] most of the narrative is set within a decaying, former plantation house in rural Terrebonne Parish, Louisiana. This dark, labyrinthine space on the edge of a swamp is the main source of horror throughout the film. While the house's status as a plantation residence is not overtly addressed in the course of the film—which establishes the origins of the house's "hauntings," somewhat vaguely, between 1915 and 1920—the antebellum architecture of the sprawling home conjures this dark legacy in diffusive ways. In the Southern Gothic, the plantation house, which Wester describes as a "stock feature" of the Southern Gothic landscape,[16] typically stands in for the more generalized haunted house of the traditional Gothic, functioning as a spatial signifier of not just an uneasily suppressed past that lingers in the present, but the specific pasts of African American oppression. As Davison suggests, "in its Southern manifestations, the haunted house regularly assumes the form of the slave plantation house, a spectralized locale whose materialist substructure is exposed by way of irrepressible ghosts."[17] Because it has long been such a prominent feature of the Southern Gothic, the plantation house is thus suggestive of the present's ambivalent relationship with the South's dark history, even when the slavery that is historically imprinted upon such houses is only vaguely addressed, as in *The Skeleton Key*.

In the film, when the house's backstory is conveyed to both the viewer and to protagonist Caroline via a combination of oral history and flashback, it is revealed that the property was owned in the early 1900s by a wealthy white banker, Thorpe. Thus, the film traces the house's history to the early 20th century—well after slavery's official abolishment—while still linking the traumatic origins of the house's spectral presences to slavery's lingering effects on southern culture. According to the house's current owner, Violet Deveraux, Thorpe was "a mean man. He made his fortune cheating the poor." Furthermore, Violet refers to the African American specters who continue to haunt the property, Mama Cecile and Papa Justify, as Thorpe's "house servants," yet vaguely links their plight to slavery by suggesting that they were dehumanized under Thorpe's employ. As she explains, Thorpe was unaware of their powers as Hoodoo conjurers and only thought of them as "the help." As Christine Buzinde outlines in her work on plantation museums and southern travel guidebooks, it is common for the terms slavery and slave to be absent from historical accounts of the plantation and substituted with euphemisms like servant, laborer, or family member.[18] As in much contemporary cultural production concerning the South's history—including both plantation museums and the Southern Gothic—while slavery is not overtly referenced in *The Skeleton Key*, it hangs over the entire film. In fact, Violet's vague references to the wealthy landowner's ignorant dismissal of his servants takes on more pointed connotations at the end of the film, once the twist has been revealed. At the climax we discover that Violet, the house's current owner, has in fact been inhabited by the spirit of Mama Cecile since she attained ownership of the house. It is thus Mama Cecile *herself* who orates the property's backstory to Caroline via the bodily and social identity of Violet, an elderly white woman. This complex dialectic of historical evasion and confrontation is characteristic of the film's layered negotiation of Southern Gothic themes.

Corporeality, History and Inter-Generational (Dis)continuities

The Skeleton Key follows the plight of protagonist Caroline, a young hospice worker from New Orleans who has come to the sprawling plantation property to work as a live-in caregiver for an elderly patient: Ben Devereaux, Violet's husband. Ben is incapable of speech and independent movement after supposedly suffering from a stroke. As we learn later in the film, however, the old man's condition is actually due to the fact that Papa Justify has inhabited Ben's body for the previous 50 years, but has recently used Hoodoo to swap souls with a young lawyer, Luke Marshall. Thus, Luke's soul is now trapped inside Ben's mute, immobile body, and Justify inhabits the body of Luke. Cecile and Justify plan to undertake the ritual again in the near future, which is why Caroline has been lured to the house. In the hope that they can soon discard Violet's aging body and swap it for a younger model, the couple plan to place Cecile's spirit within Caroline's youthful body and trap Caroline's soul within the body of the old woman.

The film thus troubles teleological temporality through its character construction and narrative structure. On first viewing, it seems as though we are watching a narrative centered on a young white woman, Caroline, who is attempting to uncover the nefarious plot of a superstitious old woman who may be keeping her husband sick or even trying to kill him. Yet the twist reveals that the elderly, white bodies of the Deveraux couple are simply a foil. These bodies have long been used to conceal the hidden black identities that have for decades inhabited them, in what Adam McGee describes as a "radical form of racial 'passing.'"[19] The assumption that Violet is an unhinged old woman and that Ben is a severely disabled stroke-victim at the brink of death is thus weaponized by Cecile and Justify to lure Caroline into their house, and also to mislead her into underestimating "Violet's" agency and strength, just as Cecile's power was underestimated in her former existence as a black woman (as "Violet" explains to Caroline when narrating the history of the property, while Thorpe dismissed the servants as merely "the help," he was unaware that they were in fact powerful conjurers, famous throughout the Louisiana bayous). Indeed, Caroline's journey to the Deveraux household is framed through such a dismissal of her elderly employers: as Caroline's friend Jill remarks when Caroline leaves for Terrebonne Parish, "They'll try and suck you into their elderly ways. I'll be around whenever you want to talk to someone who wasn't around for World War II."

Jill's dismissal of the old couple's vitality, relevance, and experiences functions as both a disregard for this specific old couple and for the Terrebonne Parish region as a whole, which is constructed in the film as largely inhabited by the elderly and marginalized (as Jill says, "they all have no teeth there"). With the revelation that Violet's elderly body houses the powerful soul of an African American woman who has been alive for well over 100 years, this dismissal is revealed as a perilous adherence to shallow cultural assumptions about the limited social value and agency of the elderly. While Violet's body is old, Cecile's lifespan, which encompasses multiple bodies and generations, has amplified, rather than quelled, her power. As a result, many of the film's horror set-pieces revolve around Violet/Cecile's unexpected strength in relation to her elderly body. At the climax, for instance, Violet/Cecile yells at Caroline as the young woman tries to escape the property, "You think you're stronger than me? You have no idea how strong I am, Caroline!" her voice imbued with a supernaturally-charged volume that underscores the futility of Caroline's escape attempt. Even after breaking both of her legs in a fall, Violet manages to claw towards Caroline with great speed, finally pulling herself up to stand on her visibly broken limbs. Such scenes dwell on the abject qualities of Violet's apparent corporeal frailty in relation to her spiritual power.

The unsettling nature of this disjuncture between corporeal frailty and spiritual vitality contributes to the film's overarching challenge to the idea that cycles of corporeal growth and decline parallel—and *naturalize*—teleological narratives of historical continuity. Augmenting the preoccupations of the Gothic supernatural cycle, the film deconstructs the manner by which dominant historical narratives are constructed and sustained across generations by powerful social groups. Initially Cecile and Justify use old age to hide their supernatural power inside bodies that have been cast to the margins of society, and subsequently to trap young white identities inside these bodies and thus into the historical cycles of social voicelessness and powerlessness that previously entrapped them as African Americans. Significantly, Cecile and Justify harness the very mechanisms that sustain inter-generational, white social power, such as property inheritance, to turn it against those who benefit from it most. They co-opt the bodies of young white people—like the Thorpe children, the once-young Deveraux couple, and Luke and Caroline—usurping their futures just as they are about to claim their powerful social position as young white adults. Possessing their bodies at a moment at which they are primed to grasp all the social privilege afforded by these identities, Cecile and Justify in turn trap these white subjects typically central to narratives of historical progression inside black or elderly bodies with limited social voice and agency.

For the Thorpe children, this corporeality-based oppression reaches a disturbing apex: as soon as Cecile and Justify swap bodies with the children, they are discovered conducting Hoodoo rituals in the attic by the Thorpe patriarch and a group of aristocratic revelers who are attending a party at the household. As punishment, the servants are lynched as a source of perverse spectacle for the party guests. On second viewing once the viewer is aware of the twist, it becomes clear that it was actually the Thorpe family's own children who were murdered in this scene, their spirits having just been trapped within the bodies of the servants. Thus, Cecile and Justify appropriate the Thorpe children's future—covertly displacing the legacy of the family—while the children experience a horrific death at the hands of their own parent's violent racism. In the film's present, when young lawyer Luke is trapped in Ben Deveraux's aging body he is left unable to speak or move (a disempowerment aided by Cecile and Justify's Hoodoo magic), and thus is unable to communicate his circumstances or true identity to Caroline or anyone else. Similarly, at the end of the film when Caroline's soul is forced into Violet's body—which now has two broken legs—Caroline is left unable to walk or speak. One of the film's final and most unnerving scenes consists of "Ben" and "Violet" (as inhabited by Luke and Caroline) being casually locked into the back of an ambulance by paramedics as they both writhe in distress, trapped by both their corporeal identities and their physical inability to communicate with those around them. It is implied that they will both be taken to a hospice center to live out their remaining days, their experiences and identities written out of the present, future—and ultimately, history—like many generations of African Americans before them.

In the scene that immediately follows, Cecile and Justify are depicted claiming another generation of ownership of the plantation house through Caroline's body via a will that they wrote on behalf of Violet. Both Caroline and the "real" Violet—who would be long dead, her soul having been forced into the aging body of one of the Thorpe children many decades ago—are powerless to protest or resist this transferal of ownership. The film's final sequence thus reinforces the broader cultural implications of Cecile and Justify's reversal of their social marginalization. There is ultimately a vague equivalence drawn in the film between the social dismissal of elderly and African American bodies, a marginalization that amounts to entrenched processes of social disenfranchisement. Cecile and Justify ironically harness this disenfranchisement to hollow out, from within, the dominant historical narratives sustained by inter-generational exchanges of property, belongings, and family legacies. This macro-subversion of historical cycles of power transferal is paralleled on a micro scale by the way that the couple have repeatedly hollowed out white bodies to transform them into vessels for their own spirits.

The Plantation House, Elderly Bodies and the Dialectic of Historical Evasion and Confrontation

It is significant that most of the film takes place within, and centers on, the decaying plantation house in which Cecile and Justify initially worked as "the help." The house itself is at the crux of Cecile and Justify's supernaturally-charged rebellion against the hegemonic structures of inter-generational continuance that tend to displace the historical experiences of African Americans. As Michael Kreyling suggests, the plantation house in the Southern Gothic can typically be read "both as an evasion of history and as the return of the history that it aims to avoid,"[20] a dialectic embedded in the way the house's history in *The Skeleton Key* both gestures to and bypasses the specific contexts of slavery. Frequently fetishized for their grandiose beauty and associated with the glamorous lifestyles of the wealthy white patriarchs who owned them, the memorialization of plantation houses has been implicated in the "white-washing" of the South's history of slavery. As Derek Alderman, David Butler, and Stephen Hanna explain in their study of the historical narratives constructed by plantation museums:

> Although the Southern plantation was, for many African Americans, the beginning of their ancestral connection with the region and the nation, managers of plantation museums have traditionally created and marketed a form of tourism that valorized the wealth and perspectives of the white planter class while ignoring, minimizing, or romanticizing the historical contributions and suffering of the enslaved who made that privileged way of life possible.[21]

They further suggest that "white-centered" historical narratives that position the plantation within teleologies of American national progress and achievement serve to "'symbolically annihilate' the histories and identities of the slave community and disinherit African-Americans from their own heritage."[22]

In *The Skeleton Key*, the beautiful but dark and decrepit plantation house functions as a powerful spatial metonym for multi-layered processes of "white-washed" historical remembrance, and the simultaneous gesturing to and evasion of darker historical legacies of African American suppression. The most obvious signifier of this suppression is the fact that the "skeleton key" after which the film is named—which Violet gives to Caroline after agreeing to take her on as Ben's hospice worker—opens all of the house's 30 rooms except for the attic. This enigmatic space underpins much of the film's mystery-driven narrative: Violet tells Caroline at one point that she and her husband have never ventured into the attic in the almost 50 years that they have owned the house, and gives Caroline strict instructions never to enter it. It is in this attic that all the signs of the house's suppressed black history and ownership lurk: this is where Cecile and Justify store (and hide) all of their Hoodoo paraphernalia. Thus, the attic both houses and conceals the "true" identities of the Deveraux couple since they obtained ownership of the property.

Throughout the film, the relationship of the "Deverauxs" to their house and its histories reinforces this overarching dialectic of confrontation and evasion. Like the attic, the old white bodies of the Deveraux couple both conceal and contain the repressed history of black suffering and agency that runs parallel to the overt history of white home ownership that initially seems to structure the film. Until the film's twist is revealed, the house metonymizes this dialectic. For instance, when "Violet" is introducing Caroline to the property—including explaining that she and Ben bought the house from the Thorpe family in 1962—Caroline notices that she has a picture of the previous "owners" of the house—that is, the two Thorpe children—on the mantelpiece. Surprised, Caroline remarks, "you keep their picture?" to which Violet replies, "I like to pay my respects to the memories of this house." As Violet leaves the frame, Caroline picks up the picture to take a closer look, and as she does so another photograph falls out of the picture-frame. In this image, Cecile and Justify stand behind the children. The image is similar to the one at the front of the picture-frame, its parallel composition reinforcing the vacillation between Cecile and Justify's absence in the displayed photograph, and presence behind their young masters in the concealed photograph. Thus, the picture-frame holds the multiple layers of the property's "memories" while at the same time disguising them, in particular obscuring the extent to which African Americans are key to both the house's traumatic past and to its ongoing preservation into the present and future. The erasure of this layer of history in the displayed photograph aesthetically conjures the complex and self-reflexive way that the film negotiates the history of the American south. On initial viewing, the narrative seems to be built around the experiences of white people, and to focus on white legacies of property ownership. However with the final twist, the viewer learns that buried beneath this narrative all along has been a story about how a black couple rebelled against their subjugated social position to claim the property for themselves.

That the exposure of this twist parallels the exposure of a buried layer of American historical consciousness is further suggested by the fact that initially it seems that Cecile and Justify are simply ghosts that haunt the house. When the characters are first intro-

Caroline (Kate Hudson) inspects the two photographs in the picture-frame on the Deveraux couple's mantelpiece: the one on display depicts the Thorpe children (right), while the one hidden behind the displayed photograph depicts Cecile and Justify standing behind the children (left) in *The Skeleton Key* (2005).

duced in the film, they are constructed as eerie specters of a dark past that continually haunts the present, raising white guilt while at the same time seeming largely incidental to the white-centered narrative that unfolds in the film's present. After explaining the house's history, "Violet" tells Caroline about these ghosts, explaining that she has removed all the mirrors in the house because she and Ben see the ghosts in them. At this point, just over halfway through the film, some of the tension seems to dissipate as Caroline and the viewer are able to associate the old couple's odd behavior with their belief that their house is haunted. It is also implied at this juncture that Cecile and Justify are only relevant in the present as spectral remnants of a disturbing history that has long since passed, a fading relevance further diminished by the film's suggestion that they may be the product of the elderly Deveraux couple's foolish superstitions (Caroline herself does not believe that the house is haunted). Indeed, Ben is presented as senile throughout much of the film, and Violet too is depicted as losing her grip on reality: at one point when Caroline condescendingly references the old woman's belief in the ghosts, Violet/Cecile informs Caroline that she is aware that the young woman believes her to be senile.

Caroline's dismissals of both the supernatural preoccupations of the elderly couple and of the black ghosts that supposedly haunt the house are simultaneously overturned when she and the viewer realize that the past represented by these murdered servants is not dead and gone. By contrast, this past continues to live on in and shape the present. Subverting the dominant white-centered narrative, the revelation that Cecile and Justify live on through the bodies of the Deveraux—and prior to that, through the bodies of the Thorpe children—transforms the relationship between not only the Thorpe household's present and its dark past, but by extension the broader relationship between the present of the American south and its history. Rather than remaining immobilized by and bound to their place in history, Cecile and Justify have occupied white bodies for almost a century in order to, in the words of McGee, "take revenge on their employers and an oppressive society in which the only way to be socially powerful was to be white."[23]

That Cecile and Justify have enacted this maneuver through sustaining multi-generational ownership of their former employer's plantation house is significant. As Stefanie Benjamin and Derek Alderman suggest, the plantation home in sites of American historical remembrance such as heritage museums is traditionally deployed in service of

> a selective and romanticised remembrance of the antebellum past that has regrettably silenced and marginalised the historical experiences and struggles of enslaved African people. This inequality at museums shapes and is shaped by a broader White-centric political and ideological contexts and worldviews that traditionally have actively forgotten and de-valued African American and Black identities, histories, and civil rights struggles.[24]

The Skeleton Key initially seems to echo such selective processes of historical remembrance, before subverting them via the revelation that Cecile and Justify have covertly written their white oppressors out of a history that on a surface level seems to revolve around them. Furthermore, as Alderman, Bulter, and Hana suggest in a passage cited earlier in this essay, the Southern plantation home is not just a site of oppression but "for many African-Americans, the beginning of their ancestral connection with the region and the nation."[25] The fracturing of ancestral connections to plantations through evasion and simplistic narratives of victimhood play a large part in the decentering of African Americans in official histories. In their usurpation of white cycles of socio-historical dominance, Cecile and Justify surreptitiously solidify their ties to the plantation. Thus, a film seemingly driven by white characters that displaces black characters to the spectral margins reveals itself with the final twist to in fact center around covert *black* legacies of property ownership.

Counter-Memory

Cecile and Justify's spectral rebellion ultimately entails a subversive incarnation of what Foucault calls "counter-memory": a form of collective memory that challenges hegemonic historical discourse by enacting "a transformation of history into a totally different form of time."[26] Counter-memory is not concerned only with adding new voices to dominant historical narratives, but with the displacement of linear, teleological forms of historical consciousness wholesale. As José Medina explains, counter-memory is "not a pluralism that tries to resolve conflicts and overcome struggles, but instead tries to provoke them and to re-energize them…. This is a pluralism that focuses on the gaps, discontinuities, tensions and clashes among perspectives and discursive practices."[27] In defining counter-memory Foucault proposes the replacement of "objective," linear historical narratives—which tend to be constructed by powerful social groups—with personal memories and genealogies. As he suggests, this involves the "insurrection of subjugated knowledges"[28]: knowledges like Cecile and Justify's mastery of Hoodoo; awareness of the cruelty of wealthy white patriarchs celebrated in official histories; and the complex combination of suffering and ancestral belonging experienced by slaves in the plantation house.

Highlighting that their counter-memories belong to a different epistemic order than the white-centric knowledges that initially seem to underpin the film, Cecile and Justify's memories are presented via aesthetics that contrast with the rest of the film. These memories are conveyed through a strange juxtaposition of charged liveness and decaying pastness, reinforcing both their position in history and their ongoing interaction with the present. This aesthetic construction also echoes the dichotomy between corporeal decline and spiritual vitality embodied by the elderly Violet/Cecile. Initially, the black couple's grisly past is depicted via a montage of what look like moving sepia photographs. Echoing the photo of the Thorpe children on the mantelpiece depicted earlier in the film, these seemingly static shots erupt into moving images with varying frame-rates to create jerky, unpredictable bodily movement that appears at once antiquated and threateningly present. This flashback sequence continually vacillates between shots depicting Cecile and Justify, and full-color scenes with largely conventional editing that depict the Thorpe family's indulgent party. This sequence thus aesthetically juxtaposes the white history retained and romanticized in official recollections of the house with the convulsive trauma of Cecile and Justify's counter-memories. The aesthetic disjuncture metaphorizes the film's overall subversion of official (white) histories with black insurrected knowledge, signaling the larger battle between perspectives that structures the film as a whole. As Medina explains: "when it comes to knowledge of the past and the power associated with it, this battle involves resisting the 'omissions' and distortions of official histories, returning to lost voices and forgotten experiences, relating to the past from the perspective of the present in an alternative (out-of-the-mainstream) way."[29]

The film's interplay between white official histories and black counter-memories ultimately works to deconstruct the historical consciousness upon which the ongoing marginalization of black experiences rest. As Buzinde suggests, the unseating of teleo-

102 II. Aesthetics of Decay

In *The Skeleton Key*, Caroline (Kate Hudson, left) listens as Violet/Cecile (Gena Rowlands) recounts the history of the house, framed by the rotting boat dock.

logical historical narratives of American culture "requires [American] society to engage in dialogue with and deconstruct its collective recollection of the plantation."[30] Thus, in self-consciously troubling ways, *The Skeleton Key* contributes to the kind of "memory-work" advocated by Benjamin and Alderman, which entails "a set of creative practices or interventions—often artistic in nature—that seek to create new forms of public memories about violence and injustice."[31] David Butler, Perry Carter, and Owen Dwyer also contend that to disrupt hegemonic historical narratives, memory-work must take place that puts forth "an alternative way of viewing and knowing the Southern plantation that holds the power to shape the understanding and the production of knowledge."[32] *The Skeleton Key* constructs such an "alternative way of viewing and knowing the Southern plantation" by revealing the dominant history of white property ownership to be a hollow front for black counter-memories.

The Aesthetics of Decay

As a result, in keeping with the features of the supernatural film cycle of the turn of the millennium, *The Skeleton Key* is structured around a subversion of audience expectations about narrative time and progression that, by extension, troubles modernist understandings of historical temporality. As Wester explains, key to the problematic and complicated "interchange of recognition and disavowal at play in daily American racial discourses" is the notion that "racism is fixed in a distant and long-past history."[33] It is this kind of association of slavery and racism with a fixed, static and long-dead past that allows for assumptions that the structural inequalities of history have been resolved. As Buzinde argues, such utopian discourses of national post-racialism might be interpreted as "a carte blanche that obviates the need to engage or sustain any dialogue on race issues because society has surpassed these struggles."[34] Key to *The Skeleton Key*'s articulation of insurrected counter-memories is an uncomfortable deconstruction of this mode of historical thought that subtly endorses a lack of critical engagement with uncomfortable historical pasts.

This subversion of teleological historical consciousness occurs not only through *The Skeleton Key*'s narrative structure, but through a complex fetishization of decay and aging that unsettles entrenched fixations with cultural progress. Just as Violet seems by turns frail and powerful, the Thorpe mansion is both beautiful and unsettling in its decay and decline, which drives the uncanny mystique throughout the film. The house is frequently framed through shots that foreground this sublime decay: significantly, during the sequence in which "Violet" tells Caroline about the history of the house, the pair stand at the edge of the swamp in front of the property, the shot framed by a rotting boat-dock that has almost completely been consumed by the swamp, the function of the structure almost unrecognizable. Dead vines cascade from the moldering beams, and atop the swamp's murky surface sits an algae-covered dinghy. Wester reads the mansion's decay as suggestive of an assumption that "the usurping black body cannot sustain the economic success of (rightfully) privileged white power. The disrepair that the Thurgood [*sic*] mansion suffers ... posits blacks as deadbeats who destroy rather than maintain ... economic stability."[35] I suggest instead that the film's fetishization of the decay of structures, bodies, and landscapes is bound up with its overarching challenge to modernist epistemologies of history. As Walter Benjamin has famously articulated, the aesthetics of decay unravel teleological historical narratives, exposing how "history decays into images, not into stories."[36] As Þóra Pétursdóttir and Bjørnar Olsen suggest, citing Benjamin, "by bringing history to a halt in a 'petrified unrest' [decaying objects, structures and images] enable involuntary remembering of that which becomes ignored or is made redundant."[37]

The preservation of a space or site as a historical monument—like a plantation museum—entails a solidification of a particular narrative of teleological history: the kind of "selective and romanticised remembrance of the antebellum past"[38] that Benjamin and Alderman identify in relation to plantation museums. Thus, while the restored houses of plantation museums are bound to a particular ideological and temporal place on America's established historical continuum, the decaying Thorpe mansion carries multiple layers of memory into the present and future through its decay. In addition, the structure's decay impels us to conceptualize the continual transition of the present into pasts that are *not* captured within sanctified historical narratives. A similar effect is acutely provoked by the film's final scene in which Ben/Luke and Violet/Caroline's elderly bodies are whisked into the ambulance and then out of the shot—and ultimately, the film—without being able to communicate their experience to anyone.

The declining mansion thus resists the conventional wisdom that the past is given meaning—or is even justified—by the progress that has been made and that continues

The aesthetics of Justify (Ronald McCall) and Cecile's (Jeryl Prescott) "counter-memories" in *The Skeleton Key*, as depicted in the flashback sequence that portrays their apparent lynching by the Thorpe patriarch.

to drive the present. As Dylan Trigg explains: "unlike the enforcement of a political agenda through the conservation of the monument, the ruin frees us from an already formed definition of history.... The false arrangement of the past, whereby the surplus remains are discarded, presenting history as an ordered, self-contained, and rationalistic project, is overruled by the emergence of the past in the ruin, as fragmented and incomplete."[39] Instead, the eerie beauty of decaying structures incarnates "the preservation of a past, manifest not by the *fulfilment* of that past, but through its decay."[40] In fact, this fetishization of decay often features in black cultural production: for instance, Rafaël Lucas identifies what he refers to as an "aestheticisation of degradation" in Haitian literature of the American occupation (1915–1934) and into the late 20th century. He suggests that this fixation with the sublime qualities of degradation signals "the definitive inadmissibility of any euphoric discourse on national identity," while allowing "us to see a veritable mystique of change in the social, physical and cultural environment."[41] The aesthetics of decay oppose processes of historical curation by empowered social groups. Instead, such aesthetics work alongside counter-memory to dramatize the raw plurality of histories. We see this in the film's ending, in which the protagonist, Caroline, is locked inside both an elderly body and an ambulance, suggesting that her true story will be lost to history. The algae-covered boat that is gradually disappearing into the swamp likewise incarnates the slow decay of the present into a past that will not be memorialized, and is—like Caroline's dual imprisonment—suggestive of a future in which part of a much larger story will be lost.

Ultimately, *The Skeleton Key* deploys the aesthetics of decay—the deterioration of both elderly bodies and grand plantation mansions—as an uncanny tool of sedition against modes of historical remembrance centered on powerful social groups, and that marginalize the extent to which past oppressions shape present structures of knowledge. That Cecile and Justify continue to inhabit the decaying plantation house without restoring it thus signals their subversive way of "paying respects to the memories of this house" (in the words of Cecile). The house's treacherous and beautiful decay metonymizes the pluralized maintenance of the many voices—oppressed, powerful, victimized, and sacrificed—that have contributed to its history. As Pétursdóttir and Olsen articulate, in the decaying ruin "things of different times and places are coincidentally gathered in a "disor¬derly" entanglement, showing how the past things remember is never linear, sequential or continuous … things' persistency—and thus gathering—renders them rather as hybrid encounters with multiple times, the piled *aesthetic durations* of the past."[42] Both the Deveraux couple's elderly bodies and the decaying plantation home at the center of *The Skeleton Key* reveal such a disorderly entanglement of temporalities, deconstructing the impression that history is an objective and linear continuity of past cultural events.

Notes

1. Kendrick, "A Return to the Graveyard," 142.
2. Weinstock, "Introduction," 6.
3. Buse and Stott, *Ghosts*, 1–14.
4. Foucault, *Language, Counter-Memory, Practice*, 160.
5. Weinstock, "Introduction," 3.
6. *Ibid.*, 5.
7. *Ibid.*, 4.
8. Davison, "Southern Gothic," 56.
9. Horsley, "The Southern Gothic Film," 7–8.
10. Sivils, "Gothic Landscapes of the South," 92.

11. Donovan-Condron, "Twisted Sisters," 347.
12. Wester, "Keys to a Hurricane," 64.
13. Greven, "Southern Gothic Film," 482.
14. *Ibid.*
15. Truffin, "New Orleans as Gothic Capital," 187.
16. Wester, "Slave Narratives and Slave Revolts," 255.
17. Davison, 56.
18. Buzinde, "Discursive Constructions of the Plantation Past," 221.
19. McGee, "Haitian Vodou and Voodoo," 247.
20. Kreyling, "Uncanny Plantations," 234.
21. Alderman, Butler and Hanna, "Memory, Slavery, and Plantation Museums," 210.
22. *Ibid.*, 211.
23. McGee, "Haitian Vodou and Voodoo," 248.
24. Benjamin and Alderman, "Performing a Different Narrative," 2.
25. Alderman, Butler, and Hanna, "Memory, Slavery, and Plantation Museums," 210.
26. Foucault, "Language," 160.
27. Medina, "Toward a Foucaultian Epistemology of Resistance," 24.
28. Foucault, "Society Must Be Defended," 10.
29. Medina, "Toward a Foucaultian Epistemology of Resistance," 13.
30. Buzinde, "Discursive Constructions of the Plantation Past," 220.
31. Benjamin and Alderman, "Performing a Different Narrative," 4.
32. Butler, Carter and Dwyer, "Imagining Plantations," 142.
33. Wester, "Keys to a Hurricane," 65.
34. Buzinde, "Discursive Constructions of the Plantation Past," 233.
35. Wester, "Keys to a Hurricane," 71.
36. Benjamin, *Arcades*, 471.
37. Pétursdóttir and Olsen, "Imaging Modern Decay," 18.
38. Benjamin and Alderman, "Performing a Different Narrative," 2.
39. Trigg, *Aesthetics of Decay*, 238.
40. Trigg, *Memory of Place*, 261 (my emphasis).
41. Lucas, "The Aesthetics of Degradation," 72.
42. Pétursdóttir and Olsen, "Imaging Modern Decay," 18.

Bibliography

Alderman, Derek, David Butler, and Stephen Hana. "Memory, Slavery, and Plantation Museums: The River Road Project." *Journal of Heritage Tourism* 11, no. 3 (2016): 209–218.

Benjamin, Stefanie, and Derek Alderman. "Performing a Different Narrative: Museum Theater and the Memory-Work of Producing and Managing Slavery Heritage at Southern Plantation Museums." *International Journal of Heritage Studies* (2017): 1–13.

Benjamin, Walter. *The Arcades Project*. Edited by Rolf Tiedmann. Translated by Howard Eiland and Kevin McLaughlin. Cambridge: Belknap Press/Harvard University Press, 1999.

Butler, David L., Perry L. Carter, and Owen J. Dwyer. "Imagining Plantations: Slavery, Dominant Narratives, and the Foreign Born." *Southeastern Geographer* 48, no. 3 (2008): 288–302.

Buse, Peter, and Andrew Stott, eds. *Ghosts: Deconstruction, Psychoanalysis, History*. Houndsmills: Macmillan Press, 1999.

Buzinde, Christine N. "Discursive Constructions of the Plantation Past Within a Travel Guidebook." *Journal of Heritage Tourism* 5, no. 3 (2010): 219–235.

Davison, Carol Margaret. "Southern Gothic: Haunted Houses." In *Handbook of the Southern Gothic*, edited by Susan Castillo Street and Charles L. Crow, 55–68. London: Palgrave Macmillan, 2016.

Donovan-Condron, Kellie. "Twisted Sisters: The Monstrous Women of Southern Gothic." In *Handbook of the Southern Gothic*, edited by Susan Castillo Street and Charles L. Crow, 339–350. London: Palgrave Macmillan, 2016.

Foucault, Michel. *Language, Counter-Memory, Practice*. Edited by Donald F. Bouchard. Ithaca: Cornell University Press, 1977.

———. *"Society Must Be Defended": Lectures at the Collège de France 1975–1976*. Translated by David Macey. New York: Picador, 2003.

Greven, David. "The Southern Gothic Film: An Overview." In *Handbook of the Southern Gothic*, edited by Susan Castillo Street and Charles L. Crow, 473–486. London: Palgrave Macmillan, 2016.

Horsley, Karen. "The Southern Gothic Film." PhD Thesis, LaTrobe University, 2016.

Kendrick, James. "A Return to the Graveyard: Notes on the Spiritual Horror Film." In *American Horror Film: The Genre at the Turn of the Millennium*, edited by Steffen Hantke, 142–159. Jackson: University Press of Mississippi, 2010.

Kreyling, Michael. "Uncanny Plantations: The Repeating Gothic." In *Handbook of the Southern Gothic*, edited by Susan Castillo Street and Charles L. Crow, 231–244. London: Palgrave Macmillan, 2016.
Lucas, Rafaël. "The Aesthetics of Degradation in Haitian Literature." *Research in African Literatures* 35, no. 2 (2004): 54–74.
McGee, Adam. "Haitian Vodou and Voodoo: Imagined Religion and Popular Culture." *Studies in Religion* 41, no. 2 (2012): 231–256.
Medina, José. "Toward a Foucaultian Epistemology of Resistance: Counter-Memory, Epistemic Friction, and *Guerrilla* Pluralism." *Foucault Studies* 12 (2011): 8–35.
Pétursdóttir, Þóra, and Bjørnar Olsen. "Imaging Modern Decay: The Aesthetics of Ruin Photography." *Journal of Contemporary Archaeology* 1, no. 1 (2014): 7–56.
The Skeleton Key. Directed by Iain Softely. California: Universal Pictures Home Entertainment, 2005. Blu-ray.
Trigg, Dylan. *The Aesthetics of Decay: Nothingness, Nostalgia, and the Absence of Reason*. New York: Peter Lang, 2006.
_____. *The Memory of Place: A Phenomenology of the Uncanny*. Athens: Ohio University Press, 2012.
Truffin, Sherry R. "New Orleans as Gothic Capital." In *Handbook of the Southern Gothic*, edited by Susan Castillo Street and Charles L. Crow, 187–199. London: Palgrave Macmillan, 2016.
Weinstock, Jeffrey. "Introduction: The Spectral Turn." In *Spectral America: Phantoms and the National Imagination*, edited by Jeffrey Weinstock, 3–17. Madison: University of Wisconsin Press, 2004.
Wester, Maisha. "Keys to a Hurricane: Reading Race, Class and Abjection in *The Skeleton Key*." *Film International* 12, no. 1 (2014): 63–75.
_____. "Slave Narratives and Slave Revolts." In *Handbook of the Southern Gothic*, edited by Susan Castillo Street and Charles L. Crow, 245–258. London: Palgrave Macmillan, 2016.
Wynn Sivils, Matthew. "Gothic Landscapes of the South." In *Handbook of the Southern Gothic*, edited by Susan Castillo Street and Charles L. Crow, 83–94.. London: Palgrave Macmillan, 2016.

III.

Elders as Others/Outsiders

Making the Hard Choices
The Economics of Damnation in Drag Me to Hell

CYNTHIA J. MILLER

The 1980s were complicated times. The activism and upheaval of the 1960s and '70s cast a long shadow over the decade, as debilitating recession yielded to the promise of prosperity, and the pendulum of collective consciousness swung sharply from rights, equality, and opportunity to unfettered economic growth and upward mobility. Little remained unaffected as late-capitalism shifted to an information economy, and conflicts abounded: The youth counterculture of the '60s gave way to young urban professionalism, characterized by high expectations and little experience; second-wave feminism propelled women into a workplace where glass ceilings were still firmly in place; the faces of both policy and sentiment turned sharply away from social welfare, even as increasing numbers of Americans fell into need; and post-recession fears for national well-being, combined with late 20th-century rejection of traditional lifeways, led to mistrust and marginalization of immigrants in spite of the increasing diversity of the nation's population.[1]

This constellation of economic forces and social attitudes both resulted from and, in turn, caused, rapid social change that echoed throughout the remainder of the 20th century as neoliberalism held sway in the Reagan years. Neoliberalism then exploded into public consciousness once again with the 2008 subprime disaster, often referred to as the Great Recession. The worldview that these economic forces shaped also served as fodder for cinematic terror tales that several scholars have termed "Recessionary Horror," and Barry Keith has designated "Yuppie Horror."[2] One of the most acclaimed among these is Sam Raimi's *Drag Me to Hell* (2009), a film that draws together a host of late 20th- and early 21st-century fears in a supernatural morality tale of intergenerational conflict.

A Tale of Capital and Curses

While released in the first decade of the new millennium, Raimi's film was co-written with his brother Ivan ten years earlier, and as a result, is deeply influenced by the zeitgeist of that era. Not simply wanting to repeat the successful gore-driven formula of *The Evil*

Dead trilogy (1981–1992), Raimi instead crafted a tale of psychological horror which, early in the narrative, implicates the shifting values and cutthroat economics that earmarked the late 20th century as the film's true horrors.

Set in Los Angeles, the story focuses on Christine Brown (Alison Lohman), a sweet, farm-raised young woman with aspirations of upward mobility. Employed as a loan officer at the Wilshire Pacific Financial Center, she seeks to advance her career; in no small part, because she overhears her boyfriend Clay's (Justin Long) mother urging him to find a woman with ambition, someone of better social standing who will be an asset to his own rising career. Christine sees an open assistant-manager position at the bank as her ticket to both personal and professional happiness. Competing with her for the promotion, however, is an underhanded colleague, Stu (Reggie Lee), who will stop at nothing, including fraud, to make her look incompetent. As they discuss her candidacy, her boss Jim Jacks (David Paymer) advises her that if she is to succeed, she must be willing to make "hard choices."

The stage is thus set for Christine to make not only a hard, but ultimately horrific, choice. When elderly Sylvia Ganush (Lorna Raver) appears at the bank, desperate for a third extension on her mortgage, Christine seizes the opportunity to prove herself and denies the request, even as the old woman falls to her knees and begs for help. Christine instead calls security and has the woman ejected from the bank, but not before the enraged crone vows revenge. Shaken, Christine questions her choice, but praise from her boss strengthens her resolve. Later that day, however, when Christine leaves work, she is viciously attacked in the parking garage by the old woman, who has hidden away in the back seat of Christine's car. Ganush rips a button from the young woman's coat and uses it to place a curse on her.

Soon, it becomes apparent that there are dark forces at work. Christine's mind and body begin to break down, leaving the young woman and those around her uncertain about her health and sanity. Flies appear out of nowhere and seem to invade her body, visions of Sylvia Ganush haunt her, sounds torment her, and an evil entity stalks and attacks her, leaving her bloodied and terrified. Christine convinces Clay to accompany her to consult psychic Rham Jas (Dileep Rao), who confirms her haunting and suggests that a curse is the cause. This moves the young woman to seek out her tormentor and attempt to make amends. She visits the Ganush home, intending to ask for forgiveness and have the curse lifted, but finds that she has arrived too late. The old woman has died, leaving her no possibility of reprieve.

A panicked Christine returns to Rham Jas for help, and he advises that she is being stalked by a Lamia, a powerful demon that will torment her for three days, and then drag her to hell for eternity. He introduces her to her last hope, the psychic Shaun San Dena (Adriana Barraza), who has confronted the demon before and failed (which viewers witness in flashback at the film's opening), and who, for a steep fee, will risk her life to vanquish it and redeem herself. During a climactic séance scene, the two psychics attempt a plan that will trap the demon and trick it into the body of a goat, which they can then kill. The demon, however, proves too powerful. San Dena banishes it from the séance, but then dies from the supernatural struggle, unable to fully conquer it.

Rham Jas informs Christine that her only hope now is to give away the cursed button to someone else—an option he had not offered before, since the act would condemn the recipient's soul to eternal torture—and places it in a sealed envelope. Although she immediately devises a plan to place the curse on her co-worker, Stu, she ultimately relents. The psychic presents the frantic young woman with one final option, informing her that the cursed button may be returned to Sylvia Ganush, even though she is dead. In one last desperate attempt, Christine digs up the old woman's grave in a horrific storm, struggles with the corpse as the grave fills with water, and finally, jams the envelope in its mouth, formally declaring that she is giving the button to it, just before the stroke of midnight on the third day.

In the aftermath, Christine appears to have a new lease on life. The tortures of the Lamia have stopped, and her vitality has returned. Stu's workplace deceptions have been discovered, she has received the coveted promotion, and her life seems back on track. To celebrate, she and Clay prepare for a romantic weekend away where he intends to propose. However, when Clay meets her at the train station, he returns an envelope that she had dropped in his car a day or two prior—one that contains the cursed button. Christine realizes that she passed the wrong envelope to the dead woman, and that the curse has not, in fact, been lifted. As she backs away from the envelope in horror, she falls onto the tracks. Helpless, Clay looks on as a high-speed train barrels toward her, but before it reaches her, fiery hands emerge from the tracks and drag her into the underworld, in clear homage to Jacques Tournier's classic *Night of the Demon* (1957), which resolves with a similar scene. The devil, or at least the restless soul of Sylvia Ganush, has had its due.

Poverty as Contagion

Through Ganush's character, Raimi both reinforces and complicates images of the elderly in horror. Cast as a decrepit stereotypical Hungarian gypsy,[3] she is the embodiment of abjection. Her character is introduced through a shot of her gnarled hands and thick, rotted fingernails drumming on Christine's desk at the bank, forecasting the horrors that are to come. As Christine's eyes search for the origin of the sound, viewers see a look of startlement and disgust cross her face upon her first glimpse of Ganush sitting opposite her. The camera shifts again to reveal the old woman—wrinkled, with filth encrusted dentures and one eye deadened by disease—her thinning, oily hair covered by a headscarf. "Vill you 'elp me?" she asks in a thick Eastern European accent. Ganush is the quintessential Other—as April Miller describes, a "grotesque, abject body that threatens to spread a kind of contagious poverty"[4]—surrounded by the crisp, efficient landscape of the finance industry; a body out of time and place that disrupts the ordered space of the bank, she signals weakness in an environment where competitiveness reigns. Her disabled body is cast as "deviant and inferior," as Garland-Thomson observes, "excluded from full participation in public as well as economic life" and "defined in opposition to a valued norm which is assumed to possess natural corporeal superiority."[5]

Ganush and the fresh-faced young loan officer are set in stark contrast—worlds, ages, and lifeways apart. In a social environment such as this where, adapting Foucault's observation, the value of the body is "bound up ... with its economic use," the value of aging bodies, particularly those that have aged "unsuccessfully," is limited, and they are often met, as Russo suggests, with "ridicule, contempt, pity, and scorn."[6] Thus, while Ganush makes an appeal to their shared humanity, Christine, and the viewer, can only see their differences, thanks to the camera's unflinching gaze.

As the scene continues, Raimi layers abjection upon abjection. Ganush leans over

Christine's desk and begins to cough, and in close-up hacks thick yellow phlegm into a linen handkerchief as they talk. She literally seems to be decomposing as the scene unfolds. As Tony Magistrale discusses, this presence of "corporeal decay" signaled by "excess and uncontrollable fluids [and] bodily wastes" is key to the terror inspired by the female monster.[7] Clutching the linen tightly in her hand, as if its contents are still part of her body, she asks again for the young woman's help. Then, when left alone at the desk for a moment, she spies a dish of candy. Removing one from its wrapper, she sets the handkerchief on the desk, and removes her dentures, dripping with saliva, to suck on it, while, unbeknownst to her, Christine looks on in disgust. Conforming once again to representations of elderly figures as "inhuman, threatening, and laughable," this brief action increases the visceral horror of Ganush's character, but through its use of dark comedy, lessens the social horror, leaving viewers off-guard for the action that follows.[8]

Sylvia Ganush (Lorna Raver) becomes the embodiment of abjection in *Drag Me to Hell* (2009).

When Christine is given the option to exercise her authority—or her compassion—and chooses to deny the woman an additional extension, Ganush stares a moment in disbelief, then rises from her chair to leave. She stops, however, refusing to absolve the young woman. She begins to speak, and falls to her knees: "I am proud woman Miss Brown, and never have I beg for anything. But now, I beg to you. I humble myself before you. I, Sylvia Ganush beg, on my mother's grave, I beg you." Grasping the hem of Christine's skirt, she kisses it in supplication. Christine panics and causes the elderly woman to fall as she calls for a security officer. Ganush gathers herself and chides Christine for shaming her—

There is a stark contrast between Old World and New, age and youth, as Sylvia Ganush (Lorna Raver, facing camera) begs Christine (Alison Lohman) for a final extension on her mortgage in *Drag Me to Hell*.

not for the public embarrassment, but for not honoring her ultimate expression of humility.

In this brief, five-minute scene—the longest her character is seen on screen—Sylvia Ganush violates a key social principle elaborated by scholars such as Laura Herd Clarke, Kathleen Woodward, and Pamela Gravagne: that older women are encouraged to recede into invisibility, so that we, as a society, might avoid having to confront the notion that "old age is bad, repulsive, and ugly."[9] She enters into the sterile, unwelcoming space of the bank, where older women are often "poor ... powerless ... and without voice,"[10] and transgresses its norms of appearance (through both her physical traits and her Old-World, working-class attire), comprehension (through her lack of understanding of language, processes, and procedures), public health (through a perceived lack of hygiene, visible disabilities, and the introduction of bodily fluids into the public sphere), and demeanor (through prostrate begging, anger, making a "scene"). In short, she disturbs the order of the financial institution, and in the process, becomes abject.[11] Fighting for her own economic security, she refuses to be invisible, regardless of the discomfort of others.

In this, Ganush departs from several of the tropes of elderly characters that have been well-established in the horror genre, which generally establish aging figures as objects of fear or pity. As Shary and McVittie point out, aging characters in horror are typically rendered as "monstrously othered objects"—dehumanized and objectified through the characteristics and performance of their advanced age.[12] While certainly a grotesque elderly character subject to violent outbursts, and one who, like many others in the genre, engages in violence or summons supernatural forces for vengeance against perceived wrongs, Sylvia Ganush does not fit comfortably in either the helpless victim or the "psycho biddy" templates established in the 1960s with characters such as Cornelia Hilyard in *Lady in a Cage* (1964), Mrs. Trefoile in *Die! Die! My Darling!* (1965), Minnie Castevet in *Rosemary's Baby* (1968), or Alice Dimmock in *What Ever Happened to Aunt Alice* (1969).[13] It is the social context of the film's narrative that has forced Ganush into her roles as both victim and terrorizer, making her simultaneously more complex and sympathetic. In this, she is similar to another displaced elderly character from several decades prior: Miss Emily in Larry Yust's horror comedy *Homebodies* (1974), who murders all those associated with her impending eviction from her urban apartment building. Like Raimi, Yust uses his elderly characters to craft commentary about the impact of social and economic forces on vulnerable individuals who become monstrous as a result. Both Miss Emily and Sylvia Ganush are victims of rapid social change—the world is simply passing them by—and both exercise unanticipated, horrific agency in response.

Old Age and the Neoliberal Ethic

The impact of neoliberal economics in *Drag Me to Hell* is readily apparent from the early moments of the film, as Christine attempts to navigate the hierarchies of class and caste vis-à-vis her position at the bank. Following David Harvey, we may think of neoliberalism as "the elevation of capitalism, as a mode of production, into an ethic, a set of political imperatives, and a cultural logic."[14] It is a project to "strengthen, restore, or in some cases constitute anew" the power of the economic elites,[15] earmarked by those transactions actively supported by large, impersonal financial institutions: privatization, accumulation by dispossession, and the association of freedom with the power of the consumer.[16] Under neoliberalism, "capital" (following Marx) represents more than merely economic variables—it is a process that shapes and influences goals, values, ethics, and relationships—it is "an ethic in itself, acting as a guide to all human action."[17] The world of Wilshire Pacific Financial Center thus stands for a constellation of values and ideologies embedded in neoliberalism and dominant notions of progress and success—notions to which Sylvia Ganush falls victim. Those notions are, of course, privileged in capitalist systems; they have no limits or ceilings, but rest on what Anthony Giddens terms "ontological security"—a sense of order and continuity, of routine, based on frameworks of meaning that provide a stable sense of self.[18] As Gullette argues, the security underpinning individual conceptions of progress and success are achieved by various means: "Some acquire this security by agency, some by luck, some by inheritance. Some conceive progress in masculinist metaphors of overcoming less fit adversaries or cruising directly on time's arrow. Some envision it through a version (relevant to their class, race, gender, ableness) of the life-course narrative called 'the American Dream.'"[19] This dream—the belief in the attainment of success—is the glue that informs the construction of the film's narrative world, and also its social critique. Embedded in that dream is the post-recession promotion of unfettered free market activity that defined Reaganomics, where "survival of the fittest" determined success and prosperity.

In particular, Allison Warwick notes that prevailing masculine notions of these concepts bind together the two female characters, as both attempt to navigate a patriarchal culture where competition thrives and weakness (conceived in feminized terms) is held in disdain.[20] Both share an economic background that is marginalized by others—Christine, the rural farm girl, and Ganush, the Romani "gypsy"—and both struggle, and fail, to avoid being defined by it. Christine is a "docile body," one that attempts to change and conform to fit expectations.[21] Early in the film, we see the care with which she manages her appearance, her diction, and her corporate demeanor. Later, we witness as she manages her personal demeanor with equal care, as she attempts to convey her "value" as a partner to Clay's parents. When advised that achieving her aspirations involves making "hard choices," Christine moves away from female-identified traits of empathy, kindness, and nurturing, sacrificing the well-being of the elderly Ganush, and placing self-interest, in the form of job success, over "community" and concern for others. In so doing, however, she is merely following the internal logic of neoliberalism as an organizing principle.

Ganush is an outsider, stigmatized on multiple levels by her ethnicity, appearance, accent, health, and most significantly, her age. Unable to participate successfully in the neoliberalism that drives both the financial institution and the wider culture of which it is a part, she exists on the margins. Even before her emotional outburst, the old woman appears as a disruptive and destabilizing force in the ordered world of the bank (and the wider society it represents) by virtue of her difference. She embodies and exposes some of the very traits that Christine successfully hides. Her poverty is visible in her very presence—not merely in the loan papers that she lacks the education to understand—and acts as a sign of her exclusion from the processes represented by the institution itself.

At the time of its release, ABC News used the film as a catalyst for an article on the moral bankruptcy of the banking industry:

> In the horror flick *Drag Me to Hell*, a promotion-hungry bank loan officer denies an elderly woman who can't make her mortgage payments the extension she so desperately needs. Though the down-on-her-luck homeowner begs and pleads, the young loan officer holds firm.... You can probably guess

where this is going: The creepy elderly woman puts a curse on the loan officer, demons begin lurking around every corner, and people who were just trying to do their jobs die. While the threat of eternal damnation doesn't enter into most workplace decisions, being asked to compromise one's values on the job is something many workers are more than familiar with...[22]

Several scholars have also examined *Drag Me to Hell* and similar films within the framework of morality and the national economy, citing its engagement with the excesses of late capitalism and the dehumanization of the banking industry.[23] The themes of "disruption, abandonment, and takeover" of homes resonate strongly with the lived realities of recession and post-recession audiences, and make these films particularly apt vehicles for social commentary on the national economy. Film scholar Tim Snelson includes films such as *The Haunting in Connecticut* (2009) and *Foreclosure* (2012) in this cluster, which he sees as echoing an earlier cycle of possessed and haunted house narratives released in the late 1970s and mid–1980s.[24] Snelson argues that these home (re)possession cycles reposition the home "as a site of threat, instability and disruption" exposing "the inequalities of recession-era households."[25] As the character through which demonic supernatural forces are introduced in *Drag Me to Hell*, Sylvia Ganush is thus made monstrous because of the socio-economic turmoil she represents. Her advanced age and decrepit state is a signal that she, in fact, is no longer able to participate in the neoliberal processes of the wider world—collateral damage from the cultural logic of capitalism.

Repressed and Oppressed

Robin Wood writes that "one might say that the true subject of the horror genre is the struggle for recognition of all that our civilization *re*presses or *op*presses: its re-emergence dramatized, as in our nightmares, as an object of horror, a matter for terror, the 'happy ending' (when it exists) typically signifying the restoration of repression."[26] While most of the scholarly discussion of *Drag Me to Hell* focuses on Christine and her (in)ability to function under the strictures of a dispassionate male-dominated finance industry without abandoning her female instincts and sensibilities, there is another figure that is equally, or perhaps more, interesting. The aged character of Sylvia Ganush, considered in scholarly literature almost solely for her abject presentation, bears additional thought in light of Wood's observation. In her brief on-screen role in the film, perhaps ten minutes in total, she is arguably the strongest character, male or female, and offers the most pointed social commentary. Ganush is firmly situated in her own identity, even as social forces swirl and change around her. The narrative makes it clear that she is not a recent immigrant—she tells Christine that she has lived in her house for 30 years—yet she embraces her Hungarian identity, in dress, accent, traditions, and belief systems. As a result, she is marginalized, excluded, and also, following Wood, the simultaneous embodiment of both repression and oppression.

While it is certainly the case that she functions as the figure of the "hag" in the film—the catalyst for the horrors that are visited upon Christine and those who try to help her—Ganush is also a signifier of tradition, and of a way of life that has seen and withstood many such shifts in the ways of the world. She represents a thru-line of continuity and durability across place and time, juxtaposed against the world of the film and its focus on youth, commerce, superficiality, and the present moment. The elderly woman serves as a reminder that there was, in fact, a time before the present, and a worldview that embraced values now barely in evidence. It is here that we find Wood's "repressed"—visible only in fleeting points of articulation between the two women when Christine responds authentically to the old woman's plight. In a socio-economic sphere that has given rise to the neoliberal ethic, qualities such as humanity, vulnerability, honor, vengeance, simplicity, trust, groundedness, and interdependence are, indeed, repressed. Barry Keith Grant discusses at length the fears and anxieties of the young urban professional, or "yuppie," in films of the mid to late 1990s (arguably, the period in which *Drag Me to Hell* was written, given Raimi's decade-long hiatus between writing and filming), observing the transformation of classic evil, which I shall expand here to include the "transgressive," from the realm of the supernatural to elements affecting the material and economic spheres.

Citing Marissa Piesman and Marilee Hartley's now-classic text *The Yuppie Handbook*, Grant notes that, for the new generation of upwardly-mobile adults, "aspirations of glory, prestige, recognition, fame, social status, power, money" in any combination "coalesced into a lifestyle, a veritable *weltanschauung*."[27] This shift, highly visible in *Drag Me to Hell*, creates the social and cultural landscape on which the film's horror unfolds. Visually, the film offers a stark contrast between the lifeways of the old generation and the new, not only through disturbing images of the body Sylvia Ganush, as it is juxtaposed with Christine, but also of Ganush's home (and that of Shaun San Dena, as well). Both are dark, run-down, chaotic spaces—gothic reminders of times and worldviews past—intended to be read as places of foreboding, netherworlds of decay tied to knowledge, values, and lifeways which, like their inhabitants, have not only lost relevance but threaten the neoliberal order. All serve as reminders of the economic and moral polarization that is repressed and hidden from view, a hell into which the unsuccessful risk descent, and as a result, are made monstrous.

At the same time, however, the character of Sylvia Ganush is also *oppressed*, and stands for a range of social identities that experienced oppression under neoliberalism. In theory, the emergent class of young urban professionals of the 1990s transcended categories of both race and gender,[28] however, both the economic and ideological realities of recession and post-recession America is that high concentrations of poverty were located among immigrants and people of color, and that the glass ceiling was very much in place, limiting the economic opportunities available to women.[29] April Miller argues that *Drag Me to Hell*, in fact, specifically engages with "the implications of race and class in our relationship with 'others' and the financial fears of the 'average' white, middle-class American family."[30] Miller points to Ganush as a "terror-inducing" stand-in for American fears about immigrant "others," noting the film's use of stereotypes and misconceptions of Romani lifeways and beliefs:

> In Raimi's film, the Hungarian Ganush is identified as a gypsy both by ... stereotypes and the frequent reference to gypsies made during the seances, fortune telling, and sacrificial processes.... Even Ganush's wake becomes a stereotype-laden exposé of Romani culture as numerous ethnicities merge together in a ribald scene of drinking, gambling, and celebration meant to both honor Ganush and terrify the naïve Christine....[31]

Added to this is the deeply-rooted fear of aging—and aging badly—that plagues the young and ambitious. Old bodies like that of Sylvia Ganush, just like her old lifeways, have no place in an industry that thrives on the young. They, like other disempowered minorities, become the uprooted and dispossessed. Ganush experiences a particularly telling form of oppression when, already marginalized, she comes to the Wilshire Pacific Financial Center seeking financial help, and is rendered fully invisible—forcibly removed from the building—as a result of her refusal to accept her fate. Her threat to the neoliberal ethic, via Christine, becomes tangible as the old woman makes physical contact, momentarily erasing the boundaries between their subjectivities.

Conclusion

In the film's resolution, we find one of the least considered, yet most significant, aspects of Raimi's tale of elder horror: Despite the narrative's focus on the status and struggles of young urban professionals, youth does not win out in the end. Although dying early in the film—at the hand of neoliberalism, it is suggested, with Christine acting as its agent—Sylvia Ganush is not the ultimate victim. She is made monstrous not by her advanced age and its attendant, disconcerting ills, but by an economic imperative in which she cannot participate—one that casts her as irresponsible, inconvenient, and disruptive—and so, she returns. Thinking back to Wood's observations on the return of the repressed—"its re-emergence dramatized, as in our nightmares, as an object of horror, a matter for terror"—we see that in her return, the elderly woman has, in fact, transformed and gained power. She physically appears on the screen once more after her death, as Christine digs up her grave to return the cursed button to her decomposing corpse, as merely an object for grotesque comedy, but her power endures throughout the film. Her curse literally breaks down the agents of neoliberalism: Clay, whose family and lifestyle motivated much of Christine's attempts at upward mobility, ends the film alone and in shock after witnessing Christine's horrific death; Stu's career ends in shambles and his final moments on screen reveal the depths of his weakness; and Christine is doomed to spend eternity in hell.

In interviews and production notes, Raimi has categorized the film as a "simple morality tale" in which the protagonist is punished after she makes a choice to "sin." He describes Christine as "a really good girl" who does one bad thing and sets in motion the events that first unravel and then end her life, and damn her soul. He neglects to

Digging up the dead in order to return the cursed button in *Drag Me to Hell*.

mention, however, that Christine's carefully-curated image began to unravel from the moment she met Sylvia Ganush and was confronted with a value system at odds with her aspirations. As the film illustrates, her refusal of an extension to the elderly woman was merely the culmination of a range of decisions leading down the path to perceived socioeconomic success. The director, as Miller observes, universalizes the young loan officer's moral dilemma, suggesting that her desire to "get ahead" makes her just like "anyone else."[32] And here, perhaps, is the film's greatest horror: Raimi's observation is as true today as it was at the time of the film's release nearly a decade ago, and at the time of its writing, a decade before that.

Notes

1. See, for example, Hainmueller and Hopkins, "Public Attitudes Toward Immigration."
2. Miller, "Real-to-Reel"; Grant, "Rich and Strange: The Yuppie Horror Film."
3. More appropriately, a Romani-speaker.
4. Miller, "Real-to-Reel," 33.
5. Garland-Thomson, "Feminist Theory, the Body, and the Disabled Figure."
6. Foucault, *Discipline and Punish*, 25–26; Russo, "Aging and the Scandal of Anachronism," 21.
7. Magistrale, *Abject Terrors*, 6.
8. Shary and McVittie, *Fade to Gray*, 83.
9. Clarke, *Facing Age*, 29.
10. Woodward, *Aging and Its Discontents*, xxvi.
11. See Kristeva, *Powers of Horror*, 4.
12. Shary and McVittie, *Fade to Gray*, 86.
13. See Peter Shelley's *Grande Dame Guignol Cinema* for numerous examples of films with characters who do fit this model.
14. Thompson, "The World According to David Harvey," 23.
15. *Ibid.*
16. David Primrose, "Contesting Capitalism in the Light of the Crisis," 6.
17. Thompson, "The World According to David Harvey," 23.
18. Giddens, *Modernity and Self-Identity*.
19. Guillette, *Aged by Culture*, 18.
20. Allison Warwick, "Damning Discipline," 4–5.
21. Sandra Lee Bartky, "Foucault, Femininity," 71, 81.
22. Micelle Goodman, "Recession Ethics."
23. See, for example, Shary and McVittie, *Fade to Gray*; Boyle and Mrozowski, *Great Recession*; Snelson, "(Re)possession of the American Home"; and Oliete-Aldea, "The Great Recession and Transnational Horror."
24. Snelson, "(Re)possession of the American Home," 161.
25. *Ibid.*, 163.
26. Wood, "An Introduction to the American Horror Film," 201.
27. Grant, "Rich and Strange," 5.
28. *Ibid.*
29. Miller, "Real-to-Reel," 45.
30. *Ibid.*
31. *Ibid.*
32. *Ibid.*, 31.

Bibliography

Bartky, Sandra Lee. "Foucault, Femininity, and the Modernization of Patriarchal Power." *Feminism & Foucault*, ed. Irene Diamond and Lee Quinby, 61–86. Boston: Northeastern University Press, 1988.
Boyle, Kirk, and Daniel Mrozowski. *The Great Recession in Fiction, Film, and Television: Twenty-First-Century Bust Culture*. Lanham, MD: Lexington Books, 2013.
Clarke, Laura Herd. *Facing Age*. Lanham, MD: Rowman & Littlefield, 2011.
Foucault Michel. *Discipline and Punish: The Birth of the Prison*. Trans. Alan Sheridan. London: Penguin, 1977.
Garland-Thomson, Rosemarie. "Feminist Theory, the Body, and the Disabled Figure." *The Disability Studies Reader*, ed. Lennard J. Davis, 279–292. New York: Routledge, 1997.
Giddens, Anthony. *Modernity and Self-Identity: Self and Society in the Late Modern Age*. Stanford: Stanford University Press, 1991.

Goodman, Micelle "Recession Ethics: Dealing With Morally Bankrupt Bosses." *ABC News*, June 25, 2009. https://abcnews.go.com/Business/Economy/story?id=7919449&page=1

Grant, Barry Keith. "Rich and Strange: The Yuppie Horror Film," *Journal of Film and Video (ARCHIVE)* (Spring 1996): 4–16.

Guillette, Margaret Morgan. *Aged by Culture*. Chicago: University of Chicago Press, 2004.

Hainmueller, Jens, and Daniel J. Hopkins. "Public Attitudes Toward Immigration." *Annual Review of Political Science* 17 (2014): 225–249.

Kristeva, Julia. *Powers of Horror: An Essay on Abjection*. New York: Columbia University Press, 1982.

Magistrale, Tony. *Abject Terrors: Surveying the Modern and Postmodern Horror Film*. New York: Peter Lang, 2005.

Miller, April. "Real-to-Reel Recessionary Horrors in *Drag Me to Hell* and *Contagion*." *The Great Recession in Fiction, Film and Television: Twenty-First Century Bust Culture*, ed. Kirk Boyle and Daniel Mrozowski, 29–49. Lanham, MD: Lexington Books, 2013.

Oliete-Aldea, Elena. "The Great Recession and Transnational Horror." *Journal of Popular Culture* 49, no. 5 (2016): 1163–1183.

Primrose, David. "Contesting Capitalism in the Light of the Crisis: A Conversation with David Harvey." *The Journal of Australian Political Economy* 71 (2013): 5–25.

Russo, Mary. "Aging and the Scandal of Anachronism." *Figuring Age: Women, Bodies, Generations*, ed. Kathleen Woodward, 20–33. Bloomington: Indiana University Press, 1999.

Shary, Timothy, and Nancy McVittie. *Fade to Gray: Aging In American Cinema*. Austin: University of Texas Press, 2016.

Shelley, Peter. *Grande Dame Guignol Cinema: A History of Hag Horror from Baby Jane to Mother*. Jefferson, NC: McFarland, 2009.

Snelson, Tim. "The (Re)possession of the American Home: Negative Equity, Gender Inequality, and the Housing Crisis Horror Story." *Gendering the Recession: Media and Culture in an Age of Austerity*, ed. Diane Negra and Yvonne Tasker, 161–180. Durham: Duke University Press, 2014.

Thompson, Michael J. "The World According to David Harvey." *Democratya* 3 (Winter, 2005): 22–27.

Warwick, Allison. "Damning Discipline: Gender, Disability, and the Aging Body in Sam Raimi's *Drag Me to Hell*." Unpublished master's thesis, 2011.

Wood, Robin. "An Introduction to the American Horror Film." *Movies and Methods, Volume 2*, edited by Bill Nichols, 195–219. Berkeley: University of California Press, 1976.

Woodward, Kathleen M. *Aging and Its Discontents: Freud and Other Fictions*. Bloomington: Indiana University Press, 1991.

"Mirror, mirror on the wall, who is the ugliest of them all?"
The Elderly as "Other" in Countess Dracula

JENNIFER RICHARDS

Throughout the history of cinema, depictions of female characters have varied sharply with the characters' age. Lead roles for women in film have, with some limited exceptions, celebrated the youth, positivity, and enthusiasm of the stereotypical female ingénue. Aging female characters have, in contrast, been depicted in largely negative terms, as figures toward whom the audience is expected to be unsympathetic, or even fearful. The age dichotomy is particularly striking in horror films, where younger women are almost invariably cast as sympathetic victims or resourceful heroines, and images of older women as nurturing grandmothers or wise mentors are less common than they are outside the genre. Elderly female characters in horror films are, overwhelmingly, reflections of archetypal figures such as the Hag or the Witch. From the old woman in the bath who propels Danny Torrance into a catatonic state in Stanley Kubrick's *The Shining* (1980) to the terrifying character of Sylvia Ganush in *Drag Me to Hell* (2009), the elderly woman has served only to instill a sense of fear and dread into cinema audiences. Such depictions frame aging women as what Julia Kristeva and Barbara Creed identify as "the Other." The fear and anxiety surrounding the aging process are examples of abjection, defined by both authors as a means of separating "the human from the non-human."[1] Abjection is a state in which the self can experience repulsion from the bodily experience. Kristeva and Creed each use the example of a person viewing a corpse to illustrate their theory. The corpse serves as a reminder of the inevitability of death, and links can be made between this experience and the aging process. While aging is a natural part of our everyday lives, women are encouraged—and often feel pressured—to strive for perfection by preserving their youthful appearance.

Hammer Studios' *Countess Dracula* (1971) explores these conflicts as it engages with the title character's endless search for, and obsession with, youth. Starring Ingrid Pitt as the widowed Countess Elisabeth Nadasdy, it uses beauty as the central theme of its plot, following her character as she accidently finds a way to reverse the aging process, and then goes to horrific extremes to transform herself from a wizened, elderly woman to one who is vivacious, young, and therefore powerful.

Chasing Youth

The film opens with the Countess newly widowed and contemplating the terms of her late husband's will, which leaves half his estate to their daughter Ilona. Angry, she argues with her chambermaid Teri over the temperature of her bathwater, and then—after ordering the girl to peel her a peach—lashes out at her when she drops a piece of the peel on the floor. The Countess' blow causes Teri to gash her own cheek with the knife, and her blood spatters the Countess' face. She wipes it away, but is astonished to discover, the next morning, that the skin touched by it is once again taut and youthful. Grasping the possibilities opened up by this discovery, the Countess sets out to obtain more blood by any means necessary. She kills Teri and, after bathing in the girl's blood, transforms herself into a radiant young woman. She takes only Julie, the castle nurse, and Captain Dobi, the castle steward who is also her longtime secret lover, into her confidence, and they reluctantly agree to help her maintain the illusion.

The Countess (Ingrid Pitt), transformed from old age to youth after bathing in the blood of virgins in *Countess Dracula* (1971).

Ilona—absent from the castle for 13 years during her education in Vienna—is scheduled to return the next morning, now a young woman of 19. The Countess, infatuated with her newfound youthfulness and unwilling to be upstaged by her own daughter, devises an audacious plan. She arranges for Ilona to be abducted from her carriage before reaching the castle, and to be held prisoner in the remote cottage of the castle's mute gamekeeper. When dinnertime arrives, the Countess makes a grand entrance, presenting *herself* as Ilona and attracting the attention of a handsome young army officer, Lieutenant Imre Toth, whose father served alongside the Count years before. The Countess' ruse, initially successful, soon turns complicated. She spends two nights in Imre's bed, but on the second morning finds that she has reverted to her true, elderly state. She flees from him, desperate for more blood to restore her youth, and Julie obliges by bringing her a gypsy dancer from a travelling circus performing in the nearby village. Youthful again, the Countess resumes her pursuit of Imre, and a pattern is established in which Julie supplies the Countess with a steady stream of fresh victims. Imre and "Ilona" fall deeper in love, and begin to contemplate marriage, even as an increasingly jealous Captain Dobi tries to drive them apart in order to have the Countess for himself.

Even as her wedding day approaches, however, the Countess' situation grows increasingly unstable. The rejuvenation treatments become less effective over time, and maintaining her youth demands the butchery of a steady stream of young women, which Count Dobi procures for her from among the castle's large staff of servants. The castle librarian, Grand Master Fabio, begins to suspect the truth, and Dobi has him killed, leading the Chief Bailiff to seal the castle and send its servant girls away until the serial murderer who preys on them can be apprehended. Cut off from her usual source of victims, the Countess begs Dobi to find her a girl, which he does—bringing her the real Ilona, who has broken out of the gamekeeper's cottage and escaped into the countryside. Having accepted the smitten Imre's proposal of marriage, the Countess plans to murder Ilona—both for her blood, and for the opportunity to permanently assume her identity.

Loyal to Ilona, who she raised from birth to age six, Julie turns against her mistress and makes plans to smuggle the girl to safety. She enlists the aid of Imre—to whom Captain Dobi, stung by the Countess' rejection of him, has spitefully revealed her true identity and appearance—and they free Ilona on the morning of the wedding. The plan initially goes smoothly, but Ilona impulsively turns back to catch a glimpse of her unnaturally youthful mother at the altar. At that moment, in the midst of the ceremony, the latest rejuvenation treatment wears off, and the Countess reverts to her true, elderly appearance. She lunges at her daughter with a knife in her hand, determined to draw the blood that will make her young again. Imre jumps between them and, to her horror, the Countess slays him instead of Ilona. The final scene shows her being hauled away to prison, derided by the townspeople as "Countess Dracula."

The Anxiety of Aging

When we are first introduced to the Countess, she is dressed in black mourning clothes with a high collar and large black hat, her body secreted under layers of fabric and her face covered by a veil. The audience's view of her is thus obscured; close-up shots provide glimpses, but we cannot clearly see her face. In the next scene, her veil has been removed and her pale wrinkled skin, covered in the stereotypical signs of aging, is revealed.

The same scene establishes that the Countess' interest has been piqued by Imre, who is named as a beneficiary in the will. The film thus sets up the pursuit of a handsome and desirable young man by a sexually aggressive, but much older, woman: a trope with a history reaching back to Chaucer's "Wife of Bath's Tale." The Wife of Bath, in telling her version of the story, presents the old woman's desire as absurd, and her pursuit of a much younger man as farcical. She does so, however, in the service of a moral story about women's deepest desire being sovereignty over their husbands. *Countess Dracula*, on the other hand, presents the title character's desire as grotesque, her pursuit of Imre as horrifying, and her story as bereft of any redeeming moral.

The Countess, like the old woman in Chaucer's tale, is subject to rejection and humiliation, but she also suffers from physical decline, becoming more haggard and fragile as the story unfolds. Once she has discovered the secret of regeneration, the physical borders separating self and "Other" begin to break down and her sense of identity becomes increasingly unstable. In her attempt to arrest the natural processes of degeneration and decay, the film suggests, she has created new forms of instability and disorder in their place. As her transformations from old age to youth grow more frequent, she becomes progressively more grotesque each time she returns to her natural state. In turn, her anxiety and desperation build as the story progresses. The slightest possibility that she might return to her true, aged form becomes abhorrent to her.

This anxiety is depicted in two scenes that involve the Countess sleeping. In the first, she has a nightmare in which she has returned to her elderly appearance. She wakes with a start, throwing her hands up to her face in order to check that it is still youthful. Only after reassuring herself that her appearance is unchanged does she settle back to sleep, confident that it was just a dream. At the same moment, the film cuts to a scene of Imre in bed with Zizi, a prostitute from the local tavern who he brings back to his chambers in the castle after a night of drinking, encouraged by the jealous Captain Dobi. This juxtaposition serves to validate the Countess' fears that, if she loses her youthful beauty, she will be rejected by Imre and her position in his life will be usurped by another woman.

The Countess' anxiety is deepened by her growing awareness that the rejuvenating effects of the blood are not only temporary, but come at a steadily escalating price. With each transformation, her face becomes more lined and drawn, her drooping skin more exaggerated, and her moles more prevalent. Warts and other marks frequently appear after her transformations, often in the center of her face, between her eyebrows, and around her mouth. Her original, aged state thus becomes—like the portrait that Oscar Wilde's character Dorian Gray keeps hidden in his attic—a mirror of her soul, its increasingly horrific appearance a reflection of the murderous deeds she has committed. The more decrepit her aged self becomes, the deeper she is pushed into the realm of the abject, intensifying her self-revulsion and redoubling her determination to keep old age at bay.

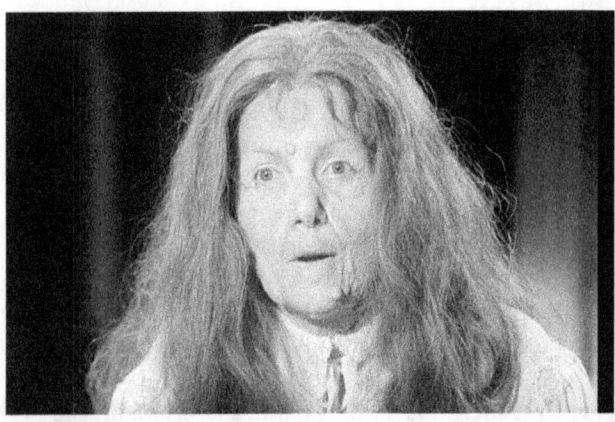

Covered with warts and wrinkles, the Countess (Ingrid Pitt) becomes abject as the effects of the virginal blood dissipate in *Countess Dracula*.

Her body's inability to remain youthful without regular blood treatments means that the possibility of reversion is ever-present. The Countess is continually vulnerable, therefore, to the collapse—at any time, and without warning—of her carefully constructed illusions, and the new life she has founded on them. She is terrified by the possibility that she will be seen in her true form and so lose Imre's love. The inevitable moment of collapse occurs, tellingly, in the final scene, when the Countess is on the verge of attaining her goal by marrying Imre. As the wedding reaches its conclusion, her happiness dissolves into horror as she transforms back to her original state. The audience does not see the transformation, but the priest's horrified reaction to the sight of her face reveals everything they need to know.

The final scene reinforces Gary Smith's argument that the film works on the "grimmest" of levels, acting as a cautionary tale about women's anxiety over aging and the resulting obsession with youth[2] The Countess takes these tendencies to monstrous extremes; she becomes more desperate, and "descends deeper into madness," as the effects of the blood ritual become progressively weaker, more costly, and ultimately unsustainable. *Countess Dracula* thus embraces the recurring horror-genre trope of the aging woman as not merely grotesque, but monstrous and ultimately—in her "unnatural" desire to hold onto youth at all costs—evil.

The Countess Reflected

Images of the Countess in mirrors and other reflective surfaces are a recurring motif throughout the film, but only in scenes where she can see herself. In one instance, she is awakened by the sound of a wolf outside her open window. She gets up from her bed and goes to close the window, only to see her "true" elderly self, reflected in the window pane. The camera creates a range of close-up shots that distort her appearance, exaggerating the shape of her face and stretching out her features within the frame. In another scene, after professing to Imre that she is in love with him, she again sees herself reflected in a mirror as an elderly woman. The cumulative effect of these images is to emphasize her grotesque appearance and encourage the audience to react to her elderly face with disgust. It is important to note than when the Countess views her reflection in her unnatural, blood-enhanced state, it is *only* the reflection that changes, her physical self is still transformed, youthful and beautiful.

This trope of mirrors revealing the truth about characters has been used throughout fairy tales and other fantastic fiction. In the tale of Snow White, for example, the Wicked Queen asks if she is the fairest in the land, and the mirror's response that she is no longer the fairest—underscored by her knowledge that the mirror is unable to lie—sets the story in motion. The link between the Countess' increasingly grotesque face and her ever-lengthening series of crimes suggest that the mirrors and mirror-like surfaces in *Countess Dracula* play a similar role, reminding her of her corrupt spirit as well as her age-ravaged body, and underscoring the depths to which she has sunk to satisfy her vanity. Like Dorian Gray's portrait, they remind her of a reality that she can barely bring herself to acknowledge, speaking the truth so forcefully that she often averts her eyes from them before she can glimpse it. The distortions that she glimpses in mirrors are, moreover, not random. Reflections lengthen her chin to a point, alter her other features, and emphasize her increasingly numerous warts and boils. These distortions do not just twist her beauty into wizened ugliness, but also transform her into the stereotypical image of the Witch: "speaking truth" not only by revealing her real physical self—old, ugly and undesirable— but also by revealing the darkness that has overtaken her soul.

The Countess and Abjection

The Countess' fear of aging stems not just from her determination to remain desirable—able to compete with younger women like Ilona for the attentions of men like Imre—but from aging's association with decay, abjection, and death. Monstrous in her selfishness, she condemns others to (unnatural) death in order to postpone her own (natural) one. The threat of death is ever-present in *Countess Dracula*, and corpses—the ultimate symbol of abjection[3]—are ubiquitous throughout the film. The story begins with the death of one of the Countess' own peasants, who clings to the side of her open carriage as it passes through his village, pleading for her aid. The Countess remains silent and unresponsive behind her veil, even as one of her courtiers smashes the man's fingers—

causing him to fall and be crushed to death by the wheels of the carriage. The Countess and her entourage drive on, leaving the man's distraught family standing over his motionless body at the wayside. The subsequent murders, though equally callous, are more deliberate and self-centered: part of the Countess' increasingly desperate campaign to gather the blood she needs to sustain her youthful looks.

The next corpse shown on screen is that of the belly dancer, which is found in the woods by two young boys. She is stripped to the waist and very pale, as if to emphasize her lack of blood. There is nothing to link the death to the Countess, however, as the discovery is made outside of the castle walls. The third corpse is that of Zizi, the prostitute employed by Captain Dobi to seduce Imre away from the Countess. Having watched the initial phase of his plan succeed, and knowing that the Countess is desperate for her next "offering," Dobi takes Zizi from the unconscious Imre's bed to the Countess' chambers. His plan, however, quickly goes awry. Zizi is killed (off-screen), her wrist slit, and her blood drained into a large metal bowl for the Countess' use, but it has no rejuvenating effect. Primly informed by Grand Master Fabio, the castle's resident scholar, that only the blood of virgins will do, the enraged Countess berates Dobi for his failure in bringing her "a common whore."

We next see Zizi's body after Imre discovers the Countess in the act of bathing in her blood. Angered by her discovery, she throws open a cupboard door, revealing the prostitute's corpse, naked and pale. In life, Zizi's exposed flesh served as a reminder of the youthful qualities the Countess herself no longer naturally possessed: firm body, unblemished face, and unwrinkled skin. In death, however, her nakedness makes her pitiable—deprived of the vibrant life that she exhibited in the tavern, and in Imre's bed—rather than desirable. Nakedness also underscores Zizi's now-abject nature. Where Imre (and, the film implies, numerous other men) once sought eagerly to uncover it, cultural convention now demands that it be covered, lest the sight of a corpse disturb those still living by reminding them of their own mortality. The Countess, obsessively aware of *her* own mortality, and rendered indifferent to the abject by her constant association with blood and corpses, has no time for such niceties. In death as in life, Zizi is, for her, a thing to be used.

The presence of Zizi's corpse within the Countess' chambers thus becomes, for her, not a horrifying intrusion but an opportunity. When Imre—aware of, and repulsed by, her secret after Dobi's intervention—threatens to break off the marriage he impulsively proposed, she reminds him that *he* was the last person with whom Zizi was seen alive, and that the girl shared his bed on the night she was killed. If he tries to leave her, the Countess explains, she will make certain that he is blamed for her murder, and (presumably) those of the other servant girls. The furtiveness the Countess exhibits earlier in the story—ordering Dobi to smuggle the body of the gypsy dancer out of the castle and dispose of it in the woods—has given way to boldness. Now confident in her own power over the situation, and inured to the presence of the abject, she is comfortable secreting the corpse in her own rooms within the palace, undisturbed by either disgust or the threat of discovery. The boundaries between the ordinary and the abject have, in the Countess' world, completely collapsed at this point, just as her true, aged self has—in her mind—become one with the abject. Determined to create distance between herself and the abjection she sees within her, she embraces abjection in the day-to-day physical world, unaware (or perhaps uncaring) that doing so renders her monstrous in the eyes of others.

The final corpse revealed in the film is that of the Countess' first victim: her chambermaid, Teri. She is discovered amongst a mound of corpses of nameless young women in the castle's wine cellar, each of them—like those discovered earlier—naked and drained of blood. The only corpse to escape this treatment is that of Grand Master Fabio, who the Countess eliminates in order to keep her actions a secret. His middle-aged male body, useless to her, is discovered fully clothed, hanging in his own library.

Although abjection is primarily discussed in terms of physical objects, such as corpses, Creed notes that it can also occur when "individuals fail to respect the law," or when a protagonist becomes "a hypocrite, traitor or liar."[4] The use of deception and manipulation in *Countess Dracula*, therefore, can be as potent a form of abjection as the victim's corpse. Throughout the film, the Countess deceives a variety of characters in order to keep her blood rituals a secret. She uses her transformed young body to entice and bewitch those around her into colluding with her and her evil plans. In her youthful state, her beauty enables her to prey on Captain Dobi's desire, harbored for the past 20 years, by persuading him to conspire with her and aid her plot. He helps to supply her with a steady stream of fresh, virginal young women to help to satisfy her constant need for blood, and is instrumental in organizing—at her orders—the abduction of her own daughter. He believes that by facilitating the Countess' plan he will win her favor, but the opposite is true. After Captain Dobi realizes that the Countess has cheated him, and her real goal is to woo Imre, he goes to her rooms and finds her in her chamber in her elderly state. In his anger, he mocks her, conveying his disgust at the sight of her old and withered body. She begs for his affection, but he spurns her, declaring that he does not want to make love to her, "like two old fools fumbling at each other."

The Countess revels in the fact that, after her transformation back to a youthful woman, she can pass herself off as her own daughter, threatening to erase Ilona's identity, and even her very existence in the process. Her actions and her ultimate goal—to seduce and eventually marry Imre—suggest that she is driven by her lust for power and her obsession with retaining control of her world. The antithesis of the culturally approved process of "aging gracefully," these qualities are traditionally considered unseemly, even grotesque, when displayed by the elderly. The absence of motherly instincts toward her daughter underscores her selfish nature and monstrous ego. Ilona figures in the film *only* as a pawn in the Countess' scheme, and—though she is discussed by many different characters—does not appear until after the Countess' discovery of the ability to reverse her aging process.

The Countess' relationship to Ilona adds another dimension to the use of abjection in the film. Creed's interpretation of the abject frames the mother's body as "a site of conflicting desires,"[5] and Kristeva argues that in order to authenticate her daughter's existence, a mother will seek to keep a tight hold over her child. Abjection becomes a "precondition of narcissism."[6] That which threatens the traditional borders between mother and child is considered abject as it threatens stability and order, yet a Mother's refusal to let go of her child also creates an environment which becomes corrupted and symbolically unclean. At the beginning of the film, Ilona has been in Vienna, isolated from the castle, for most of her life. In Kristeva's view, she has physically broken away from the grasp of her mother, and so, is free. With the Count now absent in death, the Countess is able to control her, yet simultaneously facilitates her being "lost" as she organizes Ilona's abduction. and imprisonment. When at last Ilona does attain her freedom, she is almost immediately made a captive again, this time in the castle (where she awaits her fate as the

Countess' intended next victim). This final act of desperation—the ultimate expression of her determination to preserve her youth at any cost—represents the bottom of the Countess' long downward spiral into evil.

Blood Rituals

Elisabeth Bathory, the real-life figure on whom *Countess Dracula* was based, was said to have killed over 600 women in order to bathe in their blood.[7] She was eventually convicted of killing 80 women, leaving hundreds more victims unaccounted for. The implications of the film's title aside, the Countess' vampirism thus hovers between the literal and the symbolic. Traditional vampires nourish and sustain their bodies through the physical acts of biting victims and drinking their blood. She drains the blood of her victims in order to sustain herself and renew her aging body, and, though blood may not *literally* give her life, it unquestionably gives her the ability to live life on the terms that she wishes. While the Countess obtains her victims' blood by slicing their wrists rather than biting their necks, her character still falls firmly within this vampiric tradition. The film's promotional lobby cards played up the Countess' insatiable desire for blood, proclaiming: "BLOOD. The more she drinks, the prettier she gets. The prettier she gets, the thirstier she gets."

The Countess' use of blood rituals further heightens the horrors of the body, and of the process of aging. As in other aspects of her life, the Countess draws closer to objects from which others recoil in horror. She murders several women in cold blood. Her sexual desires, and openness in pursuing them, are heightened to the point of being socially unacceptable for a woman of her station. The discovery of Zizi's lifeless corpse shocks Imre, and the Countess takes pleasure in his shock, mocking his naiveté. The unsustainability of her hunger, and its effects on her actions, set her apart from traditional vampires whose need for blood is constant, but stable. Provided they are able to satisfy their thirst for blood, traditional vampires enjoy immortality, eternal youth (in many versions of the lore) and thus a sense of stability. The Countess, however, knows no such comfort. The temporality of the rejuvenation process, and the diminishing time that the blood rituals allow her to spend in her youthful state, make her life inherently *un*stable. Rather than being rendered immortal by the consumption of her victims' blood, she uses it in an increasingly desperate attempt to buy a temporary respite from her inescapable mortality—a mortality of which she is reminded by every glance at her reflection.

Kristeva emphasizes the notion that abjection can be relative, and this is reflected in the characters of Julie, Dobi and Imre. Neither Julie nor Dobi, who spend their days in the Countess' service and are committed to meeting her needs, is visibly disquieted by the Countess' incessant need for blood. Exposure to the abject has, for them, become normalized—a routine part of day-to-day life—ceasing to produce the conventional horrified reaction. Imre, an outsider from another part of the realm, comes to the castle with his morality and innocence intact. The Countess' blood rituals are as strange to him as they are to the audience, and his immersion in the abject produces the traditional responses: revulsion and recoil. The turning point for Imre comes when Captain Dobi forces him to enter the Countess' rooms and see his fiancé in "all her glory"—an act calculated to reveal her secret and thus drive Imre away. Faced with the naked Countess covered in the blood of one of her victims, the young man responds with horror. The encounter, and his reaction, also underscores the extent to which the Countess' behavior has collapsed the distance between true self and Other. Caught unaware and surprised by her lover—naked, vulnerable and saturated in blood—she becomes instantly, crushingly aware of her own abjection, for reasons that have little to do with her aged appearance.

This scene of abjection is intensified by the connection between these elements and the bleeding woman as motif. Bodily fluids such as menstrual blood leave the body and are no longer part of the "self." Creed defines this abjection as the "gaping wound," and links the anxiety induced by it to the male fear of castration.[8] The bleeding-woman motif is a staple of horror cinema, most famously in *Carrie* (1976), where the literal blood-bath that triggers the title character's transformation from a bullied teenager into a rampaging monster is linked both symbolically and literally to menstrual blood. Captain Dobi, like Carrie's tormentors, carefully exploits his victim's sense of vulnerability, violating the Countess' sanctuary and positioning Imre to encounter her when she is at her most abject. The encounter—as Dobi intendeds—permanently destroys Imre's love for the Countess. He can no longer see her as an object of desire—only as "the bleeding woman." Once a vigorous suitor pursuing an attractive, desirable woman whom he actively sought to marry, Imre becomes a powerless male spectator who now sees his impending marriage to her not as a triumph, but as a trap.

The scene is also interesting because it includes repetitions of lines spoken, earlier in the film, between the Countess and Imre. When Imre meets the Countess for the first time in her true, elderly form, he asks for Ilona's hand in marriage, unaware that the "Ilona" he met was the Countess herself in her youthful disguise. The proposal scene closes with the Countess uttering the words "my son," which are repeated at the end of the discovery scene, with Imre now aware of the significance of the Countess' blood rituals, but no longer able to escape under the threat of blackmail.[9] The Countess repeats the words "my son" to him, but the words are now reframed by the new context and his knowledge of her abhorrent crimes. Imre is thus rendered symbolically impotent—his desire and his agency both withered.

Blood in horror film may be a physical sign of the abject but, as Kristeva argues, the function of sacred ritual is to allow the purification process to occur.[10] Ritualistic behaviors are used to cleanse the soul by purging the abject from the physical realm. In the Christian ceremony of communion, for example, wine that represents the symbolic "blood of Christ" washes away sins of those who partake of it—a symbolic echo, for believers, of the way in which Christ's literal shedding of blood at the Crucifixion redeemed believers from original sin. Christian hymns similarly use "washed in the blood of the Lamb" (that is, of Christ, "the Lamb of God") as a metaphor for redemption.[11] The Countess enacts that metaphor in a horrifically literal way: bathing in blood of innocent, virginal young women. Far from participating in a selfless act of sacrifice like that symbolized by Christian blood rituals, however, her "redemption" is purely personal and entirely selfish—the ultimate act of taking, rather than giving. Even the goals that she sinks into abject evil in order to pursue are, in the context of Christianity's traditional exaltation of the eternal and disdain for the temporal, base and trivial. She seeks not redemption and eternal life for her immortal soul, but perfection and eternal youth for her all-too-fragile body.

Conclusion

The final scene of the film shows the Countess behind prison bars. The people of the village taunt her with names like "devil woman" and "Countess Dracula," deriding her as unworthy and unholy. This marks her as a classic example of the evil older woman in cinema, drawn into corruption and degradation by her own selfish needs and desires.

The Countess' desperation is, indeed, fueled by her narcissistic tendencies. We are aware of her desire for Imre from the opening scene, and when she is granted, by accident, the means to fulfill those desires and return herself to a youthful and beautiful state, she seizes it enthusiastically. Pursuing her goal without regard for the consequences, she spirals downward into desperation and madness until the imprisonment and murder of her own daughter becomes, in her mind, not only conceivable but desirable.

The theme of vanity, and the demonization of women—especially older women—who are consumed by it plays a central role in many classic fairy tales, such as the Brothers Grimm's "Snow Drop" and Hans Christian Anderson's "The Red Shoes." Trying too hard to attain and maintain beauty is, in the moral universe of fairy tales, tantamount to refusing to abide by the laws of Nature and therefore inherently evil. *Countess Dracula* transposes that idea into horror cinema, adding Hammer Studios' trademark emphasis on blood, murder, and sexuality. Life and death are inevitable—aging will catch up with us all, eventually, no matter *how* far we are willing to go to in our vain attempts to escape it.

Notes

1. Creed, "Horror and the Monstrous Feminine," 69.
2. Smith, *Uneasy Dreams*, 56.
3. Creed, "Horror and the Monstrous Feminine," 70.
4. Ibid.
5. Ibid., 72.
6. Kristeva, *Powers of Horror*, 13.
7. Smith, *Vampires Films of the 1970s*, 63.
8. Ibid., 73.
9. If he breaks the engagement, the Countess coldly informs him, she will ensure that he is blamed for the murder of Zizi the prostitute, with whom he was seen drinking in the tavern the night she disappeared.
10. Kristeva, *Powers of Horror*, 17.
11. The phrase is a reference to Revelation 7:14.

Bibliography

Creed, Barbara. "Horror and the Monstrous Feminine: An Imaginary Abjection." *Screen* 27, no. 1 (1986): 44–71.
Kristeva, Julia. *Powers of Horror: An Essay on Abjection*. New York: Columbia University Press, 1984.
Smith, Gary. *Uneasy Dreams: The Golden Age of British Horror Films, 1956–1976*, 2nd rev. ed. Jefferson, NC: McFarland, 2006.
Smith, Gary. *Vampires Films of the 1970s: Dracula to Blacula and Every Fang Between*. Jefferson, NC: McFarland, 2016.

Old and in the Way
Torments of the Aging Male in Psycho II

HANS STAATS

In the film *Psycho II* (1983), the cinematic presentation of aging and horror poses new questions about our complex relationship with the aged, whose role as keepers of wisdom and experience is simultaneously intriguing and unsettling. In *Psycho II*, like *Psycho* (1960) before it, the representation of youth as a time that is unfettered by the limitations of senescence intersects with the figure of the aged psychopath as a portal to unexpected—even unimaginable—powers that illuminate a terrifying time of reckoning with past sins. More specifically, Norman Bates (Anthony Perkins) in *Psycho II* is a middle-aged man tormented by the past and struggling to find his place in contemporary society; he is a man who has grown out of, and back into, an obsession with murder and mayhem.

In this essay, I examine the cultural function of the figure of the aged male sociopath in the modern horror film. In *Psycho II*, the return of Norman Bates complicates the distinction between the normal and the pathological, specifically regarding the conflict between Norman, Lila Loomis (Vera Miles), sister of Marion Crane (Janet Leigh), and Lila's daughter Mary Samuels, played by Meg Tilly.[1] Ultimately, *Psycho II* is a horror film sequel that manages to effectively expand upon Alfred Hitchcock's *Psycho* by focusing on the internal conflict of the aged male psycho killer. Returning to the scene of the crime, Norman—after his release from the mental hospital at the beginning of *Psycho II*—makes his way back to the Bates Motel and the loving arms of the monstrous-feminine by film's end.[2]

The cultural function of the figure of the maniac is, to borrow from Robin Wood, the dramatization of the conceptual duality of the repressed and the other. Indeed, the figure of the madman in *Psycho II* underscores the idea that "the true subject of the horror genre is the struggle for recognition of all that our civilization *represses* or *oppresses*: its re-emergence dramatized, as in our nightmares, as an object of horror, a matter for terror, the 'happy ending' (when it exists) typically signifying the restoration of repression."[3] Building upon Wood's introduction to the modern horror film, I propose that the question of aging is fundamental to the cinematic presentation of elder horror, in which the fear of growing old takes on fantastic proportions. Regarding *Psycho II*, the return of the middle-aged male psychopath represents a unique opportunity to examine the intersection of age, gender and genre.

Norman (Anthony Perkins) goes against the grain in *Psycho II* (1983).

Aging in Psycho II *and the Modern Horror Film*

At the time of its release, Alfred Hitchcock's *Psycho* illuminated the strict conservatism of Cold War America and how it was acutely out of touch with the concept of adolescence both as a life stage and a determining factor in Hollywood's postwar marketing strategy and theatrical production. Thomas Doherty argues that moviemakers, acknowledging the "rise of television and the collapse of the old studio system," focused on "the one group with the requisite income, leisure, and gregariousness to sustain a theatrical business. The courtship of the teenage audience began in earnest in 1955; by 1960, the romance was in full bloom."[4]

Channeled through Elvis Presley, James Dean, and the musical score of *Blackboard Jungle* (1955) is, David Thompson argues, "a sense of emotional anger and brooding violence" intersected with a "curdled humanism" that was celebrated in films like *Double Indemnity* (1944) and *Sunset Boulevard* (1950).[5] According to Thompson, "the peeling away of 'Hollywood' nonsense" prepared the way for characters like Norman Bates and the cultural capital of the postwar American adolescent.[6] Taking the same line of argument further, the emergence of the juvenile delinquent as a cultural figure in the mid- to late 1950s signals the emergence of the modern horror film, populated, according to Adam Lowenstein, by "frighteningly human monsters whose carnage is depicted through graphic violence."[7]

Typically, the difference between the classic and modern horror film is understood in terms of formal change. Yet as Lowenstein points out, a strictly formalist interpretation of the classic and modern horror film tends to overlook the political and historical dimensions of horror.[8] Scholarly efforts to position the horror genre within a genealogy or taxonomy of monsters and graphic acts of violence overlook the question of *why* horror shifts from one phase or modality to another.[9] The importance of Robin Wood's interpretation, then, is that he deviates from the pioneering work of previous scholars, which was more concerned with a descriptive history of horror film and literature.[10]

The gothic and scientific worlds of *Dracula* (1931) and *Frankenstein* (1931) for example, both differ from Hitchcock's *Psycho* in terms of formal change—their fantastic characters are replaced by a frighteningly human monster and more elaborately staged acts of violence. Yet what truly distinguishes *Psycho* from the Universal horrors of *Dracula* and *Frankenstein* is the childhood trauma of Norman Bates.[11] Throughout his life, Norman is defined by a formative personal experience rather than a supernatural or mythological etiology.

The cinematic presentation of the male psychopath in relation to the dominant ideology of postwar American prosperity is vital to *Psycho* and the emergence of the modern horror film. Regarding the horror of aging in particular, Robin Wood's distinction between the child*like* and child*ish* is especially helpful when considering the historical and cultural context of *Psycho II*. In his book *Hollywood from Vietnam to Reagan*, Wood examines the connection between films like *E.T. The Extraterrestrial* (1982), the *Star Wars* series, *Raiders of the Lost Ark* (1981) and *Star Trek II: The Wrath of Khan* (1982), arguing that they used the figure of the child to "paper the cracks" created by the cultural anxieties of the Reagan Era: nuclear warfare, evil non–Americans, liberated women and the fear that democratic capitalism may not be cleanly separable from Fascism.[12]

According to Wood, the success of the above-mentioned films "is only comprehensible when one assumes a widespread *desire* for regression to infantilism, or a populace who wants to be constructed as mock children."[13] Wood argues that the films of the Reagan Era are distinguished by "the urge to evade responsibility—responsibility for actions, decisions, thought, responsibility for changing things" via the sentimental figure of the child who does "not have to be responsible, there are older people to look after them."[14] Indeed, Wood's interpretation of the modern horror film illuminates the conceptual uncertainty of the normal and the pathological in *Psycho II* at a time (1980–1989) when the dominant ideology sought to maintain a sentimental view of the nuclear family that was timeless and inviolable.

Wood, more than any scholar referred to here, is responsible for taking up the question of the cultural function of aging in the modern horror film. In his essay "An Introduction to the American Horror Film," Wood aligns the child with the figure of the monster as "the true subject of the horror genre."[15] According to Wood, the monster represents "the struggle for recognition of all that our civilization *represses* or *oppresses*: its re-emergence dramatized, as in our nightmares, as an object of horror, a matter of terror."[16] Repression was a cultural condition of the Reagan Era, and Wood's argument that "the repression of the sexuality of children ... from the denial of the infant's nature as sexual being to the veto on the expression of sexuality before marriage" is vital to understanding the figure of the male sociopath in *Psycho* and *Psycho II*. This is a point that I will return to in the following section.

Psycho II has received far less critical attention than *Psycho*—the result of Wood's distinction between the progressive and reactionary horror films of the 1970s and '80s and his valorization of the former. The progressive horror films of the '70s—Wood cites Wes Craven's *The Last House on the Left* (1972), Tobe Hooper's *The Texas Chain Saw Massacre* (1974), and Romero's *Dawn of the Dead* (1978) as examples—are imbued with a sense of social and political activism, specifically the fight against patriarchal capitalism. Horror in the '80s, on the other hand, reinforces the dominant ideology, representing the monster as simply evil and unsympathetic, depicting Christianity as a positive presence and confusing the repression of sexuality with sexuality itself. Wood's examples of the latter include Craven's *Swamp Thing* (1982), Hooper's *Poltergeist* (1982) and Romero's *Creepshow* (1982).[17] Carol Clover's analysis of gender in the modern horror film reinforced these ideas, while inspiring a new wave of feminist studies and a renewed political and historical engagement with the horror film by like-minded scholars.[18]

The above-mentioned distinction between the progressive and reactionary horror film is, however, incomplete, specifically in its implication that Norman's midlife crisis in *Psycho II* is less dramatically impactful than the image of the juvenile delinquent in *Psycho*. *Psycho II* is not a superior film to Hitchcock's 1960 masterpiece, but I propose that *Psycho II* is a frequently overlooked exemplar of the modern horror film and the cinematic presentation of aging and horror.

Building upon Wood's interpretation of the modern horror film, the question of aging is fundamental to the cinematic presentation of elder horror, specifically in terms of the frighteningly human monster and the aged male psychopath. For Wood, the gesture toward a political categorization of the horror film is typically embodied by the monster as a human psychotic or schizophrenic struggling for recognition within the single unifying master-figure of the family.[19] Likewise, Peter Hutchings and Andrew Tudor discriminate between the classic and modern horror film based upon the viewpoint that the quality of horror is closely associated with the movement from the otherworldly to everyday.[20] Indeed, the cinematic presentation of the aged madman in *Psycho II* possesses many of the characteristics of the progressive horror film—a point to which I will return.

The reason that *Psycho* and *Psycho II* still speak to us after all these years is that the figure of the aged sociopath is one of most compelling images in horror film and media. Norman Bates is a figure that speaks to a sense of moral ambiguity that overturns the facile distinction between the metaphysical categories of good and evil. By complicating the difference between the normal and the pathological, the psycho killer has captured the popular imagination and proven that the horror of aging is fundamental both to the emergence and the continuing development of the modern horror film.

What's Mother Got to Do with It: The Horror of Aging in Psycho II

The deep cultural impact of Hitchcock's *Psycho* has given the figure of the male sociopath a vital dimension of modern consciousness: rebelling against—or disturbing the difference between—the normal and the pathological. The question of whether Norman Bates is mentally stable has captured the popular imagination since *Psycho*'s initial release, and established itself as a cornerstone of the modern horror film. Norman, both as an adolescent and middle-aged man, is a frighteningly human monster, if not the outward embodiment of normality and innocence.[21] He is, in *Psycho II* in particular, wrapped in an overwhelmingly romantic notion of innocence—the perfect camouflage to blot out the monster that lurks within.[22] Hence the moral ambiguity of the figure of the madman is defined in terms of the braided, rather than discrete, identities of killer and victim.

The issue of age and its relationship to the human lifespan is incredibly important in *Psycho II*. As a middle-aged man, Norman is positioned between life and death— caught between the age of an American teenager and that of his elderly (and now deceased) mother. The problem posed by Norman's age and developmental stability is reinforced by the condition of the Bates Motel and the Victorian-style Bates home that stands above and beyond it. The motel was, even in 1960, a slightly seedy roadside motor inn located along a once-busy highway that was beginning to be eclipsed—along with countless others like it—by the emergence of the still-new interstate highway system. Decades later, with the interstate network long since complete, the Bates Motel is an emblem of the collateral damage done to small-town businesses by the federal government in the name of "progress." Worn and faded, invisible to passing travelers, the Bates Motel has little chance of prospering as a family business; modern life has passed it by, leaving it moribund, and Norman—like the workers displaced by the deregulated capitalism of the Reagan years—stranded in a cultural and economic backwater without the opportunity to go elsewhere or the means to begin again.

This point is underscored by Norman's replacement as motel manager, Warren Toomey (Dennis Franz). Unlike Norman, Toomey has allowed the Bates Motel to become a den of iniquity where locals pay by the hour to party with illegal drugs and openly engage in illicit sex. There is, he believes, no way to make a living at the now rundown property without turning a blind eye to the activities of its desperate, dissolute customers, a business model that Norman refuses to endorse. The difference between the strait-laced Norman and the morally compromised Toomey is evident in their appearance. Norman is clean-cut, well-spoken, and presentably dressed in clothes that draw attention to his tall lean frame. Toomey, on the other hand, is a corpulent, foul-mouthed, chain-smoker with disheveled clothes, greasy long hair, and a short temper.

In a halfhearted attempt to break free of the libidinal economy of the Bates Motel, Norman takes a job as a cook's helper at Statler's Café.[23] Located down the road from the Bates Motel, Statler's is—like the motel itself—a forgotten place of business located on a lost highway far from the interstate. Its proprietor, Ralph Statler (Robert Alan Browne), is a barrel-chested man with a gruff demeanor, surrounded by incompetent and ill-mannered waitresses who serve the diner's equally sullen and inarticulate customers. A sense of hopelessness hangs over employees and diners alike, brought on by a shared sense that the world has moved on without them, and that the future offers nothing but more of the same. It is at Statler's Café that Norman encounters Mary Samuels (Meg Tilly), who initiates Norman's renewed confrontation with his mother, and the monstrous-feminine in general.

Norman's first encounter with Mary takes place in the kitchen of Statler's Café. A mediocre waitress who spends more time arguing with her boyfriend on the telephone than attending to customers, she catches Norman's eye and lures him into a relationship that wavers between sexual desire and sibling rivalry. In Mary, Norman discovers a woman who suffers, as he once did, under the yoke of an elderly and unscrupulous mother: Lila Loomis (Vera Miles), the sister of Marion Crane (Janet Leigh). Norman is unaware of Mary's connection to his past, and of her complicity in her mother's attempt to emotionally destabilize Norman and force him back into a mental institution. Shortly after making her acquaintance, Norman invites Mary back to his house to spend the night. It is raining outside and a clap of thunder is heard in the distance, echoing the original film and encouraging the viewer to wonder how long it will take for Norman to dispatch Mary as he once did Marion Crane.

Instead, Norman's character arc in *Psycho II* takes an unexpected turn toward a more sympathetic and complex representation of the adult male psycho killer. Reintroducing the domestic murder weapons that Norman prefers—a tin of poisoned tea leaves and a sharpened kitchen knife—the conversation between Mary and Norman in the Bates home gets off to a rocky start. Shortly after being offered a sandwich and a glass of milk—the final meal that Marion shared with Norman in *Psycho*—Mary changes her mind and, politely refusing Norman's invitation to spend the night in the guest room upstairs, attempts to leave. Her intentions are not innocent. Having placed the sharpened knife in front of Norman, knowing full well that he is extremely reluctant to handle the utensil, Mary has effectively reversed the game of cat and mouse that Norman played with Marion in *Psycho*. In attempting to provoke Norman and place herself in harm's way in order to incriminate him, Mary undermines the power and gender norm of the killer-and-victim dichotomy, rendering Norman helpless and bewildered. If not virtuous, her actions in the scene are empowered and thought-provoking.

Norman's response to Mary's imminent departure is a fascinating example of the cinematic presentation of the aged male sociopath, not as a frighteningly human monster devoid of compassion and reason, but as a thoughtful and sensitive human being in need of companionship and solace.

> NORMAN: What if I told you that I needed you to stay?
> MARY: Why would you need me?
> NORMAN: Because this is the first night I've spent in this house in years, much less alone. A lot of my ... troubles had to do with this home. So you see I'm as scared as you are, just for different reasons.

In *Psycho*, Norman had established a dominion over the Bates Motel and Victorian home; he had removed his mother from the equation, subsumed her identity within his own psyche and acted as the sole proprietor and patriarch of the Bates family business and place of residence. He did so, for a time, at least, with no thought to the threat of reprisal or the intervention of the law. Yet during his conversation with Mary in *Psycho II* Norman is a changed man—he has been rehabilitated and expresses a legitimate need to reintroduce himself into contemporary society as an honest and law-abiding citizen. The question of whether his attraction to Mary will compel him to dress up as an elderly Victorian woman, with antiquated moral values and a propensity for violence, is (at least at first) not a point that Norman takes into consideration in *Psycho II*.

Psycho, in other words, treats the transition between young and old, or life and death, in stark terms. Norman's encounter with Marion Crane ends in murder and the wrath of the monstrous-feminine. *Psycho II* uses Norman's perspective on life as a middle-aged man to complicate these oppositions. The aging madman, unlike his youthful counterpart, is more vulnerable to—and engaged with—the world around him. Norman is no longer, as he was in *Psycho,* hiding away in a roadside motel and anachronistic home trying to live a simple life (of murder and mayhem). In *Psycho II*, he is an outpatient who is actively participating in a process of rehabilitation under the solicitous, if at times distracted, observation of Dr. Bill Raymond (Robert Loggia). The fatal weakness in Norman's attempt to embrace normality is the choice, made against the advice of Dr. Raymond, to move back into the Bates Motel and Bates home. If anything, it is the aged and dilapidated place of business and family residence, not the attractive and wayward girlfriend (or her vengeful and duplicitous mother), that emotionally destabilizes Norman.

At the beginning of *Psycho II* Norman appears in court and, after being officially declared sane, is released from custody. Dr. Raymond then drives Norman home and, after a brief discussion regarding best practices, leaves him alone in the Bates home for the first time in (following the implicit internal chronology of the *Psycho* films) over 20 years. Understandably, Norman is anxious about his return to the Bates home and wanders aimlessly from room to room. Walking upstairs, Norman looks down and notices a faded scrap of paper sticking out from under the telephone. Norman reads the letter and is horrified, a reaction that is accentuated by the music of Jerry Goldsmith—a longtime friend of original film composer Bernard Hermann. The film then cuts to a close-up of the letter in Norman's hand which reads, "Norman I'll be home late. Fix your own dinner. Love, M." Unlike the letters that appear later in the film, which are far more violent and manipulative in their choice of language, this initial letter from Norma could very well be a legitimate artifact left behind shortly before she was murdered by her son. Forgotten until Norman stumbled upon it, it is a jarring reminder of the actual past, rather than a figment of his imagination and repressed desires.

Norman's discovery of Norma's letter triggers a relapse, opening a floodgate of repressed memories and a feeling of deep anxiety that submerges Norman into a state of hallucination and abject fear. Immediately after reading her letter, Norman hears his mother's voice (voiced by Virginia Gregg) off-screen. He looks to her bedroom door, and its faded brown dissolves into a freshly lacquered version of the same door earlier in time—the very same day, we later discover, that Norman murdered his mother. In that moment, Norman's grasp of the distinction between past and present becomes thoroughly distorted. A dolly zoom further emphasizes his sense of disorientation, as the film cuts to a close-up of the door in even earlier times. The image of a young boy with blond hair and an expressionless face, Norman as a child, is reflected in the lacquered surface, as well as in the polished brass handle.

Yet, while the reflection is convincing, the image of Norman as a child reflected in the surface of the bedroom door is a head-and-shoulder shot that is more painterly than cinematic. Norman's moment of childhood rebellion is represented as if he is a ghost peering back at himself as a middle-aged man. Norman's childhood is a haunting experience, and it is fitting that his return to the Bates home coincides with a return to his childhood and a spectral figure looking out from the time and place in Norman's life that he fears most.

A similar image of a long-forgotten trauma that violently reemerges takes place later in *Psycho II*, in the bathroom of the Bates home. In the previous scene, a teenage boy has been stabbed to death in the basement of the house by a person dressed as Norma Bates. At the time of the murder Norman was locked in the attic, and the identity of the killer remains a mystery. Later, walking into the bathroom, Norman flushes the toilet and is horrified at the sight of blood spewing forth from the toilet and bathroom sink. Entering the bathroom to assist him, Mary removes an article of clothing from the toilet (belonging perhaps to the murder victim) and offers to clean the bathroom as Norman is too horrified to respond. It is ironic that Norman is unable to clean the bathroom in *Psycho II*, whereas in *Psycho* he is fully capable of mopping up the blood after he has murdered Marion Crane.

In the film *The Pervert's Guide to Cinema*, Slavoj Žižek argues that when a character like Norman looks through the façade of reality he sees "the dark other side where hidden forces run the show."[24] Onscreen, in *Psycho II*, the toilet bowl spewing forth blood literalizes this process. reflecting Žižek's argument that "in our most elementary experience, when we flush the toilet, excrement simply disappears out of our reality into another space which we perceive as a nether world—another reality, a chaotic primordial reality, and the ultimate horror of course is if the flushing doesn't work, if objects return, if remainders, excremental remainders return from that dimension."[25] Norman's reflection in Norma's bedroom door, like the blood-filled toilet, reflects the deterioration of Norman's psychic well-being in the face of the unwelcome and uncontrolled return of a chaotic and primordial reality that he has long repressed.

Norman's clean-up after the murders in *Psycho* and *Psycho II* bears a striking resemblance to his attempt to age gracefully, inasmuch as, according to Žižek, "the work of erasing the stains, [keeps] at bay this chaotic netherworld, which threatens to explode anytime and engulf us."[26] As much as Norman is struggling to clean the traces of a stain and the act of murder, he is also coping with the passage of time and the toll that it has taken upon him. In *Psycho* it was easier for Norman to repress his obsession with murder and mayhem. In *Psycho II* doing so has become a far more complicated endeavor.

In these scenes in particular, the demise of youth as a time of unfettered happiness is witnessed by the figure of the aged male psychopath as a portal to unexpected—even unimaginable—powers that illuminate a terrifying time of reckoning with past sins. Indeed, at the midway point in his life, Norman struggles with the meaning of happiness. Is happiness to be in love and to be loved by someone else? Is that love, or even a platonic friendship, possible with Mary Samuels? Or is the memory of Norma, and the perverse superego that she embodies, the only comfort and stability that he can depend upon? Norman is torn, in *Psycho II*, between two worlds that are equally unsatisfying and impossible to inhabit. Murder and mayhem were, during his childhood and adolescence, the ways in which he connected with the world. The only way that Norman was able to assert himself was to step into the form of his dead mother and kill. A quarter-century of isolation and rehabilitation later, Norman has come to terms with who he is. The system sees him as cured, and—with the guidance of Dr. Raymond and the cooperation of those around him—capable of reclaiming his sanity and enjoying a normal middle-aged life.

There are those who believe, however, that Norman has not spent enough time paying for his sins. Lila Loomis in particular believes that no amount of time will be sufficient atonement for Norman's crimes—that he should grow old and die in a mental institution. Lila is so devoted to this cause that she becomes a version of Norma Bates, transforming her daughter into a femme fatale, calling Norman on the phone and posing as his mother, and even dressing up as Norma in an effort to ruin his life. Regardless of Lila and Mary's actions, however, Norman has little chance of achieving the "normal" life of a healthy middle-aged man, having chosen to punish himself in a way that even the vindictive Lila cannot imagine. Even though he is aware that a path exists that will provide him with a chance at happiness, he returns to the Bates Motel.

Norman insists upon returning to the scene of the crime—to the most traumatic point in his life—which is filled with memories of murder. One may think that Norman is attempting to reform by confronting the memories that he has accumulated. Unfortunately, this is not the case. Norman has returned to his childhood home in order to punish himself: to remain imprisoned not within a padded cell but within a motel and home that are built upon his obsession with murder and mayhem.

Conclusion

Old age is, for Norman Bates, not exactly a stereotypical affair. There never seems to be a moment in *Psycho II* where Norman sits down and complains about becoming old and crotchety and infirm. On the contrary, Norman's confrontation with his identity, and his use of this confrontation to disguise what he *truly* is—a man still haunted by the shadows of his past, and specifically of his mother—is one of the most engaging aspects of *Psycho II*. Norman exhibits a depth of character in the film that makes him an apt representation of the aged male psychopath. *Psycho II* attempts to portray Norman's status as a middle-aged man, and what it means to be at the mid-point of one's life, confronting the onslaught of time.

Psycho II also examines a question that Hitchcock only alludes to in *Psycho*: the intersections between Norman's now middle-aged life, the Reagan-era transformation of the American economy, and the hollowing-out of the American Dream. Norman's perennial struggle to make ends meet at the Bates Motel is echoed in his job at Statler's Café. The bygone era of the American state highway, long ago forgotten by the modern interstate highway system, points to a fundamental anxiety in *Psycho II* regarding the aging of the American economy and Norman's fight to live in an age of perpetual austerity. Indeed, Norman's qualifications as a worker in the modern marketplace are very much limited, and while he is able to work as a cook's helper or motel manager, Norman's prospects in the Reagan Era (let alone today) are limited at best.

The theme of inequality in *Psycho II* is reflected by a tone of suffering and a feeling of depression, both economic and emotional, that affects many of the characters in the film. The aging of the American Dream, in particular the deterioration of the nuclear family, supports the argument that the portrayal of Norman Bates in *Psycho II* is very much an example of the progressive horror film. Each and every character in *Psycho II* is trying their very best to maintain a sense of goodwill—a sense of unity. Their efforts, in particular Dr. Raymond's, to reintroduce Norman back into a community and a greater sense of family and belonging, always seem to be a struggle. Norman, at first, wants to be reintroduced into society; he wants to participate in a story of success and prosperity.

Yet, the hurdles that Norman faces are impossible to overcome. By film's end, the crisis of the American Dream illuminates the reality that civil society, during the Reagan Era and beyond, is predicated upon the evils of inequity and the cultural logic of late capitalism rather than threatened by the mental and emotional instability of Norman Bates.[27] Both for the American Dream and for Norman, the desire to exist within the death of the family overwhelms the possibility that the aged male psychopath is destined for companionship and stability. Borrowing from Robin Wood, "the 'happy ending' (when it exists)" in *Psycho II* signifies "the restoration of repression."[28] The obsession with murder and mayhem for Norman is a family tradition that is impossible to refuse.

NOTES

1. The figure of Norman Bates in *Psycho II* points to the moral ambiguity of the aged male psychopath in the modern horror film. In his book, *The Normal and the Pathological*, the prominent philosopher of science Georges Canguilhem (1904–1995) maintains that "every conception of pathology must be based on

prior knowledge of the corresponding normal state." At the same time, "the scientific study of pathological cases becomes an indispensable phase in the overall search for the laws of the normal state." Canguilhem, *Normal and the Pathological*, 329; see also Canguilhem, *Knowledge of Life*, 121–146.
   2. Creed, "Horror and the Monstrous-Feminine."
   3. Wood, "An Introduction to the American Horror Film," 10.
   4. Doherty, *Teenagers and Teenpics*, 2.
   5. Thompson, *Moment of Psycho*, 15.
   6. *Ibid.*
   7. Lowenstein, *Shock Waves*, vii.
   8. Lowenstein, *Shocking Representation*.
   9. Clarens, *Illustrated History of the Horror Film*; Huss and Ross, *Focus on the Horror Film*; Prawer, *Caligari's Children*.
   10. Wood, unlike his predecessors, argues that cinema is an autonomous art. By virtue of his reading of genre film and popular culture, Wood has paved the way for a new generation of horror scholarship, including the work of Adam Lowenstein, Robert Spadoni and Caetlin Benson-Allott.
   11. In *Psycho*, Norman kills his mother and her boyfriend in a fit of jealous rage, only to repress the severity of his crime by internalizing his mother's identity and developing a split personality. The teenage trauma of Norman Bates was the subject of the TV series *Bates Motel* (A&E, 2013–2017).
   12. Wood, *Hollywood from Vietnam to Reagan*, 150.
   13. *Ibid.*, 147.
   14. *Ibid.*
   15. Wood, "Introduction to the American Horror Film," 10.
   16. *Ibid.*
   17. *Ibid.*, 23–24.
   18. Clover, *Men, Women, and Chainsaws*; Barbara Creed, *The Monstrous-Feminine*; Freeland, *Naked and the Undead*; Sobchack, "Bringing It All Back Home"; Williams, "When the Woman Looks."
   19. Wood, "Introduction to the American Horror Film," 16–17.
   20. Hutchings, *Historical Dictionary*, 294; Tudor, *Monsters and Mad Scientists*, 47–48, 77.
   21. The *Psycho* franchise consists of six films loosely based on the *Psycho* novels by Robert Bloch (1959, 1982, 1990), namely *Psycho*, *Psycho II*, *Psycho III* (Anthony Perkins, 1986), *Bates Motel* (Richard Rothstein, 1987)—not to be confused with television series *Bates Motel* (A&E, 2013–2017)—*Psycho IV: The Beginning* (Joseph Stefano, 1990) and the 1998 remake of the original film directed by Gus Van Sant.
   22. See Marah, "Innocence."
   23. See Lyotard, *Libidinal Economy*.
   24. Žižek, *Pervert's Guide to Cinema*.
   25. *Ibid.*
   26. *Ibid.*
   27. See Jameson, *Postmodernism*.
   28. Wood, "Introduction to the American Horror Film," 10.

Bibliography

Canguilhem, Georges. *Knowledge of Life*. 1965. Translated by Stefanos Geroulanos and Daniela Ginsburg. New York: Fordham University Press, 2008.
_____. *The Normal and the Pathological*. Translated by Carolyn R. Fawcett and Robert S. Cohen. New York: Zone Books, 1991.
Clarens, Carlos. *An Illustrated History of the Horror Film*. New York: Capricorn Books, 1967.
Clover, Carol. *Men, Women, and Chainsaws: Gender in the Modern Horror Film*. Princeton: Princeton University Press, 1992.
Creed, Barbara. "Horror and the Monstrous-Feminine: An Imaginary Abjection." In Grant, *Dread of Difference*, 37–67.
_____. *The Monstrous-Feminine: Film, Feminism, Psychoanalysis*. 1993. London: Routledge, 2007.
Doherty, Thomas. *Teenagers and Teenpics: The Juvenilization of American Movies in the 1950s*. 1988. Philadelphia: Temple University Press, 2002.
Freeland, Cynthia. *The Naked and the Undead: Evil and the Appeal of Horror*. Boulder, CO: Westview Press, 2000.
Grant, Barry Keith, and Christopher Sharrett, eds. *Planks of Reason: Essays on the Horror Film*. 1984. Lanham, MD: Scarecrow Press, 2004.
_____, ed. *The Dread of Difference: Gender and the Horror Film*. 1996. Austin: University of Texas Press, 2015.
Gubar, Marah. "Innocence." In *Keywords for Children's Literature*, edited by Philip Nel and Lissa Paul, 121–127. New York: New York University Press, 2011.
Huss, Roy, and T.J. Ross, eds. *Focus on the Horror Film*. New York: Prentice Hall, 1972.
Hutchings, Peter. *Historical Dictionary of Horror Cinema*. Lanham, MD: Scarecrow Press, 2009.

Jameson, Fredric. *Postmodernism, or, the Cultural Logic of Late Capitalism*. Durham: Duke University Press, 1991.
Lowenstein, Adam. *Shock Waves: Trauma, History, and Art in the Modern Horror Film*. PhD Dissertation, University of Chicago, 1999.
_____. *Shocking Representation: Historical Trauma, National Cinema, and the Modern Horror Film*. New York: Columbia University Press, 2005.
Lyotard, Jean-François. *Libidinal Economy*. 1974. Translated by Iain Hamilton Grant. Bloomington: Indiana University Press, 1993.
The Pervert's Guide to Cinema. Directed by Sophie Fiennes, performance by Slavoj Žižek, P Guide Ltd. and ICA Projects, 2006.
Prawer, S.S. *Caligari's Children: The Film as Tale of Terror*. Oxford: Oxford University Press, 1980.
Sobchack, Vivian. "Bringing It All Back Home: Family Economy and Generic Exchange." *American Horrors: Essays on the Modern American Horror Film*, edited by Gregory A. Waller, 175–194. Urbana: University of Illinois Press, 1987.
Thompson, David. *The Moment of* Psycho: *How Alfred Hitchcock Taught America to Love Murder*. New York: Basic Books, 2009.
Tudor, Andrew. *Monsters and Mad Scientists: A Cultural History of the Horror Movie*. Oxford: Blackwell, 1989.
Williams, Linda. "When the Woman Looks." In Grant, *Dread of Difference*, 17–36.
Wood, Robin. *Hollywood from Vietnam To Reagan*. 1986. New York: Columbia University Press, 2003.
_____. "An Introduction to the American Horror Film." In *The American Nightmare: Essays on the Horror Film*, edited by Robin Wood and Richard Lippe. Toronto: Festival of Festivals, 1979.

The Limits of "Sundowning"
M. Night Shyamalan's The Visit and the Horror of the Aging Body

STEPHANIE M. FLINT

The use of the aging body and aging characters in horror is a staple as old as horror cinema itself. From the suddenly decaying form of the female prostitute in Kubrick's 1980 *The Shining*, to the haunting image of elderly Hungarian woman Mrs. Sylvia Ganush in Raimi's 2008 *Drag Me to Hell*, to the devil-worshipping Mr. and Mrs. Ulman in West's 2009 *The House of the Devil*, to Grandma Lois who made a deal with a demon in Joost and Schulman's 2011 *Paranormal Activity 3*, elderly characters are frequently cast into antagonistic shock-and-scare roles in cinematic horror. In M. Night Shyamalan's 2015 horror film *The Visit*, the monstrousness of the aging grandparents creeps up on their grandchildren as a slow burn, increasing in intensity as the film progresses, leaving the terrified children alone to face the horrors of aging, death, mental decay, and the hazy borders that separate the normal from the abnormal.

In many ways, the lead elderly couple in Shyamalan's *The Visit* are cast into the typical role of the monstrous elder. However, the means by which the film is shot, as well as the scare scenes associated with the grandparents and the inevitable Shyamalan twist, work to provide a deeper commentary on common fears associated with aging, the aging process, and the delineations of sanity. While many elderly characters are cast in less dynamic roles of monstrous evil, the aging "grandparents" in Shyamalan's film provide insight into what—aside from surface-level monstrous actions and the abject aging body—these characters represent on a deeper, and perhaps unconscious, level for both the filmmaker and the audience.

The presence of monsters in art provides valuable space for interrogation and discussion. As figures that are physically and/or psychologically coded as outside of the "norm," monsters, by their presence, interrupt established normalcy. Rather than just functioning as antagonists to the main characters and often-frightening images to behold, the positioning of monsters also helps to expose embedded cultural and social prejudices. The context and social structure surrounding monsters, for example, can illuminate the dynamics that led to them being designated as feared and rejected outsiders in the first place. Even though not always presented in a grotesque or physically different light, these figures—at some point of the narrative—are revealed to have a terrifying difference that marks them as outside the "norm" inhabited by the majority of the other characters. In

Shyamalan's *The Visit*, the "grandparents" ultimately fill this role based on their mental difference and murderous actions, but not before horror is established as associated with the expected progression of their aging bodies.[1]

Navigating Sundowning, Delirium and Normalcy

The Visit revolves around a pair of siblings, Tyler and Becca, who visit their estranged grandparents for a vacation. Shortly after they arrive, the children start to notice their grandparents exhibiting strange behavior, which becomes more and more terrifying to them as the movie progresses. Upon the siblings' arrival, for example, the grandparents establish a rule of being in bed by 9:30 p.m. and the children soon learn that this is because the grandmother roams the house in various states of delirium throughout the evening: vomiting, scratching at closed doors while naked, and exhibiting other alarming behaviors. The characters explain the behavior as a natural part of the aging process, and even refer to her actions as the result of "sundowning," a symptom associated with certain types of dementia. However, as the film progresses, this explanation grows less convincing, since it cannot account for the elders' increasingly strange daytime behavior. Tyler finds a pile of discarded diapers (filled with excrement) that the grandfather has been piling up in the woodshed, the grandmother chases the children around under the house while partially nude, and concerned friends from the asylum where the grandparents normally volunteer begin stopping by the house to check on the family. The children are left to navigate whether this behavior is concerning or a common part of the aging process.

Although it is later revealed that these people are not actually the children's grandparents, but escaped killers from the asylum (who have slain the real grandparents and hidden their bodies in the basement), this film raises many questions regarding horror, mental ability, the aging process, and the lines that separate one from the norm. The faux grandparents are eventually revealed to be criminally insane, and thus outside the "norm," but most of the horrific behaviors they exhibit in the film could easily be symptoms of dementia, a common and naturally occurring part of the aging process.[2] The killers' alarming behavior goes relatively undetected for so long due to the grandchildren's uncertainty regarding what behavior is normal and what is threatening. The killers' ages function, in a way, as a disguise that helps them to perpetuate the lie (that they are these children's grandparents) for so long. What especially complicates this is that "sundowning" is a real phenomenon, which manifests in strange and sometimes unnerving ways. Questions of what behavior is normal and what is cause for concern can, therefore, often arise when dealing with the aging mind, body, and various stages of dementia. In highlighting these uneasy distinctions between (safe) normalcy and (unsafe) insanity, the true horror that *The Visit* evokes is the uncertain divide between sanity and insanity, normal behavior and mortal peril.

"Normal old age problems"?

As night falls on their first evening with their presumed grandparents, the grandfather walks into the children's room and announces an early bedtime. "We are old people," he says. "Bedtime here is 9:30." Despite this, Becca breaks curfew to get cookies from the kitchen, but is soon scared away by her grandmother who she finds wandering around and vomiting on the floor. Another night, the two grandchildren see the grandmother scratching at a door while naked. When Becca asks her grandfather about this, he eventually tells her that what they saw was a symptom of their grandmother's "disorder"—and therefore it's best to not leave the room after 9:30 p.m.

He explains: "She's got a diagnosed disorder. Many elderly people have it. Sometimes she gets in her head that she ate something and it's inside her and trying to crawl out. It's called sundowning. It's a kind of dementia. It's triggered by nightfall.... It's like somebody talking in their sleep.... It's probably best if we just call it a rule that you two shouldn't come out of your room after 9:30 p.m." The children's rigid bedtime is therefore connected with their first understanding of sundowning. And although Becca's conversation with the grandfather seemingly suggests that the grandmother's sundowning-related behavior will be safely kept away from the children as long as they stick to the early bedtime, both grandparents' daytime behavior continues to startle the children. The grandmother, for instance, sneaks up on the children as they are playing under the house. Crawling on all fours, naked from the waist down with hair covering her face—reminiscent of the specter of the young girl in *The Ring*—she chants, "I'm gonna getcha!" in a menacing voice. The grandfather also alarms the children; he accuses a stranger in the street of following him, and he frequently refers to an obscure "costume party" that does not exist.

Nana (Deanna Dunagan) menaces the children with her bizarre behaviors in *The Visit* (2015).

Tyler, the younger of the two, points to these behaviors as alarming, but Becca, as the older sister, seeks to soothe his nerves by explaining the behavior away as natural. "He's old," she rationalizes. "They get confused. Don't freak out. Old people get paranoid." As the antics continue, Tyler directly questions the validity of the sundowning claim regarding their grandmother: "She's weird during the day. And gets even weirder at night?" Becca again seeks to reassure him with a downloaded definition of sundown syndrome: "I'm telling you, it's okay … it's got to do with neurological reactions to sunshine and moonlight. It's literally a chemical reaction." She continues, reading directly from her laptop: "Sundown syndrome: a term for disorientation, agitation, a general worsening of mental symptoms classically described in the elderly at dusk or nightfall. It's normal, old age problems. People are scared of old people for no reason.... Just come to accept they're old people and things won't be as weird."

Although there is still some disagreement amongst researchers regarding sundown syndrome's exact timing and onset, it is generally described as the increase of delirium with the onset of nightfall. The symptoms of sundown syndrome are numerous and range from "anxiety, agitation, aggression, pacing, wandering, resistance, screaming, yelling, visual and auditory hallucinations, and so forth."[3] The children's grandparents exhibit a significant number of these symptoms in the course of the film, and what especially perplexes the grandchildren is the increasing amount of alarming behavior (including agitation, aggression, yelling, and hallucinations) that they see in the daytime hours. Tyler's questioning of his grandmother's daytime behaviors highlights a hazy border of distinction between what is deemed natural and sane versus abnormal and cause for concern with elderly patients. In a sense, the film illustrates the ongoing discussion surrounding sundown syndrome. The lines of definition around sundown syndrome vary from source to source, as its hours of measurement and daytime versus nighttime delirium are still subject to debate. Although the film later reveals that this is due to the grandparents being replaced by dangerous and psychotic impostors, it nevertheless highlights the variable definition of the syndrome as debated by researchers today.

However, even if one were to remove the grandparents as "impostors" from the story line, the majority of the horrific elements of the film would still remain. Had the children stayed with their biological grandparents, with the grandparents still going through the natural process of aging, the grandmother's frightening actions (nudity, vomiting, unexplainable laughter, and even wandering around the house in a seeming trance while holding a knife) could all reflect various stages of dementia.[4] Even the grandfather's collection of dirty diapers in the woodshed reveals an admittedly unpleasant but common part of an aging process to which we are all at risk of falling "victim."

In *The Powers of Horror: An Essay on Abjection*, Julia Kristeva defines the "abject" and states of "abjection" as moments, characters, and themes that challenge the established boundaries of self and established states of "normalcy." She identifies bodily states, such as aging, pregnancy, and birth, as well as functions, such as vomiting, excretion, and the menstrual process as particularly evocative of the feelings of unease and disgust associated with abjection—feelings also evoked by the horror genre. These references to death, decay, and excrement all work to challenge established borders of reality. Naturally, some of the horror of *The Visit* involves the fear of death. As aging beings, the faux grandparents are walking embodiments of the impending inevitability of death, particularly in contrast to their youthful counterparts, Becca and Tyler.[5] Their actions and forms remind the viewer of how close these characters are to death, and, like the abject, force the viewer to see what realities we "thrust aside in order to live."[6] *The Visit* similarly forces viewers to confront substances associated with unpleasant bodily functions, such as excrement and vomit, which occur naturally in one's lifetime, yet are "thrust aside" from day-to-day focus. As one ages, these processes are often more and more difficult to ignore, control, and contain. Kristeva notes that corpses and feces remind us of constructed borders, especially those between life and death—"the other side of the border, the place where I am not and which permits me to be"—and thus represent a "border that has encroached upon everything," forcing the viewer to reflect, "How can I be without border?"[7] The faux grandparents in Shyamalan's *The Visit* function as representational monsters of the abject by representing the inevitability of bodily decline (resulting in death) and by reminding the viewer of the hazy (and perhaps subjective) line between healthy/sane and unhealthy/insane with regard to one's mental health.

By showing the grandchildren alone navigating these shaky designations between life, health, decline, and death, the audience is confronted with the horror associated with these designations on multiple levels. On one level, the children respond to the general "grossness" associated with the grandparents' antics and are scared by the nightly activities of their grandmother (Tyler, at one point, refers to her as a "werewolf"). On a second level, the film reminds the audience of how much of what is exhibited on screen is "natural." As Becca reassures herself and her brother that their grandparents' behavior is a normal part of growing old, the audience is reminded of how common these various stages of dementia are, and that these processes could be experienced by them or someone they love someday. The film presents these grandparents' actions as terrifying through jump-scares and scary-looking nightly antics, which seeks to place the viewer into a state of fear. However, the lingering sense of horror associated with *The Visit* lies in the reality (and seeming inevitability) of the decline of one's overall mental and physical health, and this is wrapped up in the grandparents' representation.

Such fears are kept at bay to an extent through Shyamalan's inevitable twist in the story, when the children discover that the couple they are staying with are not their grandparents at all. In the scene, Becca and Tyler are on a video call with their mother, and Becca holds up her laptop's camera to show their mother a glimpse of their grandparents as they are in the yard. The mother becomes very serious, and alerts them that those are not, in fact, their grandparents. Having previously helped Becca to reassure Tyler that their grandparents' actions are just a part of being old, she reveals that his fears have been realized. There *is* something amiss, and the children's lives are in danger at the hands of these imposters. The imposters, the children later piece together, are some of the inmates at the local asylum that their grandparents cared for.

Although Shyamalan's ending seeks to provide the audience with a sense of ease that the evil is kept outside the borders of the normal and sane, the film leaves the audience with a sense of *un*ease, because the true horror had less to do with the killers than the navigation of the grandparents' mental and physical states. What lingers is Becca and her mother's reassurance that the grandparents' behavior is "natural," or "just like someone talking in their sleep." These conversations remind the audience of the likelihood of various stages of dementia affecting their lives or the lives of those they love (that is to say, if they haven't experienced this already). Although Becca and her mother use the argument of this process being natural as a way to reassure Tyler, the naturalness of what is depicted on screen is exactly what makes the film so scary.[8] It reminds the viewer that this natural process could very well happen, and once begun, is in most cases as inescapable and incurable as death itself.

Documenting the Abnormal

The style in which *The Visit* is shot contributes significantly to the realism of the fear and uncertainty surrounding the grandparents' aging process. It is presented as a documentary-style work, produced by 15-year-old Becca, an aspiring filmmaker. Scenes include her discussing her decisions in shooting the film, as well as the process of its production. Although Becca takes her role as director/producer/filmmaker very seriously, her age (and the fact that her goofy younger brother often acts as assistant) gives the film an amateurish quality. This helps to frame the grandchildren's experience in the story as they learn about the aging process, perhaps for the first time, in real time and from an inescapable first-person perspective. Their discussions about what is "normal" behavior for their grandparents to be exhibiting mirrors conversations that could very easily take place when siblings are visiting family members who suffer from dementia.

Throughout the film, Becca works to create intimate interview sequences with everyone in the family. The film actually begins with a one-on-one interview with her mother regarding her past tumultuous relationship with Becca and Tyler's grandparents. This not only sets up the very personal nature of the documentary Becca is shooting and the visit to the grandparents' house overall, but also helps the film to feel more like a working documentary, and therefore more realistic. Additionally, having the characters look directly into the camera during their close-ups and interview scenes creates a sense of closeness and connection between them and the audience. This intimacy deepens the audience's investment, not only in the grandchildren, but also in their navigation of (what the grandchildren assume to be) the realities of the aging process.

The one-on-one interviews provide telling moments of character and plot development within the narrative. The grandparents' interviews reflect their descent into madness, and document their startling behavior as it becomes more frequent and extreme. During her first interview attempt, the grandmother begins hitting her forehead when asked about her daughter, and in her second, she refers to drowning her children and sending them to another planet. Similarly, in the grandfather's interview, his narration concludes with the revelation of his experience with a man with glowing eyes that no one else could see. In each of their individual interview scenes, the children's personal struggles and regrets (largely associated with their absent father) surface and help to shed some light on the children's reactions to their supposed grandparents' behavior. The children have to face these struggles by the end of the film. Tyler has an obsessive fear of germs, and this fear is tested on multiple occasions during their visit. Becca refuses to look in the mirror after their father leaves and must ultimately confront this fear in order to fight for her life against the imposter grandmother.

Through these scenes, viewers connect with the grandchildren as characters, and watch as they are confronted with the fears and weaknesses that they reveal in their interviews. Tyler ends up with a diaper filled with excrement on his face, and Becca not only looks in the mirror to see the imposter grandmother coming up behind her, but ultimately uses a shard of the mirror in self-defense. In these personal victories, the grandchildren are forced to face their fears alongside the frightful embodiments of abject aging, and the mind gone wrong. Despite their lack of relation to the children, the faux grandparents are presented as the children's doppelgängers to an extent. This is most prominently exhibited in Becca's mirror scene. In the shot, we see her crying and holding up the camera to the mirror. As she opens her eyes, she sees the creeping face of her grandmother directly behind her. She is therefore forced to confront her sense of self—through her reflection—alongside the aging face of the imposter grandmother, who she now knows is a murderous escaped asylum inmate. Becca and her assailant are shown in parallel, through reflection, with a camera to Becca's left, and her "grandmother" behind and to her right.

Becca may be able to kill the body of the woman who represents the abjection of aging and mental deterioration, but doing so won't restore the link to her grandparents that she has been searching for through the documentary. While fighting for her life, she is simulta-

In *The Visit*, after Pop Pop (Peter McRobbie) locks Becca (Olivia DeJonge) in a bedroom with Nana (Deanna Dunagan), her camera captures chilling proof in the mirror's reflection that the old woman is right behind her.

neously lashing out at the surface level of this elderly woman's abjection, and at the loss that she helped to cause. Becca realizes that there is no "magical elixir" for this scenario; no perfect film clip that she can create to fill in the lack created by her father's (and now her grandparents') absence. She must confront all of these realities, while seeing herself and the embodiment of her sense of lack, reflected back to her.

Paul Wells, in *The Horror Genre: From Beelzebub to Blair Witch*, notes that horror films frequently utilize the home front or "domestic space" as its setting to scrutinize the hierarchical structure of relationships and to provide challenges to established social roles. Wells refers to the home as "*the* locality for the worst of horror," as it creates a miniature version of larger social hierarchies ruling our way of life.[9] *The Visit*, which takes place mostly in the grandparents' house and places a strong emphasis on family relationships throughout, similarly uses domestic space to question common social reactions to the process of aging and to call attention to the impermanent distinctions between the "normal" and "abnormal."

Time is constantly reinforced, and functions as a central point of focus in many of the scenes: the children's rigid bedtime, frequent shots of the clock preceding scenes of their grandmother's antics, the Monday-to-Friday countdown the film utilizes to distinguish between days. The structural norms of home, family relationships, and time help to give the film an easy-to-follow format and setting, but its realistic, relatable scenarios also set up its use of horror to call these structural norms into question.

Wells notes that the "representational aspects of horror" reveal the beneficial elements that only horror can produce.[10] The effective disruption of any notion of the norm (through monsters, violence, or a general sense of unease) invites the audience to ask themselves exactly what they fear in their day-to-day lives. This close-up of our hierarchical institutions "continually addresses the dysfunctional and antithetical aspects of the romantic and domestic, collapsing all received notions of predictable gender identities and social formations" and forces the viewer to examine the violent outcomes such roles can cause.[11] In this way, combining intimate shots of the characters with shots that call attention to the passage of time plays upon the horrific blurring of the already hazy demarcations between young and old, sane and insane.

The Visit's amateur-documentary style also contributes to its commentary on cinematic and genre conventions. Through its reminders of the characters' awareness of the camera and of the narrative they are trying to put together, the film creates a sense of self-awareness not often seen in horror cinema (although similar styles are admittedly increasingly popular in the wake of *The Blair Witch Project*). During Tyler's interview sequence, for example, we see Becca lead him into a clearly pre-staged chair that is positioned inside a large barn, with haystacks behind him, and a view of the snowy fields in the far distance. After Tyler looks around him, and a slight breeze passes over his face, he acknowledges Becca's use of *mis-en-scene*.[12] Even the goofy brother character is privy to the inner workings of the filming process in which he is taking part. This creates a sense of the characters and creators being "in on it," or at least perhaps more aware of what is taking place than what meets the eye. This gives the film a sense of self-awareness that not only helps to emphasize its realistic shooting style, but also opens up the possibility for it to function as a critique of the inner workings of horror cinema as a whole.

Aging, Disability and the Boundaries of Representation

The Visit plays off fears associated with aging and the deterioration of the mind and body, but it does so in a way that can, perhaps, promote interrogation of such fears. In Rosemarie Garland-Thomson's landmark text *Extraordinary Bodies: Figuring Physical Disability in American Culture and Literature*, she notes that "the fact that we all become disabled if we live long enough is a reality many people who consider themselves able-bodied are reluctant to admit," which makes the idea of disability "more fluid, and perhaps more threatening."[13] The actions of the supposed grandparents who exhibit mental deterioration act as reality-based horror for the audience, particularly with regard to physical and mental disablement. The fear and horror associated with the challenge to boundaries of self, normalcy, and self-worth are well known to disability theorists, and Lennard J. Davis even refers to mental disability as "the specter haunting normality in our time."[14] Just by performing the physical process of aging, the grandparents become abject, in the Kristevan sense, and therefore function as objects of fear.

Compounding this, the film paints the characters of the impostor grandparents as beings to fear when they are revealed to be asylum inmates. The revelation of these faux grandparents and their mentally unstable status is arguably the high point of terror in the film. Even before Becca and Tyler learn that these imposters killed their real grandparents, they are consumed by the fear of being trapped with people that they don't know, and who are identified as mentally disabled. The imposters, of course, are terrifying because of their deception even without their status as mentally unstable, but their instability contributes to the horror of their unpredictability, alongside the lingering question of what exactly they did to the real grandparents.

Using mental disability as a signifier of monstrosity is perhaps even more common than the use of the elderly as agents of fear, particularly in the horror genre. Characters who are disabled (mentally or otherwise) are frequently cast into the role of the monster, and their disability often eclipses any other aspect of them. Just as the reduction of the disabled "freak" to a one-dimensional character in the freak show or the use of stock disabled characters in literature is problematic, asserting that the fearful, "monstrous" identity of a main character can be boiled down to mental instability is equally troublesome. However, in *The Visit*, the fear that these imposters evoke remains, whether or not they are institutional inmates. Adding in the detail that these imposters have been institutionalized due to their mental instability adds depth to the uncertainty regarding the sanity-insanity divide, but they are not to be feared solely on the basis of their mental status. The fact that dangerous murderers could pass as "normal" family members for so long highlights these hazy distinctions. Their status as murderous strangers simplifies the final sequences into an us-versus-them escape narrative, but the negotiations that the characters underwent prior to this revelation regarding their sanity challenges the existence of a safe divide between the "normal" and "insane."

The Visit therefore uses two common horror-villain foils—the aging process and mental instability—yet the film is frightening in ways that do not involve these elements. The jump scares and frightening images do not rely on the villains being mentally unstable, and this fact highlights how difficult it can be to determine mental stability. Tobin Siebers points out that the "social theory" associated with disability often conflates physical disability and mental disability, establishing physical disability as "the product of mental weakness," and when mental disability is acknowledged in its own right, "the 'feeble-minded' hold rights of citizenship nowhere, and few people in the mainstream believe that this fact should be changed."[15] Ultimately, *The Visit*, through its self-aware conventions and uses of scare scenes, works to push back against the "caste system" that Siebers highlights as promoting "the vicious treatment of people with mental disabilities in most societies," which often results in associations of mental disability with clearly defined, one-dimensional evil.[16]

Prejudices are often wrapped up in designations of insanity (women, people of color, and the physically disabled are frequently cast in these roles), and therefore prejudices associated with aging could easily be channeled into the insane, imposter grandparents. Mentally disabled individuals have been frequently cast in the role of the perpetrator, and particularly in the horror genre. Joshua David Bellin, in *Framing Monsters: Fantasy Film and Social Alienation*, recognizes that fantasy film is similarly concerned, or "morbidly obsessed—with the representation of mentally unstable characters."[17] Although Bellin works primarily within the genre of fantasy, many films classified as fantasy are also classified as horror, and the "obsession" that Bellin refers to, clearly manifests itself in the horror genre.

Bellin speaks to Susan Sontag's *Illness as Metaphor* (1977), in which she describes illness as "the night-side of life" and that "sooner or later each of us is obliged, at least for a spell, to identify ourselves as citizens of that other place."[18] The persistent fear of becoming one of the perpetually ill, disabled, and aged contributes to the persistence of its separation from that which is deemed the "normal" state of life. Similarly, Sander Gilman, particularly addressing the psychiatric inmate or patient, writes: "we must construct boundaries between ourselves and those categories of individuals whom we believe (or hope) to be more at risk than ourselves…. The construction of the image of the [psychiatric] patient is thus always a playing out of this desire for a demarcation between ourselves and the chaos represented in culture by disease."[19] This necessity, Joshua David Bellin identifies, is why the insane are depicted in such frightening roles. He states: "it is little wonder that the commonest form the metaphor of madness takes is that of the inhuman, feral berserk. This image is curiously comforting: not only does it externalize the threat of one's own mind becoming a monster, turning in violent insurrection against itself, but it makes identifying the mad a stunningly simple matter."[20] *The Visit* challenges these boundaries by illustrating the horrifying lack of established boundaries between madness and sanity.

Although *The Visit* does ultimately delegate the impostor grandparents to the role of the safe outside, as abnormally insane, it simultaneously troubles this separation with its more realistic-seeming mock documentary format. The film simultaneously complicates the seemingly "safe" and divided space between the us/them relationship of the sane/insane. By bringing in these characters and letting them "pass" as sane for so long, especially with the suggestion of natural symptoms like "sundowning," *The Visit* leaves the viewer to question where exactly that line lies. If the "grandparents" weren't murderers, could this be a normal visit? For the most part, most of the scare scenes in the film could be left in, and the imposters could have actually been the children's real grandparents. By adding in their identity as escaped asylum inmates, the film seeks to relocate the fear associated with aging to the outside of the sane/insane divide. But, the question lingers as to what really separates the sane from the insane, and the film therefore illuminates the hazy line between the two designations.

Garland-Thomson notes that even in theory-based circles, such as those of feminist scholars, "the concerns of older women, who are often disabled, tend also to be ignored."[21] Just like mental instability, the representation of the aging body needs to be further addressed in various realms of theoretical discussion. This cultural process of willful ignoring certainly *is* frightening, and the inevitability and silencing tied into the deteriorating process of aging is ultimately what *The Visit* most effectively plays upon. We are all "doomed" to this end, in which both our bodies and minds veer into the terrifying realm of disability.

Although the fake grandparents are portrayed as the monsters, the film's true, lurking monster is the inevitability of mental decay and the indefinite determination of mental stability. And what's scarier than the decay of one's own mind? Especially when there is no method by which to measure whether our own mental process is "normal" or not, we tend to rely on arbitrary methods of measurement to define the normal state of mind. Shyamalan, in a sense, puts all of our grandparents, parents, and inevitable future-selves on screen, revealing the possibility of decline that we all face. And this is assuming, of course, we do not already fall into the category of the abnormal insane, who—as we learn from the demise of the impostors—must immediately be eradicated to save the normal beings who their very existence threatens.

Notes

1. For more on critical cultural considerations of the monster and the monstrous body, see Cohen, *Monster Theory*.
2. According to *DSM V*, these disorders previously classified as "Dementia, Delirium, Amnestic, and Other Cognitive Disorders" are now included under the umbrella title of neurocognitive disorders (or NCDs). According to the *DSM V*, NCDs "are those in which impaired cognition has not been present since birth or very early life, and thus represents a decline from a previously attained level of functioning" (American Psychiatric Association, *Diagnostic and Statistical Manual of Mental Disorders*, 591.)
3. Canevelli, et al., "Sundowning in Dementia," 73.
4. According to *DSM V* (606), "psychotic features are common in many NCDs, particularly at the mild-to-moderate stage of major NCDs due to Alzheimer's disease, Lewy body disease, and frontotemporal lobar degeneration. Paranoia and other delusions are common features, and often a persecutory theme may

be a prominent aspect of delusional ideation.... Hallucinations may occur in any modality, although visual hallucinations are more common in NCDs than in depressive, bipolar, or psychotic disorders."
  5. Also, the "real" biological grandparents are literal manifestations of death, having been murdered and their bodies concealed in the basement.
  6. Kristeva, *Powers of Horror*, 3.
  7. *Ibid.*, 3–4.
  8. *The Visit*.
  9. Wells, *The Horror Genre*, 18.
  10. *Ibid.*, 24–25.
  11. *Ibid.*
  12. *The Visit*.
  13. Thomson, *Extraordinary Bodies*, 13–14.
  14. Davis, *Bending Over Backwards*, 34.
  15. Siebers, *Disability Theory*, 78.
  16. *Ibid.*
  17. Bellin, *Framing Monsters*, 137.
  18. Sontag, *Illness as Metaphor*, 3.
  19. Gilman, *Images of Illness*, 4.
  20. Bellin, *Framing Monster*, 142.
  21. Thomson, *Extraordinary Bodies*, 26.

BIBLIOGRAPHY

American Psychiatric Association. *Diagnostic and Statistical Manual of Mental Disorders: DSM-V-TR*. Washington, D.C.: American Psychiatric Association, 2013.
Bellin, Joshua David. *Framing Monsters: Fantasy Film and Social Alienation*. Carbondale: Southern Illinois University Press, 2005.
Canevelli, Marco, Martina Valletta, Alessandro Trebbastoni, Giuseppe Sarli, Fabrizia D'Antonio, Leonardo Tariciotti, Carlo de Lena, and Giuseppe Bruno. "Sundowning in Dementia: Clinical Relevance, Pathophysiological Determinants, and Therapeutic Approaches." *Front Med (Lausanne)* 3 (2016): 73. doi: 10.3389/fmed.2016.00073.
Davis, Lennard J. *Bending Over Backwards: Disability, Dismodernism & Other Difficult Positions*. New York: New York University Press, 2002.
Garland-Thomson, Rosemarie. *Extraordinary Bodies: Figuring Physical Disability in American Culture and Literature*. New York: Columbia University Press, 1997.
Gilman, Sander. *Images of Illness from Madness to AIDS*. Ithaca: Cornell University Press, 1988.
Kristeva, Julia. *Powers of Horror: An Essay on Abjection*. New York: Columbia University Press, 1982.
Siebers, Tobin. *Disability Theory*. Ann Arbor: University of Michigan Press, 2008.
Sontag, Susan. *Illness as Metaphor*. New York: Farrar, Straus and Giroux, 1977.
The Visit. Directed by M. Night Shyamalan. 2015. Universal City, CA: Universal Pictures, 2016. DVD.
Wells, Paul. *The Horror Genre: From Beelzebub to Blair Witch*. London: Wallflower Press, 2000.

IV.

Fighting Back Time

"The powers of time can be altered"
The Ambiguities of Aging in Bram Stoker's Dracula *(1992)*

Thomas Prasch

When, in Francis Ford Coppola's *Bram Stoker's Dracula* (1992), Jonathan Harker (Keanu Reeves) arrives in Transylvania, his host, Count Dracula (Gary Oldman)—with his pale parchment skin seeming layered with wrinkles, his gray hair bound into a baroque sort of double bun, his fingernails so long they curl[1]—looks very nearly his age of 450 or so (since he had been a youngish prince back in 1462, when the movie began). Dracula feeds his guest, although he lets him dine alone (informing him: "I have already dined, and I do not drink"—long pause here—"wine"); rhapsodizes melancholic about his ancestral line when Harker comments on the portrait that hangs behind the table (the blood of Attila "flows in these veins," but "blood is too precious a thing in these times.... The victories of my great race are but a tale to be told. I am the last of my kind"), and then gets down to business, signing and wax-sealing the pages that give him ten properties in London ("I do so long to go through the crowded streets of your mighty London," Dracula tells Harker. "To be in the midst of the rush and whirl of humanity. To share its life, its changes, its death"). But then Dracula spots on the table Harker's pocket photograph of his fiancé, Mina (Winona Ryder)—reaching for it, he spills ink on it, and the stain puddles like blood around her neck as he caresses the image's case—and that leads to a different sort of rhapsody: "Do you believe in destiny? That even the powers of time can be altered for a single purpose? The luckiest man who walks on earth is the one who finds true love." "You found Mina," Harker responds, "I thought she was lost." And Harker thought he was talking about the photograph.

When Dracula bursts out of his earth-filled coffin in London, he is young again, like the prince of the film's first frames. When he strides out into those "crowded streets" of late–Victorian London, looking contemporary if a bit foppish, it will be Mina that he seeks (right after feasting on her friend Lucy first; a vampire has to keep his strength up, after all). And Mina, in turn, has encountered the count before: back in the fifteenth century, when she was his wife Elizabeta, "whom he prized above all things on earth." The time-altering "destiny" of which Dracula speaks is, in Coppola's remaking of the story, the reunion of two lovers, separated by war and centuries.

Coppola deploys three distinct tactics in his *Dracula* to deal with the issue of aging. The count himself both ages and seems to be able to reverse the aging process. He appears old in Transylvania (both near the film's outset and again when he returns to his castle at the end), but young in London. That youthful appearance makes it rather easier, or at least less creepy, for him to romance Mina. Meanwhile, others (at least some others) participate in a reincarnation process, whereby their bodies are reborn again. Unlike the metempsychosis preached by Hindus, Buddhists, and Platonists, where the soul migrates from body to body, this is full-scale bodily reincarnation: Mina, beyond remembering her past (when prompted, at least[2]), implying continuity of consciousness and soul, also perfectly embodies it. Both in 1462 and 1897, Mina looks exactly like Winona Ryder in 1992. The third element in Coppola's engagement with time in *Dracula* centers on the cinematic apparatus itself. Coppola on the one hand insists we notice the contemporaneity of Bram Stoker's *Dracula* (1897) and the invention of cinema (traditionally dated to the Lumière Brothers' first screening in 1895); on the other hand, by employing a range of visual tactics typical of early silent cinema, he provides a rebirth to the cinematic form that parallels the reincarnation theme and the quest across time that are the film's main themes. But before returning to these three tactics, we must trace the problem of aging in vampire cinema and review the critical reception of Coppola's film.

The Ambiguities of Aging in Vampire Cinema

We all know that vampires are eternal, or eternal until staked and/or beheaded and/or burned (either torches or the sun's rays will do), but what about aging? The cin-

Dracula (Gary Oldman, as shadow) menaces Jonathan Harker (Keanu Reeves) in Francis Ford Coppola's *Dracula* (1992).

ematic record on the point is complex and contradictory. Few films deal directly with the problem of aging in vampires. Tony Scott's *The Hunger* (1983) might be the notable exception. As Francisco Gonzalez describes it: "*The Hunger* is a film about the fear of getting old, that feeling that you get when you feel youth is slowing slipping from you and you feel the aches and pains of old age slowly creeps into your life."[3] And even then, the sudden aging process that affects John (David Bowie) in the movie appears to be something from which Miriam (Catherine Deneuve), who sired him, is immune. In the rest of the cinematic vampire oeuvre, however, two main forms dominate: the ancient vampire, looking old if not exactly their chronological age (say, like Bela Lugosi in Tod Browning's *Dracula* [1931], or even more by the time he reprised the role in *Plan 9 from Outer Space* [1959]); and the perpetually youthful vampire, frozen in development at the point of their turning (with the extreme form being the occasional child vampire, as in *Interview with a Vampire* [1994]).

In recent incarnations—since *Lost Boys* and *Near Dark* (both 1987)—the youthful vampire has dominated both the screen and the page. Ananya Mukerjea, summarizing the trend that she traces from the television *Buffy the Vampire Slayer* (1997–2003) through Stephenie Meyer's *Twilight* series and Ellen Schreiber's *Vampire Kisses* novels, notes: "While these texts vary widely in terms of their crafting, popularity, and messages ... they all share a distinctly sympathetic view of the love between a young, high-school aged human girl-woman and a blood-drinking boy-man."[4] For Mukerjea, at least part of the attraction centers precisely on the ambiguity of the vampire and age: physically frozen in perpetual youth, but mentally detached from that state, so that the romances are with "old-school gentleman vampires"[5]; it can be like dating an older man, without him having to be physically old, so that "this age-duality of being ancient in experience while also youthful in impulse renders the vampire boyfriend both wise and passionate."[6] Sally Chivers, however, writes of the reverse tendency in *Buffy the Vampire Slayer,* focusing on the relationship between the slayer and the vampire Angel. "The age difference between Angel and Buffy"—roughly 200 years—she reads as "signaling the different forms of chronological aging featured in the show."[7] In the show, Chivers notes, joking diffuses the tension around the question of age difference without quite dissipating it.

For Chivers, the agelessness of the vampire body also figures into a regularly expressed anxiety about aging in *Buffy*. She notes that "old bodies have negative meanings" and that this "must be worse for women who face what Susan Sontag calls the double standard of aging, since femininity is apparently tied to youthful appearance."[8] Jennifer L. McMahon pitches a similar argument precisely to the anxieties our society has about aging: "Aging arouses anxiety.... [Thus] the appeal of vampires lies not only in their immortality but also in their eternal youth."[9] As she notes of the *Twilight* series: "*Twilight* expresses our concern about aging and our wish to escape it. Because Bella seeks a long-term relationship with an immortal vampire, she expresses more concern about aging than most teens."[10] Simon Bacon, analyzing female vampires, transfers such anxiety to the vampire herself: "there is no monster that encapsulates and embodies the dystopian visions of a society obsesses with the perfect feminine form ... like the female vampire. Reflecting society's obsession with youth and the seemingly endless regimes of diet and cosmetics needed to maintain and/or ensure it, so too does the female vampire require a proscribed routine of care to maintain her appearance of eternal youth and beauty."[11] In such readings, even if the vampire is ever youthful, the vampire's presence in culture marks our anxieties about age.

But an alternative reading of the eternally youthful vampire underlines more positive possibilities than dire inevitability. Guillermo Del Toro and Chuck Hogan write of the vampire's perpetual appeal:

> in contrast to timeless creatures like the dragon, the vampire does not seek to obliterate us, but instead offers a peculiar brand of blood alchemy. For as his contagion bestows its nocturnal gift, the vampire transforms our vile, mortal selves into the gold of eternal youth, and instills in us something that every social construct seeks to quash: primal lust. If youth is desire married with unending possibility, then vampire lust creates within us a delicious void, one we long to fill.[12]

This parallels in some ways Rob Latham's account "consumer vampirism"—with the vampire metaphor Karl Marx employed to describe the operations of capitalism now, in a postmodern world, representing the capitalist consumer ethos—in which the vampire constellates contemporary advertising/marketing obsessions with youth culture and perpetual consumption.[13]

Even with the eternally youthful vampire, there remain ambiguities. For one, the killing of a vampire tends to re-enact, in rapid form, the aging process. Harlan Kennedy reads this reversal in moral terms (and dates its advent within vampire cinema along the way):

> But the main link to cinema is in the vampire story's overriding fascination with age and time. The Hubris of agelessness is invariably linked to evil, of course; otherwise we might all begin to like the idea too much. And it is also linked to the vampire's own tragic last-act Nemesis, which often takes the supremely apt form of a sudden accelerated aging process. (Or rapid-reverse face lift.) This is most memorably instanced in Terence Fisher's 1959 Hammer *Dracula*, where, thanks to trick photography, Christopher Lee establishes the world speed record for becoming a pile of ashes.[14]

In long-running vampire series, the agelessness of vampires proves ever more difficult to sustain, since, as Chivers points out, "while vampire characters ought not to show their characters' age, the actors who play them ... do visibly age."[15] Moreover, in a pattern detectable at least as early as *Forever Knight* (1992–1996) and still evident in recent series like *Being Human* (2008–2013), vampires in leading roles have frequently been sired by older men.[16] How those men got older is never quite clear. And in the Buffyverse as well, despite the emphasis on young vampires, there are also the Old Ones, associated with Ancient Evil, like season one's Master, who, Chivers notes, "looks monstrous but also resembles, more than any other character on the show, an old man," and later seasons' The First, who chooses age, "in effect shuffling off the immortal coil of the apparently youthful body for a similarly immortal but less youthful visage."[17] The trade-off here is youth for power, with ancient looks connected to heightened abilities.

What the ancient vampires of *Buffy*'s realm most closely resemble is the old vampires of the alternate cinematic tradition, which can be tracked from F. W. Murnau's *Nosferatu* (1922) forward through Browning's *Dracula*, Werner Herzog's *Nosferatu* (1979), and on to E. Elias Merhige's *Shadow of the Vampire* (2000). The difference between the tendency toward younger vampires and ancient ones might be rooted in source material: for the most part, the old vampires derive directly from adaptations of Stoker's novel.[18] As Nina Auerbach notes, the original, Byronic vampire was more congenial companion than monster: "Darvell [Byron's vampire] is a compelling contemporary and glamorous traveling companion, not—as Count Dracula will be to Jonathan Harker—a repulsive old man."[19] And that pattern, Auerbach contends, continues throughout the 19th century, until Stoker took on the material and abandoned the companionate vampire: "Bram Stoker's Dracula—animal rather than phantom, mesmerist rather than intimate, tyrant rather than friend—safely quarantined vampires from their human prey."[20] Coppola's Dracula, embodied as both young and old, collapses the binaries of Auerbach's catalog, functioning, depending on the circumstances as both animal and phantom, both mesmerist and intimate, both tyrant and friend.[21]

Coppola and the Critics

On its release in 1992, Coppola's *Bram Stoker's Dracula* was something of an outlier: a remake of a traditional vampire tale (the lone exoticized Other dropped into the metropole to prey in a highly sexualized way on the people whose very modernity makes them potential victims) at a time when the dominant tropes were shifting: toward the vampire conceptualized as subculture, with all its concomitant features (the chaste vampire, subcultural competition as with werewolves, and organized social structures, most evident in the requisite vampire bar).[22] It also came at a critical moment in Coppola's own career, after a decade of critically and commercially unsuccessful work. At the box office, *Dracula* was a smash, both domestically and abroad, earning enough for Coppola to save his Zoetrope Studios from looming bankruptcy.[23]

Critics were decidedly more mixed, both at the time and since. Sometimes individual critics seem pretty mixed, like Roger Ebert: "The movie is an exercise in feverish excess, and for that if for little else, I enjoyed it."[24] In the *New York Times,* Vincent Canby strikes a similar note, calling "Coppola's new extravaganza" a "dizzy tour of movie-making forces…. This 'Dracula' transcends camp to become a testimonial to the glories of film making as an end in itself." But then, Canby adds, "that's all very well and good, you might say, but shouldn't movies, even Dracula movies, be about something?" He answers his own question: "Not necessarily."[25] Hal Hinson, writing for the *Washington Post,* is more straightforwardly positive about "Coppola's magnificent, astonishing new telling," an "illuminated manuscript of Stoker's classic" by a "visionary entertainer and miracle worker."[26] But Desson Howe, in the same paper, harrumphs: "Francis Ford Coppola wins endless vam–Pyrrhic victories but loses the narrative war. Not so much a story as an endless dreamscape, this 'Dracula' is peculiarly undead…. You can't tell if this is a flawed masterpiece or an intricately designed bag of wind."[27] For Lyndon Joslin, the work "is a deeply frustrating film … an overlong, confusing film in which virtually nothing works from beginning to end."[28] There is not much of a critical consensus.

A particularly ferocious fight over the film focuses on fidelity: on the claim to more faithful adaptation, implicit in the title itself,[29] regularly reiterated by Coppola himself ("I knew enough about the authentic *Dracula* to realize that it had never been made as a movie," he told Gene Phillips[30]), and dutifully parroted by many reviewers then (like Todd McCarthy: "James V. Hart is the first screenwriter to have had the bright idea to fundamentally follow the quite wonderful 1897 novel" or Vincent Canby: "unusually faithful screen adaptation"[31]) and commentators since (for instance, James Clarke: "Given Coppola's theatrical and literary sensibilities, his adaptation … was to be one of the most faithful of the many produced, most of which deviated from the narrative"[32]). Given that Coppola's movie in fact begins by deviating from the narrative—its extended, and narratively central, opening historical sequence entirely absent from the novel to which the film asserts its faithfulness—such claims have irritated other commentators. Thus Joslin notes, near the beginning of his seven-page lacerating of the film, "Even the title is a problem.... As anyone knows who has seen virtually any film adaptation of virtually any novel ... a book is not a movie, and never can be. But even taking this title as what it's meant to be—a claim that this film is, within the limits of adaptation, the story that Bram Stoker wrote—it's misleading. Anyone familiar with the novel won't make it past the first few minutes before noticing that Stoker didn't write *this*."[33] James Welsh observes: "None of this fanciful and spectacular back story is to be found in the novel, although legend has it that Vlad's wife committed suicide in the way suggested at Castle Dracula. But this back story gives Dracula a context that seriously distorts Bram Stoker's original design, shifting the story from one of Gothic horror to one of Gothic romance."[34] Ken Gelder references that opening sequence when he notes: "By opening with this narrative—and by declaring itself as a romantic epic—the film inevitably drew attention to just how far it *departed* from the novel—even though, by putting author and text into its title, it seemed to promise (finally ...) the real thing."[35] And Cynthia A. Freeland writes: "Francis Ford Coppola's film version of *Dracula*, based upon a screenplay by James V. Hart, purports to be true to the original—it is after all titled '*Bram Stoker's Dracula*'—but it falsifies Stoker's story narratively, intellectually, and emotionally."[36] Clearly this is more than simple the-book-was-better griping.

But Freeland, while laying out that three-pronged attack, also notices the trick that makes Coppola's claims work: she notes that

> his is the first film version faithfully to portray on screen, with real emotional force, the three key scenes of erotic transgression in Stoker's novel: the scene between Jonathan and Dracula's brides, Mina's voyeuristic view of Lucy with an animalistic Dracula on the bench [although, Freeland does not note, in Coppola's film he commands Mina "Don't see me," an order he will reverse when they meet in London's city center], and the scene where she drinks blood from the vein he opens in his chest [although here, Freeland does not add, Coppola reverses the source of the impulse; she is forced to drink in the novel, demands to drink in the film].[37]

Joslyn similarly notes:

> To give credit where it's due, Hart's screenplay includes a number of details from the novel not seen in any earlier version. These range from both major themes, such a Dracula's ability (per both Stoker and folklore) to come out in broad daylight, to such trivia as the harnessing four-abreast of the horses.... This is the first version ... to depict Lucy callously dropping the little child.... And in no previous version does Quincey die. Indeed, this is the first version to feature Quincey Morris, Texan.[38]

The rampant mixture of especially careful fidelity with especially capricious infidelity seems what most riles critics like Joslin. But the central departures from the source text all relate as well to what is, for Coppola, the key characteristic of his film: its negotiation of time.

The Terms of Time: The Three Dimensions of Coppola's Vision

This brings us back to the three features of Coppola's treatment of time in *Dracula*: a vampire who can appear as either aged or young, the reincarnation trope, and the play with the cinematic apparatus. Each feature works to destabilize normal linearity of time. And the three together work to underpin the reshaping Welsh notes, turning the story from Gothic horror to romance. None of the three, however, is especially fully explicated within the film itself.

The count's differential age, his sudden youthfulness in London, is one of those details in which Coppola's adaptation is, in fact, more faithful to Stoker than most previous versions. Dracula appears, when Harker first meets him, "a tall old man, clean shaven save for a long white moustache," but when Harker sees him on the London streets, he declares: "I believe it is the Count, but he has grown young."[39] What still, however, differs between text and adaptation is the other direction of transformation: he has not just grown young, but more handsome. The fiend of the novel is never portrayed as attractive. And Dracula can shapeshift in a range of other ways as well: becoming animal (as in the garden with Lucy), turning into green mist (as he sneaks in on Lucy), appearing monstrous in ways that are not just aged (when he is surprised by the posse of vampire hunters), and even transforming into multiple rats that can then separately disperse (as he escapes them).

Exactly how this age reversal works (and then unworks, since when Dracula returns to Transylvania he is old again) is not quite clear. One is tempted to follow Hinson: "He can change shape at will."[40] That certainly seems consistent with some of the other transformations, and with his ability to force people to "see" or "don't see" him. It would also be consistent with the powers that van Helsing (Anthony Hopkins) attributes to the vampire (or at least describes as "things in the universe which you cannot understand and which are true"): "mesmerism, hypnotism, telekinesis, materialization, astral bodies." But the willed power would seem to be, finally, a control of appearance: Dracula forces others to see him a certain way (as if Dracula mentally transmitted the message to Lucy not just to "see me" but to "see me young and attractive if somewhat oddly attired"). And such an explanation does not fit the moment when Dracula first appears young: bursting out of his coffin at Carfax Abbey just after arriving in London, when no one is looking at all. It also does not address the return to agedness as Dracula heads back to his castle. Or that, in a striking rejection of the norms for most post–Hammer vampires, when Dracula dies, he doesn't age but instead returns (again) to his youthful form. What, given all this back and forth, can we take to be his "natural" state? It is not quite clear. But after all, this is one of those things van Helsing has told us "you cannot understand," so perhaps we need not try to unravel it all.

Elizabeta's reincarnation as Mina is similarly less than fully sorted out. She is, as noted, fully re-embodied, both soul and physical form reborn. Nor is she the only such rebirth: Van Helsing is also apparently a reincarnation, in his case of the priest who told Dracula that his dead wife, a suicide, could not be buried in hallowed ground (and who thus inspired the cursing of God and burying his sword in a bleeding cross that turned him into a vampire in the first place, in Coppola's account).[41] The reincarnation trope in vampire films was not new to Coppola; commentators have traced it back to Dan Curtis, who employed it in both *Dark Shadows* (1966–71) and then in his 1973 *Dracula* (with Palance as the Count).[42] Indeed, Joslin complains: "The hoary cliché of the 'reincarnation romance' was already old by the time it was spoofed in *Love at First Bite* (1979)."[43] It gives, at least, a deeper resonance to the playing out of the scene borrowed from Murnau's *Nosferatu*, where Dracula lingers over the portrait of Harker's fiancé. She's not, for him, just another pretty face.

In Coppola's case, at any rate, the reincarnation propels the romance plot, Dracula seeking out the love he had lost 400 years earlier, thus the whole discussion of how "even

"The powers of time can be altered" (Prasch) 159

the powers of time can be altered." Mina in turn remembers him, at least with a bit of prodding by the Count while drinking absinthe. She imagines his homeland: "A land beyond a great, vast forest surrounded by majestic mountains, lush vineyards, and flowers of such frailty and beauty as to be found nowhere else." "You describe my home as if you had seen it first-hand," Dracula tells her, not noticing how very vague the descriptors are in Mina's imagining. "It's your voice, perhaps. It's so familiar," she tells him. And then she seems to remember her own death (if not her old clothing choices): "There is always a princess with gowns flowing white. Her face, her face is the river. The princess, she is the river filled with tears and with sadness and with heartbreak." And that Dracula is propelled by love explains his reluctance to bite Mina—to curse her as he has been cursed—even if that seems the obvious happy ending for the pair (happier at least then the ending they get: where she stakes and beheads him to give him, finally, peace, and then presumably goes back to Harker).

But there are still gaps in this account. If both Mina and van Helsing are reincarnations, is everyone else as well? Is this norm or exception? And if it is only when he

Staked through the heart and dying, the vampire (Gary Oldman) meets his end in Francis Ford Coppola's *Dracula*.

sees the picture that he recognizes his lost love, why is Dracula already buying property in London, before that revelation (indeed, before Harker even shows up on the scene, since Renfield [a delightful Tom Waits] preceded him as real-estate agent?) Again, perhaps we are just not meant to know.

And yet, as Harlan Kennedy suggested, a decade before Coppola started filming, "Films alone—being at once animate, graphic, realistic, and unchanging—seem to have Time conquered."[44] The third element of Coppola's tangling with time in *Dracula* relates to the cinema itself, and is realized in his double move: of situating the invention of cinema within the story, and of reproducing the effects of early cinema. Dracula and Mina's first date, in a sense, is to the movies: when he wants to "see the amazing cinematograph! A wonder of modern civilization!" as the street hawker puts it and Mina somewhat reluctantly takes him there ("If you seek culture, then visit a museum. London is filled with them," she suggests before giving in to him). They find themselves in the dark spaces of what amounts to some sort of Victorian metroplex: against one wall, multiple films are cast (a softporn sex show, with a disappearing naked woman like some shadier Mèliés; something like the Lumière Brothers train film, although this one, in a more Freudian move, goes through a tunnel); in another corner, a precinematic shadow-puppet play can be seen (self-reflexively reenacting Vlad's battles with the Turks); there are dark spaces and couches and space enough for Dracula's waltz of seduction and a for a wild wolf to wander a bit before his Romanian words and Mina's touch tame it.[45] Stoker's text revels in technological modernity, filled with its artifacts (trains, telegraphs, typewriters); Coppola both reproduces that focus and adds cinema to the list.[46]

At the same time that Coppola showcases early cinema, he also reproduces it, imitating a range of the effects of silent films. Much of this benefited from the editing work of his son Roman Coppola, as Gene Phillips notes: "Roman Coppola employed such quaint cinematic techniques as double exposures, slow fades, and dissolves to achieve special effects.... Chiaroscuro lighting infuses certain interiors with vast, menacing shadows, which loom on walls and ceilings.... These artfully composed visual effects were not only economical, but they also paid homage to the magic of earlier Dracula films of Murnau and Browning."[47] Iris shots close out scenes; Dracula's first stroll in London is accompanied by the stuttering motion often seen in early film.[48] The effects—especially the creepy shadows and light effects—more recall Weimar cinema than the films of Stoker's novel's time, but given Coppola's expressed admiration for Murnau's *Nosferatu* (1922),[49] that makes perfect sense.

Reproduction of effects also permits homage, through deliberate allusion to earlier cinema and even other visual modes. Thomas Elsaesser insists that "the film's particular authenticity" is precisely in this catalog of citations, in which he has identified reference to "at last count, no less than sixty titles. Besides the 30-odd Dracula films, this still leaves a dense intertextuality."[50] As Elsaesser notes as well, this includes, in visual clues, homages to artists from Northern Renaissance figures like Albrecht Dürer to modernists like Gustav Klimt. Elsaesser concludes that "the film poses as a kind of palimpsest of a hundred years of movie history."[51] But Alsaesser's term—with its painterly suggestions of pasts covered up and uncovered again—rather misses the mark. Alternatively, it juxtaposes, or cuts between, putting Coppola in dialogue with the cinematic past.

This juxtaposition of past and present resonates beyond the cinematic referencing, affecting the central metaphors of the film as well. Consider the tropes around blood in the film. Van Helsing lectures: "Blood and the diseases of the blood such as syphilis will concern us here. The very name 'venereal diseases,' the 'diseases of Venus,' imputes to them divine origin. They are involved in that sex problem about which the ethics and ideals of Christian civilization are concerned. In fact, civilization and syphillization have advanced together." His discourse, if a bit wackily fringe in form, hearkens in its Victorian context to the debates about criminal type in which figures like Cesare Lombroso, Max Nordau, and eugenicist Francis Galton participated in the last decade of the century.[52] But to contemporary audiences, it also resonates with the AIDS crisis, at its height when the film was released.[53]

Where does this leave us? What does Coppola's multiple manipulation of time and aging in his *Dracula* suggest? Thomas Elsaesser proposes that films like Coppola's necessitate a new form of appreciation, which he terms "engulfment": "a distinct mode of consequence, of implication and interrelation," featuring a far more "attenuated kind of causality," but attuned to "ambient space" rather than "bounded space."[54] Short of new forms of spectatorship, however, Coppola's film at least necessitates a different sort of understanding. Given a set of binary choices—young or old, present or past, the list of oppositions Auerbach articulated about Stoker's *Dracula*—Coppola's consistent answer is, essentially, "I'll take both." Perhaps this tells us, mostly, about Coppola's own aging, about his refusal to accept the possibilities conventional thinking about that particular linear trajectory implied.

NOTES

1. Aside from agedness, David Glover notes, Dracula here, "with high-coiffed Kabuki hair and dressed in a long red silk tunic embossed with golden Chinese dragons," is "newly Orientalized," his appearance apt to "conjure up another popular Eastern villain, the ageless Dr. Fu Manchu" ("Travels in Romania: Myths of Origins, Myths of Blood," 132). Orientalization, however, is not new here; in some sense, this returns the vampire story to the Eastern settings of its English origin, in Lord Byron's vampire story and John Polidori's filching of the same. See Byron, "A Fragment" and Polidori, *The Vampyre* (both 1819).
2. For Plato, too, the past can be recalled through prompting; see especially the mathematical demonstration in *Meno*, where the principles are not learned but remembered. The same principle works for Tibetan lamas, whose identification as reincarnations of aspects of the Buddha is secured by their recognition of items from past lives. This process is cinematically represented in Martin Scorsese's biopic about the current Dalai Lama, *Kundun* (1997).
3. Gonzalez, "*The Hunger* (1983)." See also James Ward's essay in this volume.
4. Mukherjea, "My Vampire Boyfriend," 4.
5. *Ibid.*, 3.
6. *Ibid.*, 6.
7. Chivers, "Vampires Don't Age," 100.
8. *Ibid.*, 92. Lorna Jowett offers a parallel close reading of the ways Angel inhabits his vampire body, with its powers of "strength, speed, 'immortality,' youthfulness, and fast recuperation from illness" ("'Not Like Other Men'?" 45).
9. McMahon, "Twilight of an Idol," 195.
10. *Ibid.*, 196.
11. Bacon, "Binging," 21–22. His principal example, however, is not technically vampiric, as even he concedes: "Strictly speaking, *Countess Dracula* is not a vampire film" (27). The biopic concerns Elizabeth Bathory, who bathed in blood rather than drinking it.
12. Del Toro and Hogan, "Why Vampires Never Die."
13. Latham, *Consuming Youth*, 26, and generally chapters 1–2.
14. Kennedy, "Time Machine." This seems to work for almost-vampires like "Countess Dracula" as well; see Bacon, "Binging," 22.
15. Chivers, "Vampires Don't Age," 106.
16. The pattern resonates with that sexualized mentorship, already implicit in the homoerotic subtexts in Byron and Polidori's vampire tales, that fascinated a contemporary of Bram Stoker's, John Addington Symonds, whose exploration of Greek pederasty, *A Problem in Greek Ethics* (1883), had been appended to Havelock Ellis's *Sexual Inversion* in 1897, the same year *Dracula* was published.
17. Chivers, "Vampires Don't Age," 98.
18. The dichotomy is somewhat imperfect. As William Paul notes, a "new graphicness about the body"

corresponded to a shift in Dracula's representation: "The 1979 *Dracula* [directed by John Badham] foregrounded this new direction by casting a much younger and more dreamily romantic actor [Frank Langella] in the part of the Count," and featured as well "an elaborate and delirious lovemaking scene" corresponding to that more bodily and more sexualized perspective (see *Laughing Screaming*, 383). Post-Langella Draculas have sometimes followed this lead.

19. Auerbach, *Our Vampires, Ourselves*, 13.
20. Ibid., 7.
21. Auerbach was not amused. Her discussion of Coppola's film reduces it to a single dismissive footnote, in which she calls James Hart's screenplay derivative ("so reliant on that of the 1973 TV movie of the same name [Jack Curtis, director], starring Jack Palance, that discussion would be redundant," although she spends but a page or so on the earlier film) and concludes: "the fundamental illogic of Coppola's kaleidoscopic cinematography, and of Oldman's Dracula himself, suggests a postmodern Dracula may be a contradiction in terms. It may be that Coppola has killed Dracula at last and that he would fade out with the twentieth century." Ibid., 209 n. 16. The prediction now seems premature.
22. For a fuller discussion of the new wave in vampire films, see Prasch, "Vampirism as Subculture."
23. Gene D. Phillips, *Godfather: The Intimate Francis Ford Coppola*, 298.
24. Ebert, "*Bram Stoker's Dracula*."
25. Canby, "Review/Film; Coppola's Dizzying Vision of Dracula."
26. Hinson, "'Bram Stoker's Dracula.'"
27. Howe, "'Bram Stoker's Dracula.'"
28. Joslin, *Count Dracula Goes to the Movies: Stoker's Novel Adapted, 1922–2003*, 123.
29. Ebert, in "*Bram Stoker's Dracula*," points out, however, that the reason for the title signified rather less than a commitment to fidelity: "Another studio owns the rights to plain 'Dracula.'"
30. Phillips, *Godfather*, 287. Coppola is still making the claim, telling Joe McGovern in 2015 that previous movies "didn't really adapt the book," so he had "gone back to the source." Joe McGovern, "Francis Ford Coppola remembers Dracula."
31. Todd McCarthy, "Bram Stoker's Dracula"; Canby, "Coppola's Dizzying Vision."
32. Clarke, *Coppola*, 211.
33. Joslin, *Count Dracula Goes to the Movies*, 123. To be fair, Joslin does not blame Coppola alone for this: "Yet the awfulness of *Bram Stoker's Dracula* isn't totally Coppola's fault. Much of the blame must go to screenwriter James V. Hart, who had earlier ruined the Peter Pan story with his screenplay for *Hook* (1991)" (124). And who, by the way, did "write *this*," the back story about Vlad and the Turks and his suicide wife? Some of it is still Hart's fault, but the first modern writers to really explore the roots of the historical backstory were Raymond T. McNally and Radu Florescu, in *In Search of Dracula*, upon which foundations in turn Leonard Wolf built his *Annotated Dracula* (1976), which, Joslin suggests, was more than Stoker the source for Coppola.
34. Welsh, "*Bram Stoker's Dracula*," 23.
35. Gelder, *Reading the Vampire*, 90.
36. Freeland, *The Naked and the Undead*, 137.
37. Ibid., 138. For the scene of Mina drinking from his chest, however, Coppola is hardly first; it constitutes a key scene in Badham's/Langella's *Dracula* (1979), and that film also anticipates Coppola in turning Dracula into an object of romantic interest in that scene. Auerbach observes that he is "not coercive, but tender" (*Our Vampires, Ourselves*, 145). Contrast with Stoker, where after he "opened a vein in his breast" using "his long sharp nails," Dracula "seized my neck and pressed my mouth to the wound, so that I must either suffocate or swallow some of the—Oh my God!" (Bram Stoker, *Dracula*, 306).
38. Joslin, *Count Dracula Goes to the Movies*, 124. Other versions, Joslin further notes, do feature Morris, but do not identify him as Texan.
39. Stoker, *Dracula*, 20, 187.
40. Hinson, "'Bram Stoker's Dracula.'"
41. Although pretty much everybody notices Elizabetha's reincarnation as Mina, relatively few make anything of van Helsing's earlier embodiment as the priest. An exception is Welsh, "Bram Stoker's Dracula," 23.
42. Joslin, *Count Dracula Goes to the Movies*, 85. See also Palmer, *Vampires in the New World*, 66; Smith, *Vampire Films of the 1970s: Dracula to Blacula and Every Fang Between*, 181. McNally and Florescu suggest a deeper source, in the similar theme in another Universal monster franchise of the 1930s, *The Mummy* (*In Search of Dracula*, 176).
43. Joslin, *Count Dracula Goes to the Movies*, 126.
44. Kennedy, "The Time Machine."
45. Unsurprisingly, film scholars love to unpack the sequence. For more detailed accounts, see Weinstock, *Vampire Film*, 74–77; Gelder, *Reading the Vampire*, 87–90; Gelder, *New Vampire Cinema*, 4–5; Freeland, *The Naked and the Undead*, 139–41; Elsaesser, "Spectacularity and Engulfment," 197–199; Stewart, "Film's Victorian Retrofit," 189–191.
46. Part of Coppola's play with time in the film comes with his insistence on precise historical moments:

1462 for the prologue, 1897 for the body of the work. Other adaptations are less precise about time frame, because it matters less. Browning relocates the film to contemporary (1931) London (the automotive street noise when the count arrives in London cues us in on that fact); Murnau opts for a generalized 19th (or even 18th; there are few clear time cues) century; Badham's setting seems simply Gothic.

47. Phillips, *Godfather*, 291. See also Delorme, *Masters of Cinema: Francis Ford Coppola*, 80.
48. The London street scene Coppola filmed using an antique Pathé camera from his own collection, Freeland notes (*The Naked and the Undead*, 140).
49. James Clarke writes that Coppola "acknowledged that, in his opinion, the best Dracula movie had been WF [sic] Murnau's *Nosferatu*" (*Coppola*, 212).
50. Elsaesser, "Spectacularity and Engulfment," 197. The film's intertextuality includes citations of Coppola's own earlier work, as Stéphane Delorme points out: "The vampire, both old and young, is a paradox over which Don Corleone's shadow moves. When he exclaims, 'I am the last of my kind!,' we hear, word for word, the disillusioned soldiers of *Gardens of Stone*" (*Masters of Cinema: Francis Ford Coppola*, 78).
51. Elsaesser, "Specularity and Engulfment," 198.
52. For fuller context, and interesting connections to the conventions established for photographic identification, see Sekula, "The Body and the Archive."
53. On this point, see especially Rich, "New Blood Culture."
54. Elsaesser, "Specularity and Engulfment," 204.

Bibliography

Auerbach, Nina. *Our Vampires, Ourselves*. Chicago: University of Chicago Press, 1995.
Bacon, Simon. "Binging: Excess, Aging, and Identity in the Female Vampire." *MP: An Online Feminist Journal* 3, no. 3 (Winter 2011): 21–37.
Bram Stoker's Dracula. Directed by Francis Ford Coppola. 1992. Culver City, CA: Columbia Tristar Home Video, 1997. DVD.
Byron, Lord George. "A Fragment" (c. 1816), appended to *Mazeppa* (1819). London: John Murray, 1819. Online at https://www.bl.uk/collection-items/fragment-of-a-novel-from-mazeppa-by-lord-george-byron.
Canby, Vincent. "Review/Film; Coppola's Dizzying Vision of Dracula." *New York Times*, November 13, 1992. www.nytimes.com/1992/11/13/movies/review-film-coppola-s-dizzying-vision-of-dracula.html.
Chivers, Sally. "Vampires Don't Age, but Actors Sure Do: The Cult of Youth and the Paradox of Aging in *Buffy the Vampire Slayer*." In *Serializing Age: Aging and Old Age in TV Series*, edited by Maricel Oró-Piqueras and Anita Wohlman, 91–108. Blelefeld, Germany: Transcript, 2016.
Clarke, James. *Coppola*. London: Virgin Books, 2003.
Del Toro, Guillermo, and Chuck Hogan. "Why Vampires Never Die." *New York Times*, July 31, 2009. http://www.nytimes.com/2009/07/31/opinion/31deltoro.html.
Delorme, Stéphane. *Masters of Cinema: Francis Ford Coppola*. Paris: Cahiers du cinema Sarl, 2010.
Ebert, Roger. "*Bram Stoker's Dracula*." *Chicago Sun-Times*. November 13, 1992. https://www.rogerebert.com/reviews/bram-stokers-dracula-1992.
Elsaesser, Thomas. "Specularity and Engulfment: Francis Ford Coppola and *Bram Stoker's Dracula*." In *Contemporary Hollywood Cinema*, edited by Steve Meade and Murray Smith, 191–208. London: Routledge, 1998.
Freeland, Cynthia A. *The Naked and the Undead: Evil and the Appeal of Horror*. Boulder, CO: Westview, 2000.
Gelder, Ken. *New Vampire Cinema*. London: BFI/Palgrave Macmillan, 2012.
_____. *Reading the Vampire*. London: Routledge, 1994.
Glover, David. "Travels in Romania: Myths of Origins, Myths of Blood." *Discourse* 16, no. 1 (Fall 1993), 126–144.
Gonzalez, Francisco. "*The Hunger* (1983)." *The Film Connoisseur*, August 17, 2010. http://filmconnoisseur.blogspot.com/2010/08/hunger-1983.html.
Hinson, Hal. "'*Bram Stoker's Dracula*.'" *Washington Post*, November 13, 1992. http://www.washingtonpost.com/wp-srv/style/longterm/movies/videos/bramstokersdracularhinson_a0a7c7.htm.
Howe, Desson. "'*Bram Stoker's Dracula*.'" *Washington Post*, November 13, 1992. http://www.washingtonpost.com/wp-srv/style/longterm/movies/videos/bramstokersdracularhowe_a0af35.htm.
Joslin, Lyndon W. *Count Dracula Goes to the Movies: Stoker's Novel Adapted, 1922–2003*, 2nd ed. Jefferson, NC: McFarland, 2006.
Jowett, Lorna. "'Not Like Other Men'? The Vampire Body in Joss Whedon's *Angel*." *Studies in Popular Culture* 32, no. 1 (2009): 37–51.
Kennedy, Harlan. "The Time Machine: Death Is the Only Immortal." *Film Comment* (January/February 1984), in *American Cinema Papers: Print Archive*. http://www.americancinemapapers.com/files/TIME_MACHINE.htm.
Latham, Rob. *Consuming Youth: Vampires, Cyborgs, and the Culture of Consumption*. Chicago: University of Chicago Press, 2002.

McCarthy, Todd. "Bram Stoker's Dracula." *Variety*, November 8, 1992. http://variety.com/1992/film/reviews/bram-stoker-s-dracula-1200431014/.
McGovern, Joe. "Francis Ford Coppola Remembers Dracula, Firing His VFX Crew, and Keanu Reeves' Accent." *Entertainment Weekly*, October 6, 2015. http://ew.com/article/2015/10/06/francis-ford-coppola-remembers-dracula/.
McMahon, Jennifer L. "Twilight of an Idol: Our Fatal Attraction to Vampires." In *Twilight and Philosophy*, edited by Rebecca Housel and J. Jeremy Wisnewski, 193–208. Hoboken: John Wiley and Sons, 2009.
McNally, Raymond T., and Radu Florescu. *In Search of Dracula: The History of Dracula and Vampires*. New York: Houghton Mifflin, 1994.
Mukherjea, Ananya. "My Vampire Boyfriend: Postfeminism, 'Perfect' Masculinity, and the Contemporary Appeal of the Paranormal Romance." *Studies in Popular Culture* 33, no. 2 (2011): 1–20.
Palmer, Louis H. *Vampires in the New World*. Santa Barbara: Praeger, 2013.
Paul, William. *Laughing Screaming: Modern Hollywood Horror and Comedy*. New York: Columbia University Press, 1994.
Phillips, Gene D. *Godfather: the Intimate Francis Ford Coppola*. Lexington: University of Kentucky Press, 2004.
Polidori, John William. *The Vampyre: A Tale*. London: Sherwood, Neely, and Jones, 1819. https://openlibrary.org/books/OL7020802M/The_vampyre.
Prasch, Tom. "Vampirism as Subculture: Trends in Bloodsucking." *Ryder Magazine* (Bloomington, IN) (October–November 2010), 22–26.
Rich, Frank. "The New Blood Culture." *New York Times*, December 6, 1992. http://www.nytimes.com/1992/12/06/style/the-new-blood-culture.html?pagewanted=all.
Sekula, Alan. "The Body and the Archive." *October* 39 (Winter 1986), 3–64.
Smith, Gary A. *Vampire Films of the 1970s: Dracula to Blacula and Every Fang Between*. Jefferson, NC: McFarland, 2017.
Stewart, Garrett. "Film's Victorian Retrofit." *Victorian Studies* 38, no. 2 (Winter 1995): 153–98.
Stoker, Bram. *Dracula*. 1897. New York: Barnes & Noble, 2003.
Symonds, John Addington. *A Problem in Greek Ethics*. 1883. Rpt. online at Richard Norton's John Addington Symonds Page (1997), http://rictornorton.co.uk/symonds/greek.htm.
Weinstock, Jeffrey. *The Vampire Film: Undead Cinema*. London: Wallflower Books, 2012.
Welsh, James. "Bram Stoker's Dracula." In *The Francis Ford Coppola Encyclopedia*, edited by James Welsh, Gene D. Phillips, and Rodney F. Hull, 22–25. Lanham, MD: Scarecrow Press, 2010.
Wolf, Leonard, and Bram Stoker. *The Annotated Dracula*. New York: Crown, 1975.

"You can be young forever"
The Dread of Aging in Tony Scott's Art-Horror Film The Hunger

JAMES J. WARD

In 2005, a Stanford lab, run by a stem-cell biologist and neurologist named Tom Rando, announced that heterochronic parabiosis, or an exchange of blood between older and younger mice, rejuvenated the livers and muscles of the older ones. Vampires everywhere felt validated.
—Tad Friend, in *The New Yorker* (2017)[1]

From this cure sprang the myth that Keith regularly had the blood emptied out of his body and replaced with a fresh supply. This Dracula notion is one of the few elements of his image that Richards has gone to some pains to correct, but to no avail.
—Victor Bockris, in his biography of Keith Richards (1993)[2]

Of all the erotically charged moments in Universal Pictures' cycle of horror films that began with *Dracula* and *Frankenstein* in 1931, none may be more unsettling than the brief, but suggestive, exchange in *Dracula's Daughter* between the titular character, played by Gloria Holden, and the destitute young woman, played by Nan Gray, she has hired to pose as an artist's model. Since its release in 1936, that film has generated a large literature on its lesbian subtext. Less noticed has been its representation of vampirism as a form of punishment for the indulgence of desires which, because of their associations with cannibalism and necrophilia, must be repressed.[3] The sorrow and weariness that Holden expresses so memorably, together with her pursuit of a psychiatric cure, should instruct us that vampirism is not always a desired condition of existence and that vampires—for all their vaunted immortality—can tire and age. The implication that vampirism, rather than eternal vitality, results in drudgery and exhaustion can be detected in Francis Ford Coppola's *Bram Stoker's Dracula* (1992) and Neil Jordan's adaptation of Anne Rice's *Interview with the Vampire* (1994); in the Australian-made vampire dystopia *Daybreakers* (2009), directed by Michael and Peter Spierig, the dominant predator species has begun to panic as its human blood supply becomes more and more difficult to insure.[4] As Ken Gelder observes in his study of recent vampire films, the circumstances of contemporary life confront these fearsome creatures with a daunting array of new problems: "[B]ecoming a vampire in the modern world—notwithstanding the various excesses it can unleash—brings with it a set of often incapacitating restrictions and restraints. It is not a guarantee of freedom of movement at all; it's not even a guarantee of immortality."[5]

The dread of inevitable decrepitude that comes with living for hundreds, or thousands, of years informs director Tony Scott's *The Hunger* (1983) on multiple vectors. Scott's first full-length film, made after an early career stint shooting commercials and music videos, *The Hunger* tracks closely with the narrative line employed a half-century earlier in *Dracula's Daughter*, although without the desire for release from the genetic burden that weighs upon Gloria Holden's character. The casting of Catherine Deneuve, David Bowie, and Susan Sarandon constitutes another narrative, as each brought to the film a hypersexualized artistic identity that guaranteed emotive collisions, erotic hot spots, and intriguing extra-diegetic resonances. Finally, setting the beginning of the film in the Manhattan club culture of the early 1980s situates it in a historical moment that today is looked upon with a combination of envy and disdain.[6] Seen as ancient history by denizens of the post–2000 New York nighttime scene, this picaresque of indulgence, excess, and narcissistic display—captured best in Brett Easton Ellis' novel *American Psycho* (1991) and in the film version starring Christian Bale (2000)—fetishized youth and beauty at precisely the moment they were about to be ravished by death and disease.[7]

While not ignoring the importance of *The Hunger* as a sociocultural artifact of early 1980s New York, my purpose in this essay is to place it in a trajectory of several self-determined "art" films with which it shares narratological, stylistic, and aesthetic similarities, all focused on isolation, vulnerability, and the passage of time.[8] Scott's use of neo-Gothic and neo-Baroque trappings sets *The Hunger* firmly in the cinematic vampire tradition popularized by Universal Pictures in the 1930s and revitalized by Hammer Studios in the 1960s and '70s. By combining this familiar aesthetic with an explicit mood of lassitude and deracination, Scott appropriates at the same time the "feel" of classic works from the latter period that had transformed high-brow filmmaking first in Europe and then in the United States, above all those of Alain Resnais and Michelangelo Antonioni. Beyond this, *The Hunger* strikes chords of grief and sorrow at the inevitable loss of youth as convincing as any we encounter in far better-known films that address the same theme. In part, this owes to the performances by Catherine Deneuve and David Bowie. But it also reveals a directorial sensibility well versed in literary, artistic, and psychological treatments of this subject, which after all reaches back to antiquity.[9] As James Craig Holte wrote with considerable insight 20 years ago, "*The Hunger* depicts not only the eroticism and violence of vampire life but also the isolation and despair of the undead existence. In attempting to save her lover, Catherine Deneuve's Miriam Baylock [sic] is such a sympathetic character that the film moves toward the boundary between horror and tragedy."[10] *The Hunger* is no mere piece of movie trivia, nor is it just a vanity exercise by a newly minted filmmaker overconfident of his talents and eager to match his older brother's success.[11] Instead, as I will argue in this essay, it is a profound and moving meditation on what the British classical scholar Mary Beard has called "the dreadful truth of the human condition"—its inevitable and inescapable finitude.[12]

Labyrinths of Memory and Loss

The Hunger has sometimes been grouped with a series of films that, starting in the 1970s, transferred the vampire theme from its traditional European settings to the trendy

American locales of New York and Los Angeles. It has also been included with a small number of films released a few years apart in the 1980s that turned the vampire into a modish commodity at one with the burgeoning celebrity culture of that decade, the explosion of music video, and the experimentation with identities that produced Michael Jackson on the one hand and Madonna on the other.[13] These associations make sense if we see *The Hunger* in its usual coding as an exploitation of vampirism and lesbianism—although the two female principals are bisexual, not homosexual. The associations fall away, however, when we recognize that the film's deeper meaning involves the memory of past times, the entry into unknown worlds, and the betrayal of promises exchanged in order to transcend the limitations of mortal existence.[14]

Miriam and John Blaylock (Catherine Deneuve and David Bowie) are a no longer quite-so-young couple living in an old-wealth townhouse on Manhattan's Upper East Side.[15] Other than giving music lessons to a precocious teenager who lives across the street, they seem to have little involvement with the city around them—except for going out at night to visit dance clubs where the music is loud and the crowd is young and hip. *The Hunger* begins with an MTV-style performance by the English Goth band Bauhaus in which vocalist Peter Murphy croaks out the lyrics to their biggest hit, "Bela Lugosi's Dead." A series of quick intercuts illuminates the interior of a nightclub and, spectating from a balcony above the dance floor, Miriam and John, both wearing sunglasses, a possible Andy Warhol reference.[16] Signaling interest to a punkish couple who might be amenable to a more private exchange, Miriam and John repair to their new friends' apartment on Long Island where John romances the woman, slashes her throat, and drains her blood. In like fashion, Miriam desanguinates the man. This opening sequence concludes with an early morning ride back to Manhattan, the sunrise silhouetting the island's skyscrapers, John's and Miriam's hunger for blood momentarily satiated.[17]

The Blaylocks' mannered elegance, their predatory voyeurism at the nightclub, and the luxurious furnishings of their home—as well as the implication of secrets waiting to be exposed—bring to mind that lodestone of 1960s European art cinema, Alain Resnais' *Last Year at Marienbad* (1961), with a screenplay by Alain Robbe-Grillet. The dreamy, languorous nature of the Blaylocks' marriage recalls the extended, almost opiated scenes in which the guests who inhabit Resnais' isolated, ultra-luxe resort try to piece together their individual, and shared, destinies.[18] While nowhere as opaque as the earlier film's famously ambiguous plot, *The Hunger* reveals the mystery of the relationship between Miriam and John gradually, in brief flashbacks, and only slowly explains the reason for John's perplexity at the abrupt onset of his long-deferred aging process. Their roles may be reversed, Delphine Seyrig as an actual or intended adulteress in *Last Year at Marienbad*, Catherine Deneuve in *The Hunger* as a seductress who keeps her victims neatly boxed in an attic crypt, but the two women might as well be cut from the same cloth—literally, as Seyrig's costumes were designed by Coco Chanel and Deneuve's by Yves Saint Laurent.[19]

Miriam Blaylock is in fact thousands of years old, her lifespan reaching back to ancient Egypt. After a succession of prior lovers, she offered the promise of eternal life to John, perhaps a stable hand, more likely an aristocrat, in 17th-century France. Now Miriam's lethal secret, that eternal life is not the same as eternal youth, begins to reveal itself. Not long after the sojourn to Long Island, John notices that he has begun to age: the skin around his eyes is creasing, his hair is thinning, his sleep is fitful. A chance Polaroid photograph, taken by the music student Alice, confirms these changes. From her expression, it is clear that Miriam knows what is happening, and has dreaded it. By now both Blaylocks have become aware of the work of gerontologist Dr. Sarah Roberts (Susan Sarandon), who is researching a possible connection between sleeplessness and aging. Miriam seeks her out at a book-signing event and establishes a connection; John confronts her directly at the clinic where she works. Dismissing John as "just another crank," Sarah quickly regrets her misjudgment when he ages decades while sitting in her waiting room.

The same air of refinement, mystery, and perversity that links *The Hunger* with *Last Year at Marienbad* also connects it, much more directly, with Belgian director Harry Kümel's 1971 vampire melodrama *Daughters of Darkness*. With Delphine Seyrig again in the lead role, *Daughters of Darkness* updates the semi-mythologized story of Countess Erzsébet (Elizabeth) Báthory, who is alleged to have bathed in the blood of virgins, from the 16th century to the 20th and relocates it from Hungary to Belgium. Set in a grand beachfront hotel in Ostend, empty for the winter season, and with the North Sea providing a backdrop, the film is a mélange of familiar themes—vampirism, lesbianism, sadism, and necrophilia—that somehow works. Much of its effectiveness owes, once more, to Seyrig's performance, regal, reserved, and enigmatic. Kümel also uses deep tracking shots reminiscent of *Marienbad* and takes advantage of the long northern European winter night to create a feeling of boredom and claustrophobia. More than once, the opulence of the hotel's lobby and dining rooms, together with psychosexual impulses in play that can barely be contained behind the masks of polite behavior, suggest that Kümel had spent some time watching Luchino Visconti's *The Leopard* (1963) and *The Damned* (1969)—particularly the latter.[20] Looking at the scenes of billowing curtains, shadowed figures in the half dark, and violent collisions of black, white, and red in *The Hunger*, it is likely that Scott had as well.

The vampire's lure in *Daughters of Darkness* and in *The Hunger* is identical: the promise of eternal youth, deceptive in the latter case as John gradually recognizes what awaits him once age finally sets in. The response the new bride Valerie (Danielle Quimet) provides to the temptation offered by Countess Báthory—"Every woman would sell her soul to stay young"—answers in advance Miriam Blaylock's proposal to Sarah Roberts: "You can be young forever." John bought into that promise centuries ago, and it has allowed him a long and ageless life, filled with luxury and indolence. Now, with the price come due, his desperation drives him first to Sarah Roberts' clinic, then to a Central Park underpass where his failing physical strength deprives him of a victim, and finally to the hapless, androgynous Alice (Beth Ehlers), who mistakes him for his own aged father before he slashes her throat and drinks her blood in an effort to ingest her youth.[21] Miriam's appalled reaction when she realizes that something has happened to Alice—"John! What have you done?"—exposes why she had been cultivating the girl as a protégé; Alice was intended to become John's replacement when, inevitably, his senescence began. Here, even more than in Miriam's relationship with John and Sarah, her predatory nature reveals itself. Her plans thwarted, and with John looking on, she incinerates Alice's lifeless, and useless, body in their basement furnace.

Youth and Beauty, Love and Death

Not every piece of New York City real estate comes with an upstairs mausoleum and a downstairs crematorium. Nor does every Upper East Side townhouse display authentic

"How old do you think I am?" John Blaylock (David Bowie) asks Dr. Sarah Roberts (Susan Sarandon) in *The Hunger* (1983).

Egyptian artifacts and 500-year-old Florentine marble busts. In crafting the look of the Blaylocks' residence, Tony Scott took his lead from a director he greatly admired, Nicolas Roeg, and from Roeg's 1970 film *Performance*.[22] While far removed from that acme of late '60s London gangsterism, drugginess, and rock star decadence, it is possible to see in Miriam's and John's hermetic, self-enclosed lifestyle echoes of Mick Jagger's world-weary withdrawal into his Notting Hill mansion. It is as though the gift of perpetual youth is something not to be shared in public—save on nocturnal predatory expeditions among the club-hopping bridge-and-subway crowd. Roeg's influence can also be seen in the slash-and-bleed scenes in *The Hunger*, recalling in their suddenness and vivid coloration the shock of Donald Sutherland's death in a Venice church at the hands of a red-caped dwarf in the director's psycho-thriller *Don't Look Now* (1973).[23]

Death in Venice, Luchino Visconti's 1971 translation to the screen of Thomas Mann's 1912 novella, is possibly the most limpid film depicting the tragedy of youth and age, of beauty and decay, that European cinema has produced. As John's aging accelerates in *The Hunger*, David Bowie does not quote Dirk Bogarde's recognition of his own frailty in the earlier film. But the comparison is apt, as the composer Gustav von Aschenbach (Bogarde) succumbs to exhaustion and disease, both brought on by his obsession with a beautiful boy. As has often been noted, Visconti's film departs from Mann's text not only in making Aschenbach a musician rather than a writer, but also in the predatory character of the relationship between Aschenbach and the androgynous teenager Tadzio (Björn Andrésen).[24] What in the novel can be understood as adolescent curiosity and playfulness becomes in the film cruelty and malevolence, just as John's behavior toward Alice, initially tolerant if not benevolent, turns sinister and, finally, vampiric. While Tadzio does not, literally, suck the life out of Aschenbach, his flirtatious glances prompt the older man to increasingly desperate efforts to mask the signs of his decrepitude. The pathos of Aschenbach's inaudible confession to Tadzio—"I love you"—is echoed in John's hopeless plea to Miriam—"Kiss me. Think of me as I was." In both instances, it is too late, as Aschenbach's hair dye begins to run in the summer's heat and John's physical decay repulses Miriam. In the end, Aschenbach's fate is gentler than John's. The composer dies in his beach chair with one last evanescent image of his beloved cast against the horizon; the 300-year-old Frenchman who had been promised eternal life is entombed, still alive, for eternity.

The thematic emphasis on youth, age, and predation in *The Hunger* is often lost to the film's more sensational elements, above all the lesbian relationship between Miriam and Sarah and the extended lovemaking scene they share. Reading the film this way, especially in light of its opening scenes in the polysexual world of 1980s New York nightclubs, can make it appear both homophobic and misogynist, thereby placing it in a long context of lesbian vampire films.[25] But dread at the prospect of aging, grief at the realization of loss, and predatory instinct can find expression in films that have nothing to do with lesbians and vampires, yet are even more misogynistic and horrific in the behaviors depicted. While it is not usually coded as a horror film, Bernardo Bertolucci's *Last Tango in Paris* (1972) has acquired the reputation of having been a real-life horror as it was being made. Nineteen-year-old co-star Maria Schneider later claimed to have been traumatized—her term was "raped"—in the film's most controversial scene. Bertolucci confirmed Schneider's account in a 2013 interview that also implicated Marlon Brando (48 at the time of filming), whose performance as the expatriate American businessman Paul was widely acclaimed.[26]

Overlooked in these contentions over youth, sex, and exploitation is the core theme of Bertolucci's film—the fierce resistance Brando's character tries to mount against the loss of his potency, surrogated as anguish at his wife's suicide.[27] While in *The Hunger* John's murder of Alice is driven more by physiological than psychological need, the nature of the assault in essentially the same—the consumption of youthful vitality in an attempt to stave off the ravages of age. John does not turn on Alice because of her sexual allure. But the girl's death is no less horrifying because it is driven by the vampire's biological imperative. Paul (Brando) in *Last Tango in Paris* sodomizes Jeanne (Schneider); John, in *The Hunger*, cannibalizes Alice. When Sarah, after transfusing her blood with Miriam, discovers that she too is consumed by a cannibalistic hunger, she revolts—as John never could—and slashes her own throat, thereby escaping Miriam's controlling embrace. But rather than a repudiation of lesbianism or of vampirism, Sarah's act of independence is in fact a court rebellion. The film's conclusion reveals her in possession of Miriam's powers, and Miriam's wealth, as she entertains a pair of potential victims in an expensive high-rise overlooking the London cityscape.

The War of the Blood, or, Love Hurts

The promise of eternal youth would seem to be sufficient enticement in and of itself. But as played by Catherine Deneuve, Miriam Blaylock combines it with a mysterious, almost hypnotic, power of attraction that puts her in the company of such other legendary seducers as Duke Bluebeard in Béla Bartók's one-act opera *Bluebeard's Castle* (1911) and the evil music teacher Svengali, as impersonated by John Barrymore in the Warner Brothers' film of that name (1931). Like Bluebeard, Miriam keeps her former lovers in a secret room, and like Svengali she uses her mesmerizing allure to draw the all-business scientist Sarah Roberts first into her music room and then into her bedroom. "She's European," Sarah tells her boyfriend Tom (Cliff De Young) when he expresses unease with the budding relationship between the two women, as if that identification explains everything. Sarah is clearly off balance when she arrives at the Blaylocks' front door, ostensibly to inquire about John's strange condition, and admits to Miriam via the video camera, "I'm not sure why I'm here." From there, it's a quick segue, assisted by a glass of sherry, to "Mrs. Blaylock, are you making a pass at me?" What Sarah is discovering, through her laboratory experiments, Miriam Blaylock has known for centuries; but she is prepared to share only part of that knowledge with the younger woman, as the revealing of the full truth would ruin the seduction in progress.

It is hard to think of a vampire film both as stylized and as stylish as *The Hunger*. Even such glossy essays in the genre as *Love at First Bite* (1979), starring George Hamilton, and *Dracula* (1979), starring Frank Langella, fall short in comparison.[28] With Catherine Deneuve, Susan Sarandon, and David Bowie as his leads, it is unlikely that Scott could have gotten it wrong. In the early 1980s Deneuve was at the height of her erotic power; most film audiences would have remembered her from her indelible performances as a homicidal paranoiac in Roman Polanski's *Repulsion* (1965) and a frustrated young wife with masochistic fantasies in Luis Buñuel's *Belle de Jour* (1967). In the 1970s, with photographs by Richard Avedon and Helmut Newton, she had been the advertising face for Chanel No. 5 in magazines like *Vogue* and *Harper's Bazaar* and across American television screens.[29] Sarandon, coming off memorable performances for Louis Malle in *Pretty Baby* (1978) and *Atlantic City* (1980), was only a little less compelling. Her lovemaking scene with Deneuve picked up directly from the fetishistic attention Malle's camera had paid to her upper torso in the latter film. Bowie's allure was even more potent. His first film performance, as an ill-fated extraterrestrial in Nicolas Roeg's *The Man Who Fell to Earth* (1976), had been well received, and his appearance in the Broadway production of *The Elephant Man* (1980–1981)—without the prosthetics John Hurt used in David Lynch's film version—had elicited considerable praise. While glam rock had by then faded, Bowie's anthemic "All the Young Dudes," written for and performed by Mott the Hopple, still resonated ten years after its release, and Bryan Ferry, front man for Roxy Music, continued to reprise the *louche* lounge singer persona Bowie had briefly adopted a few years earlier.[30]

Once it has begun, John's aging process is rapid and extreme. From the vaguely gangsterish look he affects in the opening nightclub scene to his haggard expression when the music lessons with Alice become a strain to his abrupt descent into the latter stages of old age, Bowie achieved as much with posture and vocal expression as his makeup artists accomplished with latex and prosthetics. On his visit to the gerontology clinic, Bowie wears a raincoat and fedora hat that make him look like William Powell in the 1930s/1940s *Thin Man* movies, possibly a nod to his Thin White Duke phase in the mid–1970s. Crippled, desiccated, and incontinent at the end, John's abjection is complete. Miriam cannot, or will not, concede his pitiful appeals to put an end to his misery, and Sarah—remembering what she saw happen in the clinic's waiting room—has more than enough reason to rethink the compact she has entered into once she and Miriam mix their blood. As John has learned, a few hundred years of ageless youth is a small return for centuries of living death.[31]

Sarah, Tom, and their lab partners had been conducting their research using mon-

IV. Fighting Back Time

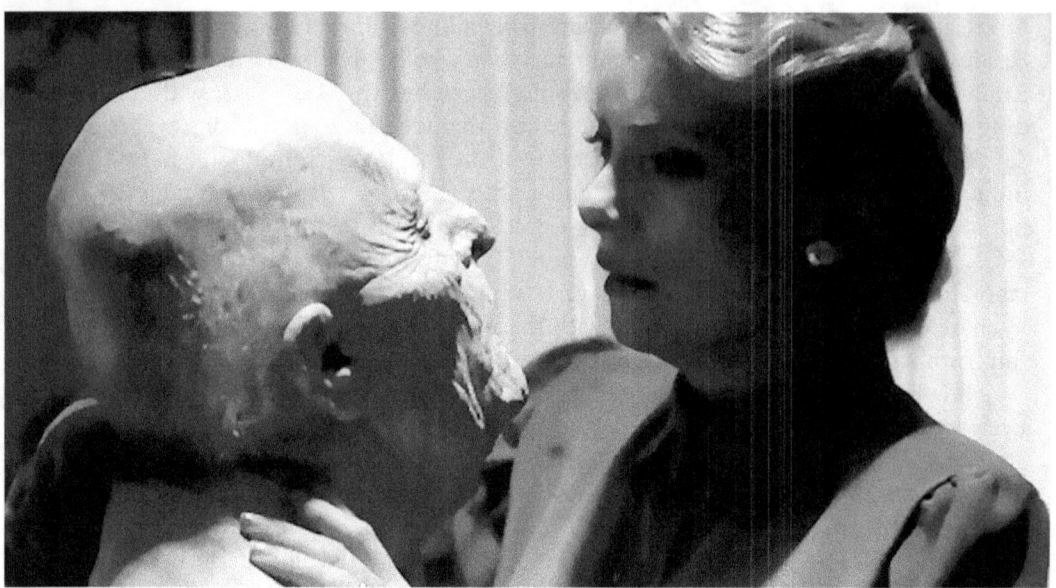

Miriam Blaylock (Catherine Deneuve) comforts her suddenly aged husband John (David Bowie) in *The Hunger*.

keys. Their experiments showed that protracted sleep deprivation produces extreme aggression—this is glimpsed in opening nightclub scene, intercut with Bauhaus lead singer Peter Murphy vamping for the camera and John and Miriam cruising the customers—followed by a fantastic acceleration of the aging process. Other than his nocturnal hunts in the dance clubs, John seems to have shown little aggression; but his behavior changes once his deterioration from beautiful semi-youth to near necrosis begins. Not fully aware of what has happened to her, Sarah tries to stanch her ravenous hunger for blood by ordering an uncooked steak while having dinner with Tom. The attempt fails, resulting in nausea, vomiting, and the recognition that, medically, something has changed. Blood tests at the clinic disclose no infection or disease; instead, Sarah is hosting an alien blood type, one that is not human, is at war with her normal blood, and is winning.

The notoriety that attaches to *The Hunger* owes above all to the sex scene between Catherine Deneuve and Susan Sarandon. Deneuve's icy elegance, patented by her performance in *Belle de Jour*, paired perfectly with the volcanic sensuality Sarandon had been developing ever since *The Rocky Horror Picture Show* (1975). Scott's staging of the scene, filmed on a closed set in the garage of a Brooklyn gas station, went well beyond what was available in the new category of "erotic thrillers"—both in theatrical release and in direct-to-video format—and anticipated the "soft porn" productions that would soon fill suburban bedrooms and hotel room pay-for-view menus.[32] The shock effect provided when Miriam bites the inside of Sarah's forearm, releasing the precious blood, is doubled by Sarah's response in kind; the fusing of the two women's blood, amidst gauzy curtains, tangled bed clothes, and soft focus close-ups suggests that Scott could have taken his career in directions other than the action adventure films for which he is remembered. For Sarah, the pleasures of lovemaking with Miriam—who learned the art in the Egypt of the pharaohs—are purchased at too high a price. Within hours, she has cannibalized her first victim, the devoted but obtuse Tom. Covered in gore, Sarah repudiates her new identity, piercing her jugular vein and drenching Miriam with her contaminated blood.

Conclusion

Anyone who has seen *Dracula's Daughter* will remember the scene where Gloria Holden seeks solace by playing Chopin's Piano Nocturne No. 5. But as the scene deepens, her playing becomes darker and more agitated, and her manservant Sandor—to whom she has promised eternal life—taunts her, declaring, "That music does not speak of release." In *The Hunger*, John Blaylock's final plea is the same, as he implores his wife, "Kill me, kill me, Miriam. Release me." John's plea is futile, for Miriam tells him, "There is no release, my darling, no rest, no letting go." In a last gesture of independence, John throws himself down the basement stairs while Alice's body burns in the furnace. To the haunting strains of Allegri's Miserere for Nine Voices, Miriam carries John's broken body to the upstairs crypt where his coffin has long been waiting. "Comfort him, all of you, all my loves, be kind to him tonight," she pronounces mournfully to the living corpses who have preceded him there. However cynical Miriam's farewell may seem—she has her sights set on Sarah Roberts—the scene of John's internment is genuinely sad, and the betrayal of her promise to be young "forever and ever" registers a degree of moral opprobrium for which there are few comparisons.[33] What John dreads the most, to spend eternity as a living cadaver, has become his fate.

In its penultimate scene, *The Hunger* collapses into familiar generic conventions. Miriam carries Sarah's dead body to the attic, to entomb her with John and her other

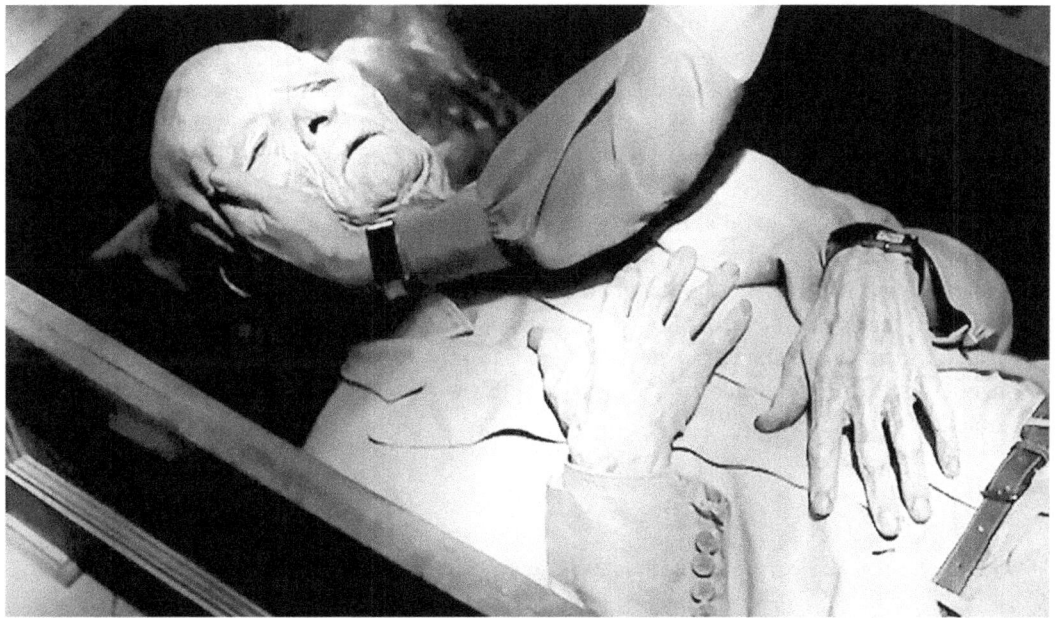

Miriam Blaylock (Catherine Deneuve) places her 300-year-old husband John (David Bowie) in his attic coffin in *The Hunger*.

past lovers. But Sarah's act of rebellion has broken Miriam's control over her victims. They emerge from their coffins in varying states of decay and try to embrace Miriam, forcing her backwards to the stairwell where, aghast and powerless, she plunges to her death. As the bodies upstairs crumble into pieces, Miriam's beauty vanishes, the centuries take their toll, and—like so many vampires before her—her face dissolves into dust.

With its obsessive attention to youth, beauty, and decay, *The Hunger* quickly became a signal for the onset of the AIDS epidemic, especially as it was set in the quaalude-consuming, role-playing, partner-swapping culture of after-dark Midtown and Lower Manhattan.[34] But while there were affinities between John Blaylock's deterioration and the first symptoms of a new disease that had begun to appear among gay men in New York—physical wastage, weakness, loss of bodily control—the relationship was coincidental rather than correlative. The metaphors of contaminated blood and the exchange of bodily fluids, central to *The Hunger*, were not yet widely disseminated; for all its cultural associations with disease, vampirism was still a matter of myth, legend, and nightmares, not a medical condition. The corruption of youth and the decay of beauty may have carried a special resonance in the gay community that enjoyed a semi-safe if not privileged existence in New York and San Francisco. But this was an old literary convention going back a century if not more; as the use of the Duet of the Flowers from Léo Delibes' 1882 opera *Lakmé* for the love scene between Miriam and Sarah suggests, *The Hunger* looks back to the time of Rimbaud, Verlaine, Swinburne, and Wilde, not ahead to the era of Larry Kramer's *The Normal Heart*, ACT UP, and Rudy Giuliani's crackdown on gay bath houses, leather bars, and swingers' clubs.[35]

Today an added poignancy attaches to *The Hunger*, beyond John's painful-to-watch decay and Miriam's hideous, centuries-overdue demise. In 2012, suffering a recurrence of brain cancer, Tony Scott leapt to his death off the Vincent Thomas Bridge, which links San Pedro with Terminal Island. A favorite shooting location for LA-based filmmakers, the bridge had figured in some of Scott's projects; only two years before the director had confirmed that he was developing a sequel to *The Hunger*.[36] In January 2016, to the surprise of almost everyone, David Bowie died in New York of undisclosed, and terminal, liver cancer. Only days earlier he had released his final album, *Blackstar*. Bowie's performance in the video version of the four-minute cut "Lazarus," filmed in what looks like a flophouse room, is eerily reminiscent of John Blaylock's last moments in *The Hunger*, enfeebled, exhausted, and about to be confined in his coffin. Lazarus, who rose from the grave and was restored to life; John, interred in his above-ground grave, never to die. "Humankind die one way," Miriam consoles John, "we another. Their end is final, ours is not. In the earth, in the rotting wood, in the eternal darkness, we will see and hear and feel." And in both, David Bowie, changeling, extra-terrestrial visitor, ambisexual and gender-fluid, forever beacon of the next cool thing—lost to the inevitable grip of age and time.[37]

Notes

1. Friend, "The God Pill," 60.
2. Bockris, *Keith Richards*, 211. The story of Keith Richards' full-body transfusion as a cure for his heroin addiction has been debunked several times, including by Richards himself, yet remains an operative part of Rolling Stones mythology.
3. See, e.g., Fleming, "Looking Back at 'Dracula's Daughter'"; Heller-Nicholas, "Seductive Kindness." For the broader context, see Weiss, "The Lesbian Vampire Film."
4. Cf. Smith, "The Grave New World." On vampirism as a wearying burden rather than a privileged condition, see Hughes, "Postmodernising the Lady Vampire."

5. Gelder, *New Vampire Cinema*, 26–27.
6. E.g., Latham, *Consuming Youth*, 111–23. On this chapter in the history of New York's nightlife, see Lawrence, *Life and Death on the New York Dance Floor*.
7. Schneier, "Don't You Forget About Me!" See also, on the resonance of the '70s/'80s club scene today, Allen, "Defiant on the Dance Floor."
8. Calling *The Hunger* an "art-horror" film raises a number of epistemological issues, as the term itself is both slippery and contested. The best introduction to the subject remains Hawkins, *The Cutting Edge: Art-Horror and the Horrific Avant-Garde*, 3–30, although *The Hunger* is not part of the discussion there.
9. Missing from the critical commentary on *The Hunger* is its mythological origin in the tragic story of Tithonus, who was granted the gift of eternal life by Eros, without the crucial clarification that "life" was not synonymous with "youth." In the modern literary tradition, the best known version of the story is Alfred Lord Tennyson's poem *Tithonus*, published in 1860.
10. Holte, "Not All Fangs Are Phallic," 172.
11. Or, as has been argued, just "another Hollywood revamping … of the Euro-sexploitation tradition." See San Filippo, *The B Word: Bisexuality in Contemporary Film and Television*, 118. On "Euro-sexploitation," see Olney, "The Whip and the Body." For a more positive appraisal of Scott's development as a filmmaker, see Bevan, "Man on Fire: Tony Scott."
12. Beard, "Wrath in the Time of Choler." The theme is literally as old as time itself, yet the scholarship on artistic and cinematic representations of the resistance against it is surprisingly sparse. The subject is broached in Cohen-Shalev, "Golden Years and Silver Screens." Further, see Armstrong, *Mourning Films: A Critical Study of Loss and Grieving in Cinema* and DeFalco, *Uncanny Subjects: Aging in Contemporary Narrative*.
13. For the former, see Abbott, "Urban Vampires in American Films of the Eighties and Nineties." For the latter, see Nixon, "When Hollywood Sucks, or, Hungry Girls, Lost Boys, and Vampirism in the Age of Reagan."
14. Admittedly these themes are more emphatic in Whitley Strieber's 1981 novel from which the film's screenplay was adapted. Still, they become clear when we look beneath the gloss and cinematic acrobatics of Scott's direction. On the differences between the novel and the film, see Auerbach, *Our Vampires, Ourselves*, 57–60.
15. Catherine Deneuve was 39 or 40 when the film was made, David Bowie was 36.
16. Some of the commentary on *The Hunger* links the opening nightclub scene with The Dom, the music, dance, and performance space on St. Marks Place in the East Village, which was occupied by Warhol and his circle of admirers in the mid-1960s. On her visits to New York in the 1970s, Deneuve occasionally socialized with Warhol, and their friendship was played up in the artist's *Interview* magazine. See the reprint of the October 1976 issue featuring Deneuve at http://www.interviewmagazine.com/film/new-again-catherine-deneuve/#slideshow_68930.1. In the self-replicating world of New York celebrity point/counterpoint, David Bowie would years later turn in a universally-praised performance as Andy Warhol in Julian Schnabel's 1996 artist biopic *Basquiat*.
17. This summary does little justice to these scenes' atmospherics, which are simultaneously Gothic, psychedelic, and '80s urban realistic.
18. In his account of the "spa life" at places like Marienbad, historian David Clay Large devotes considerable attention to the counterpoint of luxury and indolence on the one hand and sexual tension and indulgence on the other; somewhat anachronistically, Keith Richards serves as a source. See Large, *The Grand Spas of Central Europe*, 117.
19. A half-century later, the costumes Delphine Seyrig wore in *Last Year at Marienbad* continue to influence *haute couture*. See, e.g., the unsigned article "Influences: Last Year at Marienbad."
20. It is worth noting that Ostend was the home of James Ensor, painter of the masks that conceal the elemental forces that shape human behavior. On the importance of appearances, costumes, and colors in *Daughters of Darkness*, see Cherry, "*Daughters of Darkness*: Vampire Aesthetics and Gothic Beauty." For another reading of the film, arguing its feminist credentials, see Zimmerman, "Daughters of Darkness: The Lesbian Vampire on Film."
21. In his commentary on the 2005 DVD edition of *The Hunger*, Tony Scott emphasizes the "look" he wanted for the Alice character, going so far as to costume her in tights, a skirt, and a football jersey, and with a haircut as popular with teenage boys as girls at the time he made the film. For someone living in New York in the 1980s, the police investigation of Alice's disappearance had to bring to mind the abduction and presumed murder of six-year-old Etan Patz, whose body has never been found, in the SoHo neighborhood in 1979. Some of the more lurid press coverage at the time referenced vampirism and cannibalism. After a series of failed investigations and mistrials, a guilty verdict for the death of Etan Patz was rendered in 2017.
22. Scott's commentary on *The Hunger* DVD.
23. There are other echoes of *Don't Look Now* in *The Hunger*, most notably in the verisimilitude of the lovemaking between Catherine Deneuve and Susan Sarandon, recalling the at the time scandalous scene in the earlier film with Julie Christie and Donald Sutherland.
24. See, e.g., Wiehe, "Of Art and Death: Film and Fiction Versions of *Death in Venice*."

25. Creed, *The Monstrous-Feminine*, 67–72. See also Hanson, "Lesbians Who Bite: Abjection as Masquerade."

26. For Schneider's allegations in a 2007 *Daily Mail* interview and Bertolucci's response to them in his 2013 interview with *Agence France-Press*, see Victor, "Revisited 'Last Tango in Paris' Rape Scene." For the larger context, see Forshaw, *Sex and Film: The Erotic in British, American, and World Cinema*, 127–28.

27. Baker, "On Not Being Porn: Intimacy and the Sexually Explicit Art Film."

28. For a detailed analysis of the stylistics of *The Hunger*, see Phillips, "'You Said Forever': Postmodern Temporality in Tony Scott's *The Hunger*." The elegant, polished look of the Blaylocks' townhouse—"waiting for the *Architectural Digest* photographers"—has drawn the ire of some critics. See Day, *Vampire Legends in Contemporary American Culture*, 92.

29. On Deneuve's erotic allure, at age 40, see San Filippo, "Two Women: The Dialectical Sexual Persona of Catherine Deneuve." On *The Hunger* specifically, see Kelsey, "The Bourgeois Out for Blood: Catherine Deneuve in *The Hunger*."

30. Trying to fit Bowie's performance in *The Hunger* into the "lost decade" of the 1980s, Shelton Waldrep misreads his role as "passive," when, in fact, it is anything but; for example, his interrogation of Sarah Roberts, his attack on the skater in Central Park, and his murder of Alice. See Waldrep, *Future Nostalgia: Performing David Bowie*, 177.

31. It cannot be accidental that the term "consumption"—with its multiple meanings—figures in much of the commentary on *The Hunger*. See, e.g., Latham, *Consuming Youth* and Magistrale, *Abject Terrors: Surveying the Modern and Postmodern Horror Film*, 40–43.

32. For the details of this scene, see Vineyard, "Susan Sarandon on Her Vampire Lesbian Sex Scene with Catherine Deneuve." For the larger context, see Williams, *The Erotic Thriller in Contemporary Cinema* and Andrews, *Soft in the Middle*. Neither of these studies mentions *The Hunger*.

33. In Barbara Creed's reading of *The Hunger*, Miriam becomes another of the "cruel mothers" who figure notably in *fin-de-siècle* art and literature. See, e.g., Giovanni Segantini's well known painting "The Evil Mothers" (1894), now in the Österreichische Galerie in the Upper Belvedere in Vienna. Cf. Creed, *Monstrous-Feminine*, 68–69.

34. E.g., Michel, "Deviance, Decadence, and Destructive Desire."

35. According to Lawrence, *Life and Death on the Dance Floor*, 431–37, the New York club scene did not begin to turn away from all-out hedonism, excess, and experimentation until the mid–1980s, when the ravages of the AIDS epidemic could no longer be denied.

36. In his commentary on the DVD edition of *The Hunger*, Scott explained the "tacked on" ending as insisted on by MGM in the expectation of making a sequel. The film's commercial failure put that project on hold, although a television anthology series, with participation by both Tony and Ridley Scott, was spun off for the Showtime network in the late 1990s.

37. Nick Glass, CNN London correspondent, following the announcement of Bowie's death: "The simple truth is David Bowie was magnetically, agelessly cool." Quoted in Amanpour, "The Life and Legacy of David Bowie."

Bibliography

Abbott, Stacey. "Urban Vampires in American Films of the Eighties and Nineties." In *Vampires: Myths & Metaphors of Enduring Evil*, edited by Carla T. Kungl, 133–37. Oxford: InterDisciplinary Press, 2003.

Allen, Jeremy. "Defiant on the Dance Floor." *New York Times*, June 25, 2017, special section on "Pride," F8.

Amanpour, Christiane. "The Life and Legacy of David Bowie." CNN, January 11, 2016. http://www.cnn.com/videos/world/2016/01/11/remembering-david-bowie-glass-obit-pkg-amanpour.cnn.

Andrews, David. *Soft in the Middle: The Contemporary Softcore Feature in Its Contexts*. Columbus: Ohio State University Press, 2006.

Armstrong, Richard. *Mourning Films: A Critical Study of Loss and Grieving in Cinema*. Jefferson, NC: McFarland, 2012.

Auerbach, Nina. *Our Vampires, Ourselves*, 2nd ed. Chicago: University of Chicago Press, 1995.

Baker, Anthony. "On Not Being Porn: Intimacy and the Sexually Explicit Art Film." *Text Matters* 3, no. 3 (2013): 186–202.

Beard, Mary. "Wrath in the Time of Choler." *New York Times Book Review*, September 10, 2017, 18.

Bevan, Joseph. "Man on Fire: Tony Scott." *Sight & Sound*, May 2013, updated October 2015. http://www.bfi.org.uk/news-opinion/sight-sound-magazine/features/man-fire-tony-scott.

Bockris, Victor. *Keith Richards: The Biography*, reprint ed. New York: Da Capo Press, 2003.

Cherry, Brigid. "*Daughters of Darkness*: Vampire Aesthetics and Gothic Beauty." In *Dracula's Daughters: The Female Vampire on Film*, edited by Douglas Brode and Leah Deyneka, 219–34. Lanham, MD: Scarecrow Press, 2014.

Cohen-Shalev, Amir. "Golden Years and Silver Screens: Cinematic Representations." *Journal of Aging, Humanities, and the Arts* 1, nos. 1–2 (2007): 85–96.

Creed, Barbara. *The Monstrous-Feminine: Film, Feminism, Psychoanalysis*. New York: Routledge, 1993.

Day, William Patrick. *Vampire Legends in Contemporary American Culture: What Becomes a Legend Most.* Lexington: University of Kentucky Press, 2002.
DeFalco, Amelia. *Uncanny Subjects: Aging in Contemporary Narrative.* Columbus: Ohio State University Press, 2010.
Fleming, Colin. "Looking Back at 'Dracula's Daughter,' the 1936 Monster Movie That's Really About Love and Lesbianism." *Vice Magazine*, February 14, 2016. https://www.vice.com/en_us/article/looking-back-at-draculas-daughter-the-erotic-1936-film-thats-really-about-lesbians.
Forshaw, Barry. *Sex and Film: The Erotic in British, American, and World Cinema.* New York: Palgrave Macmillan, 2015.
Friend, Tad. "The God Pill." *The New Yorker*, April 3, 2017, 54–67.
Gelder, Ken. *New Vampire Cinema.* London: BFI/Palgrave Macmillan, 2012.
Guinness, Catherine, Andy Warhol, and Ara Gallant. "New Again: Catherine Deneuve." *Interview*, September 17, 2014. http://www.interviewmagazine.com/film/new-again-catherine-deneuve/#slideshow_68930.1.
Hanson, Ellis. "Lesbians Who Bite: Abjection as Masquerade." In *Outtakes: Essays on Queer Theory and Film*, edited by Ellis Hanson, 183–222. Durham: Duke University Press, 1999.
Hawkins, Joan. *The Cutting Edge: Art-Horror and the Horrific Avant-Garde.* Minneapolis: University of Minnesota Press, 2000.
Heller-Nicholas, Alexandra. "Seductive Kindness: Power, Space and 'Lesbian' Vampires." In *Hospitality, Rape and Consent in Vampire Popular Culture: Letting the Wrong One In*, edited by David Baker, Stephanie Green, and Agnieszka Stasiewicz-Bieńkowska, 201–18. New York: Palgrave Macmillan, 2017.
Holte, James Craig. "Not All Fangs Are Phallic: Female Film Vampires." *Journal of the Fantastic in the Arts* 10, no. 2 (1999): 163–73.
Hughes, Jessica. "Postmodernising the Lady Vampire: Melancholy, Isolation, and the Female Bloodsucker." *Image & Text: A Journal of Design* 18 (2011): 82–98.
Kelsey, Colleen. "The Bourgeois Out for Blood: Catherine Deneuve in *The Hunger.*" *cléo: a journal of film and feminism* 3, no. 3 (2015). http://cleojournal.com/2015/11/24/the-bourgeois-out-for-blood-catherine-deneuve-in-the-hunger.
Large, David Clay. *The Grand Spas of Central Europe: A History of Intrigue, Politics, Art, and Healing.* Lanham, MD: Rowman and Littlefield, 2015.
Latham, Rob. *Consuming Youth: Vampires, Cyborgs, and the Culture of Consumption.* Chicago: University of Chicago Press, 2002.
Lawrence, Tim. *Life and Death on the New York Dance Floor, 1980–1983.* Durham: Duke University Press, 2016.
Magistrale, Tony. *Abject Terrors: Surveying the Modern and Postmodern Horror Film.* New York: Peter Lang, 2005.
Michel, Deborah. "Deviance, Decadence, and Destructive Desire: The Proprietary Cinematic Gaze in Tony Scott's *The Hunger.*" *Acidemic Journal of Film and Media* 5 (2007). http://www.acidemic.com/id97.html.
Nixon, Nicola. "When Hollywood Sucks, or, Hungry Girls, Lost Boys, and Vampirism in the Age of Reagan." In *Blood Read: The Vampire as Metaphor in Contemporary Culture*, edited by Joan Gordon and Veronica Hollinger, 115–28. Philadelphia: University of Pennsylvania Press, 1997.
Olney, Ian. "The Whip and the Body: Sex, Horror, and Performative Spectatorship in Euro-Horror S&M Cinema." In *Screening the Dark Side of Love: From Euro-Horror to American Cinema*, edited by Karen A. Ritzenhoff and Karen Randell, 1–17. New York: Palgrave Macmillan, 2012.
Phillips, Kendall R. "'You Said Forever': Postmodern Temporality in Tony Scott's *The Hunger.*" In *Dracula's Daughters: The Female Vampire on Film*, edited by Douglas Brode and Leah Deyneka, 253–65. Lanham, MD: Scarecrow Press, 2014.
San Filippo, Maria. *The B Word: Bisexuality in Contemporary Film and Television.* Bloomington: Indiana University Press, 2013.
_____. "Two Women: The Dialectical Sexual Persona of Catherine Deneuve." *Senses of Cinema* 23 (2002). http://sensesofcinema.com/2002/the-female-actor/deneuve.
Schneier, Matthew. "Don't You Forget About Me! The Formerly Irredeemable '80s Return." *New York Times*, April 21, 2016, D1.
Scott, Tony. Director's Commentary. *The Hunger*. 1983. Warner Bros. DVD. 2005.
Smith, Eric D. "The Grave New World: Biopolitics and the Vampire Dystopia in *Daybreakers.*" *The Minnesota Review* 86 (2016): 61–80.
Unsigned. "Influences: Last Year at Marienbad." *Poetic & Chic* web site, January 19, 2012. http://www.poeticandchic.com/home/2012/1/19/influences-last-year-at-marienbad.html.
Victor, Daniel. "Revisited 'Last Tango in Paris' Rape Scene Causes Internet Outcry." *New York Times*, December 5, 2016, https://www.nytimes.com/2016/12/05/movies/revisted-last-tango-in-paris-rape-scene-causes-internet-outcry.html.
Vineyard, Jennifer. "Susan Sarandon on Her Vampire Lesbian Sex Scene with Catherine Deneuve." *Vulture*, December 5, 2014. http://www.vulture.com/2014/11/susan-sarandon-the-hunger-catherine-deneuve-sex-scene.html.

Waldrep, Shelton. *Future Nostalgia: Performing David Bowie*. New York: Bloomsbury, 2015.
Weiss, Andrea. "The Lesbian Vampire Film: A Subgenre of Horror." In *Dracula's Daughters: The Female Vampire on Film*, edited by Douglas Brode and Leah Deyneka, 21–36. Lanham, MD: Scarecrow Press, 2014.
Wiehe, Roger E. "Of Art and Death: Film and Fiction Versions of *Death in Venice*." *Literature/Film Quarterly* 16, no. 3 (1988): 210–15.
Williams, Linda Ruth. *The Erotic Thriller in Contemporary Cinema*. Bloomington: Indiana University Press, 2007.
Zimmerman, Bonnie. "Daughters of Darkness: The Lesbian Vampire on Film." In *Planks of Reason: Essays on the Horror Film*, rev. ed., edited by Barry Keith Grant and Christopher Sharrett, 72–81. Lanham, MD: Scarecrow Press, 2004.

The Brittle Body

The Elderly and Cars in The Brotherhood of Satan

BRIAN BREMS

In the darkness on the edge of town, there is a seemingly empty, broken-down old house where the town's elderly citizens gather. Up the stairs, which are nearly rotted away and speckled with cobwebs, and through an arched doorway, there is an opulent, well-maintained ballroom. Classical music plays. Black-robed figures serve drinks, carry candles; in a stone chamber beside the ballroom, children stand on pedestals, suspended in tableau.

This scene occurs in the first third of *The Brotherhood of Satan* (1971), a desert-set horror film about a cult of elderly residents of a dusty town called Hillsboro. These geriatric desert-dwellers have contracted with the Devil himself to transfer their spirits out of their aging bodies and into the youthful bodies of local children, provided they can procure 13 of them (one for each of the coven's members). The cult's sacrificial rite has taken a bloody toll on Hillsboro: 26 people have been killed in three days, and nearly a dozen children are missing. The town's Sheriff (L.Q. Jones) teams up with a few local residents and a family of out-of-towners, the Holdens, whose daughter KT is abducted, to find out who has been stealing the children, leaving a trail of bodies in their wake. He is thwarted at every turn by the town's doctor, Duncan (Strother Martin), who is secretly the leader of the Satanist cult.

The film's Satanic elements likely reflect the popularity of Roman Polanski's 1968 thriller *Rosemary's Baby*, in which the titular heroine (Mia Farrow) is imprisoned by a Satanist cult, so that she can be raped and impregnated by the Devil, as well as Paul Wendkos' *The Mephisto Waltz* (1968) featuring a concert pianist (Alan Alda) who undergoes a similar transfer of souls. They also evoke memories of Charles Manson and his "family," who called him both "God" and "Satan" and who—under his direction—ventured out from the Death Valley ranch where they lived to commit a series of brutal murders. The Manson killings reinforced centuries-old beliefs about the central role of violence and blood sacrifice in real-world Satanism, and fears of human monsters lurking in remote desert towns. Trailers for *The Brotherhood of Satan* played up the Manson parallel, calling the film "a contemporary story of family witchcraft in California."

The film's fusion of Satanic horror and the vastness of the unoccupied West is accomplished through its most dominant image: the automotive body. As the bodies of the elder residents of Hillsboro grow old and brittle, so too do the bodies of the cars that lie at the side of the highway, bent and broken nearly beyond recognition. The film centralizes images of the car—idle, in motion, and crucially, smashed in the aftermath of a wreck—each foregrounding the film's deep focus on transformation. In *The Brotherhood of Satan*, the aging, declining body is a prison to be transcended; the film's images of cracked, broken cars comment upon the viability of that transcendence.

The Young and the Restless

The film's release came at a time of transition in both film and American culture more broadly. The Vietnam War, in particular, was a cultural flashpoint that animated anger fundamentally characteristic of a generational divide. The young were at risk of being drafted, shipped out, and sent back from Southeast Asia in a body bag, while the old pulled the strings and made decisions about who would live and who would die. Protesters gathered outside the White House, taunting President Lyndon Johnson with what became one of the era's iconic chants: "Hey, hey, LBJ, how many kids did you kill today?"[1] At the same time, young people were rewriting the rules of sexuality, launching an all-out assault on long-standing societal assumptions about (and legal restrictions on) what partners could do in the bedroom. To these young people, older Americans were square, defined by conservatism that manifested itself most powerfully in the repression of their own desires, suppression of discourse that threatened hegemony, and oppression of those who would dare to transgress it.

At the same time, the revolutionary "New Hollywood" of the late 1960s and early 1970s was ascendant. This era's young directors were influenced by international art cinema and classic Hollywood, as well as the cultural upheaval going on outside the movie theatres. As these filmmakers, inspired and informed by the era's countercultural movements, began to conquer the box office, they transplanted a youthful sensibility into old forms, injecting classic Hollywood genres with new cinematic approaches. They used the radical formalist techniques of European and Asian filmmakers to breathe new life into tired stories, and fashioned critiques of narrative conventions by undermining and interrogating them. The old studio system structure was on its way out. Films like *Easy Rider* (1969) used images of the road and the wide-open country to rewrite the rules of mainstream American cinema, and "stunned the counterculture with a shock of recognition."[2] Into this swirling maelstrom drove *The Brotherhood of Satan*, itself a literalized, cinematic incarnation of Jack Weinberg's counterculture maxim: "Don't trust anybody over thirty."[3]

Cars, a potent symbol of youth culture, were integral to this process. They had, for almost half a century, been "central to young people's efforts to gain visibility, to participate in community life, and to claim public space against a sweeping tide of organized efforts to preclude such possibilities."[4] They were also, for young people, an essential tool in expressing rebellion: "They arrived and departed in their powerful, gaudily painted, 'souped-up' chariots amidst thunderclaps of noise, wildly spewing gravel, and engines usually at full throttle. Although their elders clucked disapproval, many of these teen rebels were sophisticated, knowledgeable car buffs,"[5] like the young heroes of Nicholas Ray's *Rebel Without a Cause* (1955), who use cars as a means of (temporary) escape from unhappy home lives, and George Lucas' *American Graffiti* (1973), where "driving is the key for teenage transition to adulthood."[6]

Filmmakers of the late 1960s and early 1970s seized on the iconography of the road and its lonely riders, which provided "a ready space for exploration of the tensions and crises of the historical moment."[7] Films such as *The Rain People* (1969) and *Vanishing Point* (1971) worked to capture—if not entirely re-create—the road movie genre for their own countercultural purposes. *Easy Rider*, among the most influential films to come out of the New Hollywood, picked up on the association of youth culture and driving, framing the road as a stage for rebellion against the cultural norms of the day and a setting for self-discovery. The worlds they created on film, in which the road (and the car or motorcycle) provide "mobile refuge from social circumstances felt to be lacking or oppressive in some way,"[8] mirrored that outside the theater. "The countercultural movements of the '60s are evoked by the single image of a handful of kids packed into a Volkswagen van (a microbus) in their pursuit of freedom from adult control, the oppressiveness of prevailing middle-class sexual mores, and the snare of suburban conformity."[9] In life and on screen, what was in the rearview was a prison, and it was known. Out the front windshield, there was the unknown, a horizon which offered not a guaranteed future, but something that might be better than what was left behind.

Famous body horror directors John Carpenter and David Cronenberg would later explore car culture in *Christine* (1983) and *Crash* (1996), respectively. Carpenter's film, from Stephen King's novel of the same title, the story of a nerdy teenager (Keith Gordon) made James Dean-cool through his ownership of a murderous 1958 Plymouth Fury, "makes a bid to be the definitive statement on the love affair between the American male ego and the automobile—the dark side of *American Graffiti*."[10] Christine, the car, also reinforces the association of women and Satanism. "She" is presented as inherently evil, "a diabolical presence from the start as we share the wing mirror's point-of-view of a potential victim on the assembly line in Detroit."[11] In Cronenberg's film, a man (James Spader) is drawn to an erotic underworld of car-crash enthusiasts after surviving his own violent collision with another woman (Holly Hunter). Cronenberg's camera lingers on the characters' collision-scarred bodies during sex scenes—a reflection of his trademark interest in the impact of violence on the human form—but "the road in *Crash* functions on many different levels. Among other things, it serves as a metaphor for the cultural condition of Western civilization—in this case, a bleak, gaping expanse of vacancy."[12]

Neither of these films overtly explores the car in the context of generational conflict. Both do, however, speak to the power of automobiles as subject matter for body horror. Each filmmaker is concerned with the modern world's impact on mankind, a theme which also occupies John Orr in a car-themed chapter in *Cinema and Modernity*: "The automobile is the thing owned which defines the modern persona, a mechanical extension of the self and the body."[13] Tim Corrigan sees the same thing: "Cars and motorcycles represent a mechanized extension of the body, through which that body could move farther and faster than ever before and quite literally evade the trajectory of classical narrative and twentieth-century history."[14] The human body operates the motor vehicle, but the vehicle conveys the human body; together, they synthesize experience into a transcendent moment where the limitations of the physical, emotional, and spiritual provide the possibility of renewal, rebirth, and rejuvenation.

Death on the Highways

It is the car and its association with youth culture that animates *The Brotherhood of Satan*, foregrounding generational conflict waged on the dangerous road with its lingering images of the desert and the wrecked automobile. One of the film's intertwined narrative strands involves the sheriff's search for the children who have gone missing, along with his attempts to solve the murders of other townspeople. He is joined in this effort by the visiting Holden family, looking for the missing KT, as well as Deputy Tobey (Alvy Moore) and Father Jack (Charles Robinson), a local priest. The second strand follows the cult members who hold the children captive in an abandoned house on the edge of town, preparing to sacrifice them and claim their bodies as hosts for their own transported spirits. The character that links these two narrative threads is Doctor Duncan, who poses as an upright citizen of Hillsboro, but is secretly the leader of the coven, and its intermediary with Satan. The two narratives converge in the final moments of the film, as the sheriff and his followers converge on the cult's lair—their pursuit intercut with the ritual of transformation—but the climax reveals that the sheriff and his compatriots have arrived too late. They burst through the door to find the ritual seemingly concluded, all of its iconography and paraphernalia vanished into thin air. The children, including the Holdens' daughter KT, are all that remain, their bodies—the Satanic rite having been successful—now acting as vessels for the spirits of the older citizens of Hillsboro.

This spiritual transference of old into young is foreshadowed in the automotive imagery that pervades the opening scenes. The first sound in the film, heard behind the production company logo, is that of a rumbling engine, punctuated with a high-pitched rat-a-tat. When the logo fades from the screen, it reveals a child's toy tank, sitting in the dirt, as the source of the tinny gun sounds. It lumbers towards the camera after a few spins of the turret, nearly blocking out all other visuals when, suddenly, there is a cut to the treads of a real, life-size tank (images that inevitably evoke the Vietnam War). Its noise is deafening, but the frantic screams of a man and a woman—shouting things like "It's going to hit us!" and "Get the kid out of here!"—are faintly discernable. They are too late. The tank—filmed entirely in alienating, disorienting close-up—crushes the car, the smaller vehicle's glass breaking and metal frame crunching as it gives way under the massive weight of the war machine overtaking it. The camera shifts outside the car, watching its destruction as the tank drives over it, then cuts back inside as the car's door bends in, its handle jutting out under the pressure. There is a quick cut to the toy tank, its cannon pointing straight into the lens, then back to the life-size tank as it rolls over the car, frame buckling and glass flying in slow motion. The tank grinds the car into the ground as the shrieks of twisting metal fill the air. Gasoline spills onto the ground, cascading out of the car's body. The screams of the car's occupants are long gone. The camera never shows them, until a slow tracking shot surveys the ruined aftermath; a bloodied hand sticks out from a bent car door with a rosary draped over its lifeless fingers. In the dirt beside the wreckage lie a child's doll and a comic book. Small fires crackle.

A young boy, wearing cowboy boots and a cowboy hat, emerges from the wreck and walks in the dirt away from the devastation. He walks up a hill, through the tank tracks, picks up the toy tank, and exits the frame. Then, after a cut away, he enters a new frame, joining a group of three other young children who are seven to 10 years old, like him. Smoke rises from the wrecked automobile below, filling the scene with ghostly fog. The film freezes, a yellow halo of superimposed light appears behind one of the young girls,

A hand protrudes from the grisly wreckage of a car, setting up the horror in *The Brotherhood of Satan* (1971).

and the credits begin. There is no sign of the life-size tank. The sequence is rife with images meant to contrast the world of children with the world of adults—like the toy tank juxtaposed with a real one—and, when his parents are eliminated before they are even visually present in the narrative, the boy is himself seemingly reborn as he appears out of the demolished vehicle.

The cult in *The Brotherhood of Satan*, paradoxically, uses car wrecks as tools to achieve their own rebirth, trapping unwary travelers within the town's borders. Freedom, a concern of the young and mobile, vanishes as the film's families lose access to vehicular liberty. They are stranded in a small desert town, suddenly trapped within borders beyond their control. The lack of a functioning car becomes a barrier to escape, rendering the film's youth subject to the whims of its elders. The old use their control of the roadways to reassert power, compensating for the limited mobility of their own bodies by limiting the mobility of their intended victims. Having aged into staid intransigence within the confines of the town, they imprison the children that they envy in order to reclaim their youthfulness through the sacrificial rite. The bloody hand stretching from the ruined body of the car in the opening scene, grasping in vain for help amid the wreckage, is a stark reminder of the finality of death, which the elderly cult members are determined to avoid. The victims of the tank are trapped within their car, once a symbol of freedom, as its physical body is destroyed along with their own. The film's opening sequence depicts the first stage of a rebirth, but one masked by brutal violence and chaotic destruction.

Entrapment and Sacrifice

Writers exploring the cultural meaning of car crashes describe them in terms which hold an undeniable, morbid power. Mid-century American cars, Mikita Brottman notes, featured "huge windshields that broke easily and could sever jugular veins, upright metal steering columns ready to penetrate thoraxes, enormous steering wheels that could crush chests, protruding radio knobs that could enter skulls, and crazy suicide doors that could spring open, spilling helpless bodies onto the concrete."[15] Another author goes so far as to say these horrific images inspire a kind of pleasure, as "one gleefully imagines exploding windows, crumpled steel, bodies thrown from the car, and blood on the highway"[16]—descriptions brought to life in the crushing of the car at the beginning of *The Brotherhood of Satan*.

Similar horrific yet riveting images recur throughout the film. The first post-credits sequence, which introduces the main characters—patriarch Ben Holden (Charles Bateman), his daughter KT (Geri Reischl), and his new wife Nicky (Ahna Capri)—also ends with images of a car wreck. When the family's picnic is interrupted by rain, they head toward the town of Hillsboro, driving along a mountain road lined with green foliage. The road stretches out before them, with its joyous, idyllic invitation to relaxation. The scene is largely without dialogue, but suffused with tension—a mounting sense that something is about to happen. A grinding sound on the car radio garbles the bouncing, bubbling music. Suddenly, there is silence, as Ben switches off the radio. They swerve to a stop beside a wrecked car: crumpled, strewn with clothes, burning, and splashed with blood. The car—the same one crushed by the tank in the film's opening scene—is a twisted ruin. Nicky screams.

The Holdens drive into Hillsboro to report the accident, but are met by a frenzied mob of locals, consumed by suspicion and anger after the unsolved disappearance of local children, and the deaths of several of their fellow citizens. An axe-wielding man in a green army jacket charges the Holdens' car, only to be interrupted by the timely arrival of the Sheriff. Alarmed by the growing mob, the Holdens quickly decide to leave town, gunning their car up the highway with Ben behind the wheel. The possibility of escape offered by the road, once symbolic, becomes literal.

That same road, however, soon thwarts their escape. A girl—one of the children seen with the surviving boy in the film's opening sequence—appears in the road, and when Ben swerves to avoid her, he hits a utility pole. After the crash, the girl disappears. The damage to the car leaves the family vulnerable and frightened, stranded in the harsh desert. Nicky expresses the hope that another car will come by to give them a ride, but the landscape is unforgiving and the road is desolate. The town, it becomes clear, is a dead place, the emptiness of the surrounding desert echoing the elderly cult members' empty lives. Vitality, growth, and change are a distant memory. For the town, and for its elderly residents, there is no future. The Holdens are youthful—Ben and Nicky are newlyweds and KT is not yet 10—but being on the road places their bodies at risk. The smoking ruin of their car is a reminder of the always-imminent possibility of death.

The film's staging of these two early scenes of automotive destruction in the desert taps into the intersection between car crashes and ritual sacrifice. There is, Julia Darius argues, "a quasi-spiritual component to this compulsion to immerse ourselves in the etiology of the car crash and the rituals of sacrifice surrounding it—a compulsion that is resonant of some very archaic religious practices, including the worship of magic talismans and the collecting of relics."[17] The car wreck functions almost as the first act of the Satanic rite in the film. It is a necessary precondition for the old to ensnare their young victims, eliminating their ability to escape. A dusty desert town, miles from anywhere, with just one road in and out, then becomes the perfect place for a Satanist ritual of spiritual transference, as the old occupy the bodies of the young in exchange for their fealty to the Dark Lord. When cars crash, it is not just the body that is at stake; the soul is up for grabs, too. *The Brotherhood of Satan* hinges on precisely that possibility.

New Bodies for Old

The focus on the wrecked, destroyed bodies of automobiles in the early scenes of the film anticipates the physical erosion of the film's elderly characters, who are trading in their old, used-up bodies for new ones through a Satanic rite, just as "we replace our old cars with new cars and our new cars with newer cars."[18] Cars depreciate in value when they lose their "newness"—"the moment you drive it off the lot," as the maxim holds— but also because they, much like the human body, are susceptible to the ravages of time and use. Old cars' shells are blistered and gnawed by rust, their worn-out mechanical components become undependable or cease functioning entirely, and manufacturers' annual design changes render them antiquated and unappealing long before they are shipped off to the junkyard. Cars, as Eric Laurier notes, "need repair more often than just about any other object ever manufactured. They are the feeblest of built environments."[19] The film's elder characters face the same fate: the inevitable deterioration of their increasingly fragile physical bodies, matched by a ruthless, inexorable decline in their agency and influence. Both are givens, "planned obsolescence"[20] assured by physical processes and social forces; the allure of a new model, which runs better, looks sleeker, and has more options, is obvious. Through their arrangement with Satan, the town elders are attempting to arrest the natural process of aging—a process that has marginalized them, but also allowed them to hide in plain sight as they plan its undoing.

The scenes in *The Brotherhood of Satan* that depict the sacrificial rite pay significant attention to elderly bodies. One such scene in the cult's stone chamber shows the old members of the cult confronting and killing an apostate: Dame Alice (Helene Winston), who has developed doubts about going through the rite once more and so, is in violation of her pledge to Satan. When Alice first enters the space, she is the subject of skeptical gazes from her fellow elders. She accepts a candle from a robed figure, and says, "I have nothing which is not thine." Alice's quivering voice emphasizes both her awareness that Satan has granted her the temporary bodily vessel she occupies, now aged into maturity, and her fear that she has been discovered by the other cult members. Although some of the gathered elders ignore her when she tries to speak to them, one elderly woman tells her that it has "been a long time" since they have seen each other, another stark reminder of the time that has passed since their last sacrifice. Upon confronting Alice with her apostasy, Doctor Duncan, the cult leader, reminds Alice that Satan has "renewed the very blood in your veins," as though she had pulled up to a gas station and said, "Fill her up, Prince of Darkness." Behind the kneeling Alice, a group of elders, who might ordinarily be unthreatening, surround her and obscure the room with the looming possibility of physical violence.

That threat becomes real when Doctor Duncan passes Satan's judgment on Alice, and the other elder cult members close in to kill her with their bare hands. In a parallel to the film's opening tank sequence, the camera is unstable, the lens itself under assault by the snarling, grasping old folks bent on rending their fallen compatriot limb from limb. The scene's noise becomes cacophonous, just as it was in the film's beginning moments when the tank rolled over the buckling, crunching station wagon. Alice's old body is vulnerable, and the elder cult members, though weak in isolation, are powerful enough together to destroy it, and subject Alice to a painful death. The result is not shown by the camera, but it is hard not to feel the crushing, claustrophobic weight of 12 old bodies pressing down on top of her in an effect that inevitably recalls the crushing of the car in the movie's opening sequence.

186   IV. Fighting Back Time

Later, during the ceremonial transference of old souls into young bodies, the Doctor very much has death and rebirth on his mind. He offers the members of the coven "another lifetime in the brotherhood of Satan," and—acknowledging Satan's vital role with the observation that "all time bends to thy sweet presence"—boasts of the coven's ability to escape aging and transcend the seeming inevitability of death. The Doctor's direct address to Satan also foregrounds imagery of the road: "Thirteen souls receive with joy unspeakable that golden bridge that connects the two worlds of death and life." This dialogue underscores the symbolic meaning of the automobile: behind the wheel, the driver can escape, transcend limitation of aging, and find something new out there on the horizon. It is the car itself (or here, the body) that can provide the self-realization of youthful identity: "The American love of the automobile remains very much a search for self-affirmation."[21] In this sense, it is not just the road that offers the opportunity for the claiming of an identity, but the car itself that is a vehicle for achieving it. It is not just the destination, nor even the journey; the means of transportation—the aging body—holds equal sway in self-actualization. Transferring one's soul into a newer, younger body is just like sliding into the driver's seat of a brand-new car—fresh off the lot, with every surface gleaming and every part functioning perfectly—and pressing the gas pedal.

The doctor returns the focus of the film to the elderly bodies of the coven members as he asks Satan to "possess these children with the fire of thy holy way. Fill them with the blood of your passion that will enable their spirits to move in pursuit of your holy work." The imagery of refueling thus returns, layered with the fire of youth that automobile culture has long represented. The Doctor continues his appeal to Satan: "We beg for change. Change these bodies, worn ancient in thy service, for this youth, which we have gathered for your promise, for sacrifice to your holy will." In these moments, the camera pans across the gathered members of the brotherhood, their old bodies draped in red robes, alternating with those of the children, who stand, black-clad, on their pedestals. The visual contrast foregrounds the change the Doctor seeks: Old will become young, the spirit remaining as the body changes.

The camera tracks among the gathered, again highlighting the contrasting image of

Preparing for the Satanic ceremony that will transfer the aged cult members into the bodies of the kidnapped children like KT (Geri Reischi) in *The Brotherhood of Satan*.

the elderly—bowed on their brittle knees—with the youthful vitality of the children standing upright. The Doctor declares: "Bright, shining youth stands ready. The old withers." He begs Satan to "drown our useless age in blood!" At the climactic moment of sacrifice, black-robed figures (whose deliberately shrouded identities suggest demonic forces) strike at the 13 elderly cult members, their flaming swords drawing blood. Smoke rises, as it did in the film's opening moments, amidst the burning car crushed under the weight of the tank, signifying the mobility of the old souls into new, youthful bodies. The children are taken. The ritual is completed.

The Brotherhood of Satan is cynical, as are many films of the New Hollywood period. The parents and the sheriff are too late to stop the transfer—Satan is too powerful, and by the time they arrive the elderly characters have won. That conclusion also reifies its conservatism; the elders have made their deal with the Devil, and each side upholds its end of the bargain. This transfer affords the elderly characters the opportunity to continue their domination of Hillsboro by appropriating (and thus disempowering) the youth culture that threatens them, both in the world of the film and in the countercultural historical moment of the late 1960s and early 1970s. The Satanic rite allows the elders to beat them by joining them: reclaiming the physical perfection and vigor of youth while retaining the wisdom that comes with age. Though the film ends in ambiguity, viewers conclude that the old-now-young will hide within the bodies of the children, fooling their parents into accepting them warmly into their arms until the inevitable day comes when the sacrificial rite must be repeated. Here, as in the wider culture, an older generation selfishly resists its own demise, doing so at the expense of the young.

The elders in *The Brotherhood of Satan* exchange service in Satan's army for new, youthful bodies—"this year's model"—and the new lease on life, power, and influence that those bodies will bring them. Their blood sacrifice is a subversion of the coming dominance of youth culture, accomplished through the destruction of the automobile, a youthful symbol left smashed and ruined on the side of a desert highway. New bodies make them relevant again and restore the agency that had slipped away. It is not young people who will have a chance to find themselves out there on the road somewhere, but the elders who—having stolen young bodies to convey their dark and aging souls—will enjoy lives, and control over their world, far longer than the natural order would allow them. Just as the automobile has the power to obliterate "time, space, and corporeality,"[22] so too do a group of seemingly harmless old men and women—the Brotherhood of Satan—hidden in the darkness on the edge of town, in a decaying house, up a set of creaking stairs, down a hallway lined with crumbling stones.

Notes

1. Gitlin, *The Sixties*, 302.
2. Biskind, *Easy Riders, Raging Bulls*, 74.
3. Ibid., 161.
4. Best, *Fast Cars, Cool Rides*, 9.
5. Foster, *A Nation on Wheels*, 66.
6. Borden, *Drive*, 20.
7. Cohan and Hark, "Introduction," 2.
8. Laderman, *Driving Visions*, 1–2.
9. Best, *Fast Cars, Cool Rides*, 7.
10. Cumbow, *Order in the Universe*, 128.
11. Ibid., 150.
12. Brottman and Sharrett, "The End of the Road," 201.
13. Orr, *Cinema and Modernity*, 129.

14. Corrigan, *A Cinema Without Walls*, 146.
15. Brottman, "Introduction," xxxi.
16. Darius, "Car Crash Crucifixion Culture," 308.
17. *Ibid.*, xxxviii.
18. Best, *Fast Cars, Cool Rides*, 6.
19. Laurier, "This Wreckless Landscape," 29.
20. Volti, *Cars & Culture*, 52.
21. Jakle and Sculle, *Motoring*, 31.
22. Seiler, *Republic of Drivers*, 139.

Bibliography

Best, Amy L. *Fast Cars, Cool Rides: The Accelerating World of Youth and Their Cars*. New York: New York University Press, 2006.
Biskind, Peter. *Easy Riders, Raging Bulls*. New York: Touchstone, 1998.
Borden, Iain. *Drive: Journeys Through Film, Cities, and Landscapes*. London: Reaktion Books, 2013.
The Brotherhood of Satan. Directed by Bernard McEveety, 1970. Culver City, CA: Sony Pictures Home Entertainment, 2002. DVD.
Brottman, Mikita. "Introduction." In Brottman, *Car Crash Culture*, xi-xlii.
_____, ed. *Car Crash Culture*. New York: Palgrave, 2001.
Brottman, Mikita, and Christopher Sharrett. "The End of the Road: David Cronenberg's *Crash* and the Fading of the West." In Brottman, *Car Crash Culture*, 199-214.
Cohan, Steven, and Ina Rae Hark. "Introduction." In *The Road Movie Book*, edited by Steven Cohan and Ina Rae Hark, 1-14. New York: Routledge, 1997.
Corrigan, Timothy. *A Cinema Without Walls: Movies and Culture After Vietnam*. New Brunswick: Rutgers University Press, 1991.
Cumbow, Robert C. *Order in the Universe: The Films of John Carpenter,* 2nd edition. Lanham, MD: Scarecrow Press, 2000.
Darius, Julian. "Car Crash Crucifixion Culture." In Brottman, *Car Crash Culture*, 305-318. New York: Palgrave, 2001.
Foster, Mark S. *A Nation on Wheels: The Automobile Culture in America Since 1945*. Belmont, CA: Wadsworth/Thomson, 2003.
Gitlin, Todd. *The Sixties: Years of Hope, Days of Rage*. New York: Bantam Books, 1993.
Jakle, John A., and Keith A. Sculle. *Motoring: The Highway Experience in America*. Athens: University of Georgia Press, 2008.
Laderman, David. *Driving Visions: Exploring the Road Movie*. Austin: University of Texas Press, 2002.
Laurier, Eric. "This Wreckless Landscape." In Brottman, *Car Crash Culture*, 25-38.
Orr, John. *Cinema and Modernity*. Cambridge, MA: Polity Press, 1993.
Seiler, Cotton. *Republic of Drivers: A Cultural History of Automobility in America*. Chicago: University of Chicago Press, 2008.
Sharrett, Christopher. "Crash Culture and American Blood Ritual." In Brottman, *Car Crash Culture*, 319-326.
Volti, Rudi. *Cars & Culture: The Life Story of a Technology*. Baltimore: Johns Hopkins University Press, 2004.

The Evil Aging Women of *American Horror Story*

Karen J. Renner

American Horror Story (*AHS*) has revitalized the possibilities for horror—and more specifically the horror anthology series—on the small screen. True to its name, the show takes viewers on tours of the settings and scenarios that most terrify the American imagination, each season forming its own self-contained narrative. Season 1, *Murder House*, tells the tale of a family, the Harmons, who move into an Amityville-like mansion that imprisons any who die on its premises. Along the way, it makes references to the Columbine High School shootings, the "Black Dahlia" murder, and mass murderer Richard Speck. Season 2, *Asylum*, imagines a corrupt mental institution, Briarcliff Manor, which serves as a clear stand-in for Willowbrook—the facility that Geraldo Rivera exposed in 1972 for its mistreatment of inmates. Briarcliff's staff includes a serial killer named Bloody Face, who has much in common with Ed Gein, and one of its inmates is a man who, along with his African American wife, is plagued by extraterrestrials—an obvious reference to Betty and Barney Hill's alleged abduction by aliens in 1961. Season 3, *Coven*, takes us to New Orleans, where we meet reenactments of historical characters like the voodoo queen Marie Laveau and Delphine LaLaurie, a 19th-century figure known for brutalizing her house slaves. Season 4, *Freak Show*, recalls the sideshow attractions that remained popular in America well into the 20th century and features a cast of human oddities that rivals Tod Browning's 1932 *Freaks*; it also includes a homicidal clown and a disturbing mother-son relationship not unlike Norma and Norman Bates. *Hotel*, Season 5, takes place in a California lodging that recalls the horrors of both the famous Eagles song and *The Shining*; the season additionally incorporates a character resembling the historical killer H. H. Holmes, who throws parties attended by such notorious American serial killers as Jeffrey Dahmer, John Wayne Gacy, and the Zodiac Killer. Season 6, *Roanoke*, set on a southern homestead located near the infamous lost colony, adopts a postmodern approach, the first half posing as a mockumentary called *My Roanoke Nightmare* while the second half unites the "real" subjects of the documentary with the actors who portrayed them. Season 7, *Cult*, is the most political of all: a careful detailing of the worst possibilities of Trump-era America. The appearance of characters across seasons suggests that the multiple *AHS* storylines are set in a single universe, and rumors of a crossover between *Murder House* and *Coven* have raised the tantalizing possibility that the seasons are interconnected in a deeper way as well.

One of the most striking aspects of *AHS* is its tendency to reuse actors, who play different characters in each season. This feature calls attention to the show as a fictional construction: after all, it is difficult to remain caught up in the illusion of reality when the viewer recognizes that one actor has played multiple parts. The series is also known for its intertextuality, another means by which it disrupts the fictional dream it presents: in addition to invoking historical horrors, the show references well known horror fictions, playing, for example, segments of the soundtrack from *Carrie* or *Candyman* or constructing scenes that mirror iconic moments from *Halloween* or *Rosemary's Baby*. Together, the seasons of *AHS* constitute a cross-section of specifically American horrors, both fictional and factual, but also demonstrate a metafictional awareness of the genre within which the series fits, suggesting that the show critiques horror tropes as much as it relies on them.

AHS has been revolutionary in other ways, too, cutting against the sexist-ageist grain of Hollywood. The series has been repeatedly praised for placing older actresses in challenging and complex roles. The most frequently appearing actors in *AHS* are older women who appear far more frequently than any male actors, with the exception of Evan Peters and Denis O'Hare, and together constitute the core cast.[1]

	Number of Episodes	Number of Seasons	Age in 2018
Sarah Paulson	76	7	44
Jessica Lange	52	4	69
Kathy Bates	48	4	70
Angela Bassett	47	4	60
Lily Rabe	46	5	36
Frances Conroy	45	6	65
AVERAGE AGE			57

	Number of Episodes	Number of Seasons	Age in 2018
Evan Peters	85	7	31
Denis O'Hare	60	5	56
Cheyenne Jackson	33	3	43
Wes Bentley	25	3	40
Finn Wittrock	25	3	34
AVERAGE AGE			41

Left: **Average age of female actors in *American Horror Story* Seasons 1–7.** *Right:* **Average age of male actors in *American Horror Story* Seasons 1–7.**

The fact that older women dominate *AHS* does not, however, necessarily mean that they are presented positively. In fact, the show duplicates many of the problematic tropes surrounding aging—and specifically aging women—that have long marked the horror genre, allowing only certain women, those who have achieved "successful aging," to be sexual, thus supporting the stereotype that sex is for the young or at least the young-looking. Of the older female cast, only Jessica Lange and Angela Bassett, 69 and 60 in 2018, respectively, ever portray sexual characters, and both women look remarkably young and physically fit for their ages. Online accounts report Lange to be 5'8", 134 pounds, with measurements of 36–24–36 while Bassett is said to be 5'4", 114 pounds, and measuring 34–25–37. Their physiques are exceptional considering their ages but would be even if they were 20 years younger.[2] At the same time, though the age-defying bodies of these women are frequently displayed and their sexuality is given screen time, sexually active older women are also treated with caution, especially if they choose youthful male partners who violate the norms of age-appropriate male-female relationships.

In addition, many of the show's older female characters are obsessed with age, to the extent that they will torture and torment others if it will help them to resist aging, suggesting that older woman would prefer to be anything but. This theme is particularly apparent in *Coven,* in which several women seek supernatural anti-aging formulas, no matter the cost to those around them. LaLaurie (Bates), for example, drains blood from the slaves she keeps caged in her attic and paints it on her face as part of a nighttime beauty regimen. Although *AHS* can be praised for employing older female actors, the characters they portray support a variety of unsavory stereotypes about aging women.

Desire and Desirability

Dafna Lemish and Varda Muhlbauer have argued that "the traditional 'Madonna-whore' dichotomy has now been extended to include women's later life as well as their youth." Nowhere is this more evident than in *AHS*, with Conroy and Bates taking on the roles of twisted Madonnas and Lange and Bassett playing their sexualized counterparts.[3] Indeed, the distinction frames every portrayal of older women in the series.

The characters played by Lange and Bassett, traditionally attractive women, are all frequently involved in romantic and sexual relationships. In terms of Lange's characters, Constance (*Murder House*) is shown with at least three men throughout the season, one a great deal younger. Jude (*Asylum*), who wears a red negligee under her nun's habit, lusts for her boss, the younger Monsignor, and though she only successfully seduces him in a fantasy, that fantasy is given screen time. Fiona Goode (*Coven*) is consistently featured wearing high heels and tight-fitting black attire and has a steamy relationship with the Axeman, her age-mate. Finally, Elsa (*Freak Show*) regularly has sex with one man, marries another toward the end of the season, and is in love with a third, who returns her affections. Bassett's characters have similar romantic and sexual success. Marie Laveau (*Coven*) has a lover, Bastien; Desiree Dupree (*Freak Show*) has a long-term relationship with strongman Dell Toledo (Michael Chiklis), one sexual encounter with his son, Jimmy (Peters), and later marries another man; and Ramona Royale (*Hotel*) is involved with the Countess (Lady Gaga) for a decade before meeting her new lover. In fact, of all Bassett's characters, only Monet Tumusiime (*Roanoke*) is not shown to be involved in a sexual or romantic relationship. Lange's and Bassett's youthful physiques not only grant them the right to be sexual, but also allow that sexuality to be displayed on screen.

The characters played by Conroy and Bates—who never engage in sexual relationships—are, in contrast, defined by their maternal nature, their ruthlessness, or both. In *Murder House*, Conroy portrays, Moira, a maid who acts as an additional caretaker for the Harmons. She also appears as Shachath, a benevolent Angel of Death who offers her services to the suffering in *Asylum*, and as Myrtle, a protective mother figure to Cordelia (Paulson) and the rest of the young witches in *Coven*. In *Freak Show,* she is Gloria Mott, a widow so devoted to her son, Dandy, that she will help him cover up his murders, in *Roanoke,* she is cast as Mama Polk, whose name reflects her role, and in *Cult*, she is Bebe Babbitt, who in her youth was a lover to Valerie Solanas, a historical figure best known for shooting Andy Warhol, but also the author of the *SCUM Manifesto*, a radical feminist text that advocated the elimination of the male sex. Bates plays the part of the crone as often as she does the doting mother. In *Coven*, she is Madame Delphine LaLaurie, who tortures slaves and demands complete obedience from her daughters. In *Freak Show,* she plays Ethel, the Bearded Lady, divorced from her husband (whom we later discover is a repressed homosexual and likely was only attracted to her because of her masculine features) and a caretaker of both Elsa and her son, Jimmy (Peters); in *Hotel*, her character, Iris, is a near-fanatical mother completely devoted to her son, Donovan, even though he remains entirely hostile to her, and in *Roanoke*, Bates plays the actress Agnes Mary Winstead, who in turn plays Thomasin "The Butcher" White in *My Roanoke Nightmare*, the woman who took over the Roanoke colony in the absence of her husband. In short, then, Lange and Bassett are portrayed in at least 12 actively sexual relationships, but neither Conroy nor Bates is ever placed in a sexual scene. Relegating the latter actresses to asexual roles perpetuates the stereotype that the only women who experience desire are those who continue to remain youthful-looking, and only youthful-looking women are allowed to be portrayed in a sexual manner.

Moira O'Hara in *Murder House* bridges the two categories, and thus underscores the distinction between them. Although the female characters (and viewers) see Moira as an older woman, played by Conroy, she appears to Ben Harmon and most of the male characters as a scantily clad seductress, played by Alexandra Breckenridge. The use of two actresses, 30 years apart in age, functionally transforms Moira—a ghost who can change form at will—into two distinct characters, and her role in the story hinges on that idea. In her younger form, Moira is defined by her sexuality, but in her older form she behaves as a maternal figure. Ben's shifting perceptions of her highlight her liminal state. Early in the story, when his eye is regularly drawn to women other than his wife, he sees the Breckenridge version of Moira and is tempted by her playful, seductive attention. Only after he dedicates himself entirely to his wife does he finally see Moira as Conroy—"old" and therefore implicitly undesirable.

AHS's foregrounding of women like Lange and Bassett who look years younger than their average agemates initially seems like a refreshingly positive treatment of aging women, but the choice has several problematic elements. When the older women showcased look far younger than their age, this puts pressure on the average woman to maintain media-championed beauty standards far later in life. According to Imelda Whelehan

Frances Conroy (left) and Alexandra Breckenridge play elderly and youthful versions of Moira O'Hare, the housekeeper of "Murder House" in season one of *American Horror Story* (2011).

and Joel Gwynne in their introduction to *Ageing, Popular Culture and Contemporary Feminism*, these expectations have permeated the larger culture: "While advancing age was once understood as an experience of freedom from societal pressures of physical desirability and a relaxation of body anxieties, postfeminism and neoliberalism has ensured that these concerns remain in sharp focus for women in midlife and even beyond."[4] As a result, such age-defying women could actually reinforce prejudices against aging. As Barbara L. Marshall and Momin Rahman explain, "successfully ageing celebrities embrace anti-ageist sentiments at the same time as reinforcing a resistance to *old* age."[5]

Age and Anxiety

We might assume that the older women in *AHS* who are able to maintain their youthful appearance would be confident, powerful figures, but the show treats them with great suspicion. Their desire and ability to maintain youthfulness is typically paired with an ironic combination of obsessive vanity and irrational insecurity that (in the context of the story) signals their mental instability and drives them to commit horrific acts. Lange's and Bassett's characters have not simply aged gracefully and naturally. Rather, their lives are defined by the need to remain young and their needless anxiety that they have failed. In Season 1, for instance, Lange's character, Constance, attempts to recapture her youth through her relationship with Travis, a handsome and caring but dimwitted man several decades younger. (The actor who plays Travis, Michael Graziadei, is 30 years younger than Lange.) Their relationship is hardly smooth sailing. Constance verbally abuses Travis, accuses him of having sex with Adelaide, her daughter who has Down's Syndrome, and frequently seems to only value him for his looks. Meanwhile, Travis cheats on Constance readily whenever his ego is pierced by her barbed words. Even so, Travis continually affirms that he loves Constance and even plans to marry and adopt a child with her.[6] Constance's endless concerns about her age are presented as an issue that exists only in her mind, for Travis ultimately seems unfazed by their age difference, which in turn implies that women focus on their own aging far more than do their male partners.

In *Roanoke*, it is Audrey Tindall (Paulson) who frets about the age gap between herself and her new husband, Rory Monahan (Peters), a difference that in reality is only 13 years. Although Audrey confidently proclaims, "Who could have guessed that a woman of a certain age could have landed such a handsome young stud?" when she first announces their marriage, her insecurity over their relationship quickly becomes evident.[7] When another character congratulates them and innocently says, "It's never too late for love," Audrey becomes irate. "Too late?" she asks. "What do you mean? When is it 'too late'? When your heart ossifies? When your vagina exsiccates into an ancient artifact? Or is it just any woman over the age of 29? What do you mean?"[8] When, unbeknownst to Audrey, Rory is murdered and disappears, she immediately assumes he has left out of dissatisfaction with his older bride: "I was batshit crazy to think it could work," she says. "He always said age is just a number. But I knew better. It's nothing for a man to be fifteen years older than his bride. But for a woman, it's Mount Everest. All the conditions have to be perfect for the ascent. And I guess he just ran out of oxygen."[9] Both Constance and Audrey are depicted as irrationally worrying that their age makes them undesirable to their younger partners.

Yet at the same time, *AHS* punishes men who consort with older women. Travis is killed in a particularly emasculating manner by a ghost-lover, Hayden, who is enraged by his undying loyalty to the older Constance. After they have sex, he asks, "Would you mind finishing yourself?" explaining that he is eager to return to Constance so that they can make amends. Hayden asks for a goodbye hug, which Travis happily provides, remarking, "I had a really good time." Hayden then stabs him multiple times and, staring at his dead body, says: "I had a really good time, too." This line draws a clear connection between Hayden's murder of Travis and their sexual encounter, an equivalence made even more pronounced by the fact that she murders him with a phallic knife and ends up astride his body, practically panting with pleasure. In a sense, Hayden strips Travis of his masculinity by taking his place in a symbolic sex act. Travis's emasculation is even more emphasized in that, to divert suspicion, his body is disposed of Black Dahlia-style—he is found naked, a grin carved into his face and his torso cut in half, earning him the title "Boy Dahlia." In *Roanoke*, Rory meets a similarly grisly end, killed by two undead nurses, and is found eviscerated and hanging in a tree. The message appears to be that "settling" for an older woman requires a sacrifice of manhood.

This is not to say that men never express concerns about aging in *AHS*. In *Hotel*, for example, Will Drake (Cheyenne Jackson, who turns 43 in 2018), an openly bisexual fashion designer, tells a younger male model Tristan (Finn Wittrock, ten years his junior) that "[e]very beautiful young thing is hilarious, and then you grow older and wonder why no one is laughing at your jokes."[10] He seems to be speaking from personal experience. Liz Taylor (O'Hare), the transgender bartender of the hotel, bonds with Iris (Bates) because, according to Liz, they are both "women of a certain age."[11] However, only Iris links her dissatisfaction in life directly to the fact that she is an older woman: "This world holds nothing for women like me. When you get to be my age, men look right through you. Unless they want something. It's not just them, it's everyone."[12] Liz's invisibility, by contrast, seems to result from the fact that, because he is so obviously a man dressed in women's clothing, people look away, unwilling to engage with the "otherness" he represents. Furthermore, Liz, unlike Iris, feels that her sort of invisibility is ultimately an advantage. As she puts it, "You see everything when the world doesn't see you."[13]

Significantly, Will and Liz, who share what the show presents as a feminine concern with appearances and attraction, are both queer men. Both, however, overcome any momentary worries they may have had about their ages quite easily: Will regains his creativity, and Liz is reunited in life with her son and his family and in death with her true love, Tristan. In fact, Liz and Tristan's relationship is arguably the most positively portrayed in the entire series, even though it involves a 23-year age gap between the two male actors. Concerns about aging are, in *AHS*, thus implied to be women's problems and problems of their own making.

Youth at Any Price

The most horrific depictions of older women in *AHS* involve those who seek ways to artificially alter the progress of aging. These figures have no male counterparts in the series and are a recognizable type, what Lemish and Muhlbauer term the "bitch-witch older woman." They explain: "These women possess supernatural, evil powers.... They are envious of younger, more beautiful women/girls, and they are heartless, vindictive, egocentric, and seemingly unremorseful when destroying others' lives to fulfill their personal, irrational desires."[14] *Coven* includes three such figures: Fiona Goode (Lange), Madame Delphine LaLaurie (Bates), and Maria Laveau (Bassett). No clear reason is given as to why any of these women so desperately seek youth. They simply resemble the witches of fairy tales in that "there is little or no explanation of the witch's desire for youth; her desire is simply incorporated into her evil activities."[15]

Our first encounter with Fiona establishes that a fear of aging is central to her character. In this scene, she visits a scientist who is working on a stem-cell treatment that she hopes will give her "an infusion of vitality. Of youth."[16] The sort of "vitality" that Fiona seeks has little to do with renewed health: after all, she smokes and drinks constantly throughout the season, and later in this episode we also see her snort cocaine. Kelsea Stahler, reviewer of the show for *Bustle*, praises Fiona's character for not being obsessed with her appearance. She writes, "Lange's Fiona isn't often found looking in the mirror, trying to lift her drooping eyebrows or smooth out her wrinkles. She's complaining that she feels weak and that she's deteriorating; she's losing her power."[17] I would disagree. When she realizes that the supposed miracle cure is failing to rejuvenate her appearance as she would like, she looks at herself in a mirror with disgust and cries over what she sees. Furthermore, when the scientist arrives and she yells, "You've been injecting me with your shit for five days now, and nothing, nothing has changed," the second "nothing" is suggestively accompanied with a disgusted gesture to her face. Fiona's solution is to literally drain youth from the young man. After using telekinetic powers to throw him against a wall, she kneels down and begins to kiss him. What first appears to be a passionate embrace is quickly revealed to be a murderous act: Fiona literally sucks the life force from him. The longer they remain liplocked, the more the man ages, eventually becoming a gaunt, almost skeletal figure who drops to the floor, dead. Far from sorry, Fiona simply lights up a cigarette and seats herself in front of a mirror, admiring the new youth that her stopgap anti-ageing remedy has given her.[18]

In a later episode, it becomes even more evident that Fiona is only interested in youth insofar as it means beauty and, even more problematically, that she measures her attractiveness through the male gaze. In this episode, we see Fiona sitting in a bar. In a voiceover, she gives what appears to be a very confident speech:

> It's a dance, a dance no one ever had to teach me. A dance I've known since I first saw my reflection in my father's eyes.... I make the first move, which is no move at all. I've always just understood that they will eventually find themselves in front of me. Primitive, beautiful animals, their bodies responding to the inevitability of it all. It's my dance, and I have performed it with finesse and abandon with countless partners. Only the faces change.

During this voiceover, a man begins to walk slowly toward Fiona, and we initially assume that he, too, has become another partner in her dance, powerless to resist her. However, he passes her by for a younger woman, and Fiona ends her speech with "And all this time, I never suspected the night would come when the dance would end."[19] That this rejection has done terrible harm to her ego is evident in the next scene, when we see her in a cosmetic surgeon's office, where she insists on watching a video of the procedure she is considering undergoing—presumably a facelift. Obviously, the type of "vitality" that Fiona seeks is whatever will make her attractive to men.

Although she may believe herself beyond her prime, Fiona is able to find love. She has a brief but passionate affair with the Axeman. Fiona overlooks the fact that in life the Axeman was a cold-blooded serial killer who murdered indiscriminately until he was finally brought down by earlier members of the coven—he desires her and her alone, and that is enough for her. However, even though she is in a relationship with an age-mate, Fiona cannot accept that she can be truly attractive in her older age. When the Axeman tells her that, as a ghost, he watched her grow from a small child into the woman she now is and fell more deeply in love with her over the years, Fiona only hears in his words an indictment of her lost youth. She is angered by what she describes as him explaining that "[he] watched [her] grow old" and insists their sexual encounter must have been "a mercy lay."[20] Fiona cannot believe that the Axeman could desire the older version of herself when he has had the privilege of seeing her younger one in all her glory. Like many of the older women in *AHS*, Fiona unnecessarily causes problems in her romantic relationships by wrongfully assuming that her partner is as obsessed with her age as she is. Meanwhile, the Axeman—like so many of the men in show—seems blissfully unaware of any of the indicators of age about which Fiona worries.

Coven also problematically pits older women against younger women, taking on the plot of the typical fairy tale that so frequently envisions conflict between actual or symbolic mothers and their "daughters." Fiona is the Supreme, the leader of the coven, and according to the show's mythology, "when a new Supreme starts to flower, the old Supreme begins to fade."[21] Although this supernatural rule might seem to make rivalry between older and younger women inevitable, the passing of power is usually determined by a ceremony in which the new Supreme demonstrates the Seven Wonders—seven powers of witchcraft—and is pronounced the new leader by a council. The ritualistic and cooperative nature of this ceremony ensures that the change of leadership is a mutually celebrated occurrence, no doubt sad on some level for the exiting Supreme but nonetheless affirmed as necessary for the good of the coven. Fiona, however, consistently thwarts tradition and disregards the larger community of women represented by the coven in pursuit of her own selfish ends. She first ascends to the position of Supreme by killing her predecessor, Anna Leigh. In a short flashback scene, Anna Leigh initially demonstrates what seems like authentic affection for her young apprentice while Fiona expresses nothing but disdain, even gleefully pointing out Anna Leigh's many illnesses, which signal her decline. She then slashes Anna Leigh's throat without hesitation. When she looks back on the moment, Fiona even briefly acknowledges that her behavior was the height of cruelty and selfishness: "My mentor, Anna Leigh Leighton, there was a Supreme," she says. "She was majestic and powerful. She taught me everything I know. You know how I thanked her? By cutting her throat."[22] Fiona's contempt extends beyond her immediate predecessor to all of the Supremes who came before. "Get your portrait painted when you're young," she says at one point, gesturing disdainfully at all of their pictures. "Just look at these old bats."[23] All Fiona recognizes in the long tradition of women who came before her is their age—which she feels makes them undesirable and therefore worthless, especially in comparison to herself. Rather than forging alliances with other women, Fiona instead sees them as rivals and considers herself superior, at least for as long as she believes herself to be more attractive.

When Fiona herself becomes the "old Supreme," she continues this pattern of behavior, but directs it against the young. Fiona erroneously believes that the new Supreme destined to take her place is Madison Montgomery (played by Emma Roberts, over 40 years her junior). As a result, she tells Madison: "My time is up, and you're killing me. Your powers, you've been feeling them growing? … *I'm* the source. My life force is literally pouring out of my body and into yours."[24] Rather than go gently into that good night,

Fiona, in an attempt to forestall this takeover of her position and potency, slashes Madison's throat. Fiona is not only obsessed with her looks, but, like Snow White's queen, she is also willing to murder to ensure that she continues to be the fairest of them all. Her need to remain the Supreme has nothing to do with wanting to lead the coven. Indeed, she herself admits that she's been a "shitty Supreme." "All that power, all those gifts," she admits, "I just took it and poured it back into myself."[25] And yet these realizations do little to change Fiona's values; up to her death, she still clings onto the importance of her good looks. She tells her daughter Cordelia, who ultimately turns out to be the next Supreme, "Lord knows, you'll do a better job of it than I ever did, though you won't look half as good doing it."[26]

Madame LaLaurie is another woman in *Coven* who frets about her aging appearance and who also pursues supernatural remedies for it, even when they require the pain and death of others. Whereas Fiona resorts to murdering younger rivals or literally sucking the life out of them, LaLaurie—who initially lives in the 1840s—paints her face with the blood of her slaves, claiming, "When the blood dries, my skin is supposed to be as tight as a drum."[27] LaLaurie's obsession with age is, like Fiona's, motivated by male inattention; her husband has a passion for younger woman, which he typically satisfies with the black slaves in his household.

The full extent of LaLaurie's cruelty becomes apparent in "The Dead." Learning that her kitchen slave, Sally, has just given birth to a baby boy "with a complexion as light as cream" and clearly aware that her husband is the child's father, LaLaurie tells Sally that the kitchen is no place for a new mother and asks Sally to become her handmaiden and to help her with her "beauty treatments" that evening. Once in her boudoir, LaLaurie reveals her secret anti-aging concoction and asks Sally to guess at its ingredients. Sally observes nervously that it looks like blood. LaLaurie praises her wit, then reveals that this is a special batch which "came from a boy. Newly born. Youth begets youth. I know who's been between your legs, whore. You needn't bother to give that baby a name." Heartbroken over the murder of her newborn son, Sally commits suicide by jumping out the window the next morning.[28] LaLaurie, believing that she is losing her husband because of her age not her cruelty, is entirely willing to destroy others—even a newborn—in order to forestall aging.

Like LaLaurie, Maria Laveau has achieved eternal life. What we discover, however, is that it has come with a shocking price tag. Laveau, we learn, was once happy, with a lover, Bastien, with whom she had a child. Yet her desire for eternal youth was so great that she unwittingly summoned Papa Legba, a voodoo spirit of great power. As Laveau explains, "I thought I was the *shit* back then. I had just come into my prime, and my magic was strong. Shockingly strong. I was pregnant, and I did not accept the idea of death. I was invincible. Papa must have heard me."[29] In exchange for eternal life and eternal youth, Papa Legba says he will demand a yearly payment, and Laveau agrees, not realizing that what Papa Legba wants each year is an innocent soul, starting with Laveau's newborn. Laveau is horrified at the loss of her own child, but she keeps up her side of the bargain for over a century, even though doing so requires that she steal babies to give to Papa. She even helps Fiona drown Nan, a young, innocent witch, in the bathtub, showing absolutely no remorse after Nan passes. Like LaLaurie and Fiona, Laveau's obsession with youth becomes truly monstrous, requiring as it does the sacrifice of others for its maintenance.

Ironically, these women get what they wished for—but with a horrific twist. LaLaurie is sufficiently desperate to keep her husband's attention that she drinks what she believes is a love potion in order to stop his philandering. The potion grants her eternal life, but not eternal youth, and serves as a means of torture. For almost 200 years, she is buried underground, immortality amounting to eternal suffering. In the end, she is sent to a hell in which she and her daughters become the subject of the tortures that she inflicted on her slaves. Her tormentor? None other than Laveau, who is horrified to find herself forced into the role of torturer by Papa Legba. Though Laveau insists that she has done much good in the world, Papa Legba reminds her of her of her sins: "How many little babies did you bring to me every year?"[30] By comparison, Fiona's hell seems like a mercy. She is sentenced to spending eternity in a poor, run-down farmstead with the Axeman, though a far less devoted and suave version of him than she is used to. Seeking youthful attractiveness, these three women are instead rewarded with an immortality that leaves them longing for death.

Conclusion

In *AHS*, older women are slotted into the categories of Madonna or whore, but these categories are based on their ability to remain young rather than on their behavior. While aging women are frequently targets of actual derision in society, or simply excluded from consideration, women's insecurities about aging are depicted in the series as entirely self-manufactured, linked to an irrational vanity that will never be appeased. The men with whom they couple, however, have no such shallow concerns.

AHS also promotes the problematic belief that the only older women who experience sexual desire are those who look younger, thereby supporting the belief that sex is for the young. At the same time, it is the sexual older woman, the one who can defy the aging process, who is the most dreaded object of fear. In *Coven*, older women are especially horrifying, seeking youthfulness through supernatural means, never caring if those means depend on the suffering of others, and they are sentenced to the most fitting of punishments: eternal life in the worst version of hell they can imagine. It is no surprise that of all *AHS* seasons *Coven* is the one in which these types of older women become objects of fear and disgust. After all, in fairy tales, older women cast in the roles of crone, hag, and witch have long menaced the young. *Coven* thus duplicates the most troubling stereotypes surrounding older women in society—stereotypes given horrific form in the lore in which *AHS* is so deeply embedded.

NOTES

1. "American Horror Story (2011–): Full Cast and Crew."
2. Celebrity measurements can be found on the websites *Starschanges* and *Celebsfacts*, among others. Of course, there's no guarantee that these measurements are accurate, but if they aren't, then an even more problematic myth about their physiques is being perpetuated.
3. Lemish and Muhlbauer, "'Can't Have It All,'" 174.
4. Whelehan and Gwynne, "Introduction," 8.
5. Marshall and Rahman, "Celebrity, Ageing and 'Third Age' Identities," 588.
6. "Spooky Little Girl," 9:13, 29:20.
7. "Chapter 6," 23:09–23:14.
8. "Chapter 6," 26:50–27:13.
9. "Chapter 7," 5:08–5:36.
10. "Mommy," 15:06–15.
11. "She Gets Revenge," 43:05.

12. "Room Service," 10:59–11:07.
13. "Room Service," 28:29–28:31.
14. Lemish and Muhlbauer, "'Can't Have it All,'" 171.
15. Rozario and Waterhouse-Watson, "Beyond Wicked Witches," 239.
16. "Bitchcraft," 18:08–18:14.
17. Stahler, "Right Idea about Women with Sexual Power."
18. "Bitchcraft," 16:08–22:10.
19. "The Replacements," 5:00–6:07.
20. "The Dead," 32:00–32:10.
21. "The Replacements," 2:15–2:22.
22. "The Replacements," 49:18–49:57.
23. "The Replacements," 46:20–46:27.
24. "The Replacements," 47:12–47:43.
25. "The Replacements," 48:49–49:10.
26. "The Seven Wonders," 41:13–41:19.
27. "Bitchcraft," 1:35–1:42.
28. "The Dead," 37:27–39:51.
29. "Magical Delights," 22:10–22–34.
30. "Go to Hell," 39:08–43:08.

Bibliography

"American Horror Story (2011–): Full Cast and Crew." *IMDb*.com. http://www.imdb.com/title/tt1844624/fullcredits?ref_=tt_cl_sm#cast.

American Horror Story. Season 1, Episode 1, "Pilot." Aired October 5, 2011, on FX.

_____. Season 1, Episode 7, "Open House." Aired November 16, 2011, on FX.

_____. Season 1, Episode 9, "Spooky Little Girl." Aired November 30, 2011, on FX

_____. Season 3, Episode 1, "Bitchcraft." Aired October 9, 2013, on FX.

_____. Season 3, Episode 2, "Boy Parts." Aired October 16, 2013, on FX.

_____. Season 3, Episode 3, "The Replacements." Aired October 23, 2013, on FX.

_____. Season 3, Episode 7, "The Dead." Aired November 20, 2013, on FX.

_____. Season 3, Episode 10, "The Magical Delights of Stevie Nicks." Aired January 8, 2014, on FX.

_____. Season 3, Episode 12. "Go to Hell." Aired 22 January, 2014, on FX.

_____. Season 3, Episode 13, "The Seven Wonders." Aired January 29, 2014, on FX.

_____. Season 5, Episode 3, "Mommy." Aired October 21, 2015, on FX.

_____. Season 5, Episode 5, "Room Service." Aired November 4, 2015, on FX.

_____. Season 5, Episode 10, "She Gets Revenge." Aired December 16, 2015, on FX.

_____. Season 6, Episode 6, "Chapter 6." Aired October 19, 2016, on FX.

_____. Season 6, Episode 7, "Chapter 7." Aired October 26, 2016, on FX.

Lemish, Dafna, and Varda Muhlbauer. "'Can't Have It All': Representations of Older Women in Popular Culture," *Women and Therapy* 35 (2012): 165–80. doi: 10.1080/02703149.2012.684541.

Marshall, Barbara L., and Momin Rahman. "Celebrity, Ageing and the Construction of 'Third Age' Identities." *International Journal of Cultural Studies* 18, no. 6 (2015): 577–93. doi: 10.1177/1367877914535399.

Stahler, Kelsea. "Why 'American Horror Story: Coven' Has the Right Idea about Women with Sexual Power." *Bustle*, October 24, 2013. www.bustle.com/articles/7491-why-american-horror-story-coven-has-the-right-idea-about-women-with-sexual-power.

Whelehan, Imelda, and Joel Gwynne. "Introduction: Popular Culture's 'Silver Tsunami." In *Ageing, Popular Culture and Contemporary Feminism*, edited by Imelda Whelehan and Joel Gwynne, 1–13. New York: Palgrave Macmillan, 2014.

V.
What the Old Folks Know

Disturbing the Past

Horror and Historical Memory in Ghost Story *(1981)*

A. BOWDOIN VAN RIPER

Four impeccably dressed old men, leading citizens of Milburn, Vermont, sit in overstuffed leather chairs in a darkened room lit only by firelight, sipping their drinks from cut-crystal glasses. Three of them watch and listen intently as the fourth, in a voice mixing equal parts stage oratory and campfire whisper, tells a ghost story. The tale is filled with classic genre tropes—a dark night, strange noises, a deserted cemetery, and a freshly disturbed grave—and its final line, like the final flourish of a magician's wand, reveals the horrifying truth that connects them. Haunted throughout the story by a specter that he hears but never sees, the nameless cemetery keeper learns, in that last line, the reason why it haunts him: "Alive ... alive ... buried alive..."

The ghost story told at the beginning of *Ghost Story* is, in its broad outlines, the story of the four old men sharing it. They are, like the nameless cemetery keeper, collectively responsible for the premature burial of a "body" not yet dead, and haunted by the specter of the person who died as a result. There is, however, a critical difference between them.

Ghost stories hinge on the idea that the spirits of the dead walk the Earth when, and only when, they have unfinished business with the living. The resolution of that business—Scrooge changing his ways, Hamlet avenging his father's murder—lays the ghost to rest, or at least ends its haunting of the protagonist. The nameless cemetery keeper is, the story implies, trapped by his mistake. The premature burial belongs to the unreachable, unchangeable past; it is done, no act of atonement on the part of the living can undo it, and it will—given form and voice by the specter—haunt him until he himself is dead. The specter that haunts the four old men in *Ghost Story* is more elaborately developed, and its motives are correspondingly more complex. Its unfinished business with the four old men has less to do with the accidental death of the person it was in life than with their determination erase the event—and thus the person—not just from their own memories, but from the shared, collective memory of the town in which they live.

The living have always told stories about the dead, and—because the dead are, by definition, no longer capable of objecting—shaped those stories to serve their own ends. Friends and family members, eager to display their generosity of spirit, deliver fulsome eulogies praising individuals who they found exasperating, even loathsome, in life. Organizations, eager to present the best possible face to the public, canonize their founders as wise and flawless saints. The statewide committees whose purchase orders provide the stamp of approval for schoolbook histories encourage the transformation of morally flexible politicians into statesmen and ruthlessly destructive soldiers into guardians of freedom. Revealing the dead as they actually were—and thereby, in many cases, challenging the stories widely told about them—has traditionally been the work of archaeologists, historians, and biographers. *Ghost Story*, however, imagines a world in which the dead can return from beyond the grave to directly challenge the stories told by the living, and to resist—by their spectral presence—attempts to erase them from public memory and, ultimately, from history.

Buried Secrets

The four old men at the heart of *Ghost Story*—attorney Sears James, physician John Jaffrey, businessman Ricky Hawthorne, and politician Ned Wanderley—call themselves the Chowder Society. Friends since their youth, now leading citizens of their small New England town, they meet once a month tell one another ghost stories by firelight. All four suffer sleepless nights and, when sleep does come, terrifying nightmares.

The film's unfolding of the reasons why begins with Ned's adult son David (Craig Wasson) questioning the woman (Alice Krige) who shared his bed the night before. She turns toward him, revealing the face of a rotting corpse, and he leaps back in shock, crashing through the window of his high-rise apartment and falling to his death. Returning home for the funeral, David's twin brother Don (Craig Wasson again) resumes his

The Chowder Society—(from left) Ned Wanderley (Douglas Fairbanks, Jr.), Sears James (John Houseman), Ricky Hawthorne (Fred Astaire) and John Jaffrey (Melvyn Douglas)—toast their health after an evening of ghost stories in *Ghost Story* (1981).

tense relationship with Ned, from whom he is all but estranged. The two have just begun a halting reconciliation when, on the night of David's funeral, Ned has a dream in which he is a guest at the wedding of a young woman in a long, white dress. The bride turns to him, lifts her veil, and he awakens, terrified. The next morning, stumbling through the streets of Milburn as if in a daze, he makes his way toward a bridge where the same woman, now in street clothes, stands with her back to him. He reaches out and she turns, revealing the same rotted face from which David recoiled. Like his son, Ned staggers backward and falls to his death.

Stunned, the three surviving members of the Chowder Society discuss what to do next, making oblique references a secret that they hold in common. Don, sorting through his father's belongings, finds a photograph of Ned and the other members as young men in the late 1920s, posing with a beautiful young woman in a summer dress. Ricky shrugs it off as meaningless when Don shows it to him over lunch, but meets with his friends that night to inform them of its existence. He assures them that he revealed nothing, but admits: "I wanted to. I like the boy." Sears disagrees: "The circle has held this long," he tells the other two. "Change is change for the worse."

Don interrupts the discussion, asking to "buy his way into" the Chowder Society with a tale of his own, and adding: "I think it's a ghost story." In a long flashback he explains how, while working in Florida, he fell into a passionate, all-consuming love affair with a beautiful young woman named Alma Mobley. The two had begun discussing marriage—including Alma's desire to be married in Milburn, in a long white dress, "in front of your father and all his friends"—when Don, sensing something uncanny about her, asked that they slow down. Furious with him, Alma left town without warning, only to reappear in New York as David's new lover and, soon, his fiancé.

John is deeply disturbed by the story, and by Don's observation that Alma resembled the woman in the picture. Muttering "it had to happen," he begs the others to reveal the secret, but is overruled by Sears. That night, John has a nightmare in which the corpse of a young woman come to life his autopsy table; the next morning, he finds the same woman waiting for him in the home office where he used to see patients. Descending the stairs, he suddenly collapses and, after a glimpse of her corpse-face, dies. Sears relents at last and—with Ricky's help—tells Don the Chowder Society's secret in the film's second flashback sequence.

One summer in the late 1920s, a beautiful young woman named Eva Galli came to Milburn and took up residence in a lavishly appointed house for the season. All four friends courted her, but when it became clear that she and Ned were falling in love, the other three yielded to him. Ned, humiliated by his impotence during their first sexual encounter, rejected her tender reassurances and left her to drink with his friends, regaling them with tales of his sexual prowess. Later that night, thoroughly drunk, the four decided to call on Eva as a group. She invited them into her marble-columned living room, where Ned sulked and the others flirted drunkenly with her as they danced to gramophone records and dropped broad hints about the couple's passionate tryst.

Eva, furious at Ned's violation of her trust, taunted him by returning his friends' flirtations. When she threatened to reveal the truth about their time in the bedroom, he cried "No!" and shoved her, causing her to strike her head on a marble column and slump to the floor. John, a medical student, declared her dead after a brief examination, and the four friends conspired to dispose of her body by sinking their car, with Eva laid across the back seat, into a deep corner of nearby Dedham Lake. As the car slipped below the surface, however, Eva appeared in the rear window: alive all along, and now revived by the cold water. Hands and terrified face pressed against the glass, she cried out to them for help as the car submerged, drowning her.

Don and the two survivors of the Chowder Society go to Eva's long-abandoned, crumbling house in an effort to lay her ghost to rest, but Don falls through a rotted staircase and breaks his leg. Sears drives into town to call an ambulance, but Eva's ghost intercepts him on the road and he is killed. With night approaching and Don's condition growing more serious, Ricky reluctantly leaves on foot to seek help. He locates the sheriff and, insisting that "we must save the boy," directs him not to the house but to the lake. Winched ashore, the long-submerged car breaks the surface as—back at the darkening house—Eva's ghost stands over Don in her wedding dress, taunting him about his impending death. Ricky yanks open the rear door of the car, bringing Eva's corpse and the Chowder Society's buried secret to light, and the ghost fades to nothingness as the screen fades to black.

Editing, Erasure and Collective Memory

Writing in the 1930s, Maurice Halbwachs distinguished between "collective memory" and "historical memory."[1] The former, he argued, is compounded of individual memories—direct personal experiences with the events of the past—integrated within the framework of, and given context and meaning by, the worldviews of specific social groups to which the individuals belong. Every individual belongs to many such groups (families, nations, and religions, among others) and the identities of those groups, as well as the individuals' relationship to them, changes over time. Individuals' memories of past events changes over time as well, as details fade and maturity brings new perspectives. Collective memory is, for Halbwachs, both plural and plastic by nature. It encompasses multiple pasts, whose contours and boundaries are constantly shifting. Historical memory—unitary, stable, and eternal—emerges only after "tradition ends and the social memory is fading and breaking up."[2] It is, as Susan Crane notes, "the representation of a *lost* past, and its only recollection."[3] Only when there are no more individuals with direct memories of a particular set of historical events, Halbwachs argued, can historians can abstract those memories from the multiple social frameworks within which they were formed, and integrate them into a single, objective chronological framework.

The events of *Ghost Story* span 50 years or more, with the long flashback narrated by Sears and Ricky taking place in the mid to late 1920s and the remainder of the story in the film's present, circa 1980.[4] The events of the fateful summer depicted in the flashback thus remain within the realm of collective memory. Individuals with direct memories of them—the members of the Chowder Society—are still alive, and recollections of them still fluid. The past to which they belong has not yet (quite) been lost, and the historical memory of it has not yet (quite) begun to form. The distinction matters because the four old men are implied to be the *only* still-living citizens of Milburn with individual memories of that summer, and because they have spent their lives shaping the collective memory of it to serve their own ends.

Acting in panicked, drunken haste on the night that Eva died, the future members of the Chowder Society set out to erase all evidence of their connection to her death. The first part of the process is straightforward and deliberate. "Burying" her in Dedham

Lake eliminates the only tangible link between their names and her demise. Failing to inform the local authorities of her apparent death-by-concussion in the house or her actual death-by-drowning in the lake forestalls the creation of such a link in police, judicial, or medial records. Destroying every copy of the only photograph showing the five of them together removes the last tangible reminder that she and they even were associated with one another even in life. The only remaining evidence is memories: theirs and others.

Erasing—or attempting to erase—Eva from their own memories is, like erasing the material evidence, an orderly and deliberate process. "We agreed never to talk about it again," Sears tells Don, "not even among ourselves." Ricky concurs, declaring that "we put it behind ourselves," and Sears finishes the thought: "We got back to school ... got on with the rest of our lives." The four even edit their memories of what they saw as the car slipped beneath the surface of the lake, convincing themselves that the terrified face they saw through the glass of the rear window was not real but "a trick of the light." The erasures and reframing takes place exclusively within the tightly bounded confines of their group, shaped by and in service of the group's shared worldview. The four young men—products of wealthy, privileged backgrounds—not only look forward to futures defined by power, prestige, and influence but see such futures as their birthright. They do what they do to ensure that Eva's death does not, in any way, tarnish their personal reputations or imperil those futures. The result, within their small group, is a version the then-recent past from which Eva has been all but edited out.

A similar process of erasure is, simultaneously, at work in the larger community of Milburn: more complex, less predictable, and not entirely under their control. "Wasn't she missed?" Don asks incredulously after Sears and Ricky describe their disposal of Eva's body. Sears, shaking his head, explains: "Everyone assumed that she'd grown tired of the place, and moved on. There was talk, but it died down." Ricky chimes in: "You could almost feel a sigh of relief that she was gone." The two friends' enigmatic comments reflect the social dynamics of small New England towns, more pronounced in the 1920s than in the film's present, let alone ours.[5] Eva was an outsider: a stranger "from away" whose beauty turned young men's heads and whose manner pushed the boundaries of social convention. "Talk" (a polite synonym for "gossip") about such a woman's sudden, unannounced departure would likely have revolved around the possibility that she was pregnant. The "sigh of relief" Ricky describes would have accompanied the realization that, if the father was someone local, she had chosen not to name him. Glad to have avoided the scandal such a naming might have caused, the town allowed its collective memory to close over the empty place she left behind like the surface of Dedham Pond closing over the roof of the sinking car. "It was," Sears concludes, "as if she had never existed."

All My Sins Remember'd

The four old men of *Ghost Story* know, from the moment that they pick up Eva's limp body rather than the telephone, not only that they are lying but that they are doing so for purely self-serving reasons. They conclude (as their tacit pledge of silence makes clear) that, having chosen that course, they cannot, for the rest of their lives, deviate from it, lest they bring down on themselves precisely the disgrace and ruin they sought so urgently to avoid. What they do not see; what—as young men who are, at most, a year or two into legal adulthood—they likely *cannot* see is how long the rest of their lives will be. They have, when the events of the film transpire, been living with the knowledge of what they did for a half-century or more. A quirk of casting accentuates the passage of time. The actors who play the four friends as young men look convincingly like 1920s "college boys," but three of the four who play them as old men— Houseman (79), Douglas (80), and Astaire (82)—are nearly a decade older than their characters "should" be when the film takes place.

The passage first of years and then of decades leaves the four in an unenviable position. The small-town world they (still) inhabit has moved on. Few other residents—none that we see on screen, other than John's wife Milly (Jacqueline Brooks) and Ricky's wife Stella (Patricia Neal)—are old enough to have been alive in the summer that they met (and killed) Eva, and whatever memories of her they may have possessed have faded to nothingness decades before. For everyone in town *but* them, that summer has moved from the realm of collective memory to that of historical memory: lost, forgotten, and all but unrecoverable. For the members of the Chowder Society, however, the memories of that summer are still very much alive. They remain part of the group's shared consciousness, and the determination not to talk about them remains an organizing principle of the group's day-to-day life.

As Halbwachs observed, however, collective memory is reformed and recontextualized by the passage of time and the shifts in individual (and group) perspective that come with it. The old men's memories of the night Eva died have, with the passage of time, become saturated with regret and self-reproach. "If only we'd been thirty rather than twenty," Ricky laments as he trudges through the snow toward Eva's long-derelict house; Sears, walking beside him, agrees: "What fools we were!" Ricky muses as the 1920s flashback ends: "We could have gone to the police, taken our chances, but instead we did this … obscene thing."

Disturbing the Past

The specter that haunts the four old men—both in their dreams and in the real world—is a tangible symbol of the offense they once committed, not just against human-made laws but against human decency. It takes the form of a fully dressed, half-decomposed corpse, its skin sheened with water as if it had returned, only moments before, from a long submergence. It initially appears, except in John Jaffrey's dream, as a (seemingly) normal young woman with her face turned away from the camera. Only when the victim draws closer to does the specter turn, revealing its horrific visage of rotting, distended flesh, mottled gray-green skin, and eyes bulging from shrunken sockets. This ruined face is the last thing that Ned, John, and Sears see before they die, and—the film strongly implies—the thing that robs all four old men of their sleep and causes them to wake up, screaming and sweating, in the middle of the night. *Ghost Story* never addresses whether the specter that invades their dreams is the same ghost that stalks them by daylight, or merely a projection of their own troubled minds. In the end, in does not matter. Both versions of the specter wear Eva's face, and both remind them of the "obscene thing" they once conspired to do.

There is no such ambiguity about the specter that appears to Ned's twin sons—first to Don in Florida, then to David in New York, and finally to Don again in the crumbling house in Milburn. It is the ghost of Eva Galli, risen from her watery grave in Dedham Pond to walk among the living, and the rotted face it reveals in its final encounter with each of the brothers is the same one it revealed to Ned, John, and Sears in the moments before they died. The principal face that Eva's ghost presents to the two younger men is not, however, that of a sodden, half-decayed corpse. She appears to each of them—for days, weeks, and in Don's case perhaps even months—as "Alma Mobley," a beautiful, passionate, exuberantly sexual young woman. Eva's ghost, in her "Alma" manifestation, does not merely *appear* to be alive and whole, but actually passes as a living being, holding down a job—as a secretary at the Florida university where Don teaches—collecting a paycheck, and keeping an apartment. Both Don and David hold her, sleep with her, and make love to her repeatedly without suspecting that she is anything but a living flesh-and-blood woman.[6] When she (inadvertently, the film suggests) reveals her true nature, it is in her sleep, not theirs, and only through the subtlest of flaws in her "living" persona: a voice turned suddenly odd and otherworldly, and skin turned unnaturally cold and damp.

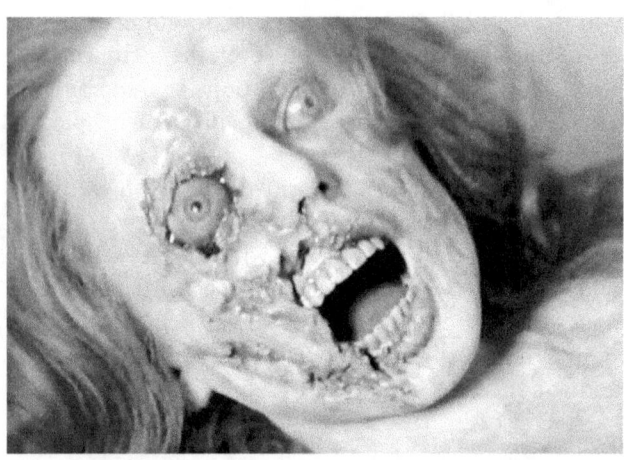

After a night spent in David Wanderley's bed as a beautiful, living woman, "Alma Mobley" (Alice Krige) reveals her true nature in *Ghost Story*.

"Alma" first appears onscreen stretched out, full-length and face-down, on the bed in David's high-rise apartment. The bedclothes are crumpled at her feet, her arms are crossed above her head, and her face (hidden by a cascade of dark red hair spread across her shoulders) is buried in the pillow. Her body language conveys a languid sleepiness that matches the morning light streaming through the windows and hints a night of vigorous activity. She is casually, comfortably nude, but the camera's gaze is coolly appreciative rather than prurient. Its cataloging of small, unexpected details—the swell of her left breast beneath her upraised arm, a scattering of freckles across her pale skin, the curve of her lower back and the flare of her hips and bottom—is miles removed from the furtive, fleeting glimpses of breasts in contemporary slasher films aimed at teenaged male audiences.

Don's long flashback narrative of his own passionate affair with Eva unfolds in similar ways, but at greater length and in more detail. The scenes in which Eva appears nude are longer and more revealing, but like her morning-after scene with David they have a higher purpose than gratuitous titillation.[7] A scene of Eva and Don sharing a bath is a case in point: The two face each other from opposite ends of the tub, smiling as they carry on an emotionally intimate conversation. She holds his left foot in both soapy hands, taking obvious pleasure in the fact that washing has given way to massaging. Her breasts, their erect nipples a startlingly bright crimson, are visible above the water—glistening with soapy water but, in a pointed departure from a decades-old Hollywood convention, unobscured by bubbles. He arches his left foot, gently caressing her right breast with his outstretched toes, and she giggles with pleasure. The staging of couple's first sexual encounter, simultaneously explicit and atmospheric, works both as erotica and as character development, like similar scenes in *Body Heat* and *The Postman Always Rings Twice* (released earlier the same year). It reveals a ferocity in Eva that, like the playfulness on display in the bath, complements the languid sleepiness she displayed with David.

The living Eva who floats, like a Jazz-Age goddess, through Sears and Ricky's flashback memories is—it quickly becomes clear—the basis for the spectral Eva's "Alma Mobley" persona. The shadings are different, adjusted for 50 years of changing cultural mores, but the mixture of playfulness, sensuality, and intensity is unchanged. When Ned playfully wrestles her to the ground during an impromptu outdoor game—falling half-beside, half-atop her—she neither squirms nor protests, but looks coolly up at him with an unsettlingly intense gaze, as if daring him to take further advantage. Later, she responds to Sears' truculent demand for a dance by declaring "you'll *get* your dance, you all will," locking eyes with Ricky (the least mature of the group) for a long moment, and then kissing him fiercely. The sexual tension in the scene escalates as she delivers a similar kiss to John, telling him: "I'm going to take a bite out of you." When she turns to Sears to pay off her promise of a dance, the exchange that follows, where Eva says, "Dance with me, you little toad…," Sears replies, "Slut," not raising his voice, and Eva slaps his face, comes off as a seamless mixture of fight and foreplay. Her subsequent taunt to Ned about their night together ("Shall I tell them all about it?") plays like a slightly sour echo of the exchange, but—whether genuine anger or a miscalculated appeal to Ned's masculinity—its intent quickly becomes irrelevant. He shoves her, she falls, and the light leaves her eyes.

Eva-as-Alma exists, in the fictional universe of *Ghost Story*, to bring Don and David face to face with the woman who, one long-ago summer, captivated their father and his friends like a Siren in a flowing summer dress, and to confront them with the horror of a vibrantly alive person becoming—in a terrible, irreversible instant—a cold, inert, lifeless *thing*. She exists, in the film-as-film, to do the same thing for the audience. "Certain memories live on," as Yosef Yerushalmi writes, while "the rest are winnowed out, suppressed, or simply discarded by a process of natural selection which the historian, uninvited, disturbs and reverses."[8] Eva, returned to almost-life as Alma, disturbs and, ultimately, reverses her own erasure from history, reminding Don, David, and us not only that she once lived, but who she once was. The four old men, of course, have no need of such reminders. They already know, and have known for 50 years or more.

Winner Lose All

Ghost Story ends with three of the four old men dead, and Ricky left to face the consequences of what the four did, together, a half-century before. That those consequences will be significant, however, seem unlikely in the extreme. The sodden corpse that tumbles from the back seat of the car, rotted flesh sloughing off its skull like melting snow from a steep roof, barely resembles a human being, let alone the woman Eva Galli was in life. She is, thanks to the quartet's long-ago actions, not even a name on a dusty file in the sheriff's office. The discovery of her body resolves no mysteries, closes no cases, and ties off no loose ends. Statutes of limitations aside, Ricky—elderly, avuncular, wealthy and respected—would be the least appealing of targets for even the most zealous of local prosecutors. At worst, he is destined to become (along with Eva and his now-dead friends) the subject of a local legend that will, in time, become woven into the town's historical memory.

The members of the Chowder Society have, in that sense, won. They lived out the bright, shining futures that stretched out before them—and that they went to extremes to protect—on the night Eva died. Three are dead, but they died in old age, wealthy and respected, with their reputations intact. Whatever details of that long-ago summer pass, through Ricky or Don, into historical memory are more likely to add an exotic patina to their reputations than an ineradicable stain.

On another level, however, the members of the Chowder Society have won nothing. The strains imposed by half a century of enforced silence about "the worst thing that ever happened" to them has warped the lives of all four men. Their inability to share their dark secret, or be honest about the torment that it causes them, has placed an impenetrable barrier between them and those closest to them. Ned's relationship with Don (and, to a lesser extent, David) is distant and cold. Milly, watching John waken from his nightmare of the animated corpse on the autopsy table, is able—just for a moment— to penetrate his defenses and ask him about his cryptic comment: "She moved." He responds cryptically that: "She was dead" and then, realizing that he is skirting the edge of the forbidden subject, falls silent. Late in the film, as Ricky prepares to confront the ghost, Stella observes: "I've been married to you 52 years, and I don't know any more about you now than I did then." There is warmth in the surface of her voice but, beneath it, a deep reservoir of sadness.

The four old men know—and *only* they know—that in covering up Eva's death in order to protect their own futures, each of them violated the core ethical principles of the professions they had yet to enter. Sears, the future officer of the court, conspired to destroy evidence and conceal an unnatural death from the law. John, the physician-in-training, made a gross diagnostic error and compounded his misconduct by failing to report it. Ned, the aspiring politician, lied to his "constituency" of three rather than admit an uncomfortable truth about himself. Ricky, the heir to a family business, sullied the reputation for honesty and uprightness that was its most valuable asset. All four men have, on the surface, achieved the lives that they dreamed of as college students in their early 20s: They possess wealth and power, and enjoy the respect and deference of their neighbors. Behind that façade, however, their lives they have been hollowed out and rendered empty by their determination to keep their dark secret hidden. They have been haunted by their individual memories of Eva Galli since the night she died, long before she returned from her watery grave to force her way back into history.

NOTES

1. Halbwachs, "Historical Memory and Collective Memory."
2. *Ibid.*, 78.
3. Crane, "Writing the Individual," 1377.
4. The internal clues are contradictory. Ricky flatly states that Eva died "in the spring of fifty years ago," but the events of the flashback clearly unfold over the course of one summer, suggesting that his memory may be faulty. He was clearly single during the events of the flashback, but Stella says that she has been married to him for 52 years, and the summer shown in the flashback clearly predates the Crash of 1929 and the Great Depression.
5. Henry Beetle Hough's *Country Editor*, a memoir of life in Edgartown, Massachusetts (population c. 1,300), from 1920 to 1939, chronicles and, in the author's carefully nuanced reticence about certain names and details, illustrates those dynamics.

6. In Peter Straub's 1979 novel, Eva is not a ghost in the usual sense of the word, but a literal shape-shifter: one of an ancient race of spirit-beings that gave rise to Native American belief in the Manitou.

7. The one genuinely gratuitous nude scene in the film is a full-frontal matte shot of David plummeting to his death.

8. Yerushalmi, *Zakhor*, 95.

BIBLIOGRAPHY

Crane, Susan A. "Writing the Individual Back into Collective Memory." *American Historical Review* 102, no. 5 (December 1997): 1372–1385.
Halbwachs, Maurice. "Historical Memory and Collective Memory," in *The Collective Memory*, trans. Francis J. Ditter, Jr., and Vida Yazdi Ditter, 50–87. New York: Harper Colophon, 1980.
Hough, Henry Beetle. *Country Editor*. New York: Doubleday, 1940.
Straub, Peter. *Ghost Story*. New York: Coward, McCann, and Geohagen, 1979.
Yerushalmi, Yosef. *Zakhor: Jewish History and Jewish Memory*. 1982. Seattle: University of Washington Press, 1989.

Becoming Dr. Caligari

ROBERT B. LUEHRS

They said the Great War would end all wars.[1] They were wrong, of course. Instead of eternal peace, the war brought only devastation, misery, and horrific carnage. It left too many survivors shattered physically and emotionally, and caused the disintegration of social institutions that had endured for centuries. Then came a global pandemic of influenza, frequently called Spanish Flu, a merciless scourge which slaughtered tens of millions more than the war had.[2] Those dying of this affliction drowned in their own blood while turning blue with cyanosis; some occasionally suffered psychotic episodes during recovery.[3] Not surprisingly, this milieu of unrelenting chaos and mindless torment engendered the first of the modern horror films, which was also the first cinematic example of elder horror: *The Cabinet of Dr. Caligari* (*Das Cabinet des Dr. Caligari*), which premiered in Berlin on February 26, 1920.[4]

This gothic masterpiece offers audiences two remarkable monsters. First there is the ancient Dr. Caligari himself, played by Werner Krauss, transformed into a hoary grotesque by heavy makeup.[5] A stout man, enveloped in a floor-length Inverness cape, with long, white hair snaking out from beneath his top hat, Caligari scowls at the world through thick, black-rimmed spectacles that accentuate his piercing eyes. He is both a malevolent psychiatrist and a sorcerer, endowed with dark, occult powers. The other demonic figure in the film is Cesare the somnambulist (Conrad Veidt), the doctor's cadaverous agent of death. Armed with a knife, Cesare is periodically dispatched by his master on homicidal errands. With his maniacal stare and pallid face, Cesare is both chilling and tragic. The images of the mad doctor and his twisted creation have haunted filmmakers ever since.

In the film, the story of Caligari and Cesare is told by Francis (Friedrich Feher), a student, to an elderly companion as the two men sit on a bench by a bleak wall.[6] Caligari first appears as a baleful showman with a freak exhibit, a somnambulist. When Caligari applies for a license to be part of the Holstenwall town fair, the Town Clerk treats him rudely; later the man is found stabbed to death. Francis and his friend Alan (Hans Heinz von Twardowski) attend Caligari's performance where Cesare, briefly awakened, prophesies Alan will live only "till the break of dawn."[7] As foretold, Alan is murdered that night, with the grisly crime shown as shadows on his bedroom wall. Horrified, Francis vows to track down the killer, whom he assumes to be Cesare under the command of Caligari. Since the police seem feckless in this situation, Francis becomes an amateur detective. As his Dr. Watson, he relies on Dr. Olsen (Rudolf Lettinger), father of his girlfriend, the demure Jane (Lil Dagover). The two investigators put the suspects under surveillance, collecting evidence.

Before they can stop Caligari, however, he sends his creature out again, this time to assault Jane in retaliation against the two individuals who love her. In a nightmare scene, Cesare peers through the bedroom window at Jane sleeping, silently breaks in, and stalking his prey with feline grace, slowly creeps up on her. He raises his knife, pauses, and then reaches down to fondle her, his face contorted into a leer. She awakes, struggles, and faints. Cesare tucks her under his arm like a limp rag doll, and, as the skirt of her nightgown billows behind them, he carries her off over the rooftops and into the countryside beyond. Chased by a mob, Cesare ultimately collapses, and Jane, unconscious but unharmed, is rescued.[8]

Francis follows Caligari to an insane asylum, discovering the doctor is not a patient but the institution's Director. With the aid of the staff, Francis finds in Caligari's papers the motive for his crimes: the psychotic psychiatrist has assumed the name and persona of an 18th-century Italian mystic who terrorized fairs with a somnambulist. Faced with this information and the body of Cesare, Caligari suffers a mental breakdown and is incarcerated for life.

Francis' tale ends at this point, but the film does not. Francis himself turns out to be an inmate in the insane asylum of his story, as are Jane and Cesare, who caresses a white flower. The Director appears, played by Krauss but looking far less menacing than the monster he has depicted up to that point. Francis hurls himself at him, screaming: "You all believe I am insane. That is not true. It is the Director who is insane. He is Caligari, Caligari, Caligari." Subdued by attendants, the hysterical Francis is wrapped in a strait jacket and locked in a cell. The Director then says with a smile, "At last I understand his delusion. He thinks I am that mystic Caligari. Now I know how to cure him."[9]

The authors of the screenplay, Hans Janowitz and Carl Mayer, were impecunious Austrian outsiders in Germany, writers who had never before worked in the motion picture industry.[10] They created a detailed script in only about six weeks and convinced Erich Pommer, head of Decla-Film, to produce it.[11] Pommer wanted a "comparatively inexpensive production," which, even if it was not up to best standards, would encourage comment. Accordingly, he encouraged the development of painted, flat, fantastic sets which would reflect the story's "mystery and macabre atmosphere of the Grand Guignol."[12] Thus Caligari's unsettling world of tilted buildings, distorted windows, jagged doors, deformed furniture, and ragged vegetation, all festooned with arbitrary glyphs, is more the result of mercenary calculation than bold, avant-garde artistic experimentation. To save further money, the film was shot on an indoor stage; that process took a mere month.[13] Yet, despite difficulties, it all worked, and *The Cabinet of Dr. Caligari* became an international success. Its expressionist spirit in particular has impressed generations of subsequent filmmakers and film critics.

Later, around 1941, Janowitz wrote that he and Mayer were very upset about a particular alteration in the script imposed by the director, Robert Wiene. Wiene had added a frame—or, more accurately had replaced the original frame—which completely altered the film's intended meaning.[14] The original Janowitz/Mayer script opens with Francis and Jane, a married couple, entertaining friends on a terrace. Seeing a gypsy caravan in the distance, Francis is inspired to tell his guests about the horrific encounter he and his wife had with Caligari some 20 years before. This version ends with Francis and Jane visiting a plaque at the site of the Holstenwall fair honoring Caligari's victims.[15] Wiene's revision turns Francis into a paranoid, relating what is only a delusion to a fellow patient. Once Francis is safely confined to a cell, there is a promise of somehow restoring his sanity.

Actually, the Janowitz/Mayer frame is rather bland while the one devised by Wiene leaves the audience with some very intriguing and very disturbing questions about the ambiguous relationship between reality and illusion or delusion. For example, one might expect once Francis is revealed as mentally unsound and once he ceases to be the narrator, the environment surrounding the characters would become "normal." It does not. Everything remains jagged and askew. Does Francis' cure merely involve compelling him to accept the illogic of Caligari's distorted world as ultimate reality?

Janowitz said Dr. Caligari's story was not supposed to be taken as the ravings of a madman but as an antiwar allegory.[16] Janowitz had served as an officer in the Austro-Hungarian army and lost his younger brother on the Italian front; Mayer had managed to avoid conscription, supposedly deceiving an army psychiatrist into certifying him as unfit. Neither had any respect for the Hohenzollern and Hapsburg regimes which had brought on the war and had fallen because of it.[17] According to Janowitz, he and his co-author had "unconsciously" intended Caligari to represent authoritarian governments, power-hungry and deranged, which mesmerize young men, turn them into puppets, and send them into battle to kill or be killed.[18] This interpretation was subsequently publicized and elaborated upon by film critic and sociologist Siegfried Kracauer in his book *From Caligari to Hitler: A Psychological History of the German Film* (1947). Kracauer wrote: "While the original story exposed the madness inherent in authority, Wiene's *Caligari* glorified authority and convicted its antagonist of madness. A revolutionary film was thus turned into a conformist one—following the much-used pattern of declaring some normal but troublesome individual insane and sending him to a lunatic asylum."[19] Kracauer proposed Caligari was a premonition of Hitler, who hypnotized the masses. Janowitz and Mayer fell down, according to Kracauer, in suggesting no alternative to tyranny except chaos, symbolized by the anarchic amusements of the fair, where the carousel never stops spinning.[20]

However, Caligari himself affirms no particular political agenda or ideology. He seeks no followers. Like his creators, he is an outsider, who has an adversarial relationship with all authority.[21] Through Cesare, Caligari attacks members of the municipal bureaucratic, intellectual, and professional elite: the supercilious town clerk, the student Alan, and the daughter of a prominent physician. He does so for personal vengeance and amusement, not to remake society. He just wants to see what he can get his somnambulist to do.

Janowitz referred to Caligari as a "spectral-looking old man."[22] Caligari is indeed old. He manifests the worst of the traits customarily assigned to the elderly by those who are much younger. His demeanor is weird and ominous. When he walks, he shuffles, hobbling on a walking stick. He is petulant, manipulative, petty, condescending, and filled with rage at the impotence age imposes. He is cruel, furtive, and selfish. Caligari can sometimes be childlike, as when, having temporarily bettered Francis and Dr. Olsen, he peers at them mischievously over the brim of his hat and chortles. Oddly appealing as he gently feeds Cesare a bowl of gruel, he turns into a lecherous gargoyle while enticing the innocent Jane into his tent to display her to Cesare. Above all, however, Caligari personifies will, an unconscious, irrational, and irresistible compulsion.

The eminent philosopher and psychologist of will was Arthur Schopenhauer, an erudite, sarcastic iconoclast. Creative individuals were often fascinated by his works, perhaps, in part, because unlike most 19th-century German philosophers, he wrote with clarity and wit and because he extolled music, literature, and the fine arts for revealing truth as well as providing a mystical, albeit temporary, escape from life's miseries.[23] Thus it is quite plausible that Janowitz, as he claimed, should find inspiration for Caligari's appearance in a portrait of Schopenhauer included in a bedside copy of one of the philosopher's books.[24] The dress of the two doctors is similar: frock coat, white cravat, high shirt collar which extends over his lapels.[25] They share wildness in coiffure. Caligari wears an approximation of Schopenhauer's muttonchops, and he displays a prominent wen on his left cheek, visible in several of Schopenhauer's photographs. One portrait even shows the elderly scholar with eyeglasses in his hand, although nothing as grand as Caligari's oversized spectacles.[26]

Schopenhauer, however, contributed more to *The Cabinet of Dr. Caligari* than just Caligari's physical appearance. Drawing inspiration from two of his philosophic heroes, Plato and Immanuel Kant, Schopenhauer made the unnerving assertion that reality is what we do not see. Our view of things is an illusion created by our perceptions which are, in turn, processed through structures imposed by our minds: time, space, and causality in particular. The evident interconnections among these perceptions we call "science."[27] As his *opus maximus*, *The World as Will and Representation* (*Die Welt als Wille und Vorstellung*, first published in 1819) boldly put it: "The world is my representation."[28] The contorted world of Holstenwall is a reflection of Caligari's mind, but the real significance of Schopenhauer for the film is his concept of will and the resultant pessimism about the human condition.

According to Schopenhauer, behind our faulty representation of the world lies a cosmic motive force called "will." Will permeates everything. It is a blind, relentless, unyielding drive, without either purpose or end. Will is chaos, and we are all trapped as slaves in this self-devouring process. Plato and Kant said our essence is reason. Here they were wrong; reason, like everything else, is driven by hidden, primitive urges that defy permanent satisfaction. Although will is a unity, it manifests itself in a variety of forms. In animals it is basic instinct, while in humans it is the maelstrom of involuntary and irrational passions, desires, hostilities, and fears which rise out of our unconscious to torture us without end, making our lives excruciatingly wretched.[29] Schopenhauer anticipated Freud by pointing out that chief among these manifestations of will is the sex drive, the drive to exist and reproduce, which sometimes masquerades benignly as love.[30] Indeed, as Schopenhauer noted, so powerful is this compulsion that it drives some people who cannot have their chosen sweetheart to suicide and even more to the "madhouse."[31] From this perspective, there is no real difference between Francis and Alan both seeing Jane as an object of love, and Caligari and Cesare both seeing her as an object of lust. Since all four could be interpreted as facets of just one personality, poor Jane is afforded no choice at all in her future mate.

Unfortunately, to satisfy one desire usually gives birth to more. According to Schopenhauer, full satiation leaves us not with feelings of contentment but feelings of boredom, the worst misery of all. Boredom is the awful realization of the utter worthlessness of life and the absolute futility of being human in a universe devoid of god or goal. That must be escaped at all costs.[32]

Increasing the torment of existence is the pain we inflict on others as we pursue what we conceive to be our self-interest, for limitless egoism is the chief motive of our behavior. Much of this damage is accidental or incidental, a product of treating people

216   V. What the Old Folks Know

Caligari (Werner Krauss, left), Cesare (Conrad Veidt), and Jane (Lili Dagover) play out classic German Expressionist horror in *The Cabinet of Dr. Caligari* (1920).

as disposable means to our own ends. We are indifferent to the feelings of our fellows as we work to indulge our own desires.[33] However, some individuals go beyond egoism into malice, deriving pleasure from the torment suffered by those around them. Schopenhauer listed a number of possible sources for such cruelty, including envy, misanthropy, hatred, desire for revenge, and "prying curiosity."[34] Here one again encounters Caligari, who wants to see if a somnambulist can be forced to commit deeds he or she would not normally contemplate. Caligari does not even try to justify his perverse experiment in the style of Victor Frankenstein as somehow benefiting mankind. "For the world is Hell," Schopenhauer remarked, "and men are on the one hand the tormented souls and on the other the devils in it."[35]

Schopenhauer's pessimism was not appropriate for his own era, but it fit the mood after World War I. Escape from the Hell of this world he found spelled out in Hinduism and Buddhism: compassion for all, denial of will, and extirpation of ego.[36] *The Cabinet of Dr. Caligari* offers us no such hope. The jagged, tormented environment through which Caligari and Cesare move proclaims that. The Great War had destroyed the comfortable positivism of the previous century and exposed the chaotic darkness underlying everything.

Janowitz and Mayer initially wanted their sets to be designed by the book illustrator and graphic artist Alfred Kubin, but he was unable to take on this project, which was unfortunate.[37] Like Janowitz, Kubin was from Bohemia and had read Schopenhauer.[38] Kubin's art was closer to symbolism than expressionism and anticipated surrealism. He admired Brueghel, Goya, Klinger, Redon, and Munch.[39] His preferred medium was pen and ink, heavy in blacks, shadows, and crosshatching. His subjects often involved a mix of fantasies, monsters, supernatural events, scenes suggested by dreams, images of death triumphant over life, and, sometimes, strange eroticism. In Kubin's pictures cityscapes loom over scurrying people, scarecrows go on afternoon promenades, the boogeyman really does lurk under a bed, and witches indulge in nefarious conjurations.[40] Curiously, one of the plates included in his 1918 publication *The Dance of Death* (*Die Blätter mit dem Tod*) depicts Death, in a formal cutaway coat and Caligari-style top hat, striding off while carrying a limp, dark-haired woman, eyes closed and limbs dangling; she appears to be wearing a flowing nightgown.[41] This drawing seems a premonition of the abduction of Jane.

Schopenhauer was fascinated by the supernatural. He believed in the legitimacy of occult manifestations such as prophesy, telekinesis, mind reading, telepathy, encounters with ghosts, and magic in general. They all provided evidence of will in action[42]

Janowitz's outlook was shaped, in part, by Prague's traditions of magic and myth, which included alchemists, astrologers, and the legend of the Golem, Cesare's ancestor. Janowitz found in his own encounters with the paranormal inspiration for Caligari. Janowitz recalled partying just before the war in Hamburg's notorious entertainment district, the Reeperbahn, and at one point following the laugh of a pretty, vivacious young woman into a park. She disappeared into the trees, and shortly thereafter an unremarkable "bourgeois" gentleman walked away from the same location. The next day the newspapers reported the rape and murder of a girl in that area. Janowitz felt that, possibly through clairvoyance, he had witnessed the situation surrounding the crime, and when he attended the girl's funeral, he had the distinct impression the killer was also there.[43] In his script he arranged to have the endangered woman, Jane in this case, escape harm.

In 1918, Janowitz had another encounter with the supernatural when he was convinced to consult a psychic by Mayer's girlfriend of the moment, an actress named Gilda Langer. The seer said Janowitz would survive the war, but Langer would soon die. Both predictions were fulfilled; Langer died of influenza at the end of January 1920.[44] Langer had urged Janowitz and Mayer to collaborate on a film script, and the role of Jane was written for her. However, after she found a new lover, the part was given to Lil Dagover instead. Janowitz claimed the scene where Cesare passes the death sentence on Alan originated in this encounter with the seer, even though the script was finished months before Langer's death.[45]

A key paranormal experience for the creation of the film involved hypnotism. Janowitz and Mayer attended a sideshow entitled "Man or Machine?" in a Berlin amusement park. There a man, apparently in a hypnotic trance, performed impressive feats of strength and told fortunes. Janowitz later remarked: "On that night the original story of Dr. Caligari was conceived."[46]

Cesare is generally seen as the pawn of a sociopathic hypnotist, and in 1920 hypnotism still had the aura of magic: a spell cast by a wizard. The 18th-century pioneer of hypnotherapy, German physician Franz Anton Mesmer, considered his techniques scientific, not mystical, theorizing that an unseen fluid, animal magnetism, emanated from celestial bodies and penetrated all things, including human beings. When one's magnetic fluid balance became disturbed, serious illness would result, and the skill of a talented healer, such as Mesmer, was required to restore the lost equilibrium.[47] Mesmer cured the psychosomatic ailments of his patients, most of them women, by transferring some of his own animal magnetism to them through stroking their bodies with a magnet, an iron wand, or his hands.[48] Mesmer claimed to be a modern doctor, but his therapeutic sessions (which he called "séances") had all the trappings of a conjurer at work. In a darkened room, Mesmer often appeared dressed in a purple robe while otherworldly music was played on a glass harmonica. His clients might experience violent convulsions, become clairvoyant, have hallucinations, speak in tongues, or seem unable to resist the doctor's suggestions. They emerged from their treatments feeling healthy and refreshed.[49] All that was missing were drawing magic circles and invoking chthonic entities. Eventually, Mesmer endorsed such extraordinary phenomena as fortunetelling, extrasensory perception, and telepathy, all examples, he said, of listening to one's inner sense and getting in tune with the cosmos. Later versions of mesmerism fully embraced mysticism, magic, and the supernatural.[50] Caligari pays homage to Mesmer when he awakens Cesare with a baton during the performance at the fair.

Even so, Caligari is never depicted mesmerizing anyone; even Cesare comes to him already "asleep." Rather, Caligari is more a practitioner of the ancient art of necromancy, the reanimating of the dead either through calling the corpse back to life, as in Cesare's situation, or by inviting a spirit to inhabit it. Those who have died see the future because they are beyond earthly time and space. Unscrupulous magicians also can send them out to attack the living.

Cesare is not hypnotized; he is resuscitated. Clues to Cesare's condition are provided by scenes of him in a coffin before being roused from what Caligari calls his "death-like" slumber.[51] In the original script as Cesare awakens, he gasps for breath as if coming back to life.[52] His movements are unnatural. His peculiar dress—black turtle-neck shirt and black tights—sets him apart from those who are genuinely alive. His face is a stylized death's-head. Caligari describes him as being 23 years old and in his somnambulant state for 23 years. It is improbable this young man has been comatose since birth. More likely, he died at 23, somehow managed to avoid putrefaction, and now has been reanimated by Caligari.

In Greek mythology Sleep (Hypnos) and Death (Thanatos) are twins. Their mother is Night (Nyx), offspring of Chaos. So it is in this film, where death and sleep are frequently interconnected and interchangeable and where murders and attempted murders occur at night as the victims sleep. Caligari dozes while Cesare attacks Jane. He also sleeps while Francis and the hospital staff rummage through his papers, exposing his true identity and killing the showman's guise he assumed. As Caligari is unmasked and destroyed, a skeleton hanging on a stand watches, bemused.

When Cesare attempts to escape his pursuers, he collapses and returns to an inanimate state, something generally attributed to exhaustion. Still, this reversion to his former condition might be due to the severing of psychic ties to his master. He is the younger extension of Caligari, who seems to treat him as a son, lavishing on him paternal care and affection. The old man is no longer capable of carrying out his darkest passions, so Cesare acts in his place.[53] Thus advanced age wages a futile struggle against decay. In the end, like his master, Cesare is unable to perform. When the sleepwalker cannot carry out whatever unspeakable plans Caligari has devised for Jane, he kidnaps her instead, and the link to Caligari is broken, as is Cesare, his ordeal ended.

Caligari has many of the customary attributes of a wizard. His mien is that of a wizard: curmudgeonly, forbidding, and dark. He wears contemporary versions of a wizard's robe and tall headgear; he carries a staff. In the original Janowitz/Mayer script Caligari arrives in town in the company of gypsies, practitioners of witchcraft in folklore.[54] His office is piled high with archaic tomes and grimoires such as an alchemist might have, and, according to Janowitz, his relentless search for occult knowledge drives Caligari mad.[55] He is mysterious. Even though he directs the regional mental hospital and thus should have a certain local prominence, no one in town appears to recognize him.

The arrival of Cesare transforms Caligari from an unnamed physician/scholar into an active sorcerer. In the transformation scene, he staggers onto a path outside the asylum, book clutched to his chest, while the phrase "You Must Become Caligari" ("*Du Musst Caligari Werden*") visibly swirls around him in the air, appearing and disappearing repeatedly.[56] What is depicted here is less an obsession become hallucination than a demonic possession. The Director's previous name and identity no longer matter. He now takes both from an 18th-century homicidal mystic whose nefarious activities have literally enchanted him. By turning into Caligari the aged Director has become united with the chaos which surrounds him.

In Francis' account the Director's efforts to become Caligari ultimately fail. He does not discover the 18th-century Caligari's secrets; he does not succeed in vicariously renewing lost youth or commanding the representative of death. He no longer has the wizard's robe and staff. As his mind disintegrates, Caligari twice attacks not his nemesis, Francis, but a venerable colleague, the epitome of a sagacious elder. According to Greek legend, among the siblings of Sleep and Death is Old Age (Geras), called "accursed" in Hesiod's *Theogony*.[57]

In the end, Caligari is vanquished, definitively in the original script and more problematically in the film. Yet, certain nightmares tend to recur. In the film's opening scene Francis and his elderly companion sit outdoors, surrounded by the shadows of nature dying. The old man says: "There are spirits…. They are all around us…. They have driven me from hearth and home, from my wife and child."[58] Dr. Caligari represents such a spirit. He is the incarnation of malevolent old age, forbidden knowledge, and darkness in an unfathomable environment devoid of purpose or hope. The ultimate horror of Caligari is not the tragedy of an elderly man who trades his sanity for wisdom no one should have. It is not even the possibility he is an omen of future totalitarianism. Rather, the enduring horror of this elder is his bleak commentary on the human condition, where Chaos rules and nothing but pain and death await everyone. The ancient Greeks believed that among the many grandchildren of Chaos—sister to Sleep, Death, and Old Age—is Oizys, goddess of misery and anguish.

NOTES

1. The slogan "The war to end war" derived from H.G. Wells' diatribe against Germany, *The War That Will End War*, published in 1914.
2. The estimate is the influenza pandemic took between 50 and 100 million lives worldwide. Barry, *Great Influenza*, 397.
3. *Ibid.*, 2, 244–45, 379–80.
4. Thompson, "Dr. Caligari at the Folies-Bergère," 138.
5. Up to this point, Krauss' acting career had involved stage productions and lesser roles in motion pictures. Hans Janowitz, one of the two screenwriters for *The Cabinet of Dr. Caligari*, said he created Caligari with Krauss in mind. Janowitz, "Caligari—The Story of a Famous Story," 226.
6. *The Cabinet of Dr. Caligari*, directed by Robert Wiene (1920; New York: Kino Classics, 2014), DVD. All references to the film are from this version.
7. *Ibid.*, act 2.
8. For an analysis of the relationship between Jane and Cesare see Thuleen, "Expression and Character in the Movements of Cesare."
9. *Cabinet of Dr. Caligari*, act 6.

10. Janowitz came from Bohemia and spent his childhood in Prague. Mayer was born in Graz, Styria, son of a Jewish businessman who committed suicide. Robinson, *Das Cabinet des Dr. Caligari*, 10–12.
11. Janowitz, "Story," 233, 235.
12. Pommer, "Carl Mayer's Debut," 128.
13. Robinson, *Das Cabinet*, 29.
14. Janowitz, "Story," 237–38.
15. Robinson, *Das Cabinet*, 22, 71, 87; Scheunemann, "The Double, the Décor, and the Framing Device," 145–46.
16. Janowitz, "Story," 224–26.
17. Robinson, *Das Cabinet*, 10–13.
18. Janowitz, "Story," 224–25.
19. Kracauer, *From Caligari to Hitler*, 66–67.
20. *Ibid.*, 72–74.
21. Scheunemann, "The Double, the Décor, and the Framing Device," 129–30.
22. Robinson, *Das Cabinet*, 23.
23. Cartwright, *Schopenhauer*, 311.
24. Janowitz, "Story," 234; Robinson, *Das Cabinet*, 23.
25. Cartwright, *Schopenhauer*, 138.
26. "Portrait Arthur Schopenhauer."
27. The full elaboration of Schopenhauer's theory may be found in his 1813 doctoral dissertation *On the Fourfold Root of the Principle of Sufficient Reason* (*Über die vierfache Wurzel des Satzes vom zureichenden Grunde*).
28. Schopenhauer, *World as Will and Representation*, 1:3.
29. For example, *ibid.*, 2: 349–60 and Schopenhauer, *Essays and Aphorisms*, 55–60.
30. Schopenhauer, *World as Will and Representation*, 1:328–30; 2:237, 485, 511, 533.
31. *Ibid.*, 2:532.
32. Schopenhauer, *Essays and Aphorisms*, 53–54.
33. Schopenhauer, *On the Basis of Morality*, 131–32.
34. *Ibid.*, 135–36.
35. Schopenhauer, *Essays and Aphorisms*, 48.
36. Schopenhauer, *On the Basis of Morality*, 162–67.
37. Janowitz, "Story," 222.
38. Kubin, "Alfred Kubin's Autobiography," xii–xiii, xxi.
39. *Ibid.*, xxii, xxiv, xxix.
40. Sebra, *Life and Art of Alfred Kubin*, 34, 40, 48, 54, 65.
41. *Ibid.*, 14.
42. For this aspect of Schopenhauer's thought see Erdmann and Cartwright, "The World as Weird." Schopenhauer believed that he himself had clairvoyant powers; see Cartwright, *Schopenhauer*, 436–41.
43. Janowitz, "Story," 226; Kracauer, *From Caligari to Hitler*, 61.
44. Janowitz, "Story," 226–27; Olaf Brill, "The Muse of Dr. Caligari."
45. Robinson, *Das Cabinet*, 13.
46. Janowitz, "Story," 233.
47. Buranelli, *Wizard from Vienna*, 35–36, 61–63.
48. *Ibid.*, 107–20.
49. *Ibid.*, 125–32; Darnton, *Mesmerism and the End of the Enlightenment in France*, 3–10.
50. Buranelli, *Wizard from Vienna*, 189–98; Darnton, *Mesmerism*, 127–35.
51. *Cabinet of Dr. Caligari*, act 2.
52. Robinson, *Das Cabinet*, 75.
53. Scheunemann, "The Double, the Décor, and the Framing Device," 130.
54. *Ibid.*, 71.
55. Janowitz, "Story," 236. David Hansen-Miller argues Caligari, on the contrary, champions the authority of science over mysticism (Hansen-Miller, *Civilized Violence*, 60–61).
56. *Cabinet of Dr. Caligari*, act 6.
57. Hesiod, *Theogony and Works and Days*, 9.
58. *Ibid.*, act 1. In the original script, Jane and Francis encounter the ghost of Alan at his funeral. Robinson, *Das Cabinet*, 80.

Bibliography

Barry, John M. *The Great Influenza: The Story of the Deadliest Pandemic in History*. New York: Penguin, 2009.
Brill, Olaf. "The Muse of Dr. Caligari." February 26, 2010. www.gildalanger.de/2010-02-26_muse_des_dr_caligari.htm.
Buranelli, Vincent. *The Wizard from Vienna*. New York: Coward, McCann and Geoghegan, 1973.
The Cabinet of Dr. Caligari. Directed by Robert Wiene. 1920. New York: Kino Classics, 2014. DVD.

Cartwright, David E. *Schopenhauer: A Biography*. New York: Cambridge University Press, 2010.
Darnton, Robert. *Mesmerism and the End of the Enlightenment in France*. Cambridge: Harvard University Press, 1968.
Erdmann, Edward, and David Cartwright. "The World as Weird: Schopenhauer's Use of Odd Phenomena to Corroborate His Metaphysics." colfa.utsa.edu/philosophy-classics/docs/Schopenhauer_Workshop_Erdmann_Paper.pdf.
Hansen-Miller, David. *Civilized Violence: Subjectivity, Gender and Popular Cinema*. 2011. London: Routledge, 2016.
Hesiod. *Theogony and Works and Days*. Translated by M. L.West. New York: Oxford World's Classics, 2008.
Janowitz, Hans. "*Caligari*—The Story of a Famous Story." In *The Cabinet of Dr. Caligari: Texts, Contexts, Histories*, edited by Mike Budd, 221–39. New Brunswick: Rutgers University Press, 1990.
Kracauer, Siegfried. *From Caligari to Hitler: A Psychological History of the German Film*. Princeton: Princeton University Press, 1947.
Kubin, Alfred. "Alfred Kubin's Autobiography." In Alfred Kubin, *The Other Side: A Fantastic Novel*, translated by Denver Lindley, ii–lxxviii. New York: Crown, 1967.
Pommer, Erich. "Carl Mayer's Debut." In *Classic Film Scripts: The Cabinet of Dr. Caligari*, edited by R.V. Adkinson, 27–29. New York: Simon & Schuster, 1972.
"Portrait Arthur Schopenhauer." http://www.alamy.com/stock-photo/portrait-authur-schopenhauer.html.
Robinson, David. *Das Cabinet des Dr. Caligari*, 2nd ed. London: Palgrave Macmillan, 2013.
Scheunemann, Dietrich. "The Double, the Décor, and the Framing Device: Once More on Robert Wiene's *The Cabinet of Dr. Caligari*." In *Expressionist Film—New Perspectives*, edited by Dietrich Scheunemann, 125–56. Rochester: Camden House, 2003.
Schopenhauer, Arthur. *Essays and Aphorisms*, edited by R. J. Hollingdale. Harmondsworth: Penguin Classics, 1970.
_____. *On the Basis of Morality*. Translated by E. F. J. Payne. Indianapolis: Hackett, 1995.
_____. *On the Fourfold Root of the Principle of Sufficient Reason and Other Writings*, edited by David Cartwright, Edward Erdmann, and Christopher Janaway. Cambridge: Cambridge University Press, 2012.
_____. *The World as Will and Representation*, 2 volumes. Translated by E. F. J. Payne. 1958. New York: Dover, 1969.
Sebra, Gregor, ed. *The Life and Art of Alfred Kubin*. New York: Dover, 2017.
Thompson, Kristin. "Dr. Caligari at the Folies-Bergère, or the Successes of an Early Avant- Garde Film." In *The Cabinet of Dr. Caligari: Texts, Contexts, Histories*, edited by Mike Budd, 121–69. New Brunswick: Rutgers University Press, 1990.
Thuleen, Nancy. "Expression and Character in the Movements of Cesare." September 21, 1994. http://www.nthuleen.com/papers/655short1.html.

"Some kind of special"
Queering Death Through Elder/Child Relationships in The Haunting in Connecticut 2: Ghosts of Georgia

OLIVIA OLIVER-HOPKINS

Queer theory has long suggested the importance of disturbing boundaries: exploring radical political potential with a view to opening up new ways of understanding and critiquing culture and sociality.[1] As critics such as Sharon Patricia Holland have shown,[2] the values of mainstream society are able to be "queered" through their encounters with minority cultures, including those in literature and cinema. This potential for queering is particularly strong in the cinematic supernatural horror genre, where plots often revolve around the veracity of folkloric and religious beliefs not widely accepted in the dominant culture.

This essay explores Tom Elkins' 2013 supernatural horror film *The Haunting in Connecticut 2: Ghosts of Georgia* through a queer lens, focusing upon the relationship between a young white child, Heidi Wyrick, and an elderly African American woman, Mama Kay. This relationship enacts a sort of queer reverse colonization, whereby Mama Kay passes on to Heidi African American folk beliefs about the existence of the supernatural and its interactions with the human world, in order to explain and support Heidi's abilities as a psychic medium. Most radically, these beliefs run directly contrary to Heidi's parents' view of her gift as an illness that can be treated with Western science and medicine, literally enacting fears of the "vampiric" queer parent who cannot reproduce for themselves (in this case, in the figure of Mama Kay, due to her age) and so instead "preys" upon the children of non-queers by sharing and encouraging ideologically-loaded behaviors. Thus, this supernatural horror film can be seen as in itself "queering" accepted systems of parenting, as well as majority conceptions of what does and does not exist in the world, in a way that assists racial minority cultures to counter the dominance of Western belief systems in the modern world.

Theocentric Worldviews and Marginalization

In *The Rise of Western Rationalism*, Wolfgang Schluchter examines the evolution of Western Christianity, particularly ascetic Protestantism, alongside new methods of scientific enquiry during the Enlightenment,[3] and argues that this resulted in the gradual transformation of "the theocentric world view ... into an anthropocentric world view."[4] Westerners thus tend to view spirituality and the supernatural as merely one dimension of a multifaceted yet strictly compartmentalized life over which humanity ultimately has primary control.[5] The presentation of alternative belief systems in which paranormal beings from religious folklore actively interfere in the material world on a regular basis in a manner that humans are powerless to stop is thus the principal way in which the supernatural horror genre challenges dominant ideologies.

The supernatural horror genre presents the possibility of individuals' continued existence after death in myriad ways, but its depiction of ghosts, spirits and apparitions is of particular significance here. These entities often return from the dead to attempt to redress a wrong from their human lives, or warn another who is in danger of experiencing the same misfortune that the spirit suffered in her human life, "reversing [...] a trenchant Western paradigm: that those who die do not come back, that the line between 'us' and 'them' is finite and, therefore, never porous."[6]

The presence of these entities suggests a longing for a means to construct a history of those who, in their human lives, were silenced,[7] and so these entities often represent individuals from disadvantaged groups, particularly African Americans oppressed by the dominant white culture: murdered and runaway slaves or Jim Crow-era servants.[8] Holland suggests that the race of these entities adds to their subversive potential,[9] and also, by drawing upon Orlando Patterson's work on slavery as social death, that "black subjects are not just marginal to the culture. Their presence in society is, like the subject of death, almost unspeakable, so black subjects share the space the dead inhabit,"[10] a point also made about queer people by Butler.[11] Indeed, Prince argues that the horror genre is fundamentally concerned with "what must be done to remain [or perhaps, in the sense I am using it here, become] human."[12] These entities could be seen to "hijack" the dominance of horror by white characters in a manner akin to Toni Morrison's figuration of black presences in white texts, providing "a subtext that either sabotages the surface text's expressed intentions or escapes them through a language that mystifies what it cannot bring itself to articulate."[13] Older people are similarly frequently marginalized in Western culture. Assumptions about their mental capacities or ability to contribute to society lead to a devaluation of our culture's elders, viewed, in effect, as "already (socially) dead." Therefore, while studies have shown that they are more valued than white elders within their own community, African American elders could be considered particularly marginalized within wider society.[14]

Queer Theocentric Parenting

Holland suggests, however, that there is power in this marginal position, akin to the power Butler sees in reclaiming the term "queer" and its challenge to normativity:

> Perhaps the most revolutionary intervention into conversations at the margins of race, gender, and sexuality is to let the dead—those already denied a sustainable subjectivity—speak from the place that is familiar to them. Moreover, speaking from the site of familiarity, from the place reserved for the dead, disturbs the static categories of black/white, oppressor/oppressed, creating a plethora of tensions *within* and *without* existing cultures.[15]

Holland argues that viewing death as the cessation of all earthly existence is very much a Western paradigm, and illustrates that point through her presentation of alternatives from various African cultures. Western rationalism argues that there are only two possible metaphysical states to be in: one is either living or one is dead; one cannot be partially dead or dead in some respects. Of course, within the horror genre, partial deadness is relatively common, manifest in entities such as ghosts, zombies, vampires, etc., who are usually termed the "undead."

But many non–Western cultures view life and death as part of a great cycle of existence on two separate planes, and suggest that communication between individuals on either side of the barrier is possible: "Although 'this world' and the 'other world' are viewed as two separate entities, the beginning of life, whose source is believed to be in the 'other world,' happens in 'this world,' and the cessation of life in 'this world' is believed to mean continuity of life in the 'other world.' Notionally there is an area of overlap between the two worlds."[16] The presence of undead entities in horror films and their ability to communicate with the living not only challenges the Western rationalist conception of death, but implicitly validates other non–Western cultures' views of death at the same time.

Theologist John S. Mbiti has suggested that many African cultures, rather than dividing the world along binary lines into "the living" and "the dead," divide humans into three categories to demonstrate the overlap between the two halves of the divide imagined by Western rationalism[17]: the living, the living-dead, and the long-dead. When someone dies, but there are still those among the living who remember that person, the person becomes one of the "living-dead"; only after the last individual who remembered the dead person has also died do they enter the realms of the revered long-dead ancestors.[18] This division is important because it acknowledges the way in which individuals can live on in the memories of those whom they have encountered in life, and by extension the role that such memories play in recording and shaping individual and cultural history, especially among oral cultures or minority cultures who may not have input into or access to the "official" recorded histories.[19]

Moreover, this division gives a particular power to older people, who literally have the power of life (or living-deadness) or death (or long-deadness) over those people who live on through their memories. In a similar manner, Ngubane suggests that those who are closer to the divide between the two worlds are considered to have a certain degree of power and hence status within the community—implicitly elevating the status of older people. In (white) Western society, older people are frequently marginalized and considered no longer relevant; however, in African American society, older people are revered. Older African American women, in particular, "hold positions of honor due to their role in raising children and weathering adversity."[20] Thus, the alternate conceptions of death implicitly promoted by the horror genre forge a history for minority groups outside of and beyond the history endorsed by the dominant culture, "queering" history, and granting a greater social power to groups marginalized due to age or race.

This troubling of temporal, linear relationships is a prominent feature of queer time. As queer people are unable to reproduce sexually and thus are often seen as lacking a history of their own, to forge a queer history, queer studies scholars have created a new way of looking at the relationship between the past and the present by taking the "castoffs" of traditional Western ways of thinking. As Elizabeth Freeman suggests, these scholars are "mining the present for signs of undetonated energy from past revolutions" and retrospectively recognizing as queer that which may not have been deemed so at the time, "gather[ing] and combin[ing] eclectically" from the potentially queer "cultural debris" on the abject edges of heteronormative society.[21]

In his book *No Future: Queer Theory and the Death Drive*, Lee Edelman queers time by arguing that queers represent the death drive of humanity, and hence anti-futurism, due to their inability to reproduce, and that the Child is paradoxically both the enemy and the ally of the Queer, representing as she does both the future and this death drive. While Edelman's theory has been criticized by various queer theorists for its inherently nihilistic, and hence analytically unproductive, stance, other theorists such as Jack Halberstam have suggested that perhaps it is possible to rehabilitate Edelman's ideas in order to contribute to "an anti-imperialist, queer counterhegemonic imaginary."[22] As the Child represents the future of mainstream society due to the assumption that the Child is in some way a continuation of the values of her parents (also assumed to embody the dominant social values) in Edelman's argument, I suggest that Edelman's argument may be utilized as part of a progressive political project of the kind that Halberstam imagines through "queer parenting" by individuals who are not blood relatives of the Child. Embodying Edelman's queer "raptors who famously feed on the young they're unable themselves to produce," individuals viewed as "undesirable" by the biological parents may colonize the future by encouraging the Child to accept their alternative value systems and thus challenge or even openly reject the patriarchy that she was created to reproduce. Most radically, if this parent is from a minority culture, the minority values that she imparts to the Child may thus ensure a future for such a culture at the expense of the majority culture that directly or indirectly contributed to the erosion of that minority culture in the first place.

The Haunting in Connecticut 2: Ghosts of Georgia

The Haunting in Connecticut 2: Ghosts of Georgia, allegedly based on a true story, reflects this queering of history, time, and parenting. The film follows the Wyrick family, consisting of father Andy, mother Lisa, daughter Heidi, and Lisa's sister Joyce, who buy and move into an historic property in rural Georgia that they discover was once a "station" on the Underground Railroad. Heidi and Lisa are able to see and communicate with the dead, and Heidi quickly makes friends with Mr. Gordy, whom the family assumes is a malevolent spirit, but who, it transpires, is attempting to help the Wyricks by warning them about the truly malevolent spirit on their property: Mr. Gordy's stationmaster ancestor. The stationmaster, a taxidermist by trade, helped some slaves to escape, but kept others locked in a hidden underground room where they would starve to death, after which he would stuff the bodies to add to his collection.

Andy and Lisa view their family's psychic abilities as inherently negative, although the visions are usually beneficial—in addition to protecting the Wyricks from his malevolent ancestor, Mr. Gordy shows Heidi where she can find part of his considerable fortune buried in the yard. Lisa is on medication to attempt to suppress her visions, which disturb her greatly and which she assumes to be the result of a psychiatric disorder. She describes herself as "sick," and encourages Heidi to "fight this," while a doctor at the local hospital—where the family takes Heidi after the stationmaster almost drowns her in the bathtub—suggests that they "consult with a psychiatrist" or, she adds as an afterthought, "a priest." The only white adult character who believes in Heidi's abilities is Joyce, who encourages Heidi to tell her about her visions, but Joyce is presented as eccentric and described by her brother-in-law as "crazy."[23]

Importantly, however, the beneficial visions are linked to a non-Western spirituality through the very different attitudes that the African American characters in the film have toward Heidi's visions. The most prominent of these characters is Mama Kay, an elderly African American woman who visits the shrine on the Wyricks' property commemorating the Underground Railroad station, which her ancestors utilized to escape slavery. At the beginning of the scene in which Heidi and Andy (and the audience) first meet Mama Kay, Heidi is talking to Mr. Gordy while Andy chops firewood. Heidi tells Andy that Mr. Gordy says that people are coming, and when he hears Prentice and Mama Kay immediately afterwards, Andy replies that the family should "take [Heidi] and Mr. Gordy on the road," implying that he thinks Heidi's alleged abilities as a medium are the product of mere trickery.

Heidi, aware of her difference, asks Andy when they finally see Mama Kay if he "see[s] her too." The jump-scare produced by the first image of Mama Kay, more pronounced due to her old-fashioned black mourning-style clothing, complete with a hat with a veil, and visible cataract-induced blindness, foreshadows the unpleasant disruption to the older Wyricks' world that Mama Kay comes to represent as the disseminator of African American spiritual beliefs. Mama Kay's antiquated clothing style also serves to underscore her age and the challenge that it, along with her race, represents to white conceptions of value and power, made explicit by the following exchange:

> MAMA KAY: You don't need eyes to see, little one. But you already know that.
> HEIDI: What do you mean?
> MAMA KAY: You asked your father if he saw me. That makes you some kind of special.
> HEIDI: My mama says I'm not supposed to talk about that.
> MAMA KAY: But you have to be careful with a gift like that because sometimes the devil looks a gentleman.

In this scene, Mama Kay is presented not only as appreciative of Heidi's abilities as a medium, but as predicting the discovery of the stationmaster's crimes—"sometimes the devil looks a gentleman"—when even Joyce refuses to believe in the danger the family faces on the property. Moreover, the archaic phrase further underscores the power that Mama Kay's age gives her in relation to communicating with the dead.

As an older person, Mama Kay is presented as one of the few, if not the only one, keeping several of her ancestors among the "living-dead" through her memories, which prove particularly important in reconstructing what happened to the slaves whose bodies are found in the hidden room. As revealed through a nightmare-like flashback, Mama Kay's great-aunt Nell and her fiancé were supposed to be meeting family in the North but never arrived, and their bodies are among those found, revealing the way that the stationmaster exploited the necessary opacity of the Underground Railroad system. This illustrates the usefulness of conceptions of the living-dead in queering history—the hints given to Heidi by the ghosts themselves combine with Mama Kay's memories of them (and hence their "life after death") to challenge the dominant culture's conception of Underground Railroad workers as selfless and morally pure while revealing a lost part

Heidi (Emily Alyn Lind, left) meets Mama Kay (Cicely Tyson) and the two quickly become friends in *The Haunting in Connecticut II* (2013).

of the history of African Americans in the South. The construction of a history grants power and validity to a group that is marginalized even today as a result of the continuing legacy of the slave system.[24]

Mama Kay is also the film's quintessential example of queer parenting, not just because of her race and disability, but because of her age. The idea of a woman past her nominal childbearing years taking on the role of a parent causes considerable anxiety in Western society, with women who do so frequently labeled "selfish," "wrong" and "irresponsible," primarily due to their perceived lack of ability to parent the child over the long term due to their age.[25] This fear is thus directly connected to the Child's mythical future, and therefore such a parent has a particular queer resonance by ensuring the future of her values by effectively reversing her biological clock; queering temporality by parenting a child after society has dictated that it is "too late" for her to do so.

While the trope of an elderly person functioning as a surrogate (grand)parent to an unrelated child is relatively common in Western film and literature, this particular relationship is framed in unusual terms. In the majority of instances of this trope, the child in question is presented as having biological parents who are implied to be unwilling or unable to perform this duty, and the surrogate is the same race as the child; or if not, the older person is white while the youngster is a person of color, resulting in a more overt "colonization" story involving the perpetuation of white values.[26] However, Heidi's parents are not only presented as competent and caring—thus, Mama Kay is framed more as a combatant in an ideological "battle" for Heidi than as a much-needed foster parent—but, most strikingly, Mama Kay is African American, and thus is disseminating minority rather than dominant values to the future through Heidi.

228   V. What the Old Folks Know

Heidi's Queer Colonization

While we only see the one brief meeting between Heidi and Mama Kay, the encounter is presented as having a profound effect on Heidi, and in particular, of causing a rift between her and her (biological) parents. After the meeting in the woods, Heidi explores the property in the middle of the night, led by the ghostly presence of Nell in what appears to be a nightmare, and falls into the hidden room in which the stationmaster hid escaped slaves, where she encounters their mummified corpses. Heidi's disappearance terrifies her parents, who call the police and are horrified to discover the history of their new property.

The family (from left, Chad Michael Murray, Abigail Spencer, Emily Alyn Lind) huddles close after Heidi is rescued from the underground room by policemen in *The Haunting in Connecticut II*.

This midnight sojourn is connected explicitly to Mama Kay, both because it is her great-aunt's ghost who leads Heidi into the woods, and because Lisa has a nightmare featuring Mama Kay (despite never having met her) just before Andy discovers that Heidi is missing. Moreover, Nell arguably only "exists," such as she does, in the world of the living due to Mama Kay's memories of her and hence her status as living-dead rather than long dead. Thus, Mama Kay takes on certain qualities of the horror "monster," threatening normality as Andy and Lisa experience it.[27] Moreover, like one of Edelman's raptors, Mama Kay is clearly co-opting a willing Heidi into a political quest: acknowledging her abilities and using them to perpetuate African spirituality while uncovering hidden elements of African American history, rather than suppressing them and perpetuating her parents' Western rationalist worldview.

After the discovery of the bodies in the cellar, a local television channel covers the story and Heidi sees the report. When she exclaims that she no longer wants to live in the house, Joyce, much to Lisa's annoyance, explains to Heidi that the spirits who were contacting her have now moved on. Lisa attempts to lead Heidi back to bed to end the conversation, but Heidi pulls away from her:

> LISA: Heidi Wyrick, you follow me right now.
> HEIDI: I can't be here anymore, Mama. I went in the hole and the bad man saw me! He knows we're here now. He's coming!
> JOYCE: What bad man, sweetie?
> HEIDI: The stationmaster. I let him out, Mama.
> LISA: Well, Mr. Gordy is wrong. Because you know very well that the stationmaster was a good man—
> HEIDI: No, he wasn't!

Clearly, not only has Heidi understood and accepted what Mama Kay has said about the stationmaster's spirit (despite Lisa's determination to attribute such ideas to the white Mr. Gordy), but the film directly connects her lack of respect for her mother to Mama Kay's warning. Moreover, Heidi is aware of the stationmaster's presence and "seeing" of her due to her psychic abilities, as made clear in the scene in the cellar where his shadowy spirit is seen and heard making malevolent sounds. This altercation with her mother is the first time in the film that we see Heidi being so overtly disobedient to her parents, and is also presented as a direct result of her parents' refusal to accept her alternative worldview, which Heidi has now realized is more akin to the African conceptions of spirituality represented by Mama Kay than her parents' scientific rationalism, with its associated pathologization of Heidi's experiences. The future of her parents' society, with its associated ideologies, is no longer guaranteed by Heidi's existence, as she becomes a queerly colonized emblem of the future for a marginalized African spirituality, thanks to her relationship with Mama Kay, and thus an embodiment of white society's anxieties more frightening to the dominant culture than any horror movie monster.

Social conventions about what is and isn't "age-appropriate" also appear in Lisa's discussions with Heidi about the stationmaster and the Underground Railroad:

> HEIDI: Why can't I know [what happened here]?
> LISA: It's just not a story for little girls, sweetie.
> HEIDI: I'm a big girl. You always say that.
> LISA: [...] Well, back when [the stationmaster] owned all this land, he was what's called a taxidermist. He also [...] would help hide people who were in trouble. People like Mama Kay's great-aunt Nell and her fiancé[.... S]ome of the other ... landowners, they found out what the stationmaster had been doing and, well, they didn't like it very much, so they did some very unkind things to him.
> HEIDI: I told you something bad happened here.
> LISA: No, it was a long time ago. All of that evil is over and done with now.
> HEIDI: It's still here, Mama. I can feel it. It's in the woods. It's coming for me!
> LISA: No, it's not. Heidi, it's all in your head. It's not real.
> HEIDI: [...] If you loved me, you'd believe me.
> LISA: It's *because* I love you that I can't, baby.

Lisa's explanation deliberately avoids all issues of race, given the pause she takes before describing the white lynch mob as "landowners" and her description of runaway slaves as "people like Mama Kay's great-aunt" rather than as African American, despite racism seemingly being one of the least disturbing things in the story that she tells Heidi, given its connotations of murder and explanation of taxidermy.

The true horror in the film is thus yet again presented as racial conflict, brought to

Lisa (Abigail Spencer, left) chastises Heidi (Emily Alyn Lind) when she attempts to explain why the stationmaster was lynched in *The Haunting in Connecticut II*.

the fore in the present by elderly people like Mama Kay, the keepers of collective historical memories, rather than the more mundane horror film elements of death and gore. The careful phrasing of Lisa's explanation suggests a desire to protect the future, represented by Heidi, from a true understanding of the racial atrocities of the past while she is at her most impressionable, thus perpetuating disadvantage into the future by foreclosing the possibility of a true reconciliation. While the "evil in the woods" that is "still here" to which Heidi refers clearly denotes the evil spirit of the stationmaster, it would also seem to connote white racism and ageism and her parents' inflexible beliefs. While white Americans may wish to believe discrimination, including ageism, racism and cultural imperialism are things of the past, "over and done with now," they still persist and cause harm. As Heidi suggests in her final comment above, if we love our fellow citizens, we would do well to believe them when they claim that something is there, even if we ourselves haven't experienced it.

Thus, through its depiction of the queer parenting of elder/child relationships in the dissemination of alternative worldviews linked to non–Western spirituality, *The Haunting in Connecticut 2: Ghosts of Georgia* allows us to observe the way that an erasure of spirituality and history can only lead to an erasure of culture, and thus embodies a form of cultural imperialism. As the film explores issues of race, culture and age, its portrayal of the utility of memory in forging alternative histories suggests the need for the dominant culture to look beyond the Western rationalist paradigm with its associated ageism in order to more fully embrace the perspectives of other cultures and the wisdom of elders, and thus the "true" reality of our world.

NOTES

1. See, for example, Benshoff, *Monsters in the Closet*, 5; Butler, *Bodies That Matter*; and Haritaworn, Kuntsman, and Posocco, "Introduction," 3–5.

2. Holland, *Raising the Dead*, 819–828; Scott, *Extravagant Abjection*.
3. Schluchter, *Die Entwicklung des okzidentalen Rationalismus*, 141.
4. *Ibid.*, 144, 145.
5. Kraft, *Understanding Spiritual Power*, 5.
6. Holland, *Raising the Dead*, 1.
7. On the ability of fear, pain and violence to silence or subsume those individuals who are subjected to them, see Humphrey, *Politics of Atrocity and Reconciliation*, 11–23.
8. See, e.g., *Candyman*, *Dead Birds*, and *The Skeleton Key*.
9. Holland, *Raising the Dead*, 2.
10. *Ibid.*, 6. See also Holland on the association of blackness with death or "disidentification with life" (*Raising the Dead*, 179). Anne Anlin Cheng not only connects blackness with death (*The Melancholy of Race*, 20), but also uses the metaphor of being haunted to describe the relationship of non-white racial minorities to the dominant culture (see, for example, 10–14, 24–28).
11. Butler, *Bodies That Matter*, 233.
12. Prince, "Introduction," 3. See also Freeland, "Horror and Art-Dread," 194, on horror's relationship to questions of communication between the dead and the living. The idea of humanity expanding beyond or transcending the individual or the bodily is also explored in critical race theory by scholars such as Scott (15).
13. Morrison, *Playing in the Dark*, 66.
14. Fabius, "Towards an Integration of Narrative Identity," 426.
15. Holland, *Raising the Dead*, 4 (emphasis in original). Cheng explores the manner in which death as choice historically was one of the few ways for slaves to defy their masters and thus, in a sense, liberatory, troubling our understanding of agency in a manner akin to the African beliefs explored below (*Melancholy of Race*, 20–21).
16. Ngubane, *Body and Mind in Zulu Medicine*, 77.
17. Leo Bersani and Adam Phillips allude to this divide (and its arbitrary nature) when they suggest that "we assume that a longing for death is a hatred of life" (*Intimacies*, 117), suggesting the manner in which the dead can long for their lives, or at least contact with the living, in a manner that does not necessarily reject their outsider status (and hence source of their abject power), as can be seen in the discussion below. See also Holland, *Raising the Dead*, 179–180.
18. Mbiti, *African Religions and Philosophy*, 25.
19. On African American oral culture, see Fabius, "Towards an Integration of Narrative Identity," 424, 428–429. On the radical potential of the (African American) dead speaking and its ability to disrupt time and create community, including through memory and storytelling, see also Newhouse, "'More Dead Than Living,'" especially 239–246; and Norman, "When Dead Men Talk," especially 136, 146–147.
20. Fabius, "Towards an Integration of Narrative Identity," 426; see also Waites, "Building on Strengths," 278.
21. Freeman, *Time Binds*, xvi, xiii.
22. Caserio et al., "The Antisocial Thesis in Queer Theory," 824.
23. *Haunting in Connecticut 2: Ghosts of Georgia*. This and all subsequent quotations are from the 2013 Gold Circle Films DVD.
24. On the value, as well as pain, of ancestral experiences and memories to the construction of African American experience, see Scott, *Extravagant Abjection*, 6–14. Holland also discusses the importance of the construction of a history through a sense of heritage and ancestry, and its denial as part of Patterson's conception of "social death" upon which she draws (*Raising the Dead*, 13).
25. Sullivan, "Gold Coast Grandmother"; Allaoui, "63-Year-Old Woman Gives Birth."
26. See, for example, fairytales involving "fairy godmothers" (usually depicted as elderly white women) to abused or abandoned children such as "Cinderella" and "Sleeping Beauty," novels such as *Good Night, Mr. Tom* and films like *Kotch*, *Mr. Holmes* and *Is Anybody There?* where a white surrogate (grand)father cares for a neglected white child, and films like *Up!* and *Gran Torino* where a poverty-stricken or emotionally needy young person of color's life is "enriched" by their encounter with a white surrogate (grand)father.
27. In one of the foundational essays of horror film studies, Robin Wood famously argued that the "basic formula of the horror film" is that "normality is threatened by the monster" (*American Nightmare*, 14).

Bibliography

Allaoui, Therese. "63-Year-Old Woman Gives Birth to IVF Baby in Melbourne." *Herald Sun*, August 2016. http://www.heraldsun.com.au/news/63yearold-woman-gives-birth-to-ivf-baby-in-melbourne/news-story/f8c206793b484170f211792989843f6d.
Benshoff, Harry M. *Monsters in the Closet: Homosexuality and the Horror Film*. Manchester: Manchester University Press, 1997.
Bersani, Leo, and Adam Phillips. *Intimacies*. Chicago: University of Chicago Press, 2008.
Butler, Judith. *Bodies That Matter: On the Discursive Limits of "Sex."* New York: Routledge, 1993.
Caserio, Robert L., et al. "The Antisocial Thesis in Queer Theory." *PMLA* 121, no. 3 (2006): 819–828.

Cheng, Anne Anlin. *The Melancholy of Race: Psychoanalysis, Assimilation, and Hidden Grief.* Oxford: Oxford University Press, 2001.
Clover, Carol J. "The Eye of Horror." In *Viewing Positions: Ways of Seeing Film*, edited by Linda Williams, 184–230. New Brunswick: Rutgers University Press, 1995.
Edelman, Lee. *No Future: Queer Theory and the Death Drive.* Durham: Duke University Press, 2004.
Fabius, Chanee D. "Towards an Integration of Narrative Identity, Generativity, and Storytelling in African American Elders." *Journal of Black Studies* 47, no. 5 (2016): 423–434.
Freeland, Cynthia. "Horror and Art-Dread." In *The Horror Film*, edited by Stephen Prince, 189–205. New Brunswick: Rutgers University Press, 2004.
Freeman, Elizabeth. *Time Binds: Queer Temporalities, Queer Histories.* Durham: Duke University Press, 2010.
Haritaworn, Jin, Adi Kuntsman, and Silvia Posocco. "Introduction." In *Queer Necropolitics*, edited by Jin Haritaworn, Adi Kuntsman, and Silvia Posocco, 1–27. Oxon, UK: Routledge, 2014.
The Haunting in Connecticut 2: Ghosts of Georgia. Directed by Tom Elkins. 2013. Santa Monica: Gold Circle Films, 2013. DVD.
Holland, Sharon Patricia. *Raising the Dead: Readings of Death and (Black) Subjectivity.* Durham: Duke University Press, 2000.
Humphrey, Michael. *The Politics of Atrocity and Reconciliation: From Terror to Trauma.* London: Routledge, 2002.
Kraft, Marguerite G. *Understanding Spiritual Power: A Forgotten Dimension of Cross-Cultural Mission and Ministry.* Maryknoll, NY: Orbis Books, 1995.
Magorian, Michelle. *Good Night, Mr. Tom.* New York: HarperCollins, 1986.
Mbiti, John S. *African Religions and Philosophy.* London: Heinemann, 1969.
Miles, Tiya. "Introduction: A Ghost Hunt." In *Tales from the Haunted South: Dark Tourism and Memories of Slavery from the Civil War Era*, 1–20. Chapel Hill: University of North Carolina Press, 2015.
Morrison, Toni. *Playing in the Dark: The William E. Massey Sr. Lectures in the History of American Civilization.* Cambridge: Harvard University Press, 1992.
Newhouse, Wade. "'More Dead Than Living': Randall Kenan's Monstrous Community." In *Undead Souths*, edited by Eric Gary Anderson, Taylor Hagood, and Daniel Cross Turner, 236–247. Baton Rouge: Louisiana State University Press, 2015.
Ngubane, Harriet. *Body and Mind in Zulu Medicine: An Ethnography of Health and Disease in Nyuswa-Zulu Thought and Practice.* London: Academic Press, 1977.
Norman, Brian. "When Dead Men Talk: Emmett Till, Southern Pasts, and Present Demands." In *Undead Souths*, edited by Eric Gary Anderson, Taylor Hagood, and Daniel Cross Turner, 136–147. Baton Rouge: Louisiana State University Press, 2015.
Prince, Stephen. "Introduction." In *The Horror Film*, edited by Stephen Prince, 1–11. New Brunswick: Rutgers University Press, 2004.
Schluchter, Wolfgang. *Die Entwicklung des okzidentalen Rationalismus.* Heidelberg" Verlag J. C. B. Mohr, 1979. Rpt. as *The Rise of Western Rationalism: Max Weber's Developmental History.* Translated and with an introduction by Guenther Roth. Berkeley: University of California Press, 1985.
Scott, Darieck. *Extravagant Abjection: Blackness, Power, and Sexuality in the African-American Literary Imagination.* New York: New York University Press, 2010.
Sullivan, Rebecca. "Gold Coast Grandmother, 51, Gives Birth to Fifth Child." September 2017. News.com.au. http://www.news.com.au/lifestyle/parenting/pregnancy/gold-coast-grandmother-51-gives-birth-to-fifth-child/news-story 4a2293aae09df48b0c3228aadd41c142.
Waites, Cheryl. "Building on Strengths: Intergenerational Practice with African American Families." In *Practice Perspectives with Racial and Ethnic Minorities*, edited by Jerome H. Schiele and June Gary Hopps, special issue, *Social Work* 54, no. 3 (2009): 278–287.
Wood, Robin. *American Nightmare: Essays on the Horror Film.* Toronto: Festival of Festivals, 1979.

Flowers in the Attic
The Elderly as Monster
Liam T. Webb

V.C. Andrews' 1979 gothic horror novel *Flowers in the Attic* has been filmed twice, once for theatrical release in 1987 and once as a Lifetime Network made-for-television movie in 2014. It weaves familiar gothic plot elements—a sprawling mansion, a locked room, dark family secrets, and a contested inheritance—into a multi-generational family saga driven by incest, imprisonment, and the abuse of the young by their elders. There are no supernatural elements in *Flowers in the Attic*; the monsters that menace the four Dollanganger children—teenaged Chris and Cathy, and six-year-old twins Cory and Carrie—are their own mother, Corinne, and their grandmother, Olivia.

Flowers twists a formula made familiar in gothic novels, fairy tales, and their respective screen adaptations. Traditionally, the innocent young protagonists of such stories (usually female) are separated from loving, elder family members by death or circumstance and forced into a situation where they are menaced by (usually female) evil outsiders: witches or stepmothers. The children in *Flowers* lose their father and their home, and are forced to live in an isolated manor house where their happiness, their sanity, and even their lives are under constant threat, but the evil elders who threaten them *are* their family. Their grandmother, who is never named in the film, is the ultimate source of all their suffering, though their mother changes and turns cold, then actively malicious, to them later.

This essay examines the 1987 film, focusing on Olivia's role as the perpetrator and source of the horror. Horrified that her four grandchildren are products of an incestuous relationship, and obsessed with preventing it from staining the family's name or corrupting its bloodline, Olivia haunts her grandchildren from the moment they enter her foreboding mansion. Psychologically warped by the experiences of her own past, she becomes their jailer, abuser, and would-be murderer. She is determined, like a vengeful demigod, to visit the sins of the fathers upon their children. *Flowers in the Attic* manifests its horror in multiple ways, all of which—even those involving Corrine—ultimately lead back to Olivia, the evil at the heart of a dark, modern-day fairy tale.

In a Dark Place

The 1987 film adaptation of *Flowers* begins with the death of Corrine's husband and her decision to move into her parents' house, Foxworth Hall, to avoid homelessness. By the film's conclusion, viewers are left to wonder whether homelessness might have been preferable to Foxworth Hall. The children's grandmother, wealthy matriarch Olivia Foxworth (Louise Fletcher), is cold and severe to them from their first meeting, and within hours of their arrival, locks them in an attic room with barred windows. Their mother Corrine (Victoria Tennant) assents to this, explaining that she was disowned by her father, Malcolm (Nathan Davis), for marrying *their* father Christopher Senior (Marshall Colt), who was also her uncle. Corrine explains to the children that she and Olivia will hide them—the evidence of her scandalous marriage—from their now-dying grandfather so that he will reconcile with Corrine and write her back into his will. Corrine promises that once she has been re-established as an heir and the children's financial future is secure she will release them from the attic.

Corrine's visits to the attic grow less frequent as the children's captivity drags on, and they are left at the mercy of Olivia: an ostensibly religious woman who loathes them because they are products of their mother's incest. She becomes obsessed with the idea that the two older siblings, Chris (Jeb Stuart Adams) and Cathy (Kristy Swanson) have become lovers and, when she discovers them sleeping (innocently) in the same bed, she smashes the music box that is Cathy's last legacy from her father. Later, after finding Chris talking to Cathy (again, innocently) as she takes a bath, she locks Chris in a closet and forcibly hacks off Cathy's long hair.[1] As a further punishment, she withholds food from all four children for a week, forcing Chris to feed six-year-old Cory (Ben Ganger) with Chris' own blood in order to keep the younger boy from starving to death. Their meals eventually resume, but all four are frequently sick.

Chris and Cathy discover that they can remove the attic door's hinge pins, and so sneak into the main house one night. They find that Corrine, having reconciled with her father, is living a life of luxury and dating a lawyer named Bart Winslow (Leonard Mann). On Corrine's next visit to the attic they confront her over her neglect without revealing what they know, and she storms out, angry and defensive. Soon after, Cory becomes severely ill. Olivia and Corrine agree to take him to the hospital, but Corrine later informs the other children that he died. When Chris discovers that their pet mouse has died after nibbling a cookie that Cory left unfinished, he investigates further and discovers that the sugar sprinkled on their cookies has been laced with arsenic.

Knowing they are being poisoned, Chris and Cathy plan to escape, bringing their surviving young sister Carrie (Lindsay Parker) with them. Sneaking downstairs that night to steal money for the escape, Chris discovers that Corrine and Bart will be married at the estate the next day and proposes that they leave the house during all the commotion of the people coming in and out. As they leave, they discover the truth that Olivia and Corrine had concealed: their grandfather has been dead for months, and before dying made a will stating that Corrine would lose all of her inheritance if it was ever revealed—even after his death—that her incestuous marriage had produced children. Realizing that Corrine, not Olivia, was behind the poisoning, reveal their secret to the astonished guests and horrified groom. Cathy confronts Corrine with the remains of the poisoned cookie, and, approaching Corrine, trying to get her to take and eat the cookie to prove whether or not Corrine is lying about her ignorance, Corrine backs away onto the balcony. Cathy follows her, and the two begin to struggle. Corrine topples over the railing, falls, and is strangled to death by the train of her wedding dress when it snags on a flower trellis below. The children then walk out of the house of horrors as their evil grandmother looks on, powerless to stop them.

The Horror of Seeing and Knowing

Flowers belongs to the subgenre of psychological horror. There are no ghosts, witches, or non-human monsters in the film. When Carrie, upon seeing her grandparents' mansion, declares, "Witches in there, Mama. Witches and monsters," she is correct, but only in the figurative sense. The horror in the film, and all the terrible events that unfold in it, can be traced to the manipulative and diabolical intentions of the children's grandmother (and, after some time, their mother as well). The horrors of *Flowers* are those that humans inflict on one another. We may consider *Flowers* almost as a "prequel" to a haunted house movie, in that in haunted house films, the hauntings usually begin with a grave injustice, crime, wrong, or abuse done within the house, which the house has "absorbed" and cannot expel.

Psychological horror relies heavily on the audience being able to see and know things that are vital to the characters' survival, but that the characters remain ignorant of until it is (almost) too late. *Flowers* ties discovery and knowledge specifically to seeing, and—embodying the ocular theory of horror—creates terror by having the characters (and, through them, the audience) see things that are horrifying in themselves, in their implications, or both.[2] Chris refuses to see his mother's betrayal until it is no longer possible to deny (and one could argue even past that point for a while), and both Chris and Cathy are in the dark regarding the grandfather's death and the terms of the will until the very end of the film when they see it for themselves, in point of fact looking at it with their own eyes. To continue this theme, in exposing their mother's doings to the entire crowd at the wedding, the children are revealing her publicly for all to see.

The Dollanganger children are kept in the dark, both literally (in a dimly lit attic) and figuratively (by their mother's and grandmother's lies of omission), throughout virtually the entire film. It is by repeated discoveries brought about through observation—that is, by "seeing things"—that they discover the truth about their situation and eventually free themselves of the elder characters' manipulations of their reality, mental and physical abuse of them, and (eventual) threat to their lives. Chris and Cathy learn that their mother has been neglecting them and living in luxury by seeing her opulently furnished room, and that their grandfather has died (unknown to them) by seeing his room empty and his bed dismantled. Chris learns of Corrine and Bart's impending wedding when he glimpses a celebratory party in progress at the mansion, and uses science—a deeper form of "seeing"—to make the connection between Cory's illness, the dead mouse, and poison.

Corrine's evil scheme to secure her inheritance by ensuring that her children remain unseen (and eventually erasing them from existence entirely) is, likewise, confirmed by things seen. The audience, but not the children, sees Cory being buried in an unmarked grave on the estate with three identical graves prepared alongside it, so the audience "sees" the future that awaits the kids if they do not escape. Reading the will (also an act of seeing) establishes Corrine, not Olivia, as their (active) would-be murderer, and establishes her motive. The children's exposure of their mother's actions takes place at the wedding, transforming the entire crowd into witnesses to the poisoned cookie and Corrine's horrified recoil from it.

There are, however, limits to the power of sight. Olivia, whose vision of the world is warped by her corrupted religious convictions and revulsion at what the children represent to her, repeatedly "sees" evidence of an incestuous relationship between Chris and Cathy that (in the film) is not there. Chris and Cathy are contrasted as characters because

Cathy readily accepts what she sees, but Chris resists seeing his mother as evil until the last possible moment, when it is too late to save Cory. He is able to clearly "see" the conclusions that naturally follow from scientific observation, but is less able to "see" those involving human emotions, leaving him blind to the horrors which Olivia and Corrine have proven themselves capable.

Grandmother as Monster

Olivia's hatred of her grandchildren is immediate and palpable. She greets them (and enters the story) for the first time holding a small Bible in front of her as if the children were monsters and it is a shield that will keep them at bay. A mean and vindictive woman, obsessed with propriety and public image, she is incapable of seeing the children as innocent, let alone as family members worthy of her love. They are, to her, living embodiments of sin: Corrine and Christopher's incestuous relationship, Malcolm's unnaturally close relationship with Corrine (in which she may also see the shadow of incest), and her own failure to control her husband and wayward daughter.

Freud described the uncanny as "nothing new or foreign, but something familiar and old—established in the mind, that has been estranged only by the process of repression," that terrifies because its sudden return is unexpected.[3] The uncanny threatens the individual's sense of self, he argues, because in an encounter with a double "one possesses knowledge, feeling and experience in common with the other, [and] identifies himself with another person, so that his self becomes confounded, or the foreign self is substituted for his own."[4] The children are, to Olivia, uncanny and unwelcome intruders whose presence in her meticulously managed world threatens her sense of self by continually and visually reminding her of her greatest failure.

A grandmother (Louise Fletcher) terrorizes her daughter's children in *Flowers in the Attic* (1987).

Cathy becomes a particular focus of Olivia's hatred because her age, appearance, and long blonde hair make her, for Olivia, an uncanny double of Corrine. In much the same way, Chris—close to Cathy in age, and close to her both physically and emotionally because of their confinement—becomes an uncanny double of his father/great-uncle, whose name he carries.

Olivia's forcible cutting of Cathy's hair represents an attempt to undermine the girl's reflection of her wayward mother. Long hair in women is a symbol of youth, fertility, and sexual availability; in short, of maidenhood. Taking Cathy's hair is, for Olivia, equivalent to taking her youth, and rendering her less attractive and (at least in a symbolic sense) less sexually available to Chris. It could also be intended as a mark of shame: a visible symbol of her (imagined) sins. Similarly, after Christopher has died, Olivia punishes Corrine by forcing her to strip to the waist and, as her father looks on at Corrine's front, whipping Corrine's naked back until it bleeds.

Corrine (Victoria Tennant) displays the scars of her "punishment" for forbidden love in *Flowers in the Attic* (1987).

Ignoring the biblical principle that fathers and sons should not be held accountable for one another's sins,[5] Olivia embraces—out of context—God's proclamation in Exodus 20:5 that punishment for "the sins of the fathers" will be visited upon three or even four generations of descendants. This twisting of the text, which in context applies only to those who *knowingly* allow themselves to be led astray by their elders, enables her to absolve herself and blame her grandchildren, while at the same time blasphemously putting herself in the position of God by meting out what she sees as justice.

Olivia's corrupted religious beliefs also render the children uncanny in a deeper sense. She hates them for their very existence, which represents a stain on her bloodline. The horrors that Olivia inflicts on the children are likely a result of the horror she herself experiences. She acts the way she does because, to her, the *children* are a horror. They are a subversion of her genetic line, and—fearing for the survival of her bloodline—she seeks to rid herself of them in order to marry Corrine off to another man and produce new, "untainted" children. This sense of bloodline horror that drives Olivia is more specific to the aged: She sees the transgressions of her adult child as a negation of all of the effort and sacrifices made in raising her, and this is the concomitant source of the "sin" that taints her grandchildren and her genetic survival. Unable to cope with this horror, she redirects it onto the children and onto her daughter as well, turning Corrine into another version of herself to "ensure" things are done "correctly" for the remainder of Corrine's life. Olivia's age helps to motivate her cruelty: her husband is dying and she may not be far behind, so she has no time to engage in subtle manipulations or Machiavellian schemes—she decides what she is going to do immediately and locks the children away in the first hours of the first day.

The film ends with all of Olivia's worst fears realized: her daughter is dead, her grandchildren survive and escape, and all chance of creating an untainted bloodline is gone. The disapproval, resentment, and bitterness on her face at the end of the film as she watches the children leave exists because, to her, the children's prosperity signals the final destruction of her "house." Olivia, for the first time in the film, is powerless—reduced to helplessly watching events unfold in the brightly lit world beyond while she stays imprisoned the dark walls of the house she "haunts."

Inter-Generational Conflict and Baby Boomers' Fears

Flowers in the Attic is a story about inter-generational conflict; the struggle of the young to escape from the control of their corrupt and murderous elders. Such conflict is a perpetual source of dramas, but this film's presentation is specific and historically grounded. Released in 1987, *Flowers* was filmed mostly in 1986, when older members of the Baby Boom generation were in their 30s.[6] For Boomers, especially for those born before 1955, who had shaped the youth culture of the 1960s and early 1970s, aging raised a disturbing possibility. They worried that they might become their parents: versions of the conformist, rule-bound authority figures that, in their youth, they had collectively referred to as "The Man." The horror of such a transformation was, for a generation whose members had warned each other "don't trust anyone over 30," political as well as personal. Having derided the system that their elders had created, a system that sent America's young into wars many believed to be immoral, practiced and defended legalized prejudice, and underwent the Watergate scandal, they faced the prospect of becoming cogs in a new iteration of that system.

The minimal age gap between Corrine and her husband—Christopher is 36, Corinne a year or two younger at most—suggests that it was a relationship of equals, and that theirs was a love embraced as an act of rebellion against the domineering family elders.[7] The happy family life depicted in the first minutes of the film reinforces the idea that, though the marriage was incestuous, Corrine and her husband were not objectively "bad people," and their children—who, not knowing the truth, see their parents as perfectly normal—carry no psychological scars from the incestuous relationship.

Olivia and Malcolm are, in contrast, framed as the embodiment of everything Baby Boomers hated about what they felt of which the older generation was guilty. Controlling and judgmental, the grandparents impose their rigid views of what is "natural" and "correct" on those around them without regard for the pain and suffering that imposition causes. They are aggressively materialistic, accumulating vast wealth as their mansion-like home, sprawling estate, and lavish parties suggest, and they use that wealth to exert control over Corrine even as she and the children face homelessness and starvation. The film hints, however, that Malcolm and Olivia's stiffly proper façade and obsession with "scandal" hides behavior that is not merely scandalous, but monstrous. Like the supposedly corrupt Establishment against which the elder members of the Baby Boom generation rebelled, they persecute the young for supposed "crimes of birth" which the children had no control over, while quietly tolerating or actively encouraging the evil done by the old.

Corrine's character arc in the film dramatizes this nightmare in particularly stark, literal fashion. Having left her parents' home at 18, burning her bridges by committing the ultimate affront to their authority and sense of propriety, she returns (seemingly) without hesitation when Christopher Sr.'s death shatters her idyllic life. Once back in her parents' home, she not only accepts the dominance of the elder generation (embodied by stern, rule-obsessed Olivia), but becomes its agent. She cooperates with Olivia in confining and abusing the children, denies the children's existence (along with her youthful rebellion), and ultimately engages in a careful, premeditated attempt to murder them. She does this, moreover, not to penetrate the "Establishment" and destroy it from within, but to become part of it. Seduced by the wealth and luxury that Foxworth Hall represents, and eager at 36 (as she was not at 18) to possess it, she embraces the evil—embodied by Malcolm and Olivia—that lies at its core. In the end, she does not simply *become* her parents, but surpasses them.[8]

Flowers *as Dark Fairy Tale*

Taken together, these elements make *Flowers*, beneath its modern-day trappings, a story more akin to a dark fairy tale. Royalty often married close relatives, as Corrine married Christopher, and the attic in which the children are imprisoned is a modern house's equivalent of a tower. Olivia fills the role of the "evil queen" role who seeks to erase or destroy the children's existence. When Chris and Cathy try to make their first escape, they do so by climbing down a long rope they've fashioned, not unlike Rapunzel. These elements nearly qualify the film for inclusion as a *märchen* story: while no true supernatural abilities are present in any character, the grandmother's evil is nearly otherworldly in its intensity and ability to warp life within Foxworth Hall.

In keeping with the film's fairy tale quality, the children consistently refer to "*the* grandmother" and "*the* grandfather" using the definite article, and never to "our grandmother," let alone use "Grandmother" or "Grandma" as a title. This helps to make the grandmother character in this story a more-than-human, or even non-human, entity, and allows her to represent not just one person but a type. Their descriptions of her, taken out of context, might well apply to evil grandmothers or just evil old women as archetypal figures.

The abuse and horror in the film originate with the grandparents, primarily the grandmother. She is a stern and forbidding figure from the moment she appears onscreen and never once displays happiness. She exhibits no affection for, or warmth toward, the children, and is actively aggressive to them due to her firm belief that the two eldest will eventually commit incest. This belief, while informed by her experience with their mother, can also be seen as age's jealousy of youth. As the story unfolds, other reasons for Olivia's behavior come into view: her jealousy of Malcolm's close relationship with Corrine, which resurfaces as she once again grows close to him and actively attempts to "win back his love," her twisted religious beliefs, and her obsession with protecting her family bloodline. She spends the film attempting, by nearly every means available to her, i.e., "civilized" means for propriety's sake, to force Corrine and the children to conform to her vision of what is right and moral, but her attempts to do so make it clear that she has lost any sense of what those concepts truly mean.

Her actions demonstrate that, in old age, a moral rot has settled into her soul. This loss of moral compass turns the act of "forcing the old rules upon the young," a routine part of aging, into something dark and horrible. Many children chafe at the traditions of their families, arguing that they are outdated and irrelevant even as their elders respond that they, because of their youth and lack of experience, simply don't understand. The four Dollanganger children are in a different, darker place. They must rebel against their elders if they are to physically survive. The film suggests—explicitly in the scene of Corinne's whipping, and implicitly in scenes with her father that hint at sexual attraction—that Corrine herself may once have been in a similar position. The suggestions are too ambiguous for the viewer to be sure whether Corrine, in fact, felt that she had to escape her parents if she was to survive.

Corrine falls victim to the same corruption as her parents soon after the film begins. As the story unfolds, she reveals herself to be as selfish as Olivia, and just as willing to make the children suffer in order to satisfy her own needs. Initially it appears, to the children and to the viewer, that her selfishness is latent: that she is allowing their imprisonment to drag on, and passively tolerating Olivia's abuse of them, in order to not to imperil her inheritance. As the story reaches its climax, however, it becomes clear that she has become as evil as her mother. Even if Corrine was, initially, merely acting under Olivia's tyrannical control, she has, by the climax, revealed herself to be actively, monstrously evil in her own right. Time spent with Olivia makes Corrine steadily more like the elder woman, distinguished primarily by the focus of her obsession: material wealth, rather than intangibles such as reputation and posterity. The transformation, though driven by proximity to her elderly mother, is made possible by the fact that Corrine herself is growing older.

Significantly, *Flowers* ends with the death of Corrine but not Olivia, and with the children escaping their imprisonment without taking legal or physical revenge on their grandmother. The original ending of the film—shot, but rejected by preview audiences—left both Olivia and Corrine alive, but was changed to give audiences the satisfaction of watching at least one of the villains get her comeuppance. The film as it exists is thus a compromise between reality (the children's escape leaving the grandmother alive and untouched) and wish fulfillment fantasy (the confrontation with Corrine, which leaves her dead and Cathy blameless). Olivia's survival also reflects the *märchen* nature of her character: like other embodiments of fairy-tale horror, she is "too evil for mortals to kill" which her appearance in the final scene of the film reinforces. When she attempts to intervene in the children's departure from the attic, Chris beats her unconscious with a chair leg, but when she appears at the wedding—a mute witness to their departure—she shows no signs of the assault: no blood, not even a hair out of place.

The grandmother's role as source of terror and evil is rooted in her—and our—perceptions of reality. Noel Carroll notes that "there is a necessary bond between our beliefs and our emotions. In order to experience the relevant emotion—whether of grief or of indignation—we must have beliefs about the way circumstances lie, including beliefs that the agents entangled in those circumstances exist."[9] Because the grandmother believes the children are "devil spawn," she is able to act the way she does. Because the audience believes the children are innocent and believes cruelty to children and murder are wrong, they react the way they do. And because the children believe in their mother, they tolerate the abuse at first, but later are just left with horror and emotional scars when they finally realize that the elder members of their family are determined to kill them. The shift is most visible in Chris, who clings to the belief that his mother is their defender, not their betrayer, until well past the point when a rational assessment of the evidence should have convinced him.

Olivia's unchanging appearance mirrors that of the old, unchanging house: a visible symbol of wealth and power of which she is not just the unchallenged ruler but, in many ways, an extension. She is a reflection of the house that she rules over and never leaves, visibly showing the ravages of time despite attempts to remain presentable, and surrounded by a cloud of somberness. The two are, the film hints, inseparable at some level. Olivia can also be viewed as a stand-in for the predatory ghost of traditional haunted house films. She permeates the house as a ghost would, generating a similar sense of all-encompassing evil. The last words of the film, spoken as voiceover by an older Cathy, draw the notion of grandmother-as-ghost into the foreground: "I sometimes wonder if Grandmother is still alive, still presiding over Foxworth Hall, still awaiting my return."[10] Cathy's voiceover describes Chris graduating from medical school and becoming a doctor, suggesting that she is speaking a decade or more after the events of the story, and leaving the answer to her rhetorical question ambiguous. The final image of Olivia at the window suggests, however, that it may not matter. No matter how long Cathy waits to return, Olivia will be there waiting.

Complementarily, the house mirrors Olivia. The attic is full of disused items, it is dark and filled with dust and cobwebs. The lower floors, when the children sneak through them, are mostly dark. The only bright parts of the house are the room seen during the wedding, and the spaces the children inhabit. The house as a whole is a grim, emotionally dark place, something that Carrie picks up on in her comment about "witches and monsters" when she first glimpses it. The house may be only an observer, not an actor like Olivia and (later) Corrine, but it has witnessed terrible things. Malcolm, Corrine, and Cory all die, while Chris, Cathy, and Carrie escape death by the narrowest of margins. Corrine's maternal sense, and the children's innocence, also die in the time they spend at the house. If its walls could talk, to adapt a familiar expression, they would weep in despair or scream in terror.

Conclusion

Horror produces an emotional response by subverting our expectations of what is natural or normal, confronting us instead with sights calculated to elicit fear and disgust. It overturns our sense of the natural order of things, and our expectations about fundamental elements of the human experience, such as love, justice, and pain. Psychological horror further disturbs us because it confronts us (through the story's characters) with an imaginary world where we can neither predict nor control what will happen to us next.

While psychological horror traditionally focuses on the destabilization of a single character's mind or the relationship between two principal characters, *Flowers in the Attic* tells a more expansive story, involving the destabilization of an entire family—an unraveling of intergenerational relationships that quickly move beyond discord and dysfunction into horror and outright evil. Olivia, the matriarch of the family and the unquestioned ruler of the dark and brooding house, is the source and the instigator of the horror. She menaces the children from the moment they set foot in her domain, making no secret of her loathing for them. The film also suggests, however, that she was complicit in—if not solely responsible for—the abuse that, a generation earlier, drove Corrine from the house and set in motion the horrors that befell the next generation.

The malevolent grandmother's perversion of both Biblical principles and her maternal role is at the heart of the psychological horror of the film. Instead of a loving protector, she becomes a predator. It is Olivia who turns *Flowers* from a gothic film about innocents trapped in a dark and menacing house filled with mysteries into a horror story about the elderly corrupting their children and torturing their grandchildren. Determined to prevent her daughter's "sin" from "staining" future generations of the family, Olivia commits acts worse than those she sought to expunge. Determined to clear her name, she proves instead that "the evil that [wo]men do lives after them."

Notes

1. In the novel and the original script, Chris and Cathy do become lovers, but the scenes suggesting that their incest was real (rather than a fantasy brought on by Olivia's obsession) were cut after preview audiences responded negatively to them, as well as to ensure a PG-13 rating that would make the film accessible to its target audience of teenaged girls.
2. The ocular theory of horror has multiple dimensions, some which are explored in Crary, *Techniques of the Observer*; Mulvey, "Visual Pleasure and Narrative Cinema"; and Perrello, "A Parisian in Hollywood."
3. Freud, "The Uncanny," 13, 9.
4. *Ibid.*
5. Deuteronomy 24:16 and Ezekiel 18:20.
6. The Baby Boom generation is traditionally defined as consisting of Americans born between 1946 and 1964, but the Pew Research Center, as well as other researchers, have noted significant differences between those born before and after 1955.
7. The film establishes that Christopher was 36 when he died. Given the ages of the two oldest children—both in their late teen years—Christopher could not have been more than 18–20 when they were conceived. Cathy, for her part, was at least over the age of consent, or the marriage never would have occurred against her parents' wishes.
8. The history of American culture from the late seventies to early nineties—the cocaine-addled heyday of Studio 54, the era of "greed is good" materialism, the corporatization of music, and the widespread cover-up of sexual misconduct across the entertainment industry—suggests that many Boomers fully embraced once-hated values.
9. Carroll, *Philosophy of Horror*, 61.
10. This is one of the very few times the word "grandmother" is spoken by the child characters without the definite article preceding it, possibly indicating that Cathy has, at least in part, gotten over her fear of her grandmother and sees her grandmother as just a human again, and not an extra-human monster.

Bibliography

Carroll, Noël. *The Philosophy of Horror: or, Paradoxes of the Heart*. London: Routledge, 1990. https://guionterror.files.wordpress.com/2010/11/philosophy-of-horror.pdf.
Crary, Jonathan. *Techniques of the Observer: On Vision and Modernity in the Nineteenth Century*. Cambridge: MIT Press, 1990.
Flowers in the Attic. Daily Motion Site. http://www.dailymotion.com/video/xvz997 and http://www.dailymotion.com/video/xvzc7c.
Freud, Sigmund. "The Uncanny" (1919). http://web.mit.edu/allanmc/www/freud1.pdf.
Mulvey, Laura. "Visual Pleasure and Narrative Cinema." *Screen* 16, no. 3 (Autumn 1975): 6–18.
Perrello, Tony. "A Parisian in Hollywood: The Ocular Horror in the Films of Alejandro Aja." *American Horror Film*, edited by Steffen Hantke. Jackson: University of Mississippi Press, 2010.

About the Contributors

Jessica **Balanzategui** is a lecturer in cinema and screen studies at Swinburne University of Technology in Australia. Her research examines the intersections of childhood, technological change and nostalgia—particularly in horror and gothic media—and the cultural, historical and industrial negotiations between cultural institutions and entertainment industries.

Brian **Brems** is an assistant professor of English and film at the College of DuPage. He specializes in film and literature. His film writing can be read online at *Vague Visages, Bright Wall/Dark Room,* and other film sites.

Stephanie M. **Flint** is a doctoral student in comparative studies at Florida Atlantic University, where she teaches courses in English literature and interdisciplinary studies. Her research focuses on representations of monstrosity in literature, film and popular culture, particularly through the lenses of gender and disability studies.

Dawn **Keetley** is a professor of English at Lehigh University. She is the editor of *"We're All Infected"* (McFarland, 2014) and the coeditor (with Angela Tenga) of *Plant Horror* (Palgrave Macmillan, 2016) and (with Matthew Sivils) of *The Ecogothic in Nineteenth-Century American Literature* (2017).

Robert B. **Luehrs**, a retired professor who taught courses concerning early modern Europe and European intellectual history is the teaching excellence coordinator for Fort Hays State University. His publications include articles on witchcraft in the 17th century, utopianism and deism in the 18th century, religious skepticism in the 19th century, and children's literature in the 20th century.

Sue **Matheson** is an associate professor of English literature at the University College of the North in Canada. She teaches American film and popular culture, Canadian literature, and children's literature. She is the editor of *A Fistful of Icons* (McFarland, 2017) and the author of *The Westerns and War Films of John Ford* (Rowman & Littlefield, 2016).

Maddi **McGillvray** is a doctoral student in cinema and media studies at York University in Canada. She writes extensively on the horror genre, with topics including gender and sexuality, gothic horror, 21st-century horror, the New French Extremity, and online horror. Her other research interests include feminist film theory and transmedia studies.

Cynthia J. **Miller** is a cultural anthropologist, specializing in popular culture and visual media. Her writing has appeared in numerous journals and collections and she has edited several essay collections. The editor for Rowman & Littlefield's *Film and History* book series, she serves on the editorial advisory boards for the *Journal of Popular Television* and *Bloomsbury's Guide to Contemporary Directors* series.

Martin F. **Norden** teaches film history and screenwriting as a professor of communication at the University of Massachusetts–Amherst. He has more than one hundred publications to his credit and has presented his film research at dozens of professional conferences across North America and Europe. His books include *The Cinema of Isolation* (Rutgers University Press, 1994) and *The Changing Face of Evil in Film and Television* (Editions Rodopi, 2007).

About the Contributors

Olivia **Oliver-Hopkins** is a lecturer and tutor at the University of Sydney and Queensland University of Technology in Australia, having previously lectured at Avondale Collage and the University of Canberra. She has presented at numerous international conferences.

Thomas **Prasch** is a professor and chair of history at Washburn University. His publication topics include neo-noir/screwball fusion films of the mid–1980s, Michael Palin's travel documentaries, Robert Eggers' *The Witch*, and Alfred Russel Wallace's spiritualism and evolutionary thought.

Karen J. **Renner** is an assistant professor at Northern Arizona University, where she teaches classes in American literature and popular culture. Her work combines horror and childhood studies. She is the author of *Evil Children in the Popular Imagination* (Palgrave Macmillan, 2016) and editor of *The "Evil Child" in Literature, Film and Popular Culture* (Routledge, 2012).

Jennifer **Richards** is a lecturer at Manchester Metropolitan University. Her research interests include the Gothic mode in visual communication with a particular interest in fashion, stage and screen. She has published a range of practice-based projects and academic work examining the rise of mysticism and witchcraft in popular culture and the digital realm.

Isaac **Rooks** is a graduate school fellow and doctoral student in the cinema and media studies division of the University of Southern California's School of Cinematic Arts. His research frequently explores the depiction of space and place in popular genre cinema, particularly in horror fiction. He has presented at numerous conferences and has published in several journals and anthologies.

Philip L. **Simpson** is the provost of the Titusville campus and eLearning of Eastern Florida State College. He is the president of the Popular Culture Association/American Culture Association and serves on the editorial board of the *Journal of Popular Culture*. He is the author of two books and numerous journal articles and book chapters on film, literature, popular culture, and horror.

Hans **Staats** is a humanities teacher at the Austin Waldorf School. His writing has appeared in a variety of journals and collections, including *CineAction*, *Offscreen*, *Journal of the Fantastic in the Arts*, *War Gothic in Literature and Culture* (2015), *What's Eating You?* (Bloomsbury Academic, 2017), and *Cruel Children in Popular Texts and Cultures* (Palgrave Macmillan, 2018).

A. Bowdoin **Van Riper** is a historian who specializes in depictions of science and technology in popular culture. He is the author or editor of a wide range of volumes, ranging from science to science fiction to horror. His collection *Learning from Mickey, Donald and Walt* was published by McFarland in 2011.

James J. **Ward** is a professor of history at Cedar Crest College where he teaches courses in European history, German history, urban history, and film and history. He has published in the *Journal of Contemporary History*, *Journal of Interdisciplinary History*, *Central European History*, *Journal of Popular Culture*, and *Film & History*, among others.

Liam T. **Webb** is a writer, editor, and teacher. He has been an English professor, city bus driver, and has worked as an accounting clerk in various medical technician positions. He has been published in 15 academic or creative works, focusing on comic books academically and science fiction and horror creatively.

Steve J. **Webley** is a lecturer and researcher in games design, war studies, and psychoanalysis in the School of Computing and Digital Technologies at Staffordshire University in the UK. His teaching specializes in military games design and development, interactive narrative design, and psychoanalytic game and film criticism.

Index

the abject 4, 6, 61, 72, 74–75, 77–78, 81, 84–85, 89, 92, 110–114, 119, 122–127, 135, 140, 143–147, 171, 225
actresses, aging 189–198
adaptation 70, 155–163, 165, 233
African Americans 6, 8, 24, 92–104, 189, 222–230
ageism 230
Agency 5, 7, 12, 16–21, 97, 99, 112, 127, 185, 187
aging, cultural context of: 1960s 112, 180–181, 187, 238; 108–117; post–World War II era 24–25, 130–131; Reagan era 108–117
aging metaphors: automobiles 179–187; structures 23–25, 49, 82
aging, as process 1–2, 119, 180, 185–187, 238–239; and as disease 25, 103, 180; and economics 23, 110; and exploitation 23, 68; fear of 12, 15, 22, 30, 82, 85, 116, 129–132,170; and gender 6, 58–67, 70–79, 119–128, 190–198; hopelessness 15–16, 23–24, 26; reversal 119–128, 152–161; revulsion 30, 58–67, 70–79, 82, 85, 112, 119–128, 140–149; slowing/stopping 7, 119–128, 152–161; successful/unsuccessful 15, 58–67, 110, 190–198; *see also* body; mental health
Alderman, Derek 98, 100, 102–103
Alvarez, Fede 22
Alzheimer's disease *see* mental health
American Dream 113, 137
American Horror Story (TV series; 2011–2018) 7, 189–198
anxiety, cultural 15, 66
Auerbach, Nina 155–156, 161

Bacon, Simon 154
Balanzategui, Jessica 6, 93–105, 243
Barrymore, Lionel 5, 32, 34–40
Bassett, Angela 190–195
Beard, Mary 166
beauty *see* youth
Bellin, Joshua David 148
Benjamin, Stefanie 100, 102

Benjamin, Walter 58, 103
Beugnet, Martine 2–3
body: breakdown 22; deterioration 73–74, 85–86, 104, 147, 172, 174, 185, 195; disability 2–3, 22, 28–30, 37–38, 92, 110, 147–150, 227; *see also* mental health
body horror 181; *see also* horror films
Bowie, David 154, 166–167, 171–174
Bram Stoker's Dracula (1992) 7, 33, 152–161, 165
Brems, Brian 7, 179–187
The Brotherhood of Satan (1971) 7, 179–187
Brottman, Mikita 183
Browning, Tod 5, 32–43, 154–155, 160, 189
Bubba Ho-Tep (2003) 5, 12–20
Burn, Witch, Burn! (1933) 32–34
Buse, Peter 93
Butler, David 98, 102, 223
Buzinde, Christine N. 97, 101–102

The Cabinet of Dr. Caligari (1921) 8, 212–219
Canby, Vincent 156
cannibalism 4–5, 46–53, 71, 165, 170, 173
capitalism 3, 47, 108, 112–114, 131–133, 137, 155
Carter, Perry 102
children 6–8, 12, 15, 47, 52, 70–79, 92, 97, 99–101, 140–149, 179, 182–187, 222, 224, 233–242
Chivers, Sally 2–3, 154–155
Clarke, Laura Herd 112
"cinema of attractions" 59, 65, 67
Cohen-Shalev, Amir 2–3
Conroy, Frances 191–192
"corporeal decay" 111
Coscarelli, Don 5, 12
counterculture 108, 180
counter-memory 93, 101–104
Countess Dracula (1971) 6, 120–128
Crane, Susan 205
Creed, Barbara 71–72, 74, 77, 119, 125, 127
cultural imperialism 14, 225, 230

Daughters of Darkness (1971) 168
Davis, Lennard J. 47
Day, Lori 62
Dead Silence (2007) 59, 66–67
death: cheating 1, 60, 65; denial of 30; desire for 48, 54, 225; fear of 1, 143; unnatural 88, 123, 210
DeFalco, Amelia 30
Dein, Edward 58
Del Toro, Guillermo 155
dementia *see* mental health
demons 6, 48, 50, 53, 58, 71–72, 77, 83, 109, 114, 128, 140, 187, 212, 219
Deneuve, Catherine 154, 166–167, 170–173
Detroit 5, 22–30, 181
The Devil-Doll (1936) 5, 32–43
Doherty, Thomas 130
Don't Breathe (2016) 5, 22–30
Dracula's Daughter (1936) 165–166, 173
Drag Me to Hell (2009) 6, 71, 108–117, 119, 140
Dwyer, Owen 102

East, exotic 13–14
Ebert, Roger 90, 156
Edelman, Lee 225, 228
Eisenstein, Sergei 66
elderly: and anger 61, 112, 184, 209; and discrimination 148, 193, 230; as harbingers 1, 71; as keepers of dark secrets 5, 8, 22, 26, 60, 76, 89, 124–126, 167, 179, 182, 203–205, 210, 219, 230; as keepers of wisdom 1–2, 5, 129, 230; as protectors of legacy 230; as surrogate parents 227; as victims 1, 5, 71, 112, 119
Elsaesser, Thomas 160–161
excrement 53, 136, 141, 143, 145

fairy tales 70, 123, 128, 195–196, 198, 233, 239–240
family 4–8, 12–13, 15, 22, 25, 35, 46–55, 60, 67, 72, 81–90, 93, 97–101, 115–116, 124, 131–137, 141, 145–148, 179, 182, 184, 189, 194, 202, 225–226, 233–242
fascination 29, 53, 84, 155, 214, 217

Fernandez-Vander Kaay, Kathleen 13
Flint, Stephanie 7, 140–149, 243
Flowers in the Attic (1987) 8, 233–242
folklore 70, 85, 157, 219, 223
Foucault, Michel 95, 101, 110
found footage 6, 70–79
Freeland, Cynthia 157
Freeman, Elizabeth 224
Freud, Sigmund 46–51, 54, 63, 70

Garland-Thomson, Rosemarie 110, 147, 149
Gelder, Ken 157, 165
Get Out (2017) 23, 65
Ghost Story (1981) 7, 202–210
ghosts 6, 8, 71, 82–87, 94–100, 135, 192, 194, 196, 202–219, 223–230, 241
Gilman, Sander 148
Gonzalez, Francisco 154
Gore 5, 46–47, 52, 108, 173, 230
gothic 25, 49, 52, 54, 70; Southern 6, 92–104
Grand Guignol 39, 65–68
grandparents 4–8, 70–79, 119, 140–149, 227, 233–242
Gravagne, Pamela 2, 112
Greed 49, 54–55
Greven, David 96
grotesque 3–4, 6, 23, 33, 46, 48, 52, 54, 66, 74, 77–78, 110, 112, 116, 121, 123, 125, 140, 212
Gunning, Tom 59, 65–66
gypsy *see* women, aging

hag *see* women, aging
Halberstam, Jack 225
Halbwachs, Maurice 205, 207
hallucinations 135, 143, 218–219
Hammer Studios 6, 119, 128, 155, 158, 166
Hanna, Stephen 98
"Hansel and Gretel" (1812) 70, 75
Harbinger 1, 71
Hart, James V. 156–157
Harvey, David 112
haunted houses 95, 100, 114, 235, 241
The Haunting in Connecticut 2: The Ghosts of Georgia (2013) 8, 222–230
hauntings *see* ghosts
health care 15–16
Hinson, Hal 156, 158
history: continuity 92, 95, 104, 113; hidden 92–104; queering 225–226; trauma, historical 94–97, 99
Hogan, Chuck 155
Holland, Sharon Patricia 222–224
horror films: progressive 132, 137; psychological 66, 81–90, 109, 140, 235, 241; reactionary 132
"horror objects" 61–62
Howe, Desson 156
The Hunger (1983) 4, 7, 154, 165–174

identity 3, 12, 15–20, 47–48, 53, 62–63, 67–68, 84–85, 96–98, 104, 114–115, 121, 133–137, 146, 149, 166–167, 173, 186–187, 205, 218–219
immortality 6–7, 13, 76, 126–127, 154–155, 165–166, 198
incest 8, 233–242
infantilization 131
insanity *see* mental health
Insidious (2010) 58
intergenerational conflict 22, 108, 241
intertextuality 160, 190
interviews [as storytelling technique] 71–75, 145, 147
invisibility 4, 47, 62, 112, 116, 133
isolation 25–26, 72, 74, 81–82, 89, 136, 166–167, 185, 233
It Follows (2014) 23, 58, 64–65

Johnson, Diane 81
Joslin, Lyndon 156–158, 162n2
jump scare 60, 65, 67
justice 27, 30, 42, 102, 235, 237, 241

Keetley, Dawn 6, 58–69, 243
Kendrick, James 94
Kennedy, Harlan 155, 160
Kennedy, John F. 12, 14–17, 20
Kervyn, Emmanuel 47, 49, 51–55
Kilker, Robert 85
Klimpton, Peter 81
Kracauer, Siegfried 214
Kreyling, Michael 98
Kristeva, Julia. 72, 77, 85, 119, 125–127
Kubrick, Stanley 6, 61, 81–91, 119, 141

Lacan, Jacques 47–48, 53–54
Lange, Jessica 190–193, 195
The Leech Woman (1960) 58–69
love 61, 161–162n18, 241; death transcended by 152, 154, 158–160; familial 19, 48, 229–230, 236; for inanimate objects 181, 188; romantic 14, 22, 68n3, 120, 122–123, 125, 127, 136, 142, 144, 166–167, 172–174, 191, 193–198, 204, 208, 213, 237–239
Lowenstein, Adam 130–131, 138n10
Lucas, Rafaël 104
Luehrs, Robert B. 8, 212–221, 243

madness *see* mental health
Magistrale, Tony 111
Malabou, Catherine 58–59, 62–63, 68
Manchel, Frank 89
marginalization 78; of the economically disadvantaged 25, 113–114; of the elderly 1, 13, 16, 116; of racial and ethnic minorities 97, 100–101, 104, 108; 223–224, 227, 229
marriage 82, 167, 191, 193, 204; happy 167, 210, 213; incestuous 8, 234, 237–239, 242; as "prize" 120–122, 124–125, 127, 193; unhappy 17, 60, 89
Martin, Charles 13
masculinity 5, 18, 33, 194, 209
Matheson, Sue 6, 81–91, 243
Mbiti, John S. 224
McGee, Adam 92, 100
McGillvray, Maddi 6, 70–80, 243
McMahon, Jennifer L. 154
Medina, José 101
memory 88–89, 166–167, 224, 228, 231n19; counter 9, 101–104; failure 1, 52, 86; historical 7, 179, 202–211, 230; personal 17; repressed 135–136; traumatic 42, 82–83
mental health 4, 8, 23, 27–27, 30, 81–82, 86–87, 89, 109, 122, 128, 136, 140–141, 144, 148–149, 214, 219, 223; Alzheimer's Disease 75–77, 88; dementia 6, 73, 78, 81, 86, 141–145, 149n2; post-traumatic embitterment disorder (PTED) 42; sundowning 7, 73, 140–150
Merritt, Abraham 32–34, 43, 44n9
Miller, April 115, 117
Miller, Cynthia J. 6, 108–118, 243
mimicry 47, 53–55
mirrors 47, 73, 146; and supernatural beings 84, 100; as reminders of aging 1, 62, 123, 195
monstrosity 28, 30, 83–85, 89–90, 140, 144, 146, 179, 212, 213, 217; economics and 115–116; of family relationships 5, 233–239; mental disability and 147–149; of old men 22, 29, 155, 158; of old women 6–7, 58–69, 70–78, 111–112, 114, 123–125, 154, 197, 228–229; of supernatural creatures 13–14, 39; sympathy and 129–139
"monstrous-feminine" 71–72, 75, 129, 133–134
mothers 35, 52, 76–77, 84, 87, 197, 225, 229, 235–236, 239–240; abusive 4, 27, 72, 121, 125, 234–236; domineering 49, 79n27, 132–137, 138n11, 189; estranged 72, 145; mythological 218; protective 5, 73, 89, 144, 191–192
Mukerjea, Ananya 154
mummies 6, 12–21

"narratives of decline" 2
neoliberalism 108, 112–116, 193
New Hollywood 180–181, 187
New Orleans 96–97, 189
Ngubane, Harriet 224
Nickel, Philip 68
Norden, Martin F. 5, 32–45, 243

Oliver-Hopkins, Olivia 8, 222–232, 244
Olsen, Bjørnar 103–104
oppression 3, 94–95, 97, 100, 104, 114–116, 129, 131, 180–181, 223

Index

Other 14, 54, 156; elderly as 1, 63, 84–85, 117, 119–128

patriarchy 55, 98, 101, 103, 132, 225; and authority 23, 27, 47, 50, 89; disrupted by women 71–72, 79
Peele, Jordan 65
Pétursdóttir, Þóra 103–104
pollution 49, 74, 84
possession 6, 71, 72, 76–78, 93–94, 116, 219; *see also* demons; witches
poverty 22, 110, 112–113, 115, 198, 231
power 28, 46, 54, 63, 181, 183; attractiveness as 170–171, 195; of language 47; personal 18–19, 48, 116, 124–125, 134, 155, 158, 223–224, 240; political 16, 196, 214; social 13, 97–98, 101–103, 112, 115, 187, 206, 210, 226–227; *see also* patriarchy
Prasch, Thomas 7, 152–164, 244
Presley, Elvis 12–14, 17, 19, 130
Psycho (1960) 4, 6, 58, 129–132, 134
"psycho biddy" 112
Psycho II (1983) 129–139
psychoanalysis 51–55
purification 127

queering, of the elderly 8, 222–232

Rabid Grannies (1988) 5, 46–56
race 15, 22, 46, 65, 94, 96–97, 102, 113, 223–227, 229–230, 231n10
Raimi, Sam 108, 109, 110, 112, 115, 116–117
"Recessionary Horror" 108
reincarnation 89, 153, 157–158, 161n2, 162n41
religion 8, 46–48, 68, 184, 222–223, 234–235, 237, 239
remembrance 98, 100, 103–104
Renner, Karen J. 7, 189–199, 244
repression 3, 30, 54–55, 65, 90n17, 114–116, 129–132, 135–137, 138n11, 165, 180, 191, 238
resurrection 27
revenge 6, 32–42, 61, 71, 100, 109, 216, 240
Richards, Jennifer 6, 119–128, 244
rituals 48, 127, 196; blood 4, 120–128, 152, 154–155, 157, 167–168, 170–173, 185–187, 191, 197; demonic 7, 76, 182–184, 187; family 5, 50; magical 13, 35, 60, 96–96
Roach, Marilynne 77
Robitel, Adam 71, 75–76, 78
Rooks, Isaac 5, 22–31, 244

sacrifice, human 6, 30, 61, 76, 182–187
Sarandon, Susan 166, 171–172, 175n23, 176n32

Satan 179–188
Schluchter, Wolfgang 222
Schopenhauer, Arthur 214–216, 217
Scott, Tony 165–166, 168–169, 171–172, 174, 175n11, 175n14
secrets 5–6, 8, 89, 167; family 233–234; personal 22, 26, 76, 120, 124–126, 170, 203–205, 210, 219; societal 60, 179, 182
security 112–113
sexuality 47, 52, 55, 70, 128, 156, 160–161, 162n18, 180–181, 215, 236; aging and 12, 17–19, 121, 126, 190–194, 196, 198, 204, 208–209; demonic 72; dysfunctional 28, 31n7; heteronormative 60–61, 64, 66–67; illicit 131–133, 240; queer 79n27, 166–168, 170, 172, 174, 175n11, 223–224
Shary, Timothy 2, 31n6, 112
The Shining (1980) 4, 6, 58, 81–91, 119, 140, 189
shock 6, 29, 58–69, 140, 172, 203
Shyamalan, M. Night 7, 70–80, 140–150
Siebers, Tobin 148
Simpson, Philip L. 5, 12–21, 244
The Skeleton Key (2005) 6, 92–106
slavery 8, 94–95, 98, 102, 223, 226, 229
Sobchack, Vivian 61–62, 68
Sontag, Susan 148, 154
spirits of ancestors 1, 221–230; *see also* ghosts; supernatural
splatter cinema *see* gore
Staats, Hans 6, 129–139, 244
Stott, Andrew 93
subjugation 99, 101
suburbs 22, 25–26, 181
subversiveness 47, 55, 78, 92–94, 98, 101–104, 187, 223, 237
suicide 35–36, 40, 81, 157–158, 162n33, 170, 197, 215
supernatural 1, 4, 5, 13–15, 33–35, 43, 50, 70, 79n3, 92–93, 96–98, 102, 108–109, 112, 114–115, 131, 191, 194, 196–198, 202, 217–218, 222–223, 233, 239; dark magic 13, 33, 36; elixirs 146; hoodoo 92, 95–98, 101; psychic powers 82, 109–110, 217–218, 222, 225–229; talismans 184; voodoo 34–36, 189, 197; *see also* demons; mummies; Satan; vampires

The Taking of Deborah Logan (2014) 6, 71–72, 75–79
temporality 93, 96, 102, 126
Thompson, David 130
Thompson, Hannah 14, 18
Thomson, Rosemary Garland 110, 147, 149
Trigg, Dylan 104
Troma Entertainment 6, 46–56
tropes 7, 54–55, 123; aging 4, 38, 65, 112, 121, 207; horror 5, 13–14, 71, 122, 156–158, 160, 190–202

uncanny 3–4, 8, 13, 24, 30, 48, 51–55, 64, 66, 70, 83, 89, 92–104, 204, 236–237

vampires 7, 33–34, 72, 126, 152–164, 165–178, 224
Vander Kaay, Chris 13
Van Riper, A. Bowdoin 1–9, 202–211, 244
The Visit (2015) 6–7, 70–80, 140–150

Wan, James 58, 59, 68
Ward, James 7, 165–178, 244
Warwick, Allison 113
Webb, Liam 8, 233–242, 244
Webley, Steve J. 5, 46–56, 244
Weinstock, Jeffrey. 92–93
Wells, Paul 146
Welsh, James 157
Wester, Maisha 94–95, 102–103
Williams, Linda 61
witch *see* women, aging
The Witch of Timbuctoo 32, 34, 36, 44n11
women 19, 108, 115, 131, 148, 167, 181, 217, 236; crones 1, 6, 70–80, 90n8, 109, 191, 198; evil stepmothers 70, 233; gypsies 70–71, 110, 113, 115, 120, 124, 213; hags 4, 60, 63, 70, 84–85, 90n8, 114, 119, 198; invisibility of 112; mad scientists 38; as narrative device in horror 59–69; as objects of desire 17, 19, 28; portrayals of aging in 2, 4, 6–7, 20, 31n7, 70–72, 77–78, 119, 149, 164, 187, 189–199, 224, 227, 231, 239; as predators 16, 41, 120–128, 171–172; witches 65, 70–72, 75, 77–78, 84, 90n8, 119, 123, 179, 191, 194–198, 217, 219, 233, 235, 241
Wood, Robin 3, 30, 114–116, 129, 131–132, 137, 231n27
Woodward, Kathleen 78, 112
Wynn Sivils, Matthew 94

Yerushalmi, Yosef 209
youth 2, 30, 87, 108, 111, 116, 134, 184, 236, 239; contrasted with age 48, 134, 143, 190–192; eternal 153–155, 167–172, 193–195, 197–198; lament for loss of 18, 25, 59, 136, 174, 196; magical preservation 6–7, 59–61, 96, 119–128, 161, 179–180, 182–183, 186–187; quest for 65, 71, 219; revitalization 4–5, 12–20, 126, 154, 157, 168–169, 195, 197; valorization by society 2, 54, 62, 65, 90, 114, 119, 129, 166, 181, 238
"Yuppie Horror" 108, 117; *see also* horror films

Zizek, Slavoj 136

www.ingramcontent.com/pod-product-compliance
Lightning Source LLC
Chambersburg PA
CBHW080803300426
44114CB00020B/2806